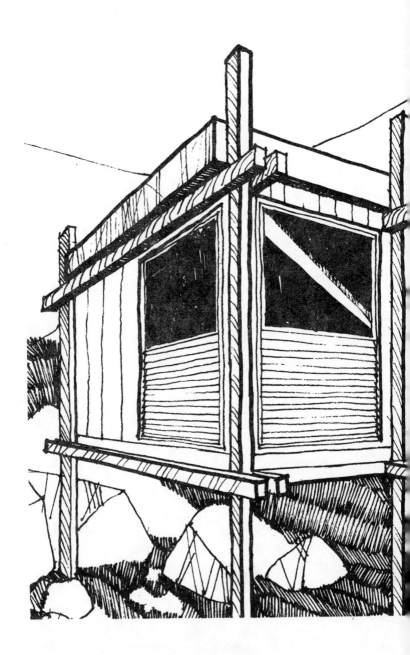

No. 1154
$12.95

HOW TO PUT UP YOUR OWN POST-FRAME HOUSE AND CABIN

by Alan D. Roebuck

TAB BOOKS

BLUE RIDGE SUMMIT, PA. 17214

FIRST EDITION

FIRST PRINTING—MAY 1979

Copyright © 1979 by TAB BOOKS

Printed in the United States of America

Library of Congress Cataloging in Publication Data

Roebuck, Alan D.
    How to put up your own post-frame house and cabin.

    Includes index.
    1. Wooden-frame houses—Design and construction. 2. Log cabins—Design and construction. I. Title.
TH4818.W6R63   694'.2   79-14657
ISBN 0-8306-9804-3
ISBN 0-8306-1154-1 pbk.

To my friends: without friends, we would have nothing.

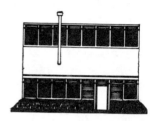

Foreword

For me, building is a very positive experience. It is more than just doing something constructive. It is more than figuring out the design puzzles and then working and watching as a two-dimensional design becomes a three-dimensional structure.

Building is many things. It is raw grit muscle-building physical labor; it is also spiritual. Sometimes it is artistic; often times it is not. When done right, building is one-third muscle and two-thirds brain. Because it is all the above, it is exhilarating.

No one builds by oneself. You may build your own home, yet so many factions of society are involved. Maybe it's just the material suppliers and the previous owner of the land. Most often it also involves certain dependencies on what has been done in the past. Usually the neighbors and local building department help—sometimes by just staying out of the way as much as possible.

I started building my house by myself. As time progressed, I was surprised to find out how many people actually were involved directly or indirectly with the construction process. Indirectly, millions of people are involved: The people who planted the trees that have now grown into construction material, the lumbering companies, the transportation firms, the people who make the transportation, and so on...

Many people are directly involved, too. I'd like to thank all of those people; without them, I'd have no house and this book would never have been written. My life would be very different. Since I'm content, these people have helped me build and have helped me personally. Sometimes the two are hard to separate.

Extra special thanks go out to Terry Lee Alexander, who used to work at the Ann Arbor Building Department. He approved my esoteric blueprints and served as a consultant for design alterations. He has helped with some of the illustrations in this book and is a good friend. The entire building department, in fact, helped me to build a better house. Thanks especially to Jack, Ernie, Carl, Larry, and Lloyd—a group of honest, sincere, and knowledgeable people.

Loads of appreciation go out to Pete Carr, who helped me work for a long time. I saw you grow in so many ways. It seemed like you turned into an adult when you found out what you were capable of doing. Thanks, too, to Dave Crandall, who helped me for many weeks.

My next door neighbors, the Angells, supplied the electricity and water I needed until my own were hooked up. Without this, everything would have been much more difficult. All the neighbors helped by being patient. No one likes looking at a construction zone, let alone living next to one. Thanks for not complaining.

Thanks go to my parents, who raised me without putting me into a mold; to my brother, Charlie, whose spirit never ends; and to my sister, Shirley, who contributed some beautiful drawings to this book.

Thank you Karen DeHosse, for helping me live while building and for tolerating me coming over to your apartment after working thirteen hours day after day—dusty, beat, and with dried sweat.

Thanks, too, to Buce who delivered my concrete. Although Buce is 68 or so, he works like a teenager. Working through a light rain, he struggled until after 8 p.m. to make sure that everything would turn out right. Thanks to John, too, the driver of the other truck, who worked some unexpected overtime.

Thanks go out to Ken Floyde, too. Armed with his backhoe, he helped me hook up my water line and drains without charging an arm and a leg.

So many people have helped me. Building is a process that is personal; yet at times it seems very public. It is positive, and we do nothing alone.

I hope the reader benefits from this book and has a building experience as positive as mine.

Thank you all,
Alan D. Roebuck

Contents

1 **What Is a Post-Frame?** 11
Easier To Build—Costs Less

2 **The Site** 21
Percolation Test—Investigate Zoning

3 **Determining Property Lines** 41
Find a Starting Point—Setback Requirements

4 **Treatment Processes** 51
The Plant Forms—The Animal Forms—Other Treatments—
Identification—Field Treatments.

5 **The Footings** 71
The Size—Digging the Holes—Types of Footings.

6 **Foundation Systems** 85
Moisture—Frost Heave—Normal Earth Pressure—Design
Number One: The Elevated Floor—Design Number Two: The Slab
On Grade—Design Number Three: Below-Grade Structure—
Conclusion.

7 **The Posts** 99
Spacing—Depth

8 **The Wall Structure** 109
Wall Design Number One—Wall Design Number Two—Wall De-
sign Number Three—Wall Design Number Four—Wall Design
Number Five—Wall Design Number Six—Wall Design Number
Seven—Wall Design Number Eight—Wall Design Number
Nine—Wall Design Number Ten.

9 **The Roof** 127
The Basic Form—The Construction—Overhangs—Conclusion.

10 **The Floors** 151
The Concrete Floor—The Wood Floor—Floor Trusses—The
Beamed Floor—Wood Floors Vs. Concrete Floors—Conclusion.

11 **Exterior Design** 171
Design Number One—Design Number Two—Design Number
Three—Design Number Four—Design Number Five—Design
Number Six—Design Number Seven—Design Number Eight—
Conclusion.

12 Interior Design.. **189**
Floor Plan Number One—Floor Plan Number Two—Floor Plan Number Three—Conclusion.

13 Insulation **207**
Moisture Barriers—"R" Value—The Fill Insulations—Urea-Formaldehyde—The Rigid Insulations—Insulation Concerns—Conclusion.

14 Planning.. **233**
Subcontracting—Work in a Logical Order

15 The Procedure **243**
Determining the Building's Location—Leveling the Site—Spreading the Sand—The Sanitary Hook-Ups—Determining the Exact Perimeter of the Building—The Interior Holes—Digging the Perimeter Trench—The Rough Plumbing—Setting Up the Posts—Installing the Foam—The Plastic—The 1x8 Splashboard—The Drains—The Backfill—Making the Beams—Trimming the Posts—Hanging the Beams—The Rough Heating—The Roof Planking—Laying the Slab Floor—The Wall Structure—The Windows—The Number 30 Felt—The Siding—The Interior Walls—The Rough Heating, Plumbing, and Electrical—The Insulation—The Drywall—Painting—The Cabinets—Finish Heating, Plumbing, and Electrical—The Interior Doors—The Interior Trim and Molding—The Finish Grade—The Carpeting.

16 The 1980s Survival Cabin... **299**
Determine Location—Ready to Live In

17 Charts and Tables... **313**
Working Stresses for Joists—Floor Joist Spans—Ceiling Joist Spans—Fir and Pine Spacing for Wind Loads—Plywood Floor and Roof Spans—Fiber Stress Values—Load Capacity; Timber Beams—Load Capacity; Roof Beams—Size of Plates, Purlins and Girts—Circle Diameters and Square Feet for Footings—Concrete Footing Thicknesses—Soil Types and Design Properties—Plywood Grades and Thicknesses—Supported Weights for Pine and Fir Posts—Post Sizes—Post Depth—Concrete Coverage Per Cubic Yard—Plate Footing Sizes—Insulating Values; Rigid Materials—Insulating Values; Fill Materials—Insulation Installation Prices—Properites of Structural and Insulating Materials—Survival Cabin Materials

Glossary **365**

Index... **369**

About the Artists... **373**

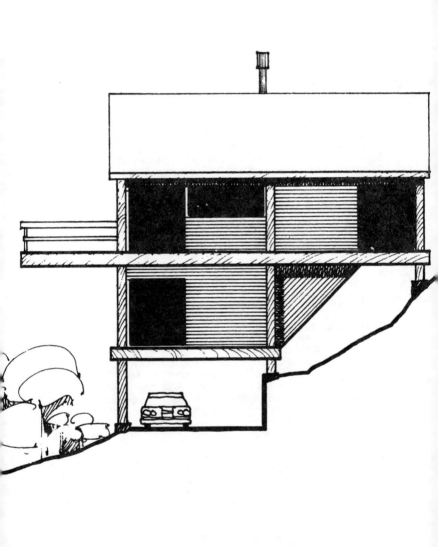

What is a Post-Frame?

A post-frame home uses treated square posts set into holes which have been dug into the ground. The roof beams are hung from these posts, as is the wall material. The posts serve as the foundation, roof support, and wall support for a structure. With proper treatment, posts are protected against deterioration (Fig. 1-1).

The posts can also support floor levels. Wood floors can be bolted to the posts for one story, two story, tri-level, or multi-level structures (Fig. 1-2). Concrete slab floors, though, are also used effectively in post-frame construction (Fig. 1-3).

The roof can be constructed with planks and beams, trusses, or can be conventionally framed. Although each offers inherent advantages, in many instances the plank-and-beam roof combines especially well with post-frame buildings. When an elevated building is not needed, the concrete floor offers an economical solution to an expensive problem.

The least expensive and often the most satisfactory design, then, incorporates the slab floor with a plank-and-beam roof (Fig. 1-4). By using these roof and floor designs in conjunction with the post-frame building technique, the building process is simplified so construction can proceed quickly

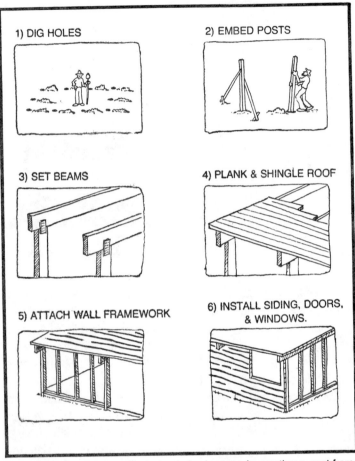

Fig. 1-1. These diagrams illustrate six basic steps in erecting a post-frame home.

even when being done by people who are not experts on residential construction.

For those people, this book attempts to communicate all the essential information needed to construct a post-frame home.

This book, *How to Put Up Your Own Post Frame House and Cabin*, is written in response to the increasing demand for alternative methods of building. As new, single-family homes priced under $50,000 become a rarity, society necessarily leans toward apartment living. Young people who find themselves dissatisfied with apartment living often find it extremely

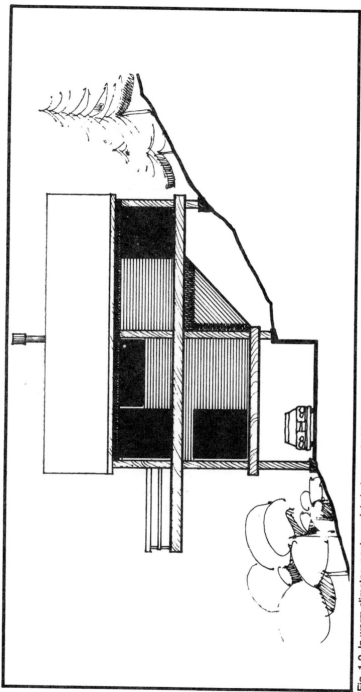

Fig. 1-2. In warm climates, posts sunk in holes can hold up an elevated wood floor. Especially for a hillside site, the elevated floor produces an effective design.

13

difficult to pay rent and to save enough money to secure a house and a mortgage. With the value of single family homes increasing an amazing 10 percent a year, the buying power of the money that is saved diminishes in value every day.

These people have few options. A minimum down payment with a maximum length mortgage can be assumed. The first few years will involve many financial sacrifices, but generally everything works out because of the escalation in the home's value. In a few years, another home is usually purchased with another mortgage. The mortgages never expire, but at least one has a home to live in.

In lieu of taking out a large mortgage, some people choose to rent an apartment while saving up for a home. As time progresses, their savings might increase by about the same amount as the increases in homes' prices. When this is the case, the balance between what they have and what they need stays the same. These people either live in apartments all their lives, rent out older homes, or make the jump and end up taking out a mortgage anyway—after wasting their early years in an apartment.

There is one other option and it applies to everything in life. If you cannot afford to buy something that is needed, then it must be made. If liveable houses are not to be produced for reasonable, affordable prices, something must be done. We must do for ourselves what others can not or will not do for us.

EASIER TO BUILD

Building a house is a large project. Through the use of conventional construction techniques, insurmountable problems are definite possibilities. Alternative forms of construction can offer to a novice builder a much more viable design that is easier to build. Post-frame construction is one such alternative; not only is a post-frame building easier to build, it is much less expensive. Importantly, a shelter can be established quickly.

This book, though, is not written exclusively for those who need to build their own homes. Hopefully, this book will encourage builders and architects to re-evaluate their thinking about their work. There is a demand for low-cost

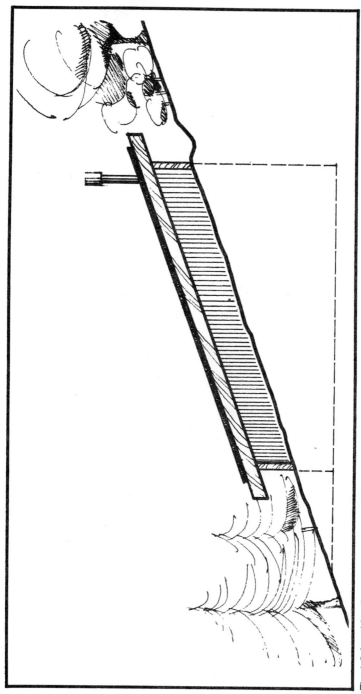

Fig. 1-3. In colder climates, a concrete slab floor provides the most economical design. When the building site is hilly, the house can be sunk into the hill. The dirt is used as insulation to keep the slab warm.

15

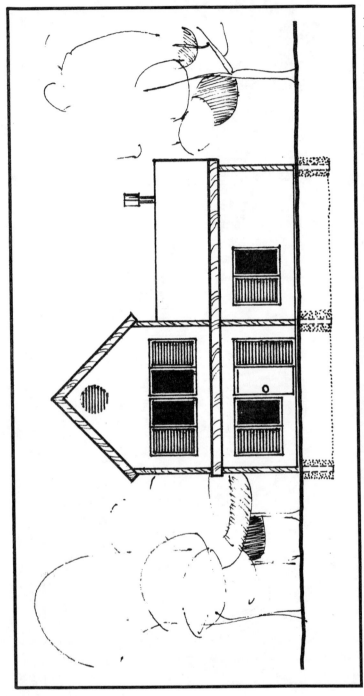

Fig. 1-4. For flat sites in frost areas, the posts are set into a trench which is then filled with gravel. The gravel keeps out the cold and insulates the slab floor.

housing. And low-cost need not mean stifling. Once we get beyond the idea that typical homes are the best because they are abundant, and once we get beyond the idea that people like what is built because they buy it, then we can get beyond our building problem.

COSTS LESS

Once mastered by the professionals, the post-frame can be erected at a cost much less than that of traditional housing. The total lack of masonry simplifies the construction process by involving one less trade. And, there is no waiting for masonry to cure before construction again progresses. With some designs, there is no need to establish a grade, dig trenches, lay storm drains, do rough plumbing early in the construction phase, backfill or worry about leaky basements. Since the surrounding area is left undisturbed by the lack of

Fig. 1-5. The post-frame home can take on many looks. It could be an extremely rustic shelter like the one above .

bulldozers on the site, there is no need for landscaping. Everything can be left natural for the buyer to change.

By the building of post-frames, or by doing anything that is alternative, we conserve by easing the demand for the norm. Perhaps the most severe demand is felt when one is looking for building sites. Ideal sites are snatched up quickly, and for top dollar. The sites which are low, heavily treed, rough, and lack good bearing soil are listed at give-away prices for years, sometimes before a buyer comes along. And, if the buyer is not cognizant of the site's complications, often the land is back on the realtors' lists after a few builders shake their heads at its pecularities.

On these sites a post-frame can be built. The side and construction method are inexpensive. It is for these reasons that post-frame structures should be incorporated into the

Fig. 1-6. The post-frame house might also look sleek and modern. The finished structure will reflect your tastes .

Fig. 1-7. The builder must arrange for a number of holes to be dug in an accurate pattern. Posts, set into the holes, provide the home's vertical structure. Besides the simplicity of the task, the major benefit is the builder can see immediate progress .

house building trade. By having more alternatives in design, the architect, builder, and ultimately the homeowner will be in a much better position than he or she has occupied in the past.

Does it make sense to build a home? Should you take the time and money to create a shelter? If you want "all the conveniences," a $50,000 home may be a real bargain. Really.

But, if you get beyond the gadgetry that is designed for no-hassle comfort and desire to create a less artificial environment, buying a house may not be such a good deal.

If you don't feel comfortable in box-type housing and are willing to work hard to get out of the box, then you may be the type of person to build a home.

The Site

Looking for a building site is more than just checking around until you find a place that looks nice (Fig. 2-1). There are many factors which must be considered before a final choice is made. The choice should be a good one if you are going to be content living there. Also if you are looking to make a good investment by the building of a house, the location is of primary importance.

One of the first steps that should be taken is to contact several real estate agents. Tell them what your realistic expectations are, i.e., how much you expect to spend and what type of site you want. Pinpoint the locale in which you desire to live. Make sure you receive the agents reactions to your expectations so you are able to know how much help you can expect to receive. Often times agents will scoff at one who desires to find a low-priced parcel; don't let this intimidate you. No one said it would be easy to find what you need. If an agent scoffs at your expectations, simply don't expect too much help from him or her.

Good deals are hard to find, but if you expend a lot of energy looking for a bargain, the chance increases that one will be found. The first place to begin looking is in the "multi-lists." This is a publication, issued weekly, which is a composite of many different realtors' listings. It is cooperative-type publication which serves the purpose of disseminating much of the information realtors have about what is on the market. Besides the advantage of having many realtors' listings all in one publication, the multi-list is good because everything is classified according to price. It takes little time, then, to find the items in one's price range.

After consulting the multi-lists, it is a good idea to check out a few available parcels—even if they aren't exactly what you want. By doing this, you get a good idea of what is available and what to expect in certain price ranges. Through this action, you gain a perspective on real estate, allowing intelligent comparisons. Also, by driving around and keeping tuned in to the areas you pass, you can get a better grip on the surrounding areas and what they have to offer. Areas previously unknown to you might be found; one of these areas could offer the attributes you are seeking. The other advantage of checking out available parcels is that you often find parcels that are not listed. Some realtors are not members of the multi-list, so many listings will not be included. And, parcels that have just gone up for sale are most easily found by driving, as are offerings "by owner." By locating the available parcels and by briefly checking them out before calling the realtor who is handling the property, you are able to see many properties; and, while requesting information on the properties you have seen, you can meet other agents. The more agents you contact, the better the chance of finding exactly what is desired.

Once some property is found that seems appealing, many things must be checked out. The issue of greatest importance, of course, is whether or not the site is buildable. The soil must have a bearing capacity capable of carrying the load the house will exert upon it. Areas with poor soil, such as silt, and those which have been filled will present special problems (and added expenses) to the builder.

There are usually many restrictions that must be adhered to before you can even get a building permit. The most stringent restriction is whether the site is capable of handling sewage, either by accessibility to the city's sewers or by being able to contain a septic system.

Fig. 2-1. This attractive place may not necessarily be perfect for a post-frame home.

If the lot is within the city limits, most likely there are sanitation facilities. The city has maps of all the sewers, as well as their depths and the places on the sewers where there are tees for connections. It is the city, then, that should be consulted about the accessibility of sewers. You need to know not only if there is a sewer in the area, but also its depth. A sewer at a twenty foot depth in sand with a high water table will be of little help to you since it would be extremely difficult to reach. Just the same, a sewer that is across a large, paved street might just as well be deemed inaccessible. Or, if lines would have to be run down the block, the cost may offset any savings the site might otherwise offer. It must be figured out whether the expense to reach the sewer is prohibitive. Any extra expense it might take to make the site buildable lessens the value of the site. Ask the city what the hook-up charge might be. Many cities perform the sewer and water taps themselves; they may be able to give you an estimate of that cost.

PERCOLATION TEST

Before rural sites should be considered buildable, a test for the percolation must be done. This "perk test" determines the surrounding soil's capability of absorbing water. If no sewers are present, the soil must perk in order for a septic system to work.

The perk test is very simply done. The county will give you their own specifications, but basically it involves digging a hole, filling it up with water, and measuring the amount of time it takes for the level of water to lower. Since clay-type soils retain moisture, the passing of water through clay is slow. It is in the clay soils, mainly, that perk tests will not pass. You should try the perk test in several locations before a negative determination is made for the area. On even a small lot, one area may perk well while another will hardly perk at all. Through the poor soil might run a band of sand or gravel, which, if large enough, will give passage to water.

For those sites which are marginal in passing the perk test, a larger septic field must be installed for the system to adequately work. The extra expense of installing a larger field, and the increased possibility of failure, lessens the value of these sites.

Before you begin digging holes for the perk test, the county should be consulted to see if they have any records of perk tests having been done on the property. Often times a piece of land that looks buildable will have had percolation tests. The tests done on the surrounding properties can give some indication on the possibilities of percolation in that area. The county may also have done soil tests throughout its jurisdiction; this is information which may be very valuable to you. They also are aware of sanitation problems of existing homes, so use the county's resources as much as you can. It can save much time.

As was mentioned earlier, even a low lot prone to flooding can be suitable for an elevated post-frame. But, if the lot doesn't perk, it doesn't matter much. If the lot is in the city, though, it may be considered buildable as long as there are city sewers. A low lot should have a low price—since it has its limitations as far as what type of building could be put there. Especially if it is sometimes swampy, you should be able to buy it very cheaply.

Places which are bone dry in June may be covered with a foot of water in April. If you are looking for a site in June, then, be cautious. Unless you are in love with red-winged blackbirds, there is little advantage to building on a low lot. Maybe you can grow great celery, but that is little consolation. There are several ways to tell if a lot is prone to dampness. First, check the surroundings. Is the site at the

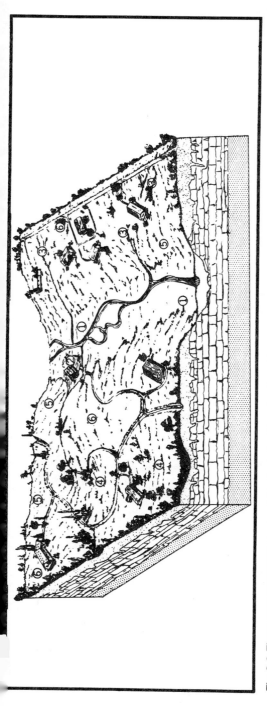

Fig. 2-2. These topographical features might affect a building site. Area 1 is a flood plain. It is subject to flooding during heavy storms. Ask yourself: If it should rain hard, where would the water flow in relation to the proposed house and site? Area 2 is an alluvial fan. The soil has been forming over the years as a result of water eroding material from the watershed above and depositing it near the mouth of the waterway. An alluvial fan can be hard hit by flash floods after heavy rains unless an adequate water-disposal system has been provided to control the runoff from the watershed above. Area 3 is an upland waterway where water flowing from the higher surrounding land will concentrate. Natural waterways should not be used unless an adequate ditch or diversion terrace has been constructed to divert water from the site. Area 4 is a low depressed area where water accumulates from higher surrounding areas. These soils remain wet and spongy for long periods. Area 5 is a steep hillside. Many soils on steep slopes are shallow to rack. Some are subject to severe slippage. On all slopes, one must be careful of soil movement through gravity or by water erosion. Yet some steep hillsides can be used safely as building sites. The problem can be solved by studying the solid and avoiding the bad ones. Area 6 is a deep, well-drained soil found on ridge-tops and gently sloping hillsides. Generally these areas have the smallest water-management problems. They are the best building sites, other things being equal.

25

bottom of inclines? Is it any kind of basin? Does it drop even a foot below the surrounding areas? Look for traces of where water has flowed. Can any areas be found where water has sat (Fig. 2-2)?

After the terrain has been examined, check out the foliage in the area. Certain species grow in damp soils. Among the species that are abundant are the following (Figs. 2-3 through 2-8).

INVESTIGATE ZONING

There are many other considerations which must not be overlooked. Obviously, before a perk test is done, you must check out the zoning to be assured that a single family home is permissible there. Some areas are designated as strictly for commercial buildings or multiple dwellings. Many of these areas will permit a single family home, but the locale's zoning might be a negative factor to consider. If you are going to make a wise investment, the surroundings are important. Not many people want to live next to a hog farm or a commercial chicken farm. No one wants to live next to a junk yard either, or a landfill. The proposed future of the surrounding area must be considered. Unrestricted areas should be thoroughly checked out since anything could be planned for the area, such as an airport.

When the zoning is being checked out, one can also find out the area's tax base. Some tax bases may be very expensive. A high tax base can easily add $1,000 a year onto a homeowner's overhead. The amount of taxes you pay is determined by the value of the property. An average for an urban area is somewhere around $25 for each $1,000 value of the property. At this rate, the owners of a $60,000 house would pay $1,500 in taxes each year. This calculates to be 2½ percent of the value of the house paid each year in taxes. As the property appreciates in value either through inflation or through improvements, more taxes will have to be paid. Vacant land, for example, will have a relatively low tax payment. Once the land is "improved" through the addition of a house, the increased value will warrant a huge jump in the tax payment. This is unavoidable. You can control, though,

Fig. 2-3. This northern white-cedar is very smooth and can be used for shingles and siding.

the amount of taxes that must be paid by not moving into an area with a high tax base. Tax bases can range from as low as ½ percent in rural areas to as high as 8½ percent in some densely populated areas. In the high tax base area, the owner of a $100,000 home will owe $8,500 each year in taxes! The records of proposed building sites should be examined so one is assured that the tax base is stable. Like everything else, tax bases often change; rarely do they lower.

People sometimes sell property on which they owe back taxes. The city records should also be checked to make sure that this is not the case with a piece of property one is going to buy. If back taxes are owed, the buyer assumes the responsibility of paying the taxes. Make sure that if there are back taxes, they are figured against the price of the property.

The owner of the property may also owe back assessments for a sidewalk being put in, for having the street paved, for having a curb and gutter put in, or for having the sewer installed. Again, if back assessments are owed, the amount owed should be deducted from the property's price. Also, you should determine if there are any assessments that the new owner will have to pay. Often, assessments for improvements (sidewalk, etc.) are spread over many years.

This is an added expense that should be calculated as part of the expense of buying the property.

You should also inquire about future improvements for which you may have to pay. The street in front of the property may now be dirt, but perhaps there are plans to pave the street within the next year. The cost will be your expense. Just the same, if sewers are constructed even after you have installed a septic tank, you may be assessed for the expense. The future plans for an area, or the lack of plans, should not come as a surprise to a new homeowner.

Besides the sewage disposal situation, one should look into what other utilities, including telephone service, are available. We've probably all heard of at least one situation when someone who has built a house has called to find that the nearest line is a mile away and that it would take $5,000 to supply electricity to the newly built home. Call the electric company before you buy land and find out how much it will cost to have the electricity hooked up. There can be various charges besides the hook-up charge to which you may be liable. For example, if there are underground lines running across your property, you will probably have to pay between a dollar and two dollars per foot for the width of your property. Then, it may be another $2 per foot from the line to your house as the hook-up charge. Just make sure that you are aware of these charges before you purchase property.

With today's complex and expensive heating dilemmas, one should consider how the home is to be heated before land is bought. If natural gas is desired because of its relative economy, this limits the areas one needs to look for property. Call the gas company to find out where their lines run. Without natural gas, the expense of heating a home rises greatly.

The other major criteria is whether there are water lines running to the property. If there are no lines, one must be assured that a good well can be constructed at a reasonable cost. Typically, if there are sewers running to the property, there is city water available.

Once these crucial questions are answered, and if you receive information that leads you to believe that the site is

Fig. 2-4. Blackgum, sourgum, pepperridge and tupelo are names by which this tree is known. It is common along moist roadsides and in woods.

indeed buildable and up to your requirements, factors of lesser importance can be checked out. You should inquire if there are lumber and other building materials available locally at a fair price. Call the suppliers and get their prices on some items you will need so that their prices can be compared. Ask a local builder or two, if available, where they purchase materials. And, if you plan to subcontract out some of the construction work, ask the builder how the labor situation is. Is labor available at a fair price? Often enough, they will be able to answer many of the questions posed in this chapter.

As well as being able to purchase materials, are there stores nearby that you will feel good about purchasing food and other staples? Or, is everything marked up tremendously? If you have children, where are the nearest schools that they will be going to as they grow? How good are these schools? Are there buses if the schools are not within walking distance? If the site is on a private road, who maintains it? Is snow plowed from it in the winter? Are there many bugs around? How about mosquitoes, flies, bees, wasps, hornets, ticks and chiggers? Are there dangerous wild animals around? How about dangerous people? What is the crime rate? Have any homes been broken into in the immediate area recently?

Is there corruption in the town's politics? Are the building inspectors politically appointed? Will they be difficult to get along with? Are the town's people the type of people with whom you are able to socialize? Is there any blatant social or racial prejudice? What do the local papers have to say? Read some letters to the editor and the more popular columns. Get a good idea on what type of community you may be moving into.

After these items have been checked out, find out about fire protection. Is a fire department near? How much is fire insurance? Must you pay extra for fire protection in the community? Are there dangers of other natural causes? Are there occasional high winds, tornados or hurricanes? Is it a flood area? How much snow and rain annually falls?

Where are the recreational facilities? How are they maintained? Are there any parks within walking distance? Where will the children play?

I've posed many questions, I know, but these are all things that must be dealt with at one time or another. It would be a shame to build one's dream house only to find that the area floods with 3 feet of water every year...or that there are no schools for the kids. Most of these questions can be answered by talking to the people in the neighborhood. Besides, having a few questions to ask will give you the chance to meet potential neighbors. Neighbors are generally much more impartial than the people at city hall, whose job, partially, is public relations. Talk to the people in city hall, too, and find out their perspective. They must be dealt with every now and then anyway. And, while you are receiving information on the tax base and fire protection and police protection, etc., you might ask them about the neighborhood into which you may move.

After these major questions are answered, some of the less crucial requirements should be checked out. Is the top soil sufficient to grow grass or a garden, if desired? Are there any natural wind buffers or noise buffers, if needed? From what direction does the weather usually come? Does the lot

Fig. 2-5. American holly is prevalent in the Southeast. The bright, red fruits grow only on the female tree. In winter and early spring bluebirds, catbirds, and mockingbirds enjoy eating the fruits.

face the sun? If the weather generally comes from the west, what is to the west? If it is farmland, good clean air will pass by your home; if there are factories, you may be sweeping dust off from your car every morning—to say nothing about air quality.

These are the major considerations. You may be more particular about some of these than others. You may not care about the schools because you have no children; but if you plan on selling your home, the school system in the area may be a huge detraction or attraction. You may have considerations that are wholly individual. For example, you may be allergic and your major requirement might be that no one in the area grows tulips. There is a lot to consider before making a purchase that will have such a tremendous influence upon your life.

Once it has been determined that a certain building site is within your expectations, a purchase agreement can be drawn up. The realtor who helped you find the site, if this is the case, will help you close the deal. If the site was found on one's own volition, choose the realtor who helped you most.

Realty agents do a lot of running around, often to no avail, so when one has tried to help you out, try to return the favor.

If the asking price for the property is $5,000, and if you are hesitant to buy it because of a minor complication, one might offer $4,000. If the offer is accepted, the savings will negate the complication. On the other hand, if the property is truly desirable, a higher offer may be in order. Often times, a seller will modify the offer and sign the contract in acceptance of the modification. For example, the seller might cross out $4,000 and write in $4,500. If this is agreeable with you, then it's yours for the modified amount.

Whenever you are buying property, you can write on any contingencies you desire. Typically a building site has the following contingencies listed: it must be buildable and be approved for a house; it must pass the perk test or have city sewers; and it must have city water or a well must be found. If there are any complications with any of these contingencies, then the deposit must be returned.

Just the same, the seller can write on deed restrictions. A seller may specify that he or she is allowed access to Porkey's grave every October 14th to mourn the death of the family's pet hamster. The seller might also specify that Porkey's grave remain untouched. Or, a seller might specify that a certain tree, planted by the late grandfather Oakly, shall never be damaged maliciously. Land might also be sold with the agreement that access to the "back 40" be kept open so that the fields may be worked. This is called an easement.

Whatever the arrangement might be, an agreement must be made to which both parties can agree. After this agreement is made, a deposit can be made on the property. This financial arrangement will be carried through by the realtors involved. Usually, the taxes for the year are pro-rated so that the buyer begins paying taxes on the property from the date of purchase. The seller pays the taxes up to this date of purchase. If this were not the case, a tax bill for the last six months could come one week after purchase, and the new owner would be liable. Insure yourself, then, that the taxes are paid to date.

Land is usually sold by a land contract. Through this arrangement, a down payment of an amount specified by the seller is paid by the buyer. The sales agreement specifies the amount of money due at the end of each month and the interest rate involved. The seller can specify the interest rate; typically it is around 8½ per cent, which is fair considering that the land's value will rise by about that amount every year. In other words, if you were to wait a year to buy the land, it would probably cost 8½ per cent more. The interest you pay on land, then, is a fair amount and not a losing proposition.

It is relatively easy to figure out the amount of interest you pay every month. It is necessary to determine this sum so you know how many dollars are knocked off the principal every month. Take the example of a $5,000 purchase with a $1,000 down payment payable at $125 per month at 8½ per cent. If you gave $1,000 down, that leaves a principal of $4,000. To figure the first month's interest on this amount, you multiply 4,000 by .085. This comes to $340. This amount is then divided by the number of months in a year, 12. This comes to $28.33. If you are paying $125 per month, the amount breaks down to $96.67 off from the purchase price

Fig. 2-6. Alders are fast-growing and prefer moist soil along streams or in swamps.

and $28.33 in interest. The total should be checked to make sure it comes to $125.

To figure this same calculation out for the next month, then, we start with $4,000 minus the $96.67 which was knocked off from the principal.

FIRST MONTH

1. 4,000   (Principal)
   × .085   (8.5% Interest Rate)
   ———
   340   ($340 Interest/Year)

2. 28.33   (Interest Due This Month)
   12)340

3. 125.   (Amount Due This Month)
   − 28.33   (Interest)
   ———
   96.67   (Principal Deduction)

4. 4,000   (Principal)
   − 96.67   (Amount of Principal Paid This Month)
   ————
   3,903.33   (New Principal)

These calculations become very simple with the use of a calculator. For the second month, one would take

$$3903.33 \times .085 = 331.78$$
$$\div 12 = 27.64$$
$$125 - 27.64 = 97.36$$
$$3903.33 - 97.36 = 3805.97 \text{ (New Principal)}$$

If you are planning on paying the exact same amount every month, you can get from any bank a payment book with all these figures in it. Sometimes, though, people pay more than required on some months; in this case, it is necessary to figure out the payment schedule every month.

Fig. 2-7. Swamp white oak is irregular and found in swamps and other moist areas.

It should be remembered that the amount of interest paid in the beginning will be a greater proportion of the payment than it will be after much of the principal gets paid off. Don't let it shock you that out of a $125 payment, some $27 goes towards interest. Later on, this amount will be much less. In a year, or so, there will only be a $3000 principal due. The interest would be $21.25. On $2,000 it would be $14.16. On $1,000, it will be $7.08 per month.

I took out a land contract for $2,300 payable at $100 a month with the interest at 8.5 per cent. The interest I paid was around $200, which I consider well worth it. If I would have waited until I had enough money to pay cash for the property I bought, the price would have been at least $200 higher. And, at that later time, all of the supplies I needed would have been much higher in cost. Building materials rise in cost about 12 per cent per year. Even if only $10,000 were spent in building materials, by waiting the two years it took to pay off the land contract, the bill would come to $13,440 instead of $10,000.

Besides this $3,440 difference, you could figure in the amount of money saved in rent by starting to build two years sooner. It makes good sense to buy land on a land contract. It is like borrowing money at 8.5 per cent, which is absolutely the lowest interest rate you can find. And, by paying for something every month, you know where the money is going. It is like a forced savings plan.

Once you are sure that the tax situation is straight, make sure that there are no unpaid assessments, deed restrictions or easements that you feel will hinder your freedom. Also, make sure that the title is free and clear; there could be a mortgage or liens against it. When all these questions are cleared, you should get a warranty deed for the property. Also, for a few dollars, you can buy title insurance. With a warranty deed and title insurance, there is no question that the property belongs to you. If there is, the title insurance company will go to bat for you.

The other two types of deeds are called tax-title deeds and quit-claim deeds. Neither of these are advisable. A tax-title deed only shows that the seller paid taxes on the site for a number of years. Heirs could come along and claim rights to the property. A quit-claim deed passes from the seller to you. Claims can come up against the property, such as long-standing indebtedness on pavements or sewers. It is best not to purchase if the seller can only produce a quit-claim deed.

In this chapter we have covered everything from looking for a building site to how to buy it. Since there is so much to remember, what follows is a list which will be handy to refer to when needed. The list is in the order that these areas were discussed in this chapter:

- Do you like the immediate area?
- Check the multi-lists and want-ads.

Fig. 2-8. Bitternut, a common tree, is sometimes called swamp hickory because of its preference for wet soils.

- Is there sufficient bearing soil?
- Does the lot seem prone to dampness?
- Is it zoned for a single family dwelling?
- How are the surroundings zoned?
- What is the tax base?
- Has the tax base stabilized?
- Are all back taxes paid?
- Are all assessments paid?
- Are there any projected future improvements (assessments)?
- Is telephone service available?
- Is electricity available?

- Are there any extra charges for electric service?
- Is natural gas available?
- Is there city water accessible or can a well be made?
- How much will water cost?
- Are building materials locally available at a fair price?
- Is labor available at a fair price?
- Are there food stores nearby?
- Where are the schools?
- Is there an abundance of nasty bugs?
- What is the crime rate?
- How are the town's politics?
- Do you think the building inspectors will be fair with you?
- Are the townspeople decent?
- Is there any prejudice?
- Will you have fire protection?
- Can you get reasonably priced fire insurance?
- Are there any dangerous natural elements?
- Where are the recreational facilities?
- Is there good topsoil?
- Any needed wind or noise buffers?
- From where does the weather come?
- Does the lot face the sun?
- Is the air fresh?
- Are there any deed restrictions?
- Any easements?
- Have the taxes been pro-rated?
- Do you understand the sales agreement?
- If on a land contract, do you understand the terms?
- Is the title free and clear?
- Is there a warranty deed?
- Have you received title insurance?
- Have you received a copy of the purchaser's closing statement?

Also, find out about these matters:

- Check with the highway department to make sure that no roads are planned for the immediate area.
- Check to make sure that there are no condemning possibilities for any reasons.

- Check to make sure that no utility companies plan on coming through your property with overhead lines or underground pipelines.
- Make sure that the boundaries of the property are well defined, done by a competent surveyor and are agreed upon by the neighbors. You don't want to get in the middle of a private war!
- Find out if there is garbage pick-up.

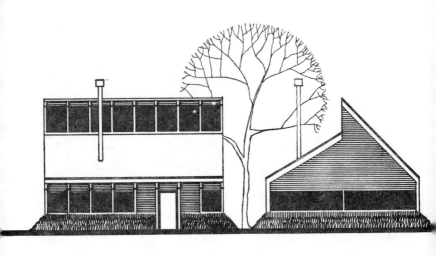

3

Determining Property Lines

Determining property lines is essential before a proposed building's perimeter can be established (Fig. 3-1). Unless the building site is an acre or more and the building is to sit near the center of the site, it is necessary to determine the boundaries so there is no possibility of encroachment. Buildings must be built at least 4 feet within the property line; no projection, like an overhang, can come closer than 2 feet. When a driveway is scheduled to provide access to the back of a small lot, accurate determinations must be made so that adequate room will be provided.

When land is surveyed, iron pipes are pounded into the ground at the corners of the property lines. A problem arises, though, when excavation is going on in the area. Often these corner stakes are lost. It is wise, though, to search the area to find missing stakes. If you have access to a metal detector, this can be a valuable tool.

If no corner stakes can be found, it will not be necessary to hire a surveyor to determine the property lines if you are at all competent at mathematics. Absolutely accurate calculations will not be necessary. Getting within six inches is tolerable and not hard to do. A map of the subdivision with all the surveyor's calculations can be obtained from the city hall. Also, if there is a house next door, your neighbors probably have a plot plan that locates their house on their site. If there is a fence on the block, it is likely that these neighbors have determined their property lines. All that is needed is an accurate starting point. Once this starting point is found, whether by subdivision maps, neighboring plot plans, a fence, or ideally by a surveyor's pipe, the other corners are easily established.

FIND A STARTING POINT

A few tools that will be needed to make these determinations are two 100-foot tape measures, some mason's line, a sledgehammer, preferably with a short handle, a felt tipped pen, chalk, a grass whip, some pointed stakes, 8d nails and a hammer. The subdivision map with all the surveyors' calculations will be used to provide the figures. If no corners of the property to be surveyed can be accurately located, the subdivision map is used to find a starting point. By beginning in the middle of the nearest street intersection and measuring up the sidewalk, using the chalk to mark the sidewalk in 100-foot increments, the first corner of the property can be found. If feasible, a measurement from the other street corner will insure accuracy. Usually city property lines begin at the sidewalk, but by measuring the right of way distance (usually 30 feet) from the middle of the street in front of the lot to the front of one's property, this front corner for the property will be precisely determined. Drive a stake at this point and hammer a nail into the butt end of the stake, leaving ½-inch of the nail exposed to hook the tape measure onto. This is stake #1.

From this point, the other front corner is easily determined. Any weeds that are in the way should be removed with the grass whip. Light brush is easily removed with a machete. Hook the tape measure onto the nail at the end of the first corner stake and measure down the front line of the property the distance of the frontage. Then start from the middle of the street directly in front of this second corner and measure the number of feet for the street right-of-way. The second corner is now established. After pounding in stake #2, attach a line between these two stakes onto the stakes' nails.

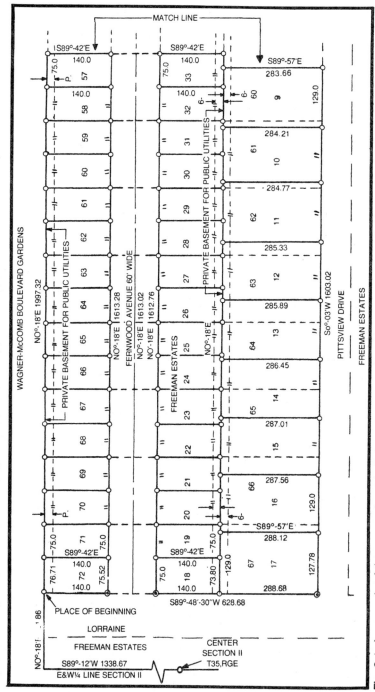

Fig. 3-1. An example of the surveyor's work. Surveyors take great pains in determining accurate property lines.

43

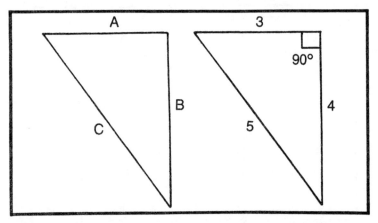

Fig. 3-2. According to the Pythagorean Theorem, the illustrated triangles are right triangles. The square of the hypotenuse (c) equals the sum of the squares of the other two sides (a and b).

If one of the corners is 90 degrees, it is easy to figure out the other two property corners by using the Pythagorean Theorem. This theorem staes that a right triangle exists when the square of the side opposite the right angle equals the sum of the squares of the other two sides. For a triangle with the sides of a, b, and c, a right triangle exists if $a^2 + b^2 = c^2$ (Fig. 3-2).

For the above triangle with sides equaling 3, 4, and 5, we have a right triangle since $3^2 + 4^2 = 5^2$. (9 + 16 = 25) This principle holds true whether we are talking about millimeters, inches, feet, miles, or light-years (Fig. 3-3).

When determining right angles for construction purposes, generally we use the measurement of feet. If a stake is placed on point a^1 and another stake is placed at point b^1 exactly 3 feet from point a^1, by measuring 4 feet from a^1 and 5 feet from b^1, the intersection of these measurements is point c^1. The line a^1, c^1, is exactly perpendicular to line a^1, b^1; in other words, a right triangle has been formed (Fig. 3-4).

For greater accuracy when determining right angles in the field, instead of using the lengths of 3, 4, and 5 feet, one can use the measurements of 30, 40, and 50 feet. Measure 30 feet down the front line from stake #1 and place stake #3. Hammer a nail into the end of this stake and attach a tape measure. Measure 50 feet diagonally toward the side line.

Attach the other tape measure to stake #1 and measure 40 feet down the side line. Where the 50-foot mark intersects with the 40-foot mark, drive a stake. This is stake #4. Hammer a nail into this stake precisely at the intersection point. A 90-degree angle has been established (Fig. 3-5).

To extend this line the length of the side line, a string is hooked onto stake #1 and unrolled a distance of 100 feet. The string is marked with the felt tipped pen at the 100-foot point. Move the string toward the nail in stake #4 until it touches the nail. Drive a stake at this point. Continue this procedure until the distance of the side line is reached. Drive a stake. Three corners have now been established.

As long as the front line and one side line have been established, no further information is needed to determine the location of the proposed building since all measurements can come from these two lines. If you want to determine the fourth corner, though, it is easy to do. Assuming that the side line is longer than the back line, you need to measure a length of string the distance of this other side line (50 feet or 100 feet at a time) with both the string and the tape measure, as was done for the other side line. Stakes are again sunk at these points so there is something on which to hook the tape measure. These stakes, though, do not designate the side line; they only designate the distance from stake #2. When

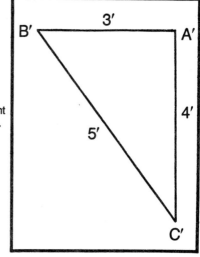

Fig. 3-3. This triangle is a right triangle because $3^2 + 4^2 = 5^2$.

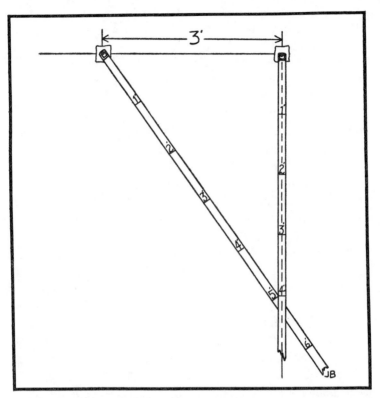

Fig. 3-4. The diagram illustrates formation of a right triangle for construction purposes.

the correct distance from stake #2 is reached, the string should be marked with the felt tipped pen. Now hook the tape measure onto the third corner stake and measure the distance of the back line. With the string in one hand and the tape in the other hand (making sure that both are taut and not interfered with by land growth), establish the point where these two measurements intersect. At this point is the fourth corner.

What if neither of the front angles is 90 degrees? After establishing the 90-degree angle, one must measure down the side line 57 feet 4 inches and sink a stake on the line exactly perpendicular to the front line. This is most accurately done by first tying a string onto stake #1. Take this string out to the 57 feet 4-inch mark. As the string is moved toward stake #4, watch closely so that it can be precisely

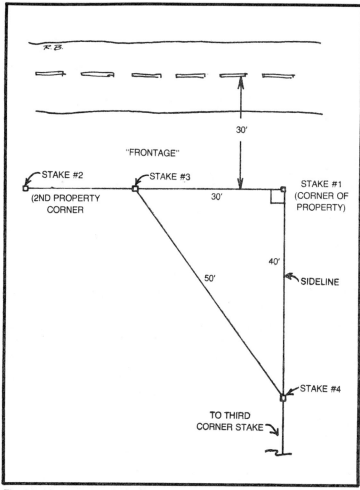

Fig. 3-5. You may use the measurements of 30, 40, and 50 feet when you are finding right angles on your property.

determined when the string touches the nail of that stake. At that point, the line is perpendicular. Pound a stake on this line at the 57 feet 4-inch mark.

The 57 feet 4-inch line designates the radius of a circle 360 feet in circumference. For each foot you move this line from the stake at 57 feet 4-inches, the angle will change one degree. If the corner, then, has an angle of 100 degrees, this angle will be designated by moving the string 10 feet to the right (Fig. 3-6).

For future reference, or in the event that heavy overgrowth would make difficult the moving of the string to make the degree change, instead of using 57 feet 4 inches, a 57 inch radius will make a circle with a circumference of 360 inches. Each inch the string is moved changes the angle by 1 degree. By using the larger measurements, there is more tolerance for error; i.e., you will be more accurate.

When the corners have been determined, examine the immediate area as a final search for the surveyor's stake. The discovery of one of these stakes is insurance that you have done a good job. If no stakes can be found, they may have been pounded in long ago. The stakes that you have sunk should be rechecked to make sure that all measurements are accurate. Be positive that the correct angles have been made in the proper direction.

After you are assured that the measurements have been done accurately, pound in some permanent stakes so that you always know where your corners are. By using metal stakes sunk deep into the ground, you never again will have to survey your property. If 18 inch lengths of pipe are used and are driven so that only 2 inches stick out of the ground, no one will ever pull them out and they will be there if you ever need to determine your corners again.

SETBACK REQUIREMENTS

Once the property lines have been established, the proposed building's perimeter can be delineated. Through the use of the same "3-4-5" method, square angles can be formed. Most areas have setback requirements which define the distance a building is allowed to be from the front property line. Usually there is some leeway of at least a ten foot tolerance; in other words, a building may be required to be within 15 to 25 feet of the front property line. This setback requirement must be known before a building's perimeter is defined.

The exactness with which you must make the proposed building's perimeter is determined by the exact form of post-frame construction that will be utilized. There are many types of footings, foundations, wall structures, and roof

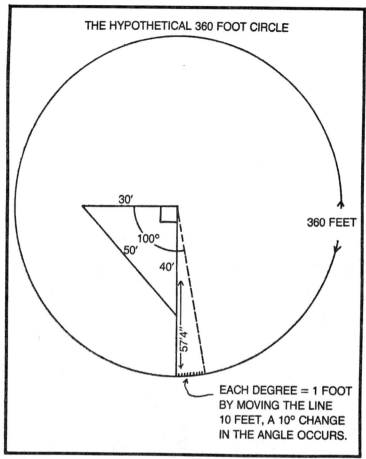

Fig. 3-6. You may need to consider the circumference of a circle when making angle measurements.

systems that can be employed. Post-frame construction is a technique which can be applied in many fashions. Before the actual building techniques are discussed, the options of the designs will be covered.

First, the treatment processes available for the posts of a post-frame will be presented. The different types of design will then follow. At the end of the book, a sample house will be presented in full detail along with the information you will need to erect your own piece of post-frame architecture.

Treatment Processes

A permanent structure is built by using treated wood in places where the wood either comes in direct contact with the ground or is within 6 inches from the finish grade. The treatment process protects the wood from decomposition caused by life forms that either feed upon its substance or seek its structure for shelter. These life forms include decay fungi, a plant form, as well as animal forms like termites, powderpost beatles, carpenter ants, and such water creatures as the pholads, limnoria, and other marine borers. Through the impregnation of the wood with chemicals toxic to these life forms, the wood is guaranteed against their attack. By being made invulnerable to these attacks, wood retains its structure and strength.

THE PLANT FORMS

The term "dry-rot" actually is a misnomer since wood must be damp in order to rot. Dry-rot is caused by plant forms of decay fungi. These fungi cannot live in dry, desert conditions; nor can they live in soaked or submerged areas. Constant dampness accompanied by warmth becomes an ideal breeding condition.

In ideal conditions the decay fungi produce millions of wind-blown spores which send out microscopic tubes to dissolve the wood cells. This fungi lives on the celluose fibers of the wood, converting the celluose into food sugars. The invisible tubes branch out, forming networks of tubes which work to dissolve the wood into nutrition for themselves.

Some forms of fungi have tubes which can carry water from nearby soil to the surface of the wood, thereby providing the moisture needed to decompose the material. Areas near to the ground, as in the case when a house is built over a crawl space, can be susceptible to the work of these fungi. For this reason, these areas should be built of treated wood in locations where decay fungi are prominent.

In desert locations, wood has been known to last thousands of years. The dry climate provides a natural protection against the decay fungi. Just the same, with the absence of marine borers, submerged wood will last indefinitely—as is the case with many sunken ships.

It can be seen then, that only certain conditions are receptive to decay fungi. Designs of buildings should be engineered to disallow those environments conducive to the growth of this plant form. Especially when heat and moisture are trapped, the lifespan of a building can be drastically shortened; by keeping these areas well ventilated, growth of the fungi can be deterred.

THE ANIMAL FORMS

Termites, carpenter ants and other insects are most notorious for their destruction of wood. These insects can completely eat through roof and floor joists within short periods of time. Figure 4-1 shows the concentrations of termites, and serves as a good guide for the necessity of taking preventive measures.

Even in the north, great care must still be taken. I've seen Michigan homes less than ten years old that have had entire walls eaten away by carpenter ants. One ceiling I took apart exposed hundreds of carpenter ants. In the middle of the span, these creatures had completely eaten through three 2 × 8s.

The subterranean termites require moisture to live. These termites, grayish-white in color, build access tubes

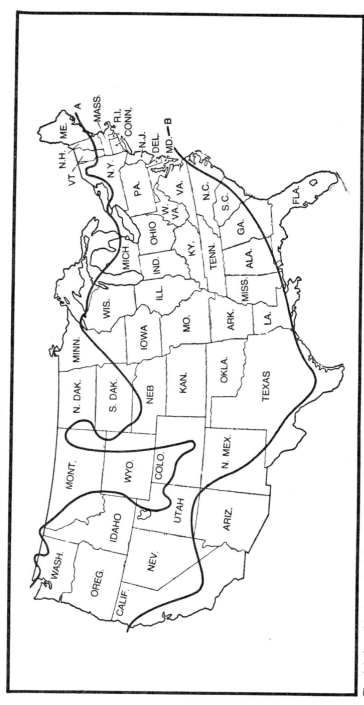

Fig. 4-1. Area A is the northern limit of recorded damage done by subterranean termites in the United States. Area B is the northern limit of damage done by drywood or nonsubterranean termites.

from the ground into the house. These tubes can be built through separations less than 1/64th of an inch between pieces of wood or through hairline cracks in foundation walls. Their colony remains underground while they traverse back and forth between meals. They, like the fungi, live on the celluose of the wood.

Although subterranean termites require moisture and stay away from light, drywood termites do not—allowing them to enter higher places of the house. Access to the roof joists can be made through air vents or through places where the facia board does not butt tight against other parts of the house. Carpenter ants allow themselves the same freedom. These ants do not live on the wood fibers, though, but destroy the wood to modify it for their own shelter.

Marine borers live in salt water and mainly attack seawalls and dock piles. A following picture shows the effect such animals can have on a large piece of wood.

The major amount of damage comes from the limnoria tripunctata, a creature that grows no larger than ⅛ of an inch. This animal, a member of the lobster family, shortens the life of an undertreated pile to eight years. Once the creosoted layer of a pile is opened, the pile can be riddled in a matter of months. Creosote alone will not stop these attacks. With a dual treatment, though, a pile can be made to last. A waterborne solution of copper, chromium, and arsenic salts comprises a second treatment. This treatment, called green-salt, in combination with the creosote has been determined to be successful.

This dual treatment is also effective against the ship-worms called teredo and bandia. These members of the mollusk family (clams, oysters) live in the pile, attacking it from beneath the water's surface, whereas the limnoria tripunctata bore from the surface. The piles must be treated to refusal, i.e., they must be saturated with the treatment oils. Most treatment processes obtain a treatment level of around 8 pounds per square foot (psf). Under the adverse conditions of wood when submerged in seawater—especially seawater infested with either the limnoria tripunctata and the teredo—the treated wood should obtain a level of at least 18 psf.

Freshwater conditions are hardly as adverse. Yet, the creosote treatment, especially when used in conjunction with another treatment, is the best protection offered. The second treatment can be modified to meet specific adverse conditions. Even in freshwater, then, submerged poles or posts should be creosoted to insure long life. The creosote treatment is the most effective against the rinsing action of the waves—guaranteeing a well-treated pole or post for the life of the structure. A retention of 12-14 psf is needed.

OTHER TREATMENTS

Even under the worst conditions, treated wood can be made to retain its original strength. The treatment must be modified to work under the conditions it will be subjected to. In the above case, a dual treatment was needed. Generally, this is not the case. Besides the type of treatment, the extent of treatment is an important factor. To stop the sea creatures, a maximum retention was needed. For most purposes, a retention of 8 psf is all that is required.

Most posts are treated with some form of penta. This chemical is added to either a light petroleum solvent or fuel

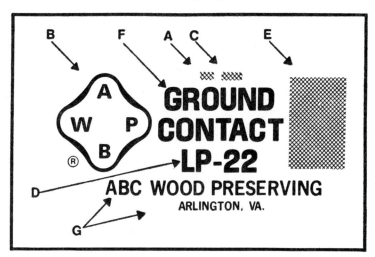

Fig. 4-2. This is a sample American Wood Preserves Bureau (AWPB) quality mark. A is the year of treatment. B is the AWPB trademark. C is the preservative used for treatment. D is the applicable AWPB standard. E is the trademark of the inspection agency. F is proper exposure conditions. G is the treating company and plant location.

oil. The penta comprises 5 percent of the solution. Penta dissolved in fuel oil produces a product that is dark colored, unpaintable, and possesses an odor. When this product is used, barriers must be set between the posts and the finishing materials of the house since the treatment will bleed. For these reasons, this treatment process is objectionable.

The most widely used process—and the one that produces the best product—dissolves penta in a light petroleum oil. This results in a clean and relatively unchanged appearance of the wood. Some odor is present in newly treated wood, but this odor diminishes in time. This treatment process also affords the user the options of leaving the posts natural, staining them, or painting them.

The penta is highly toxic to fungi and insects and is insoluble in water. It can be used in fresh water, but the high retention dual treatment of creosote is better. For post-frames built in fresh water, only the lower portion of the posts should be cresoted—leaving a clean, penta-treated post to build against. Typically, penta-treated wood is pressure treated to a retention of 8 psf.

This penta treatment in light oil is the most available and the least expensive treatment process that can be used for posts in contact with the earth. For many reasons it is the most satisfactory. Yellow pine, when handy, is used for its strength. This combination of penta in light oil, treated to a retention of 8 psf, in yellow pine gives the post-frame builder a very satisfactory product and a good, strong building material that is easy to handle and capable of dealing with wood enemies.

Penta can also be dissolved in liquid petroleum gas (volatile petroleum solvent), making this a gas-borne treatment. This process provides a clean, paintable, and relatively odorless product. This is a new treatment process and is not widely available. Many telephone poles are now treated by this method, and the results are satisfactory. Because of its newness, it is not widely available for the treatment of millcut posts. Where available, though, it may be used for wood in contact with the ground.

One problem with penta is that it is highly toxic, which is why it is so effective in protecting wood against destruction by life forms. Some problems have developed with pole-barns that have posts exposed from the inside. Cows and other animals find the penta adds a little spice to their routine diet, and so they lick the posts. Especially with milk-producing cows, a danger of tainting is possible.

For the cleanest possible treatment process, one should specify water-borne salt preservatives, generally referred to by the product name "wolmanized." This treatment process produces a clean, odorless, and paintable product. Generally, most treated lumber is wolmanized, and it is used exten-sively for outdoor decks, sills, and in areas of a building where termites or other creatures present a problem. A

Fig. 4-3. Tie the posts to a tree for stability.

post-frame could well benefit from the use of salt-treated wood for the entire floor structure.

When left exposed to the weather, the water-borne salt-preserved wood turns a bluish-grey—which makes it the most attractive of the treatment processes. This color can be used in combination with other colors to co-ordinate. the color scheme of a home. Since there is no need to paint or stain salt-treated wood as it is well protected by the treatment process, salt-treated wood is a logical choice.

IDENTIFICATION

Treated lumber is stamped to identify the type and extent of treatment. The AWPI (American Wood Preservers Institute) mark is found on much of the wood that is treated. This mark shows that the wood adheres to the Wood Institute's standards and designates the treatment process. The treatment process's code is shown on the Institute's stamp. The legend of the code is shown in Figure 4-2.

The double-digit numbers insure the buyer that the wood is treated with enough preservative to be used in contact with the ground. Regardless of the type of treatment, if not enough treatment is used, the wood is not adequately treated. Be sure that the retention pcf is of a satisfactory amount.

Wood should be examined to make sure that the treatment is not spotty. Untreated areas provide access for pests. Treatment processes are sophisticated and produce good results, but the lumber should be checked to be sure that good treatment has been done.

The treatment generally does not penetrate the heartwood. Only the outer layer of the wood is preserved. For this reason, any cuts that are made into the treated wood should be field treated. Penta can be bought in gallon cans and should be brushed onto the areas that are cut. Three coats of penta, with adequate drying time between coats, provides decent protection. Long posts that must be cut should be placed so that the pressure treated end is in the ground. The field treated end should be above ground level

Fig. 4-4. Pressure treated cylinder at a lumber treating plant (courtesy Koppers Company, Inc.).

whenever possible. All cuts into pressure treated lumber should be field treated—thereby blocking access into the untreated portions of the wood.

Through the proper selection of an adequate preservative and by specifying the amount of retention of the preservative in the wood, a satisfactory product will be obtained. Lumber with spotty treatments should be rejected. Under these stipulations, treated lumber can be placed in direct contact with the ground so that it will last the lifespan of the structure—a minimum of 40 years. If rotting were to occur after this length of time, failing posts could be sawn off and replaced with newly treated posts securely anchored onto the old ones.

FIELD TREATMENTS

Because the treatment processes are done while the wood is kiln-dried, it is not an expensive process. Treated lumber is often less expensive than untreated lumber. This is determined by your locale. Usually the southern pine which is used for the treatment process is much less expensive than varieties of fir that are used for other structural purposes. In Michigan, for example, the expenses to ship fir from the west coast are high. Since southern pine comes from the south, shipping costs are less. Adding to the cost of fir is its popularity. It is a more attractive lumber, but southern pine matches the remarkable strength of fir. For these reasons, treated lumber is often cheaper than untreated lumber.

If, though, there is a problem with obtaining treated lumber, there are field methods which can be used to treat wood. Most building codes allow a builder to use wood field-treated with creosote. Creosote can be obtained in 5-gallon buckets and is usually brushed onto the portions of the wood which will be below or within 6 inches of finish grade. For the best results, three liberal coats of creosote is advised. The instructions on the can should be religiously followed.

If this product cannot be found or cannot be afforded, a creosote solution can be made. Creosote is the material that coats the inside of a fireplace's or wood stove's chimney.

Fig. 4-5. Effects of termites on wood (courtesy Koppers Company, Inc.).

Creosote is made through a distillation process, which essentially is what occurs inside the chimney. This material can be removed from the chimney and placed in a pail. Alcohol is added to the material to act as a solvent. Under low heat—preferably outside—the contents can be heated. During the heating, the material should be stirred quickly. The chunks of creosote should be mashed into small particles. When the material turns into a paste, it can be applied to the wood. Application is best done with a large, heavy spoon. The paste should be applied with enough pressure to fully crush the creosote particles—forming a crust on the outside of the wood. After this is done, the posts should be dipped into hot tar to protect this creosote coating and to add another barrier.

As was mentioned earlier, tar alone will act as a preservative. It is best to heat the tar before application. Great care must be taken, though, since tar is flammable. Tar should be heated without a lid under very low heat and should be stirred during the warming process. Protective glasses and clothing should be worn as a precaution. If a gas burner cannot be found to heat the tar, a charcoal fire can be used. Kindling fires are not recommended because of their inconsistent tendencies. If wood must be used, the fire should be allowed to turn to coals before the tar is placed over it. If the tar does ignite, a lid can be tossed onto the container to smother the fire.

Another method of field-treating lumber is to char it. The part of the lumber that will be in contact with the ground is placed into a fire pit until the outside is fully charred. The char becomes a barrier that protects the wood. For added protection, the charred end can then be dipped into tar.

You may also treat wood by buying containers of penta and brushing or rolling it onto the surface of the wood. Paint rollers are preferable since a roller tends to squish the liquid into the pores of the wood whereas a brush will often neglect the small cavities of the wood's surface. Three liberal coats of penta is preferable. For a better treatment, the wood can be soaked in penta. Penta is available in containers as small as gallon cans and it can be obtained in bulk. If twenty or so posts are to be treated, a 5-gallon container of penta should

Fig. 4-6. Effects of decay and rotting on wood (courtesy Koppers Company, Inc.).

be obtained. The cost for this is approximately $20. All the posts can be stood up in a 55-gallon drum and the penta then poured into the drum. The posts should be tied to a tree or building to stabilize them (Fig. 4-3).

If enough penta is not obtained to fill the drum, cheap oil (even used motor oil) can be poured into the drum to "top it up." Since the penta solutions which are used to pressure treat lumber generally contain only 5 percent penta, the slight dilution of the penta is warranted.

Since most drums are only 36 inches high, and since most posts will have to be treated to about a 4 foot height, two drums can be welded together to get the proper height. In lieu of this, they may be adhered to each other. Run a liberal bead of clear silicone around the lip of the drum before placing the other barrel section on top of it. Then run a bead of silicone on the inside and outside of the lip. A well-sealed joint will occur.

Silicone can be obtained in half-barrel tubes that fit into a caulking gun. After it is applied, silicone should be allowed to cure for a few days. After a day, though, the posts can be placed into the barrel, which can be filled to somewhere below the joint. The posts can begin their treatment, and, if the seal is broken while the posts are being placed into the barrel, it can be easily redone.

Some woods are naturally resistant to rottage. Redwood and cedar contain preservation oils which act in the same manner as the oils used to impregnate other types of woods. When redwood is milled, though, it is not as durable. Only the red portions of the wood contain the preserving oils; these are the heart portions of the wood and the most expensive. Other portions of redwood are streaked with white wood. This wood is not naturally resistant to rottage.

Cedar, which is used for clothes chests and closets because its aroma is toxic to moths and other insects, can also be used in the ground. This wood is popularly used for fence posts. Care should be taken when working with cedar if extensive sawing is being done. Adequate ventilation must be provided since the substance which is toxic to moths is also toxic to humans. Some humans, especially, are sensitive to

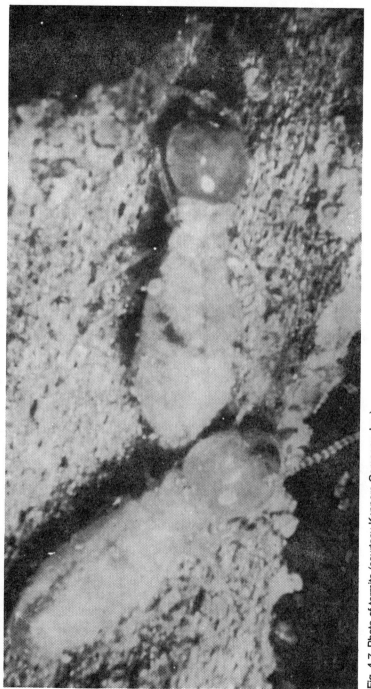

Fig. 4-7. Photo of termite (courtesy Koppers Company, Inc.).

this substance, which can cause respiratory failure. Ideally, you should saw cedar outside and should position yourself so that the sawdust blows clear of your face.

Although redwood, cedar, and, to a lesser extent, locust, can be used without any treatment, for a permanent structure it is advised that even these woods be treated. The wood is being used for the foundation of a building, and if a foundation fails, the building fails.

All of the field-treatment processes that have been mentioned are rather impromptu, and really only should be used if necessary. One is assured when factory-treated wood is obtained that a well-preserved product is being used. Not one of the field treatments can be trusted to this extent.

Although in some cases the same materials are used to field-treat, the method of application is certainly not as well controlled as when wood is treated in a factory. Factory treatments do not generally apply coatings; they actually impregnate the wood with preservative. A cresote treatment may penetrate as much as 3 inches into the wood. Sometimes the wood is incised to aid in the penetration of the treatment material. The major factor which cannot be duplicated is the use of pressure to impregnate the wood. A high-pressure airless sprayer is about the only tool that begins to approximate pressure treatment.

Since the foundation of a building is so important, and since pressure-treated wood can often be obtained without additional cost, builders are well-advised to purchase it. If pressure-treated lumber needs to be cut, though, any of the above methods will help treat the cut. When the protective shield of treatment is broken, access is provided to the untreated portions of the wood. All cuts, then, should be field-treated.

Steel has a tendency to rust, and so we treat it. Wool has a tendency to be eaten by moths and must also be treated. In the same way, wood is treated to make it last. Treated wood resists both the plant and the animal forms that it can potentially host.

Since factory-treated wood is readily available, its purchase is warranted. Yellow pine (also called southern

Fig. 4-8. Photo of subterranean termite building pattern (courtesy Koppers Company, Inc.).

Fig. 4-9. Photo showing termite cavities in wood construction (courtesy Koppers Company, Inc.).

pine) is the best choice because of its economy, receptivity to the treatment process, and its strength. Because of the wide usage of the penta in a light oil treatment of yellow pine to a net retention of 8 psf, it is the ideal choice for use as the posts of a post-frame.

For absolutely the best protection, these factory pressure treated posts can be coated with creosote at the areas where the posts will be in contact with the ground. They should also be coated 6 inches above the ground since this is a critical area. The area from a few inches below grade to a few inches above grade is important since this area is exposed to the life forms that feed on wood and experiences large variations of moisture.

The field treating of factory treated posts may well be extraneous; yet, it doesn't take much time or money and it guarantees that the building will last a long, long time.

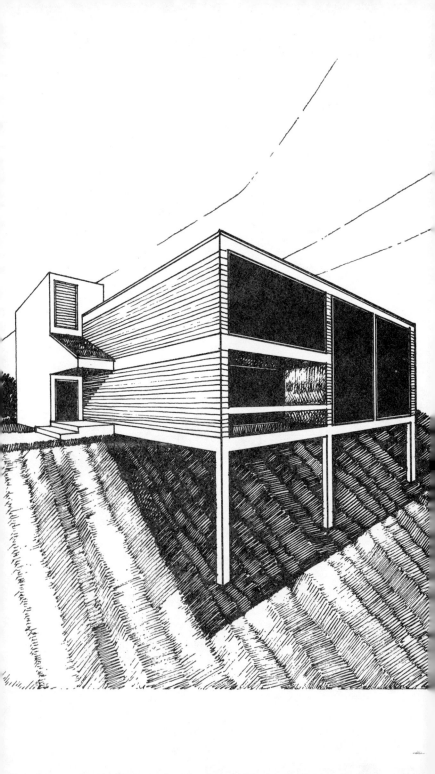

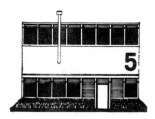

The Footings

The building site's soil will directly affect the size of the footings that will be required to support the building (Fig. 5-1). Most circumstances call for footings of less than 18 inches, which is a common diameter for augers. After the post holes are dug, footings are set at the bottom of the holes to help distribute the weight of the structure to more ground. The posts are then set upon these footings. The end of the post alone does not have sufficient bearing surface, meaning it would have a tendency to poke its way down into the ground—resulting in severe settling of the structure. Through the use of footings of the proper size, this critical problem is alleviated (Fig. 5-2).

THE SIZE

Although post-frames are generally much lighter than conventional structures which use masonry, the post-frame may have less than twenty points of load concentration. Whereas conventional structures spread their weight around the entire perimeter of the building as well as having points of support inside the perimeter, the post-frame's load is concentrated at the end of the posts. For this reason, footings are essential.

The footing size depends upon the weight of the structure and the nature of the soil on which the footing will rest.

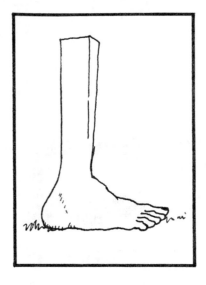

Fig. 5-1. Footings must be large enough to effectively anchor a post-frame house.

Poor, unstable soils require larger footings. Table 5-1 shows the bearing capacity of the different types of soils.

As can be seen, there is a wide variance in the bearing capacity of soils. With all other factors neutral, a footing for a soil capable of holding 2,000 psf should be four times larger than one for a soil capable of holding 8,000 psf.

Before we can figure out how large the footing must be, we must figure out how much weight will be exerted upon the footings. This weight includes the weight of the structure itself (dead load) and any weight that might be imposed upon the structure (live load). The roof's live load will include possible snow loads and wind loads. If a wood floor is hung from the posts, the dead load weight of the floor itself must be calculated as well as the weight of interior walls and the live load from furniture and the occupants.

The calculations for floors generally include 40 psf (pounds per square foot) live load and a 10 psf dead load. The roof calculations also will calculate in 40 psf live load and a 10 psf dead load. Each, then will be calculated at 50 psf.

Lesser design loads are often used to make these calculations. Steep pitched roofs, for example, can often be calculated at 35 psf combined (live and dead) load even in snow load areas, since any appreciable amount of snow would slide off from a steep pitched roof. The 50 psf figure, then, is used since it covers virtually all areas and circumstances.

Greater roof loads than 50 psf will have to be used only in special circumstances, such as when winds reach above 95 miles per hour or when a flat roof is designed to pond water or to hold a layer of dirt for insulation. Greater floor loads may be needed when heavy objects such as grand pianos and billiard tables are to be held by the floor or when heavy-duty partying and dancing are anticipated.

Under most circumstances, the 100 psf figure is more than sufficient to calculate the design load for a structure with an elevated floor. Without an elevated floor, the design load can be tabulated at 50 psf.

To keep things simple, suppose we must figure out the size for the footings for a 1,000 square foot house with 20 posts. The soil bearing capacity has been figured to be around 2,500 psf. If we figure on 50 pounds per square foot for a house without a wood floor, then the entire load will weigh around 50,000 pounds. By dividing 50,000 by 20 (posts), it is tabulated that there will be 2,500 pounds on each post. Since the soil is capable of taking 2,500 pounds per

Table 5-1. This Table Provides Load Carrying Capacities of Circular Concrete Footing Pads in Different Soils (Courtesy Northeast Regional Agricultural Engineering Service).

Soil Description	Bearing Capacity ksf[a]	Pad Diameter, inches								
		8	10	12	14	16	18	20	22	24
		Minimum Pad Thickness, inches								
		4	4	5	5	6	6	7	8	8
		Load Carrying Capacity, 1000 pounds								
Soft limestone, partially cemented gravels and hardpan	16	5.6	8.7	12.6	17.1	22.3	28.3	34.9	42.2	50.3
Well drained gravel or gravel sand mixtures in natural thick beds with little clay or silt (GW, GP)*	12	4.2	6.5	9.4	12.8	16.8	21.2	26.2	31.7	37.7
Well drained sand with little or no clay or silt (SW, SP)*	8	2.8	4.4	6.3	8.6	11.2	14.1	17.4	21.1	25.1
Well drained gravel with silt or clay (GM, GC)*	6	2.1	3.3	4.7	6.4	8.4	10.6	13.1	15.8	18.8
Well drained sand with silt or clay (SM, SC)*	4	1.4	2.2	3.1	4.3	5.6	7.1	8.7	10.6	12.6
Well drained soft clay, silts or fine sand (CL, MH, ML)*	3	1.0	1.6	2.4	3.2	4.2	5.3	6.5	7.9	9.4
Poorly drained soft clay (CH)*	2	0.7	1.1	1.6	2.1	2.8	3.5	4.4	5.3	6.3
Organic soils, fills	By test only	*	*	*	*	*	*	*	*	*

*Unified Soil Classification System

[a]ksf equals 1000 pounds per square foot

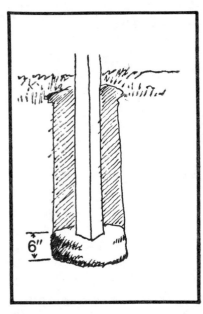

Fig. 5-2. Make sure that footings are adequate to prevent any possible settling of the house.

square foot, the footing under each post must be at least 1 square foot large. A circle with a 14-inch diameter has about the same area as a 12-inch square, so the bottom of the hole would have to be at least 14 inches across. Generally, the holes will be larger than this anyway, so making a footing for the building will present no problems.

If the building is going to have an elevated floor, the floor weight will have to be tabulated into these calculations. By figuring the floor at 50 pounds per square foot and by adding this to the 50 psf for the roof, we arrive at the 100 psf figure. The entire house, if 1,000 square feet, should be calculated at 100,000 pounds. Dividing this by 20 (posts), each post will hold 5,000 pounds. If the soil holds 2,500 psf, the footing must be at least two square feet to adequately support the structure. Since interior posts are usually used to help support a wood floor, more posts can often lighten the load per post, keeping footings from becoming too large.

This conversion table aids in the tabulation of the footing size. By remembering that the area of a circle is calculated by the formula πr^2, the area of circles is easily tabulated. Table 5-2, though, contains the most commonly used diameters and their proportion to the area of a square foot.

CIRCLE DIAMETER	NUMBER OF SQUARE FEET
13	.9
14	1.0
15	1.2
16	1.4
17	1.5
18	1.7
19	1.9
20	2.2
21	2.4
22	2.6
23	2.9
24	3.1
25	3.4
26	3.7
27	3.9
28	4.2
29	4.6
30	4.9

DIGGING THE HOLES

The holes for the footings and posts are most easily dug with an auger. Through the use of a machine especially made to dig holes or through the use of an auger attached to the pto

Fig. 5-3. An auger powered by the "power take off" of a tractor works fine to dig post holes. Other machines are made especially for this purpose.

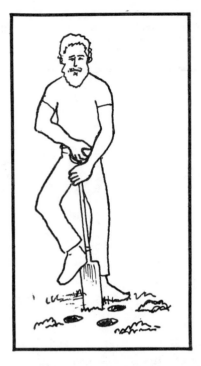

Fig. 5-4. Hand-held gasoline-powered post-hole diggers work fine in most soils to dig post holes. When the diameter of the needed hole is greater than the diameter of the auger, three holes can be dug. The dirt between the holes is then easily broken away with a shovel. Trenching shovels work the best for carving out the hole.

(power take off) of a tractor, all holes can be bored in just a couple of hours (Fig. 5-3).

If one of these machines cannot be located or if the site is inaccessible for this equipment, other approaches can be taken. Gasoline powered hand-held post-hole diggers offer an effective means by which to dig the holes. These machines can be rented for about $20, yet they do not dig holes of a large enough diameter. They are effective, though, in getting the hole started to eliminate much of the hand digging.

The use of hand-held post-hole diggers can be modified to do the majority of the excavation. Instead of boring only one hole and then hand-digging the hole wider, the post-hole diggers can be used as in Fig. 5-4.

By boring three small holes around the stake designating the post location, much of the hand-digging is eliminated. Depending on the soil, generally one should leave at least 4 inches between the holes so that the auger cuts a new hole instead of breaking into one of the other holes. If the holes are to be dug in this manner, a small (6-inch diameter) auger should be used. Hand-held augers also come in 9-inch diameters. Generally, the auger bits are 42 inches long. For deeper holes, a secondary bit is attached to the primary bit. Once the three holes are bored, the dirt between the holes can easily be broken away.

In most soils, hand digging is extremely difficult. The one advantage of hand digging, though, is that the roots of nearby trees can be worked around, thereby insuring a minimum of damage to the trees. If concrete is going to be poured around the post, the roots should be protected from contact with the concrete. This can be done by wrapping the roots in burlap. If footings larger than the diameter of the hole are needed, the bottom of the hole can be dove-tailed instead of digging a larger hole. Smaller holes offer to the builder the advantage of needing less backfill. For this reason, the diameter of the holes should be kept less than 18 inches, if possible (Fig. 5-5).

The bottom of the hole should be made as flat as possible. All loose dirt should be removed from the bottom of the hole. When the holes are dug to the proper depth, are of the proper diameter, and are clean of loose dirt the footings can be installed.

TYPES OF FOOTINGS

The footings can be made from poured concrete, large chunks of broken concrete, large flat stones, or treated

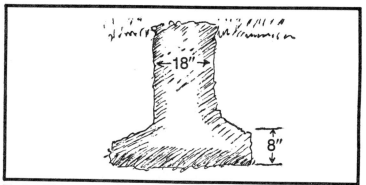

Fig. 5-5. When extremely large footings are needed, the bottom of a hole can be belled out. This permits the use of less backfill while still permitting a large footing to be poured.

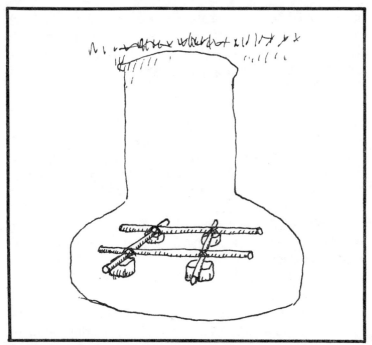

Fig. 5-6. Large footings should be reinforced with steel. "Re-rod" can be set upon bricks to hold it up from the bottom of the hole. The intersections of the rods should be wired together.

wood. If a concrete footing is used, it should be from 6 to 10 inches thick. Pads more than 18 inches in diameter should be reinforced with steel to strengthen the pad as a precaution against breakage. One-half inch reinforcing rod (called re-rod) placed in the following pattern will insure against breakage (Fig. 5-6 and Table 5-3).

The intersections of the rod can be wired together to insure against the rods moving when the concrete is poured over them. This reinforcement should be located approximately 2 inches above the bottom of the footing. By laying the reinforcement on small pieces of brick, this approximate height can be obtained. The brick pieces can be left in as part of the footing. The reinforcement can also be hung with wire (Fig. 5-7).

It must be remembered that before any footing is installed, the bottom of the hole should be cleaned of loose dirt and should be made flat. Especially if a poured footing is

Table 5-3. Use This Chart for Determining Needed Thicknesses of Concrete Footings.

WEIGHT EXERTED UPON FOOTING	THICKNESS NEEDED
2,500 pounds	6″
3,500 pounds	7″
4,500 pounds	8″
5,500 pounds	9″
6,500 pounds (or more)	10″

not used, it is essential for the bottom of the hole to be flat because any footing lying in an uneven hole would be supported only by the high parts of the ground. This set-up would soon sink. For this reason, a poured footing is easiest to do. The ground should still be level, but this factor is not as critical as it would be if footings were placed in the bottom of the holes.

When poured concrete footings are desired, 60-40 sand-gravel mix (60 percent sand, 40 percent gravel) should be used. By mixing four shovels of this mix in with one shovel of cement, a strong batch will be made. Sixty-forty mix can be obtained from most sand and gravel yards. In lieu of obtaining this pre-mixed substance, sharp masons' sand and gravel of about ½ inch in diameter should be used. Three shovelfuls of sand to one of gravel approximates correct proportioning.

Mixing is most easily done in a wheelbarrow. By throwing in two shovels of the 60-40 and then adding the cement between the next two shovels, the combining of these substances is simplified. This should be blended together while it is still dry. By using a hoe and a rake—preferably a small four-pronged rake—this mixing is easily done. It is critical that the cement is fully mixed in with the 60-40, since unequal proportions of cement will greatly weaken the finished product.

After these substances are combined, add water to fully wetten the mixture. The mixture should not be too fluid;

there should be no excess water on top of the mix. The mix should slump in the wheelbarrow but it should not be runny since a mix that is too wet makes very weak concrete. A gallon paint pail is best used to measure the water. By keeping track of the amount of water needed, each batch will be correctly proportioned. If a runny mix is accidently made, sufficient material should be added to make it of the proper consistency. After the mix is fully homogenous, it can be poured in the hole. Most holes will take more than one batch. Each hole should be finished before other holes are begun (Fig. 5-8).

If extremely large footings are needed, transit mixed concrete may be desirable. Although there is an extra charge for small loads, large footings can take enough concrete to justify the expense. Mixing a lot of concrete by hand is tiresome.

Portable mixing machines offer a nice alternative when large footings are needed. Through the use of one of these

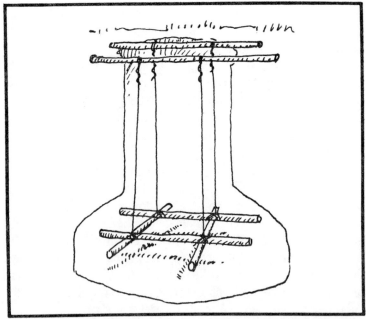

Fig. 5-7. Instead of setting the "re-rod" upon bricks, it can be suspended with wire. Sticks or "re-rod" sections can be used to hold up the reinforcement. It should be elevated approximately 2 inches above the bottom of the hole.

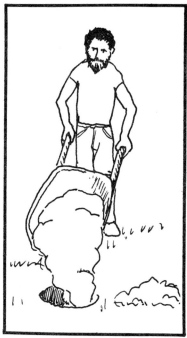

Fig. 5-8. After the bottom of the hole is cleaned of all loose dirt and made as flat as possible, a poured concrete footing can be installed. The concrete should be made stiff, not watery. The surface of the concrete footing should be made smooth by patting it with the end of a 4x4.

machines, the footings can be quickly made. If a machine is accessible, it should be used.

In place of using poured concrete footings, either pre-cast pads or broken chunks of concrete may be used to achieve a concrete footing. Broken concrete is easy to find and can offer a quick way to install footings. Care must be taken to insure that the chunks used are free from cracks. As long as it is strong concrete, it will make a strong footing.

Pre-cast pads can be purchased and are used extensively in the construction of pole-barns because they save time. Only when time is a factor is the purchase of pre-cast pads necessitated. Although you must wait overnight to begin aligning the posts if poured concrete is used, this is not a major problem for most home builders. With pole-barn builders, though, this would be a delay.

Large flat stones should have sufficient compressive strength to withstand the pressures that will be exerted upon them. Brittle stones, such as sandstone, would prove unsatisfactory.

Fig. 5-9. Laminations of treated wood can serve as a footing. The entire footing should be coated with three coats of creosote to insure its longevity.

For a non-aggregate footing, a builder can use treated wood. Especially when only small footings are needed, two 1-foot lengths of 2×12 cross-laminated will work fine. Figure 5-9 shows the all-wood footing.

By cross laminating the 2×12s, a strong footing is made—plywood achieves its strength through its cross-laminated design. Treated plywood can be substituted for the second 2×12, if desired. All fresh-cut edges should receive three coats of creosote for positive protection.

For drainage, the all-wood foundation should set upon at least 4 inches of gravel. This gravel insures that full bearing is achieved by providing a smooth surface for the footing to rest upon. The gravel should be well tamped, which can be done with a 4×4.

Through using any of the above mentioned designs, adequate footings will be achieved. It is essential to use a footing of the proper size. Over-sized footings are not necessary, although they present no harm. If larger footings are just as easy or easier to make—as is often the instance when using poured concrete—then they can be used (see Tables 5-1 and 5-4).

If a building code should require a continuous footing to be provided around the perimeter of the house, this requirement can be satisfied by making a trench footing. For some foundation systems, a trench is needed around the perimeter of the house anyway. A trench footing can easily be made in the bottom of this trench.

Table 5-4. The Diagram Gives Types of Soils and Their Design Properties (Courtesy National Forest Products Association).

Soil group	Unified soil classification system symbol	Soil description	Allowable bearing in pounds per square foot with medium compaction or stiffness[1]	Drainage Characteristics[2]	Frost heave potential	Volume change potential expansion
Group 1 Excellent	GW	Well-graded gravels, gravel sand mixtures, little or no fines.	8000	Good	Low	Low
	GP	Poorly graded gravels or gravel sand mixtures, little or no fines.	8000	Good	Low	Low
	SW	Well-graded sands, gravelly sands, little or no fines.	6000	Good	Low	Low
	SP	Poorly graded sands or gravelly sands, little or no fines.	5000	Good	Low	Low
	GM	Silty gravels, gravel-sand-silt mixtures.	4000	Good	Medium	Low
	SM	Silty sand, sand-silt mixtures.	4000	Good	Medium	Low
Group II Fair to Good	GC	Clayey gravels, gravel-sand-clay mixtures.	4000	Medium	Medium	Low
	SC	Clayey sands, sand-clay mixture.	4000	Medium	Medium	Low
	ML	Inorganic silts and very fine sands, rock flour, silty or clayey fine sands or clayey silts with slight plasticity.	2000	Medium	High	Low
	CL	Inorganic clays of low to medium plasticity, gravelly clays, sands clays, silty clays, lean clays	2000	Medium	Medium	Medium[3]
Group III Poor	CH	Inorganic clays of high plasticity, fat clays	2000	Poor	Medium	High
	MH	Inorganic silts, micaceous or diatomaceous fine sandy or silty soils, elastic silts	2000	Poor	High	High
Group IV Unsatisfactory	OL	Organic silts and organic silty clays of low plasticity.	400	Poor	Medium Medium	Medium High
	OH	Organic clays of medium to high plasticity, organic silts.	-0-	Unsatisfactory	Medium	High
	Pt	Peat and other highly organic soils.	-0-	Unsatisfactory		

[1]Allowable bearing value may be increased 25 percent for very compact, coarse grained gravelly or sandy soils or very stiff fine-grained clayey or silty soils. Allowable bearing value shall be decreased 25 percent for loose, coarse-grained gravelly or sandy soils, or soft, fine-grained clayey or silty soils. See Table A-1, Appendix A.

[2]The percolation rate for good drainage is over 4 inches per hour, medium drainage is 2 to 4 inches per hour, and poor is less than 2 inches per hour.

[3]Dangerous expansion might occur if these soil types are dry but subject to future wetting.

The trench is dug down below the frost line, which is generally less than 4 feet deep. The trench is typically 16 inches wide and should reach firm ground. The bottom of the trench should be free of loose dirt and should be flat. With this done, the trench is filled with an 8-inch layer of concrete. In this manner, a continuous footing is easily provided.

For peculiar situations, reinforcing rod can be embedded in the concrete. Two ½-inch re-rods should be located approximately two inches up from the bottom of the footing. These re-rods should be placed approximately 8 inches apart. The steel-reinforced continuous concrete footing is absolutely the best footing for a post-frame. Most frequently, though, the making of this footing is extraneous.

A strong footing is an essential part of any permanent structure. By making sure that stable earth is reached, that the footing is below the frost line, and that a well-structured footing is composed, the building built on top of the footing will not shift, sink, or become otherwise dislocated. With a proper footing, a building is well on its way to becoming permanent.

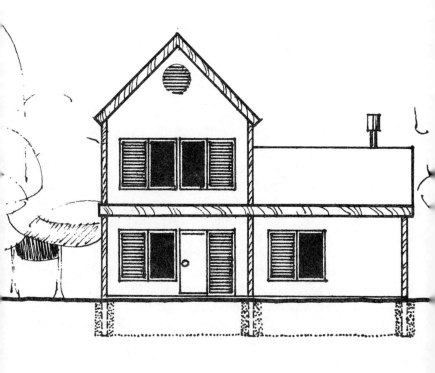

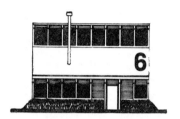

Foundation Systems

A foundation is the lowest division of a building or wall, usually of masonry and partly or wholly below the ground's surface. Lacking a proper foundation system, any building's longevity is drastically shortened. Serious disturbances of a building's structure can occur as a result of moisture penetration, frost heave, and normal earth pressure. These three factors are culprits which must be checked to insure long life for a building. Longevity, though, is only one aspect that must be considered; just as important is the occupants' comfort. Some structural disturbances may not kill a building, yet these disturbances may make living less comfortable than planned. A cold, damp floor, for example, is no reason to destroy a building; yet the building as a living environment is less ideal. For a building that lasts and for one that contains comfort, a builder must prepare a strong defense against moisture penetration, frost heave, and normal earth pressure.

The building site will determine the extent to which a builder must prepare to thwart these three factors. Some sites will have all three factors working in conjunction; having a multiplicative type of effect, the potential of failure is heightened. Other sites, though, may not have any of these potentially dangerous problems; on these sites a building is more easily and more economically created. The harsher environments are those that present the more complex problems. A structure must be programmed to shield out the undesirable elements which may impinge themselves upon the building.

MOISTURE

Generally we think of moisture penetrating roofs, but moisture can penetrate the lower parts of buildings, too. This can cause multitudes of problems: walls may leak; a constant dampness provides a living environment for mold and mildew; untreated wood parts of a structure become susceptible to rottage; water can stain or totally destroy interior finishing materials; water can also short out electrical wires and increase the possibility of fire; minor floods can ruin valued possessions; and water can erode the soil beneath the footings, causing the entire structure to begin to sink.

These factors are generally prime considerations. Although some areas have little rain, most areas have enough to destroy a building. It is in the areas that have over 3 inches of rain per annum that moisture problems become paramount. The more rain an area is subjected to, the more seriously one must consider how to seal it out.

FROST HEAVE

In locales subjected to freezing temperatures, precautions must be taken to prevent the ground from freezing beneath the footings and beneath the floor—if the floor is a concrete floor resting on the ground. The swelling of the earth caused by water in the ground turning to ice will lift any object resting on it. If the ground beneath a post's footing were to freeze, the footing and post would be forced upward, making major disturbances in the house's structure. Likewise, if the ground beneath a slab were to freeze, the slab would become dislocated. This is especially dangerous when there are water pipes inside the slab or when hot water baseboard heaters are installed just above the slab. The frost heave undoubtedly is bound to burst the pipes.

The effect of frost heave can often be seen in broken up concrete patios. Portions of the patio are sometimes raised

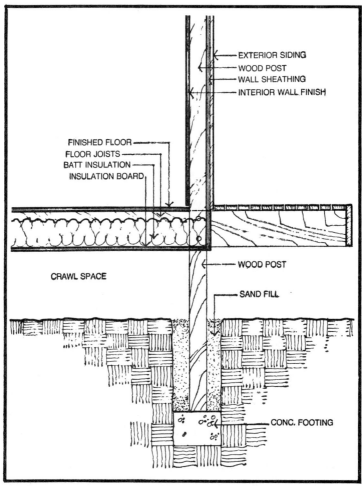

EXTERIOR SIDING
WOOD POST
WALL SHEATHING
INTERIOR WALL FINISH

FINISHED FLOOR
FLOOR JOISTS
BATT INSULATION
INSULATION BOARD

CRAWL SPACE

WOOD POST

SAND FILL

CONC. FOOTING

Fig. 6-1. Treated wood posts are sunk into holes containing concrete footings. The elevated wood floor's joists (or beams) can project past the wall structure to form a deck. The elevated floor is insulated with batt insulation; a ridig insulation board protects the batts.

three or more inches, dislodging anything in the way. Steps are often set upon patios, and, if the patio is heaved, the steps will become tremendously off level. Porch slabs can rise so much that the front door can no longer be opened. Although the ground returns to its approximate position when it thaws, in many circumstances the time span is too long to wait and the slab must be removed. This is a minor inconvenience, though, in comparison to the complications brought on with the heaving of a home's floor. For this reason, great precaution must be taken to prevent the freezing of a home's slab. And, just the same, assurance must be provided so that the posts do not heave. With a proper design, these disastrous events can be circumvented.

NORMAL EARTH PRESSURE

If the earth is piled against the wall of a house, constant pressure will be exerted upon that wall. The higher the earth is piled, the greater the amount of pressure that will be exerted upon it. When a building is partially buried in a hill, the wall on the uphill side will have the greatest amount of pressure against it; not only will it be buried deeper than the other walls, but also there will be a downhill force in action. The walls against a hill, then, warrant the greatest precautions.

Moisture, frost heave, and normal earth pressure are all forces which must be countered by the foundation. As long as the foundation is designed to endure these forces, a successful, comfortable and permanent structure will be created.

DESIGN NUMBER ONE: THE ELEVATED FLOOR

The elevated floor design is often the simplest method of building a post-frame house (Fig. 6-1). With this design, the foundation of the building consists of the footing and the portion of the post which is below grade. Obviously, this is the most simplified form of foundation that exists.

Because of the elevation of the floor, there is no worry about moisture problems. In areas prone to flooding, this system of building cannot be paralleled. By building on stilts, the building is high and dry. This is the type of foundation that must be used in low areas. Conveniently, the price of low land is cheap; in areas conducive to the building of an elevated building, this foundation system can promote the lowest cost design available.

If a floor is elevated in cold climates, the floor must be insulated. The floor itself does not necessarily have to be insulated to be structurally sound; only the plumbing in the floor must be insulated. For comfort's sake, though, the floor should be insulated in the colder climates. With this design, preventive measures in frost areas need only be taken for the building's footings. As long as the footings of the building are below the frost line, the building will be secure.

Since this building is elevated, there will be no normal earth pressure exerted upon it. The elevated floor design, then, makes for the most simplified foundation system. Since there is no concern for normal earth pressure or for potential moisture problems, it is often the most easily built. And, the danger of frost heave is pinpointed down to one feature—the depth of the footings. Again, the footings must be below the frost line.

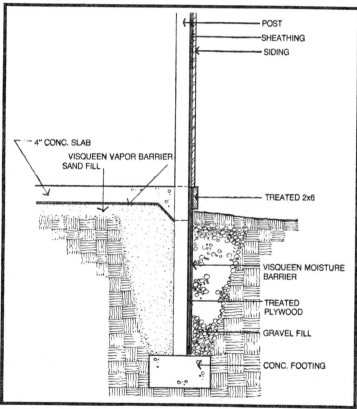

Fig. 6-2. For the "slab on grade" design, footings are placed at the bottom of a trench below the perimeter of the house. Treated plywood is nailed onto the face of the posts; plastic covers the plywood. The trench is then filled with gravel, which forms a frost barrier. Sand fill is used beneaty the slab to insulate it and to raise it slightly above grade.

DESIGN NUMBER TWO: THE SLAB ON GRADE

The slab on grade design is best suited for sites that are relatively flat (Fig. 6-2). As was mentioned in the last chapter, the slab floor has many benefits. Besides being the least expensive floor system, in cold areas the slab floor can be much warmer than an elevated wood floor.

The slab floor is kept dry by being protected by visqueen moisture barriers. The sand or gravel fill, too, helps barricade the moisture by raising the level of the floor and providing distance between the ground and the floor. Notice that the floor is slightly elevated above the exterior ground level. By doing this, the possibility of having an absolutely dry floor is increased. Because water seeks its own level, water will not be prone to seep to the floor; more likely, it will stay away from the floor because of the floor's height.

For absolutely positive protection in areas which may be slightly low, this design incorporates a membrane of treated plywood sunk below grade. In areas which are not prone to be damp, this plywood may be eliminated. An adequate moisture barrier may be composed of visqueen and felt paper. The felt paper's purpose is to protect the plastic. The plastic/felt system will take more time to fabricate, but in circumstances when time is less important than money, this system offers a nice alternative.

First of all, the posts are not sunk into holes; a trench is dug around the perimeter of the house. The footings are cast (which can be done by casting concrete in holes dug at the bottom of the trench) and then the posts are set and aligned. Instead of nailing on the treated plywood, felt paper is attached to the posts. This felt can be stapled onto the outside face of the posts. It is best to start at the bottom of the trench and work up to a point about 6 inches above ground level. This distance will usually be about 4 feet. After the felt has been wrapped around the house's perimeter, a layer of four mil visqueen is then attached to the posts over the felt. It is best to glue the plastic onto the felt, but it can be attached by folding over the top edge a few times and then sinking a nail through the folded area into the post. The plastic is hung from these nails. A second layer of felt is then applied over the plastic. This layer can be held in place with thin strips of wood applied vertically over the face of the posts. A nail in the top and bottom of the wood strip is sufficient to hold the felt in place. With this arrangement, no holes are punched through the plastic. The purpose of the felt is to insure positive protection for the plastic membrane so that it isn't punctured when the trench is backfilled. With the plastic sandwiched between the layers of felt, it will be relatively puncture-proof.

Before the trench is backfilled, storm drains can be placed at the bottom of the trench, although this isn't absolutely necessary except in areas with a high water table. As long as the slab is above grade, drains are not required in most areas. Storm drains, though, are inexpensive and easily installed. Their installation will be covered with design #3's explanation.

With the sandwich of plastic and felt, great care should be taken during backfilling. Two people should be on hand to do this job. One person takes care of filling the trench from the inside of the house, the other person fills the trench from the outside. The trench should be filled with sand and gravel since they promote drainage, can be compacted, and are not liable to rip through the felt. With the two people backfilling, equal amounts of fill are shoveled into the trench from both sides, keeping the felt and plastic membranes straight. The fill should be stomped on occasionally to pack it down. This tramping is also best done with two people, one on each side of the membrane.

By production standards, the use of treated plywood is a more labor-efficient design; yet essentially the same effect can be obtained with the felt/plastic membranes. The plywood, though, is more easily installed and it simplifies backfilling. Still, it is covered with a visqueen membrane which is glued onto it, and care must be taken during backfilling so that the membrane doesn't become punctured. For the best possible system, a layer of felt is applied over the plastic for protective purposes.

Gravel should be used on the outside of the water barrier since gravel promotes better drainage than sand. It also composes a frost barrier. Remember that precautions must be taken to insure that the ground beneath the slab doesn't freeze. This gravel "wall" barricades the frost. The gravel acts as insulation. As long as a wall of gravel surrounds the perimeter of the house, the ground beneath the slab won't freeze. For areas where severe winters are the norm, this gravel wall should be made at least a foot wide. The sand fill on the other side of the moisture barrier also helps barricade the cold; but it should be looked at as a back-up system—and not one that should be highly relied upon.

This gravel wall also serves the purpose of cushioning any earth movement. Although there normally will not be vast earth pressure with the slab poured above the finish grade, the gravel does serve this secondary purpose.

Foundation design number two, then, is well-equipped to combat moisture, frost, and natural earth movement. The treated 2 × 6 which covers the edge of the moisture barrier insulates the slab's edge from the cold. For extra protection, styrofoam can be placed between the posts before the slab is laid. This added protection is a good idea in the extremely cold climates.

Simplifications of this foundation system can be made in those climates which aren't subjected to severe winters, especially if the sites are well drained. Instead of having a trench dug around the perimeter of the house, post holes are dug. The posts are set on top of footings and, after being aligned, can be backfilled with the same dirt that was excavated. With this modified version of foundation system #2, there is no moisture or frost barrier. It is imperative, then, that this simplified version be limited to those areas which are dry and do not experience freezing temperatures.

DESIGN NUMBER THREE: BELOW-GRADE STRUCTURE

Foundation design number three is for a below-grade structure (Fig. 6-3). A below-grade design is often needed on sloped sites since extensive excavation would have to be done to level out the entire site to make it appropriate for a structure built on grade. There are some very positive advantages of having portions of a structure below grade: there is never any worry about the slab freezing since it can be made below the frost line; less siding is needed for the

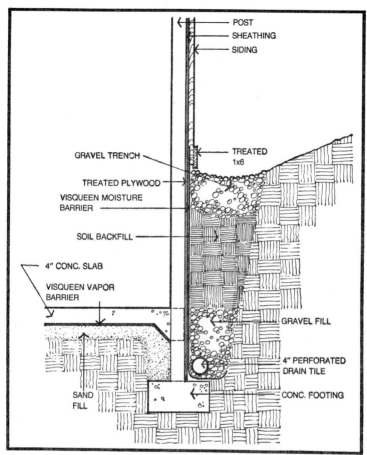

Fig. 6-3. For a building partially below grade, drains must be used around the perimeter of the building. Gravel fill insures proper functioning of the drains. A layer of soil backfill functions to keep some potential moisture from reaching the lower portions of the wall. By being below grade, the concrete floor is kept warm.

building since much of it is below the ground level; and it is easier to work on the building since all parts are lower to the ground level. The disadvantages include the necessity of using treated wood for the building portions below grade, the increased chance of having moisture problems, and the accounting that must be made for the earth pressure exerted against the below-grade walls.

All wooden portions of the wall that are below grade must be composed of treated wood. Depending upon the type of wall structure that the builder chooses, the wall's girts or studs should also be treated wood. To counter the earth's forces, the studs or girts will have to be either spaced closer together or be of larger stock. The deeper the house is buried, the greater will be the earth's pressure. Table 6-1 shows the relative materials to use dependent upon the height of the fill. If girts are used, the girted wall design #6, where the girts are fit between the posts, is suggested. For this wall design, the girts' spacing can follow the same spacing as is listed for the studs.

For below-grade walls, attaching the girts onto the outside face of the posts becomes impractical. It should not be done with the posts spaced typically eight feet on center. Instead, the posts should be spaced at four feet on center. With this post spacing, the girts can follow the spacing requirements listed in the above chart. It is wiser, though, to use wall design #6 and to fit the girts between the posts—leaving the post spacing at 8 feet.

When using the below-grade design, it is best to place the slab below the frost line. When this is done, no extra precautions need to be taken to protect the slab from freezing—the gravel frost barrier trench can be totally eliminated. As with all designs, the bottom of the posts' footings must be below the frost line—which is usually the case anyway. The posts should extend about a foot below the slab to make them rigid. The below-grade design generally results in a warmer house. The slab is not only protected from freezing, it is kept warm from the earth piled against the wall. The dirt serves as extra insulation for the wall, too.

Although the slab is kept warm by being underground, precautions must be taken to insure that it remains dry. The deeper a house is sunk into the ground, the greater is the possibility of dampness. A well-built underground structure is needed to keep the walls and floor dry. When the treated plywood is applied over the wall framework, the seams of the plywood must be well caulked with a high quality butyl caulk. Galvanized nails should be used to attach the plywood; the nails should be #8 for ½-inch plywood and #10 for ¾-inch plywood. These nails should be spaced 6 inches apart at the seams and 12 inches apart on intermediate supports (the girts or studs). The plywood's seams should break on the posts.

After the plywood is secured and caulked, it must be covered with a six mil plastic membrane secured to the plywood with asphalt adhesive. Other adhesives may be used as long as they are capable of securing plastic to plywood and plastic to plastic. The asphalt adhesives are generally the least expensive, being readily available in five-gallon containers. The wall is coated with the adhesive and then the plastic is applied to the wall. The plastic must be overlapped a minimum of 6 inches.

With the above specifications, a waterproof wall is composed. Adequate drainage, though, still must be provided. Whenever a building's floor is below grade, storm drains are required above the footings. There are many types of drains, but the perforated plastic drains are inexpensive and easily installed. A continuous loop of drain surrounds the house, outletting to a storm drain, dry well, or to daylight in non-frigid areas. This drain is set upon approximately 3 inches of crushed stone or pea gravel. Twelve inches of gravel is then shoveled atop the drains. The drains should be pitched slightly downhill toward the outlet to assure proper drainage.

Instead of backfilling the entire trench with gravel, some soil backfill is used. This soil creates a slight water barrier to inhibit the penetration of some of the water. This way, less water is allowed to reach the lower portions of the wall. The soil backfill—since its purpose is to provide runoff—should taper downhill. The top 8 inches or so of the trench should be filled with gravel to provide a channel for this runoff.

An abundance of dirt is not needed to compose this natural water barrier. The trench should be backfilled mostly with gravel. This gravel helps absorb the pressure the earth exerts against a below-grade wall. By using gravel to back-fill the majority of the trench and by beefing up the structure of the wall, the pressure the earth exerts is controlled.

Notice in the drawing that the hill does not slam right into the building's wall. A pocket is provided so no water is

Table 6-1. This chart lists minimum plywood grades and thicknesses for foundation construction and corresponding heights of fill and stud spacings (courtesy National Forest Products Association).

Height of fill (inches)	Stud spacing (inches)	Face grain across studs[2] Grade[3]	Minimum thickness[1]	Identification index	Face grain parallel to studs Grade[3]	Minimum thickness[1,5]	Identification index
24	12	B	1/2	32/16	B	1/2	32/16
	16	B	1/2	32/16	B	1/2 (4.5 ply)	32/16
48	12	B	1/2	32/16	B A	1/2[6] (5 ply) 1/2	32/16 32/16
	16	B	1/2	32/16	A B	5/8 3/4	42/20 48/24
72	12	B	1/2	32/16	A	5/8[6] (5 ply)	42/20
	16	A[4]	1/2[6]	32/16	B	3/4[6]	48/24
86	12	A	5/8	48/24	A B	5/8[6] 3/4[6]	42/20 48/24
	16	B	3/4	42/20	A	5/8[7]	42/20

[1] Minimum thickness 1/2 inch except crawl space sheathing may be 3/8 inch for face grain across studs and maximum 3 foot depth of unequal fill.

[2] Minimum 2 inch blocking between studs required at all horizontal panel joints more than 4 feet below adjacent ground level.

[3] Plywood shall be not less than the following minimum grades conforming to U.S. Product Standard PS 1, Construction and Industrial Plywood;

A. Structural I C-D

B. C-D (Exterior glue)

If a major portion of the wall is exposed above ground, a better appearance may be desired. The following Exterior grades would be suitable:

A. Structural I A-C, Structural I B-C or Structural I C-C (Plugged)

B. A-C Exterior Group 1, B-C Exterior Group 1, C-C (Plugged) Exterior Group 1 or MDO Exterior Group 1.

[4] For this combination of fill height and panel grade, only Structural I A-C or Structural I C-C may be substituted for improved appearance.

[5] When face grain is parallel to studs, plywood panels of the required thickness, grade and identification index may be any construction permitted under Article 2.2 except as noted in the table for minimum number of plys required.

[6] For this fill height, thickness and grade combination, panels which are continuous over less than three spans (across less than three stud spacings) require blocking 2 feet above bottom plate. Offset adjacent blocks and fasten through studs with two 16d corrosion resistant nails at each end.

[7] For this fill height, thickness and grade combination, panels require blocking 16 inches above bottom plate. Offset adjacent blocks and fasten through studs with two 16d corrosion resistant nails at each end.

held up against the house's wall. Ideally, the hill should be tapered back ½-inch per foot for 6 feet or more; in many circumstances this is not possible. When it is possible, though, it should be done. The idea is to keep as much moisture and pressure as possible away from the house.

For steep grades and for those areas in which there are great amounts of water, an interceptor trench can be made. An interceptor trench intercepts water runoff before it reaches the house. A trench is dug up-grade from the building. This trench, which can be as small as one foot wide and one foot deep, is dug out of the hill and filled with gravel. It should gradually work its way downslope and should lead away from the house to a water retention pond or to any area where a little extra water will do no harm.

CONCLUSION

There are, then, three different foundation systems (elevated floor, slab on grade, below-grade structure) for post-frame structures. Each one is successful at meeting the demands of being moisture resistant, frost proof, and able to counteract earth pressure. Each has advantages and disadvantages; the demands of the site will generally determine which foundation system is most ideal. With these three systems to choose from, a successful foundation system can be found for virtually any site. And, since each tends to lend itself to very different architectual effects, the builder can select the system that best meets his visual demands.

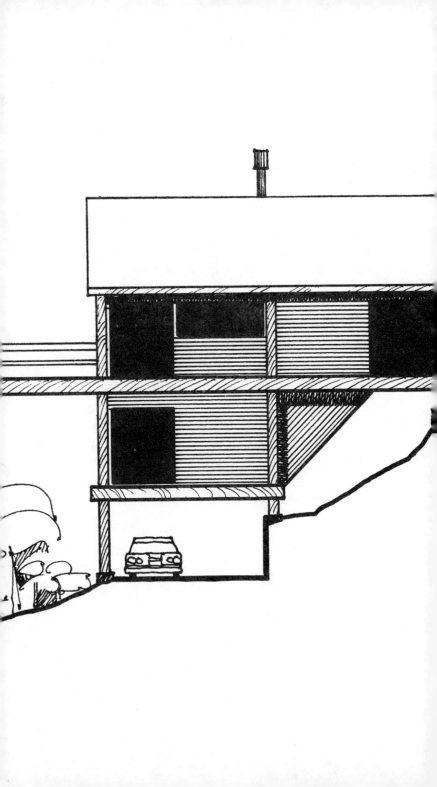

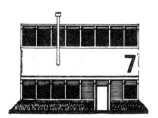

The Posts

Treated posts can be obtained in virtually any size (Fig. 7-1). Douglas fir trees from the west coast grow in excess of 200 feet tall! The determination of the size of the post hinges on the following factors: the spacing between the posts; the amount of weight each post must hold; the height of the eaves; the wind's velocity upon the building site; and any other lateral forces that might be exerted upon the building. Increases in these factors must be counteracted by an increase in the posts size.

For well-engineered designs, the smallest dimension post possible should be used. The smallest obtainable size is 4×4, which can be used in many circumstances. Table 7-1 shows the weight capacity of the various dimensions of posts.

To use Table 7-1, suppose the post size must be determined for a structure with a trussed roof and floor fully supported by the outside walls. The structure has two elevated wood floors, creating a height of 20 feet for the posts. The posts are to be 8 feet on center and the trusses are to span 36 feet.

Since the posts are 8 feet on center, two posts will support each 8 foot section of the building, that section being 36 feet long (the span of the trusses). The area of that section is 36×8 or 288 square feet. The number 288 is

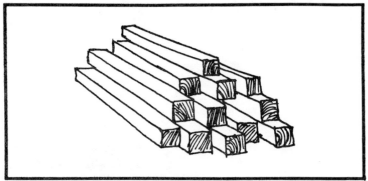

Fig. 7-1. Treated posts are readily available.

multiplied by the design factor of 50 psf for each floor and the roof, or a total of 150 psf. Multiply 288×150 to get 43,200 total pounds per 36 foot by 8 foot roof section. Since this load is supported by two posts, each post will be holding one-half of 43,200 or 21,600 pounds. Additional pounds may also have to be added for extreme wind load or snow load. If an extra 10 psf were to be added to the roof load for the increased wind load, a total of 288 square feet times 10 or 2,880 pounds per roof section would have to be added to 43,200. This creates a total load of 46,080 total pounds and divided by two posts equals 23,040 total pounds per post. For the 20 foot length, 8×8s would be needed.

For that same roof area, (which happens to be the roof area per section for the home described in the procedure chapter), if only the roof is to be held by the posts, the total load is 288×50 or 14,400 pounds. Each roof section for that building is supported by two interior posts as well as two exterior posts, so the total load of 14,400 can be divided by four which equals 3,600 pounds per post. Four-by-fours as long as 14 feet could be used to support this load, so 4×4s are well suited to do the job.

As can be seen, the 4×4 post is capable of handling 11,328 pounds when it is extended 8 feet. This limit can be adhered to in most circumstances when a slab floor is employed in the design. Wood floors not only exert more load on the posts; they also fail to provide the strength offered by the slab floor.

Many warehouses will be built with concrete floors for various reasons pertaining to operation. Such floors, by restraining poles at the ground line, tend to raise maximum bending moment in poles to a point near the surface, and to increase slightly the height of the point of inflection above the surface, while decreasing the amount of the bending moment. A concrete floor also reduces the total horizontal thrust taken by poles in an outside row. The slab directly takes the wind reaction otherwise taken by the pole itself in bending. A note of caution is necessary here, because the slab surrounding poles must be capable of taking, in bearing, the entire thrust of the wind against them. This may require a thickened slab adjacent to the poles, some reinforcement for distributing the thrust, or both. Savings in the size of poles needed effected by use of a slab may be a deciding factor in determining the type of floor to be used in a building.[1]

When an elevated wood floor is needed, the posts will also have to be larger to support the floor. And, the extra elevation raises the height of the eaves, resulting in a longer post. Under these circumstances, 4×6s or 6×6s should be used.

Table 7-1. The Chart Shows Total Allowable Weight in Pounds to be Supported by Yellow Pine or Douglas Fir Posts.

	POST SIZE				
	4×4	4×6	6×6	6×8	8×8
6'	14,528	21,792	35,352	47,136	64,000
7'	13,264	19,896	34,776	46,368	
8'	11,328	16,992	33,912	45,216	62,848
9'	9,021	13,531	32,688	43,584	
10'	7,307	10,960	30,924	41,232	61,120
11'	6,039	9,058	28,584	38,112	
12'	5,074	7,611	25,488	33,984	58,112
13'	4,323	5,592	21,888	29,183	
14'	3,728	4,871	18,872	25,163	53,056
15'	3,247	4,281	16,440	21,920	
16'	2,854		14,449	16,857	45,312
17'					
18'			11,417	15,272	36,082
20'			9,247	12,330	29,227
22'					24,154
24'					20,296

[1] Donald Patterson, *Pole Building Design* (McLean Virginia: American Wood Preservers Institute, 1969), p. 24.

Table 7-1. The Chart Shows Total Allowable Weight in Pounds to be Supported by Yellow Pine or Douglas Fir Posts.

Post Size in × in[b]	Wind Load psf[c]	Wind Speed mph	Effective Building Height[a], feet					
			9.0	10.5	12.0	13.5	15.0	19.0
			Maximum Spacing[d], feet					
5.5×9.5	10	62	X	X	38.3	30.3	24.5	15.3
	12	68	X	X	31.9	25.2	20.4	12.8
	15	76	X	X	25.5	20.2	16.3	10.2
7.5×7.5	10	62	X	X	32.5	25.7	20.8	13.0
	12	68	X	35.4	27.1	21.4	17.4	10.8
	15	76	38.6	28.3	21.7	17.1	13.9	8.7
6.0×8.0	10	62	X	38.7	29.6	23.4	19.0	11.8
	12	68	X	32.3	24.7	19.5	15.8	9.8
	15	76	35.1	25.8	19.7	15.6	12.6	7.9
5.5×7.5[e]	10	62	X	31.2	23.9	18.9	15.3	9.5
	12	68	35.4	26.0	19.9	15.7	12.7	7.9
	15	76	28.3	20.8	15.9	12.6	10.2	6.3
6.0×6.0	10	62	29.6	21.8	16.7	13.2	10.7	6.6
	12	68	24.7	18.1	13.9	11.0	8.9	5.5
	15	76	19.7	14.5	11.1	8.8	7.1	4.4
5.5×5.5[e]	10	62	22.8	16.8	12.8	10.1	8.2	5.1
	12	68	19.0	14.0	10.7	8.4	6.8	4.3
	15	76	15.2	11.2	8.5	6.8	5.5	3.4
4.0×6.0	10	62	19.7	14.5	11.1	8.8	7.1	4.4
	12	68	16.5	12.1	9.3	7.3	5.9	3.7
	15	76	13.2	9.7	7.4	5.8	4.7	2.9
3.5×5.5[e]	10	62	14.5	10.7	8.2	6.5	5.2	3.3
	12	68	12.1	8.9	6.8	5.4	4.4	2.7
	15	76	9.7	5.4	5.4	4.3	3.5	2.2
4.0×4.0	10	62	8.8	6.4	4.9	3.9	3.2	2.0
	12	68	7.3	5.4	4.1	3.2	2.6	1.6
	15	76	5.8	4.3	3.2	2.6	2.1	1.3

[a]For roof slopes 4 in 12 or less the effective height is the vertical distance from grade level to the eave. For roof slopes greater than 4 in 12 the effective building height is the vertical distance from grade level to eave height plus half the roof height.

[b]The larger post dimension is in the same direction as the wind or parallel to the building width.

[c]In areas with 20 lb/sq. ft. (psf) wind loads (88 mph) use half the 10 psf spacing.

[d]Spacing greater than 20' not recommended.

[e]These sizes are commonly available in most areas.

Just the same, two story post-frame structures must be designed to hold up the elevated wood floor(s) while maintaining an eave height of 17 or more feet. Eight-by-eights are generally needed to supply this function. Table 7-2 helps to show the relation between building height and post size.

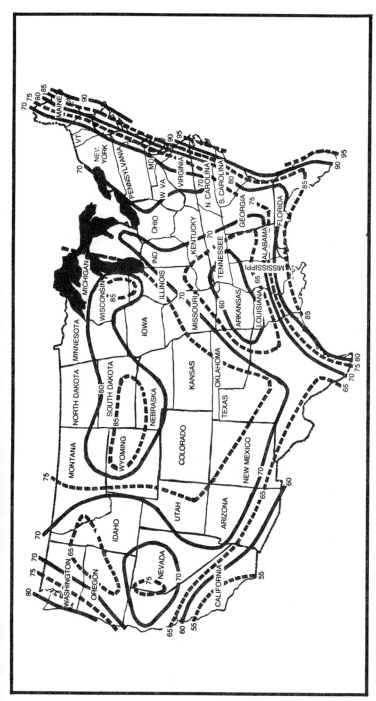

Fig. 7-2. Locate your area and find the wind velocity.

The chart also shows the relation between the post size and the wind velocity. Areas of extreme wind velocity must have larger posts to thwart movement by the wind. Figure 7-2 shows the wind velocity for the continental United States.

As can be seen, the wind velocity varies greatly, affecting the design of a post-frame building. This type of construction, though, is the most suitable for areas with severe wind conditions. The only structures that often survive the force of hurricane winds are those with this type of construction. The poles or posts that extend from deep into the ground up to the building's eaves serve to anchor the building while caging the structure inside the pole-type framing. The forces of the wind must influence the design of the structure. Strong winds mean strong posts.

SPACING

The other factor that influences the dimension of the posts is the spacing. Larger spacings mean larger posts since, with larger spacings, fewer posts will be used. With fewer posts, each post will have to support more load. Although spacings of up to 20 feet are conceivable, only under peculiar conditions would such extreme spacing be warranted. If, for example, the ground was difficult to excavate, then larger spacings might be warranted.

The problem with larger spacings is that every part of the structure must be larger to adapt to the spacing. The posts must be larger, the footings for the posts must be larger to support the increased weight, and the members spanning between the posts must be larger to make the increased span. For these reasons, the most economical designs do not space the posts too far apart; nor is it wise to space the posts too close together. The ideal arrangement, under most circumstances, is to have the posts spaced eight feet on center. In this manner, enough posts are used to distribute the weight efficiently and the members spanning between the posts can be of a nominal size. By keeping to a dimension that is a multiple of four, there will be a minimum of wastage in material. Table 7-3 gives the general sizes of post needed for the amount of spacing and the height of the eaves.

POST SPACING

		4'	8'	12'	16'	20'
E A V E	8'	4×4	4×4	4×6	6×6	6×6
	10'	4×4	4×6	6×6	6×6	6×8
	12'	4×6	6×6	6×6	6×8	8×8
H E I G H T	14'	6×6	6×6	6×8	8×8	8×8
	16'	6×6	6×8	8×8	8×8	
	18'	6×6	8×8	8×8		
	20'	6×6	8×8			

MINIMUM POST SIZES

The posts must be deep enough to be below the frost line. The frost line is the maximum depth of frost penetration. The ground does not always freeze down to this point. To protect against frost heave, the posts' footings must be below the frost line. This generally presents no problem, though, since the frost line in most areas is less than 42 inches deep. (Fig. 7-3). Usually the posts must be at least this deep anyway.

DEPTH

The depth of posts is largely determined by the type of soil they will rest upon. Posts need to be embedded deeper in the poorer soils since the greater depths reach more stable soil. The footings must rest upon stable soil since unstable soils can change as a result of moisture. The soft clays, when wet, turn mushy—resulting in a poor bearing surface.

Posts must be sunk deeper, then, in poor soil. Larger posts, presumably holding more weight, must also be sunk deeper since the greater amount of weight would tend to displace the bearing soil more than posts holding less weight. Larger footings, too, can help counter this effect (Table 7-4).

Another factor that influences the depth of the posts is the slope of the site. The posts holding up a house on a steep slope should be deeper to counteract the lateral downhill force. A rule of thumb is that for every 1/12 pitch in the slope, the depth of the posts should be increased 10 percent. For a 5/12 slope, then, a 50 percent increase in depth is

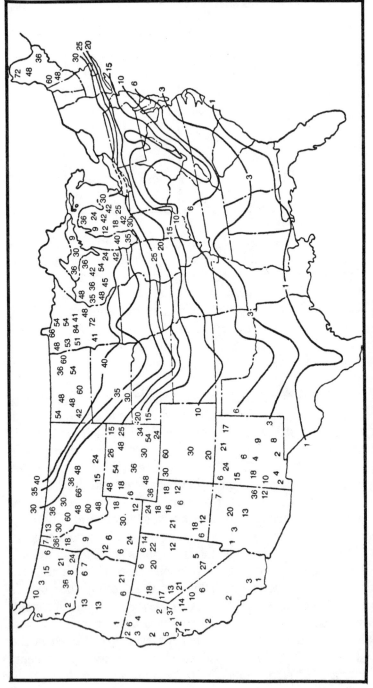

Fig. 7-3. Find your locale and note the average depth of frost penetration in inches.

Table 7-4. Use This Chart to Determine How Deep to Insert Posts.
Depth of Embedment

Post Size	10,000 PSF Soil	6,000 PSF Soil	2,000 PSF Soil
4×4	3'	4'	5'
4×6 6×6	4'	5'	6'
6×8 8×8	5'	6'	7'

Refer to Table 5-4 on soil classifications.

needed. Instead of placing the post 4 feet deep, a 6 foot depth would be warranted. This is often necessary anyway, since the ground on a hillside will often freeze deeper. This is especially true for hillsides that face north and for those not protected by buffers.

Whenever steep slopes are being considered as building sites, they should undergo soil tests to insure the builder that the hill is composed of stable soil. One form of landslide occurs when an entire shelf loses its footing on the slope. The shelf, which often is more than 8 feet deep, and anything resting upon it all slide down the hill together. This is most likely to occur during torrential rains. Thin shelves represent less of a problem. If the posts can project past the shelf and into good, stable earth, then the house will be well-anchored.

The posts should be deep enough, then, to anchor the building to the hill. They should also be larger to counter the lateral force. An elevated post-frame will have this exertion upon the posts, while a partially below-grade building will have this force against the walls as well. For the non-elevated building built upon a hillside, the wall structure must be stronger to resist this force.

The treated posts, then, should be of a dimension large enough to support all the forces that might be exerted upon the structure and strong enough to hold up the building's weight. The spacing of the posts should usually be eight feet on center. The posts' depth should be determined by the frost heave potential, the soil type, the weight exerted upon the soil, and the slope of the site.

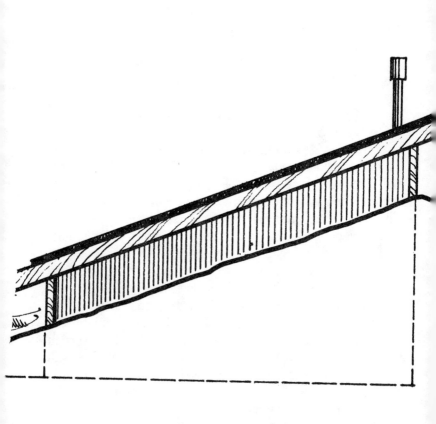

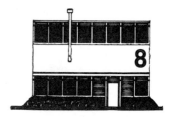

The Wall Structure

The wall structure of a post-frame can take many forms (Fig. 8-1). This versatility in wall design promotes the ability to choose an effective wall system to meet the other demands of the structure and builder. Since the posts serve the load-bearing function of the walls, the wall material only has to support itself. This material, though, provides bracing for the posts.

WALL DESIGN NUMBER ONE

Almost all pole buildings are built with girts—horizontal braces applied to the face of the poles (Fig. 8-2). Although 1×6s are most often used, 2×4s provide a firmer backing and are less expensive. These girts are placed 24 inches on center for most materials. When 1-inch thick boards are used as the siding, the girts can be placed four feet on center. By some codes, ½ inch drywall and ½ inch plywood siding may be placed on four foot centers, but a flimsy and often wavy wall usually results. Girts could be placed with four foot centers and finished with ½ inch material, but for a solid wall it is not suggested. For strong walls, ½ inch material should be limited to a span of 24 inches.

Since typical pole buildings have a spashboard affixed to the pole's lower portion, which serves as formwork for the

Fig. 8-1. Countless designs exist for walls. Be sure the walls are sturdy.

concrete slab, the splashboard takes the place of one girt and provides nailing surface for the siding. The roof support generally consists of an inner and outer plate bolted to the top of the poles; the outer plate serves as another girt. For 1-inch thick siding, then, only one girt is needed approximately four feet high to supply adequate support.

For storage structures, this exterior siding system is all that is needed. The interior walls do not have to be treated with further details. The girts and the back of the siding are left exposed from the inside. This structure is adequate for barns, garages, sheds, and other utility buildings. For our homes, though, most of us need interior finishing.

WALL DESIGN NUMBER TWO

Since the typical roof design incorporates an inner plate along with the outer plate, this inner plate is the beginning of the inside wall structure (Fig. 8-3). If 1-inch thick paneling is desired on the inside of the walls, two rows of girts will supply the needed backing. The one row of girts will be at the half-way point up the wall; the other row will be just above the slab.

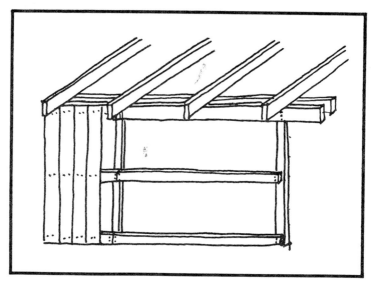

Fig. 8-2. One-inch thick wood siding is nailed onto the 2x4 girts which are secured to the outer face of the posts.

So far, though, this is a rather basic structure. The builder is likely to apply felt paper as a moisture and draft barrier to the exterior girts before the 1-inch thick paneling is affixed. Better yet, a ½-inch insulation board should be applied to the girts in place of the felt paper. By the

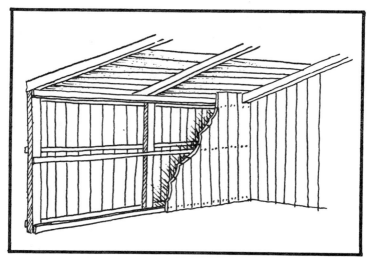

Fig. 8-3. Girts applied to the inside wall allow for a more finished inside wall structure.

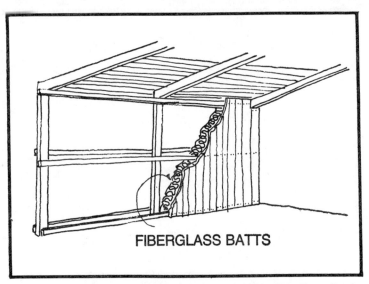

FIBERGLASS BATTS

Fig. 8-4. Batts of fiberglass insulation can be used to insulate the walls of a post-frame structure. A wall structure like this is capable of using 6-inch thick batts—giving the wall great insulating value .

application of solid sheathing, a much better insulated structure will result. Before the interior girts are nailed in place, the wall cavity should be insulated with a batt or fill insulation. The finished wall structure might look like Fig. 8-4.

The advantages of this type of interior and exterior wall structure are that it takes relatively no skill to complete the job in a substantial workmanship-like manner. Both the interior and exterior surfaces require little or no maintenance. Also, the structural materials offer rigidity and insulation value to the wall. Finally, the construction of this type of system can be completed in just a few days.

The only major drawback of this type of system is that the 1-inch thick paneling will cost quite a bit of money. Unless the builder has sufficient finances to purchase new 1-inch thick paneling or desires to use reclaimed siding such as barnwood, another approach to the wall structure must be taken. Besides, this type of wall structure is limiting in that 1-inch thick paneling must be used; although the interior partition walls could be finished with other materials, the use of paneling on the inside of exterior walls would be against some people's desires.

WALL DESIGN NUMBER THREE

In some areas—those where extensive insulation is not needed—Fig. 8-5 offers the finishing of the inside with drywall and the outside with 4×8 foot sheets of exterior siding, which is much less expensive than using 1-inch thick boards. With this design, the girts are applied to the interior face of the posts. The splashboard should also be applied to the wall's inside face so it can serve as a girt. In this case, the top of the splashboard must be at least an inch, preferably 2 inches, above the slab level. The interior plate serves as the drywall base at the top of the wall. Between the splashboard and this interior plate must be three rows of girts, since drywall works best with backing placed no more than 2 feet on center. The middle row of girts must be 4 feet from the floor to serve as backing for the drywall seam. Typically, drywall is applied horizontally since fewer seams will result. Besides, horizontal seams are less noticeable than vertical seams.

Although this design allows the use of drywall on the interior of the wall and sheets of sheathing on the outside wall, 2×4 girts will allow only 1½ inches of batt or fill

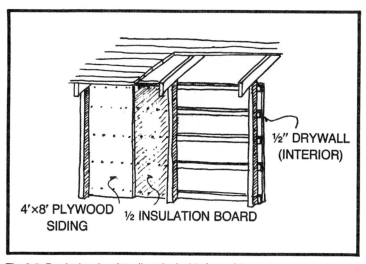

4'×8' PLYWOOD SIDING   ½ INSULATION BOARD   ½" DRYWALL (INTERIOR)

Fig. 8-5. By placing the girts all on the inside face of the posts, enough girts can be applied to give adequate backing for ½-inch thick drywall. Insulation board and plywood siding are applied to the outer face of the girts. The posts are left exposed from the outside of the house.

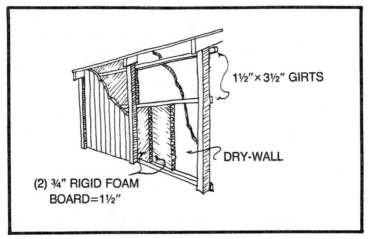

Fig. 8-6. When 1½ inches of rigid foam is secured between the girts, fewer girts are needed to give adequate backing for the drywall. Besides helping insulate the wall, the foam contributes to its structure.

insultion. When coupled with ½-inch insulation board applied before the exterior siding, this system will offer adequate insulation; but in the colder climates a thicker wall is preferable.

An appealing aspect of this design is that the posts are left exposed from the outside of the house, which can lend itself to an interesting effect. When this is the case, great care should be taken to choose only straight posts, since crooked posts will create gaps between the posts and the siding. For this reason, too, greater care must be taken to insure that the posts are perfectly plumb, since out-of-plumb posts would cause the same problem. Gaps can be remedied through the use of molding, but this expense should be avoided if possible.

WALL DESIGN NUMBER FOUR

If a thin wall is desired, yet one wants a well-insulated wall, Fig. 8-6 is sufficient. Especially if drywall and paneling are desired as finishing materials, this wall design offers solid backing without many girts.

Only three girts are needed for this wall structure. The girts are attached to the inside face of the posts, as was done in design #3. Instead of insulating with batt insulation, though, this wall is insulated with two-¾ inch layers of rigid foam. The foam not only offers superior insulation, it also offers a firm backing for the finishing materials. With this arrangement, ½-inch drywall can be attached to the girts at 4 feet on center without having a flimsy wall. Just the same, ½-inch exterior paneling can finish the outside of the wall.

The two-¾ inch pieces of rigid foam are fit between the girts. The faces of the foam will lay in the same planes as the faces of the 2×4s, because 2×4s actually are only an inch and a half thick. This arrangement is most easily built by applying the exterior panels first and then gluing the foam to the back of the panel. For the best insulation value, the foam's joints should be staggered. The inner piece of foam should be cut leaving a little tolerance to form a chase for electrical lines. These lines can run on the top of the middle girt.

WALL DESIGN NUMBER FIVE

A further variation between these designs is the incorporation of the interior system of design #3, which allows for the use of drywall, with the exterior system which needs 1-inch thick paneling (Fig. 8-7). Through this system, a large wall cavity is formed which is fine for insulation. Although

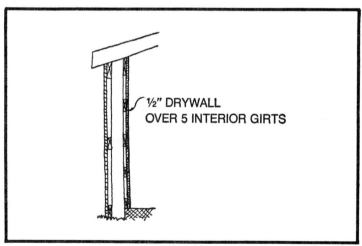

Fig. 8-7. If a thick wall is desired with drywall interior finishing, five girts are used for the inside of the wall. For exterior finishing with 1-inch thick siding, three girts are used. This wall is quickly composed and can be economically insulated.

115

many girts are used, the application of the girts in this manner is quick work. As long as the posts are evenly spaced, virtually no cutting must be done.

It is ironic that with the purpose of saving material, i.e., finding a way to get around using 1-inch thick paneling, the addition of girts is usually needed. For this reason, I will detail other plans that radically differ from what has been presented so far. These next plans have no inner or outer plates. The ceiling beams are attached directly onto the posts, making these plates unnecessary. These plans not only eliminate many girts; they also eliminate the need for the plates, which represents a tremendous savings in material. The following plans, although they differ drastically from conventional pole-frame techniques, are very well-suited for dwellings.

WALL DESIGN NUMBER SIX

In this plan, the splashboard is placed on the inside of the wall (Fig. 8-8). The top of the splashboard will serve as formwork for the concrete; the concrete can be taken from the top of this board. With the top of the board level with the top of the slab, a place is provided for securing the tack strip which will hold the carpet in place. Instead of the girts being nailed to the face of the posts, they are secured between the posts. The wall is only as wide as the posts themselves. The inside of the girt provides a nailing surface for the drywall; the outside of the girt provides the nailing surface for the exterior sheathing.

In this plan, five rows of girts are needed. For an 8-foot wall, then, the girts are 24 inches on center. The girt in the middle of the wall, as before, must be 4 feet high to provide the backing for the drywall's edge.

The attaching of these girts will be more difficult than if they were nailed to the face of the posts. These girts will have to be trimmed to fit in between the posts and it will take two people to secure them. The trimmed girts should be drilled to take a nail. As one person backs up the nailer with a sledgehammer, the girt can be secured. The posts should be pre-marked so that no measuring or leveling need be done while the girt is being installed.

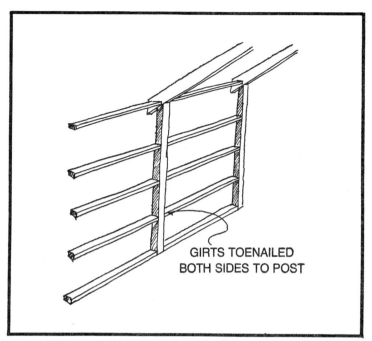

GIRTS TOENAILED
BOTH SIDES TO POST

Fig. 8-8. To get a strong 3½-inch thick wall capable of being sided with plywood on the outside and ½-inch drywall on the inside, the girts are secured between the posts. The girts can be toenailed to the posts or, since the girts will have to be trimmed to fit between the posts, the trimmings can be nailed to the posts. The girts can then be nailed onto the blocks.

The most adept manner of securing these girts would be to pre-cut many girts in assembly-line fashion (Fig. 8-9). The girts should then all be pre-drilled and nails should be placed into the holes. With the posts marked at the correct levels, the girts can quickly be applied.

The main advantage of this system is that the walls inside and out can be finished in any way desired. The horizontal surface of girts provides a strong backing for 1-inch thick boards or for any type of 4×8 exterior sheathing. Likewise, the interior wall can be finished with drywall or paneling.

Through the placement of the girts with the narrow edge facing the wall, each girt is stronger. Since the girt will only receive lateral pressure, it makes sense to position the girt so that it has the greatest resistance in that direction. Because of the manner in which the girts attach to the posts,

LEVEL USED WHEN
ATTACHING SPLASHBOARD/
MEASURE UP FROM SPLASHBOARD
TO DETERMINE GIRT HEIGHT:
CHALK LINE CAN BE USED TO
SPEED MARKING.

Fig. 8-9. If two people are available, a chalk line can be used to mark the posts. If a helper isn't around, 2x4s can be cut to the proper lengths. Each length 2x4 is set upon the splashboard. A mark is then made at the top of the 2x4 .

lesser quality girts could be used without sacrificing strength or wall straightness. Although construction grade wood is generally easier to work with because of the lack of gross defects, utility grade lumber is a possibility. Most defects in utility grade lumber are in the face; with the manner in which the girts are attached, face defects would present no drawbacks. All the girts will have to be trimmed.

This system, then, offers to the builder a viable alternative to the conventional installation of girts. Besides the need for fewer girts, the possibility of using lower quality girts, and the stronger arrangement, the greatest advantage is that the wall thickness can be normalized. For single story homes, most often 4×4s will be used for the posts. 2×4s, then, would be used for the girts. The typical 3½ inch thickness for walls would then be achieved.

By maintaining the typical thickness, later construction is simplified. The windows and doors, especially, will be more easily installed. The area will also be easily insulated. These same factors are realized in the next plan which is, I believe, often the most viable wall design a post-frame home can have.

WALL DESIGN NUMBER SEVEN

This next design eliminates the horizontal girts (Fig. 8-10). In their place, vertical studs are employed. As in the last design, there are no inner or outer plates—the beams are attached directly onto the posts. The vertical stud wall—completely non-load bearing—needs only a single top plate and a single bottom plate. The posts serve the dual purpose of supplying the needed backing for both the interior and exterior finishing materials—they function as studs.

This design offers many advantages. As well as possessing the advantages of the last design—the 2×4s are placed with their edge out resulting in a stronger design, fewer boards are needed, the exterior can take 4×8 sheets of exterior paneling, the interior can take drywall, the wall thickness is typical, and lower quality wood can be used—this design also incorporates ease of construction. This wall framework can be fabricated on the floor and tilted up into

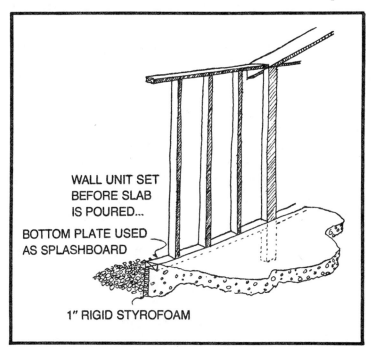

WALL UNIT SET
BEFORE SLAB
IS POURED...

BOTTOM PLATE USED
AS SPLASHBOARD

1" RIGID STYROFOAM

Fig. 8-10. A stud wall can be fit between the beams with the top plate secured to the roof planks and the bottom plate secured to the posts. The bottom plate can serve as formwork for the slab .

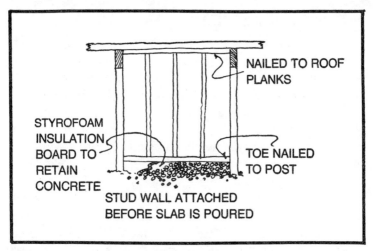

Fig. 8-11. A styrofoam insulation board is secured below the bottom plate to retain the concrete and insulate the slab. Rocks or stakes can help hold it in place. Gravel is also used to relieve back pressure and to fill in the void below the bottom plate .

place. The bottom plate serves as both a bottom plate for the stud wall and as the splashboard.

Because a separate splashboard is eliminated, this design is the most economical for most purposes. Shorter 2×4s can be used, seven footers in most cases, which are much less expensive than eight footers; through the use of seven foot 2×4s, there is less cutting.

By constructing this unit on the ground, assembly will be quick. Two #16d nails through the plates into each end of the 2×4s will secure this system. The plates should both be marked for the placement of the studs. Although the bottom plate should fit tight against the posts, the top plate can be given some tolerance. Since this top plate will be anchored to the roof decking, it will not have to fit tight against the posts. If tolerance is given to the top plate, minor adjustment can occur so that perfectly plumb studs will result.

Since the bottom plate serves as the splashboard, provisions should be made to contain the concrete from seeping under the splashboard and to insulate this concrete from cold weather. To do this, 1-inch or thicker styrofoam should be placed underneath the splashboard. It can be anchored by either pounding stakes against it or merely by backing it up with rocks, bricks, or gravel. After the slab has set, gravel will help the styrofoam insulate the slab and fill the gap under the splashboard. There must be 6 inches of space, free from dirt between the bottom of the splashboard and the ground, for moisture protection; for this reason, gravel should be shoved against the splashboard so that dirt will not become lodged next to the wood (Fig. 8-11). The splashboard is best made of treated lumber.

In windy areas, extra bracing may be needed. T-shaped metal bracing that is "let in" to the wall provides an adequate system. When the corners of the building are braced, the wall becomes rigid. This metal bracing is efficient and low-cost (Fig. 8-12).

WALL DESIGN NUMBER EIGHT

This design is fine for building the wall after the slab is poured (Fig. 8-13). By reversing these steps, the wall can rest upon the slab, which eases construction. If this is done, a splashboard will have to be used. The splashboard would be applied to the outside of the posts so that the slab would continue between the posts.

If closing in the building is not a primary consideration, this design method may be the most worthwhile in some

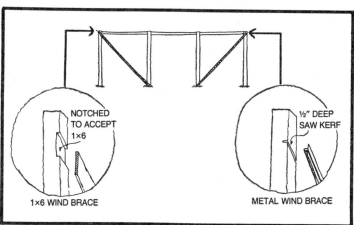

Fig. 8-12. Wind bracing is cut into the wall structure to create a rigid wall. Only the ends of a wall need this bracing. The wall is braced from the top of the outside corner to the bottom of the next post. The brace is cut into each wall member it intersects.

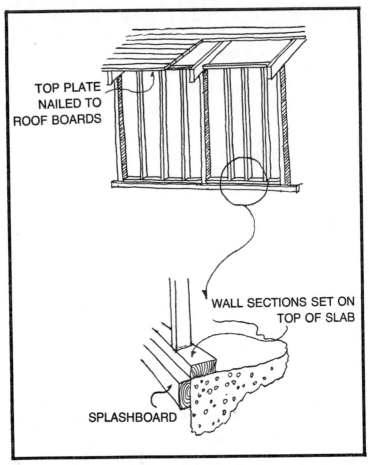

Fig. 8-13. The stud framework of this wall structure sits on top of the concrete slab. The bottom plate of the wall is glued to the slab; the top plate is nailed to the roof's planks. A splashboard is affixed to the face of the posts to retain the concrete .

circumstances. The primary disadvantage, though, is that the below-slab work (heating, plumbing) is done while the structure is still open. The other disadvantage is that a separate splashboard must be used. It is advantageous to have a structure closed in when the plumbing and heating work is being done because of the higher possibility of vandalism when a building is open. Not only is the plumbing and heating equipment expensive, youngsters can cause problems that can't be noticed until the system is tested, which may not occur until long after the slab has covered it up. Below-slab heat vents, especially, serve as receptacles for any object onto which a youngster can get his hands. For this reason, it may be wiser to complete the mechanical tasks within an enclosed building, which means building the wall before the slab is laid.

WALL DESIGN NUMBER NINE

This next wall design incorporates the 3½ inch thick wall plan with a modification of the roof (Fig. 8-14). In some circumstances, one may not want to attach the beams onto the posts. Although this system is viable for either 2-inch thick planking (or with purlins so that the ceiling could be well-insulated), it is a possibility that the exposed beam effect might not always be desired. When this is the case, this design can be used.

Generally the plates are bolted to the inside and outside of the posts. This design has the plates sitting on top of the posts. Through the use of two 2-inch thick boards with a piece of ½ inch plywood sandwiched between them, a very

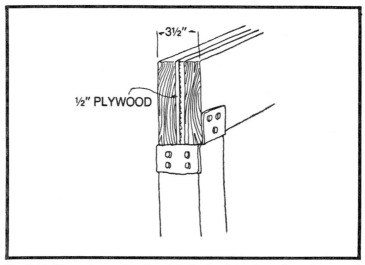

Fig. 8-14. When a beamed roof is not desired, a glulam beam is made on top of the posts around the perimeter of the house. Trusses can sit on top of this beam. If joists are used for the roof, they can be secured to the top of this beam, projecting over it to form an overhang. When an overhang is not desired, the joists may be hung from this beam.

strong beam is made. By using the ½ inch plywood as part of the beam structure, the beam's width equals that of a 4×4 post. It is necessary with this design to have the beam flush with the sides of the posts so that the beam serves as backing for finishing materials and can be securely anchored. The beam is fastened to the posts with a post cap.

Smaller lumber can be used to make the plates into a beam. The beam ideally should be glued and nailed together, making a "glulam" beam. Through the proper lamination of this beam, a stronger beam is made. You can use smaller material to achieve the same load capacity when the beam is properly laminated.

If possible, a continuous beam should be made—one that extends from one side of the house to the other side. Not only is this beam capable of carrying more load, it is stronger because of the lack of joints. This beam can either be fabricated on the ground and then lifted into place, or it can be fabricated in place. If enough people (around seven) will be available to help lift the beam into place, it should be fabricated on the ground since it is easier. Otherwise, it will have to be fabricated in place.

WALL DESIGN NUMBER TEN

Since fabricated beams can be laminated either "on the flat" (as one would stack pieces) or "on the edge," it will

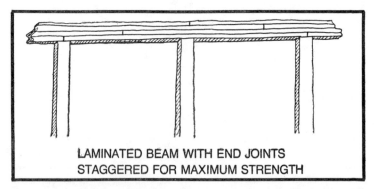

LAMINATED BEAM WITH END JOINTS
STAGGERED FOR MAXIMUM STRENGTH

Fig. 8-15. A perimeter beam can also be laminated "on the flat." The first boards' splices should all occur over posts. The advantage of making a beam on top of the posts instead of attaching plates to the posts' sides is that the wall can be made as thin as the posts .

124

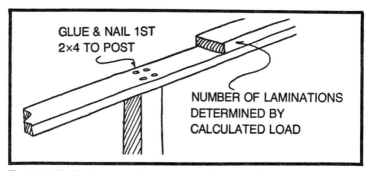

Fig. 8-16. The first course of boards is glued and nailed onto the end of each post. The glue helps since nails have the least amount of holding power when nailed into the butt end of a piece of lumber. The direction of grain for the laminations should always be parallel to the force that will be exerted upon the beam.

generally be easier to laminate the beam in place (Fig. 8-15) by laminating the members "on the flat." In this manner, it is simply a matter of building the beam up piece by piece; this is much easier than building the beam out sideways.

If the beam is to be laminated on the flat, a very secure attachment is possible (Fig. 8-16). The first row can be nailed directly into the butt ends of the posts before the second row is applied. No gusset plates or 90-degree brackets will generally be needed. The first row should be glued to the top of the posts and anchored with 20d nails. The ends of the first row should terminate over the posts; subsequent rows should stagger the joints.

In this chapter on walls, there have been many wall forms discussed. Although the flush wall designs probably will offer the most economical wall systems to the builder, the girted systems which were first mentioned may offer advantages under certain situations. Variations of any of the wall systems that were covered may solve highly individual, demanding problems.

Design #7 with vertical studs does not lend itself to the application of vertical 1-inch thick boards because of its inherent vertical structure. If vertical 1-inch thick boards are desired in one room, the use of one of the horizontal systems may be better for that area. By using these different systems next to each other, or in conjunction with each other when necessary, a suitable wall framework will evolve.

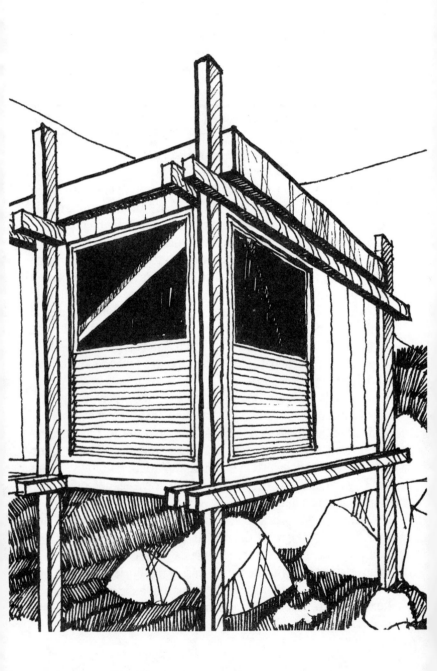

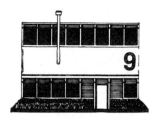

The Roof

What would a house be without a roof? We'd have to watch television while holding umbrellas, make sure we were clothed when airplanes flew overhead, wear coats when it was cold, brace our walls so they wouldn't flap in the wind, and occasionally protect ourselves from falling objects. But we wouldn't have to worry about ventilation.

What is it, then, that a successful roof does? It seals out the rain, gives us privacy, keeps the house warm, strengthens the structure and stops falling objects, but the roof can make it stuffy inside. We expect a lot from our roof. It is used to protect us and the entire structure. If a roof is allowed to deteriorate, the rest of the structure will quickly follow.

THE BASIC FORM

The roof is often the most expensive part of a structure. And, the space it occupies is usually wasted space. Yet there have been no drastic changes in roof design since the roof was first constructed. With the advent of steel, and later with the incorporation of steel with concrete, new materials have been found to supply the old functions. But these new materials have led to virtually no new designs. In fact, these materials support the trend of evolving back into cave-type dwellings. Especially through the use of reinforced concrete, earth-covered abodes seem to fulfill more of some people's needs than can any other type of structure; here the roof is concrete and earth, not much different from the earliest shelters. Our incredible lack of advancement in roof structure indicates one thing—it is a very complex problem.

The Flat Roof

The most simple roof form is the flat roof. The flat roof is the easiest to construct and uses less material than any other type of roof. But flat roof homes are mostly confined to areas which have little rain. In areas of inclement weather, the flat roof can present leakage problems and must be built to hold heavy snow loads. Frequent and sometimes constant moisture tend to test a roof's impermeability.

Built-up roofing, made by layering three to five layers of asphalt roll roofing applied hot after being soaked in a hot tar tank, is the most widely used form of roofing for flat roofs (Fig. 9-1). These roofs should be coated with some form of roof coating every year to increase their longevity. Still, these roofs soon begin to age. Through the use of stone or slag ballast, the damage from the sun's rays can be hindered. However, this ballast makes it difficult to coat the roof and is liable to puncture the roof if it is walked on occasionally. For these two reasons, the ballast is often not used.

When built-up roofing is used, the roof should be slightly pitched to provide for water run-off. Too slight of a pitch will create areas that will tend to pond water. If the building settles, a slight pitch may be totally invalidated. These roofs, then, should be pitched at least ⅛ inch to a foot. A 32-foot roof, then, would be pitched four or more inches. Without this pitch, the water will pond and will, before long, find an entrance into the structure. This usually occurs at the worst time—in the winter—when it is difficult to find the source of the leak. Even if it is found, the leak is hard to repair in cold weather. The leaks tend to happen in the wintertime since the heat loss though the roof will melt the ice on top of the roof while the cold weather will keep the surface frozen. The melted ice has nowhere to drain. This trapped water stands on the roofing seeking an outlet. Even with a slight pitch, this water often cannot drain.

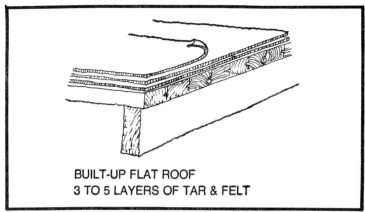

BUILT-UP FLAT ROOF
3 TO 5 LAYERS OF TAR & FELT

Fig. 9-1. Membranes of unsurfaced felt roll roofing material are layered on top of each other, staggering the splices. This type of roof is usually applied with hot tar. The rolls of felt are saturated with hot tar and then applied to the roof.

When possible, flat roofs should be pitched a little more than ⅛ inch to a foot. With concrete block buildings, this pitch is created by tapering down the last row of blocks. If the roof is trussed, the pitch can be built into the trusses; if the roof is built with laminated beams, the same is true. When building with joists, though, obtaining a pitch is more difficult. The increased cost of obtaining even a slight pitch begins to detract from the economy of the flat roof.

Because all the conditions must be right for the built-up roof to be successful, another system is often preferable. Instead of using the age-old asphalt and tar routine, one can use a plastic membrane. The plastic is generally PVC (polyvinylchloride), although CPE (chlorinated polyethylene) or EDPM (ethylene propylene diene monomer) are occasionally recommended. The plastic sheets are 30 mils thick, butted together, and then taped with plastic tape. This system should be professionally applied; some companies are giving a ten-year guarantee with the job. The costs are comparable to the cost of built-up roofing.

The least expensive system uses the PVC material with a stone ballast. The plastic—which is right along the lines of a swimming pool liner—is loose-laid and then held down by the ballast. As with the built-up roofing, the ballast provides protection against the ultra-violet rays of the sun. With this roofing material, and especially with a 10-year guarantee, a flat roof becomes much more viable. Pitching the roof is not as necessary; in fact, the roof can be made to pond water.

The Monoplane Roof

The mono or single plane roof is a variation of the flat roof (Fig. 9-2). Tipped at a pitch of 1/12 or greater, this roof is an easy to build design. By this simple design, though, the walls, especially the internal wall structure, are made more difficult.

Unless a separate ceiling is structured to create a plane parallel to the floor, the internal walls (if they are to fully enclose rooms) must angle to meet the ceiling. If the rooms do not need to be fully enclosed, the walls can be built to one specified height, making partition walls. Although serving as sight barriers, they fail as sound barriers.

If a level ceiling is installed, the internal wall problem is alleviated. The space above the ceiling can serve as storage space, the same as any attic. All walls can meet the ceiling and no complications will arise. The attic space serves as added insulation and the roof is pitched enough to provide for water runoff.

The construction of a separate ceiling, though, takes extra material. Without it, the underside of the roof can serve as the ceiling to create a simplified roof structure. Although the wall structure is more challenging, it can be successfully worked out. Some of the rooms—preferably those under the lower part of the roof—should be fully enclosed. By being under the lowest part of the roof, it will take less wall material to enclose them. These rooms should be fully enclosed when separate, incompatible activities are expected to take place at the same time. If a child wants to practice trombone, a parent wants to read, and someone else wants to watch TV, trouble is bound to erupt.

The monoplane roof is ideally suited for hillside, multi-level sites. Here, the roof can follow the natural grade, with the rooms carved out of the slope below (Fig. 9-3).

The monoplane roof has several other advantages. If the roof faces the wind, the wind will ride up the roof without exerting much force upon the structure. If the high part of

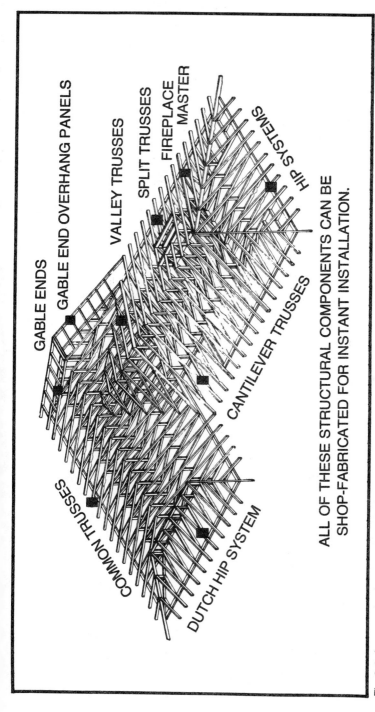

GABLE ENDS

GABLE END OVERHANG PANELS

VALLEY TRUSSES

SPLIT TRUSSES

FIREPLACE MASTER

HIP SYSTEMS

CANTILEVER TRUSSES

COMMON TRUSSES

DUTCH HIP SYSTEM

ALL OF THESE STRUCTURAL COMPONENTS CAN BE SHOP-FABRICATED FOR INSTANT INSTALLATION.

Fig. 9-2. An example of a mono or single plane roof.

Fig. 9-3. Levels of a house can step down a hill. The higher story can contain closet space under the low part of the roof.

the house faces the sun, provisions can be made to collect the sun's rays, when desired. Windows high on the southwest side can let in evening light as well.

Without an added ceiling, the natural slope of the roof provides an interesting effect for the interior of a home. It seems to un-box a room. The extra height adds an open feeling to the floor plan. Small rooms seem (and feel) larger.

The Gable Roof

Two monoplane roofs put together, meeting at a peak, create a gable roof, the "gable" being the triangle at each end (Fig. 9-4). This roof, which can be built with any pitch from 1/12 up, follows the logic that "what goes up, must come down." It is the most over-used roof structure we have because it is the most versatile design. Without regard to site, sun, or aesthetics, the gable roof monopolizes and monotonizes the landscape.

The post-frame technique simplifies the construction of the gable roof. A center support wall or a beam supported by posts holds up the ridge. In this manner, no separate ceiling need be made. Typically, a gable roof needs collar ties to

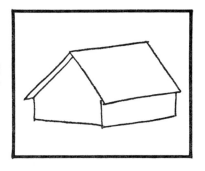

Fig. 9-4. This gable roof is formed by two monoplane roofs coming together at a peak.

inhibit the outward thrust the roof exerts on the walls. A ceiling is then needed to cover the collar ties unless the ties are nicely crafted. Through the central support of the structure—or through roof support at some point along the joists' span—thrust is thwarted (Fig. 9-5).

The gable roof system, actually, makes a lot of sense. The mean level of the ceiling is lowered, resulting in less heat waste and fewer interior materials needed if floor-to-ceiling walls are desired. The gable roof, though, typically is used with no sympathy to the conditions of the site or environment.

The gable roof is most often built with a separate, flat ceiling. Because of the bracing conventional construction needs, the ceiling joists serve to tie the structure together. Then, too, all interior walls are simply built to the ceiling, which is easier but it creates "boxy" rooms. Since post-frame construction needs no internal ties, the erection of a flat ceiling would have little purpose.

The Hip Roof

The hip roof, an obvious adaptation of the gable roof, is a bit more attractive (Fig. 9-6). This form makes for easier construction of overhangs all the way around the house, as compared to the gable roof, where it is easier to do without overhangs on the gable ends. Especially for the amateur carpenter, though, this roof system is complicated. Every joist angles up, with many different lengths involved. Experienced carpenters can build these roofs simply enough—they have built so many that they know all the dimensions by memory. The formulas are sometimes written on carpenter's

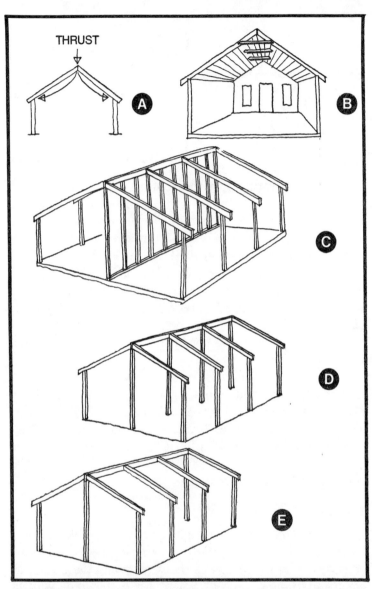

Fig. 9-5. A) The vertical force of gravity is converted into horizontal thrust by the shape of the gable roof. B) Collar ties thwart thrust by tying opposing roof beams or joists together. Nice ties can be left exposed. C) Through the central support of the structure, there is no horizontal thrust. Collar ties are not needed. A frame wall can supply this support. D) Posts can be used to supply central support for a structure. E) When central support is not desired, the ridge board's size must be increased. It then becomes a ridge beam. The beam must be of a large enough dimension to make the span and be adequately supported at both ends .

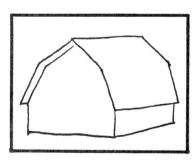

Fig. 9-6. An illustration of a hip roof.

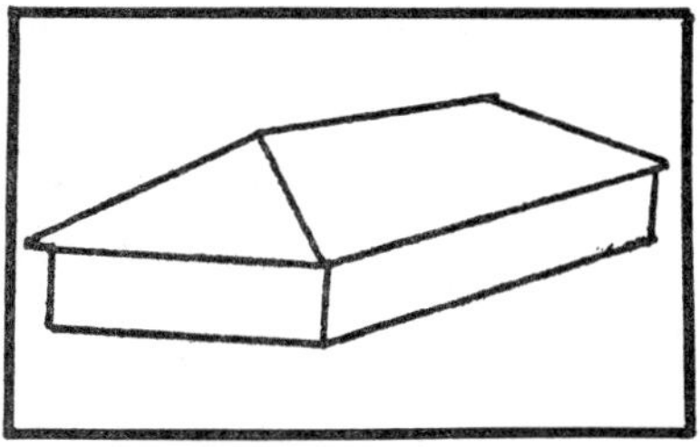

squares. But this type of roof system offers little positive value. Besides the confusing framing, the sheathing of such a roof structure is no easy task. It takes extra shingles to cover the roof. And roofers charge more for the job.

Flat ceilings are almost always placed under these roofs, but the attic offers little room. Because of this form's added expense, problems, and limitations, it is a roof form that should be avoided by the novice.

The Gambrel Roof

The gambrel or barn roof was created by the farmer to achieve the most space for the least amount of material (Fig. 9-7). With this type of roof, the attic was totally accessible and could house bales of hay stacked to the roof's peak. This roof is very efficient with its use of material, but it is difficult to construct. The roof does need collar ties, as does the gable roof, and the break in the roof needs reinforcement. For the farmer, this was no large problem. The braces could be made out of scrap wood and it didn't matter if they were not perfectly aligned. On the inside of a house, though, these factors become very important considerations.

Many homes have been built with the gambrel roof. Some have the top floor with plumb walls meeting the break

Fig. 9-7. Gambrel roofs are popular with farmers.

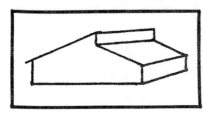

Fig. 9-8. The duo-plane roof, though seldom used, is a very handy system.

in the roof. Although this is a solution to the problem of how to brace the roof, the addition of a secondary (knee) wall seems to void the ecnomical factors of this design. The construction of dormers, of course, is difficult. Often only the ends of the upper floor possess windows. These limitations, along with the complicated construction, leave the gambrel roof out in the pasture.

The Duo-Plane Roof

The duo-plane roof is the most unused, yet one of the most practical roof systems (Fig. 9-8). This design incorporates some of the best features of both the monoplane and the gable roof, and it is well-used with the post-frame technique. Like the gable roof, the mean height of the ceiling is less than the mean height of the mono-plane. Unlike the gable roof, the duo-plane roof has style. Its similiarity to the monoplane roof is that it uses simple framing techniques. It needs a center support wall, which extends up to form the vertical part of the roof. The roof joists either hang from this center support wall and from the top plate at the eaves, or the joists can project past these points to form overhangs. The lower roof will generally always hang from the support wall at the middle of the house.

This design, of course, rarely uses flat ceilings. When flat ceilings are used, the essence of this design is ruined. The ceilings should remain open, providing various heights throughout the house. The vertical part of the roof is ideal for clerestory windows; the projecting overhand shields the entrance of the summer sun.

Multi-level structures, as with the monoplane roof, are readily adaptable with this design. The side with a higher roof obviously suggests the possibility of two floors underneath it. Again, hillside sites benefit from this roof plan (Fig. 9-9).

Fig. 9-9. The duo-plane roof is readily adaptable for two-level structures. Both levels can have equal ceiling heights. A band of clerestory windows can be installed in the vertical part of the roof.

THE CONSTRUCTION

As long as we have decided that the hipped roof and the gambrel roof are to be avoided for simplicity's sake, any of the potentially usable roofs may be built using planks over beams—the most simplified form of construction (Fig. 9-10). With this technique, the beams are usually attached to the posts of the post-frame (Fig. 9-11).

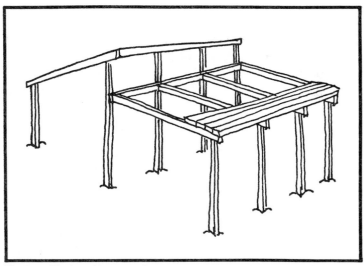

Fig. 9-10. Plank and beam roofs are easy to install. When the roof is finished, so is the ceiling.

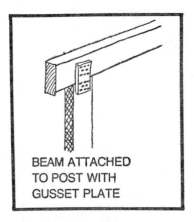

Fgi. 9-11. Metal gusset plates are often used to secure a beam to a post. Some gusset plates have holes in them through which the plate is nailed to both members. Other gusset plates have built-in fasteners. Plywood can also be used as a gusset plate.

BEAM ATTACHED
TO POST WITH
GUSSET PLATE

By Plank and Beam

With the use of beams, fewer, but larger, pieces need to be used. Because of fewer pieces being incorporated into the plan, there is less cutting to be done. Straighter roofs usually result due to the simplified construction.

After the beams are up, tongue-and-groove planks, usually 2 × 6s, are nailed to the beams. This process is very simple, yet it results in a very strong roof. The 2 × 6 tongue-and-groove can span distances of up to eight feet. The beam size is calculated according to the roof load and the span, but usually a 4 × 10 spanning some 16 feet is normal. This plank and beam structure is left exposed to the living area, resulting in an attractive, no maintenance ceiling. A primary advantage of this type of structure is the "one-process" aspect of it. Once the roof is constructed, the ceiling is finished too, eliminating some of the most difficult work.

The Raftered Ceiling

Instead of using big beams and thick planks, the raftered ceiling uses many smaller pieces covered with a thin skin (Fig. 9-12). The boards in this ceiling are usually 2-inch thick ones and placed 12 inches, 16 inches, or 24 inches on center. They are typically covered with ½ inch plywood on the top and ½ inch drywall on the bottom.

Generally, these ceilings are very successful. The 6-12 inch space between the plywood and the drywall is filled with insulation, creating an extremely well-insulated roof.

Because of the cutting and the need to finish the underside of this ceiling, this system offers more construction problems to the novice. However, the end result may well be more satisfactory. The primary benefit is that the insulation-minded person has a low-cost, low heat-loss roof.

This design is very efficient with its use of wood. Because of the lack of separate ceiling, much less lumber is used than when an attic is constructed. The sloped ceiling (in all cases except for the flat roofed house) provides an element of interest. And, because of its excellent insulating value, a slightly higher ceiling offers no drawbacks in regard to heat loss.

Beam and Purlin

An alternative to building with plank and beam or with rafters is to build with beams and purlins (Fig. 9-13). After the beams are set into place, purlins are anchored to the tops of the beams at 90-degree angles. The most economical plan usually involves placement of the beams at 8 feet on center with 2 × 4 purlins set on their edge over the beams at 24 inches on center.

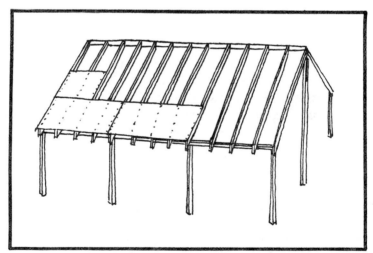

Fig. 9-12. Joists can be covered with inexpensive plywood graded CDX (one side is graded "C" and the other side is graded "D;" the "X" stands for "exterior"). The bottom of the joists is covered with drywall after the area between the joists is insulated. Without an attic, this is a closed-joist system. Like an attic, this area must be ventilated.

Fig. 9-13. When a beamed ceiling is desired but plywood is needed for the roof, purlins are set perpendicular to the beams. Drywall or 1-inch thick tongue-and-groove can be used for the ceiling finishing material.

With this design, overhangs are easily made on every side of the house. The primary advantage, though, is that beams still can be used for the roof's structure and left exposed to the inside of the house while the area between the purlins can be insulated. Through this technique, a well-insulated beamed ceiling results.

Purlins are rarely placed more than 24 inches on center since this would dissallow ½ inch plywood from being used as sheathing. Often times, though, the purlins are of larger stock than 2 × 4s so that there is a greater area to insulate. When a heavily insulated roof is desired, it is possible to space the primary beams more than 8 feet and to use 2 × 6 or 2 × 8 purlins. Generally, though, beams 8 feet on center with 2 × 6 inch purlins at 24 inches on center, filled with 6-inch foil faced fiberglass insulation or blown cellulose make an economical, adequately insulated roof (Fig. 9-14).

The spacing of the purlins at 24 inches also allows for the finishing of their undersides with ½ inch drywall. And, by spacing the beams no more than 8 feet, the drywall (which comes in 4 × 8 sheets) can be applied with few seams. Although drywall can be obtained in greater lengths, the application of long pieces of drywall on the ceiling is difficult. Generally, some kind of molding is required where the drywall meets the beam, since it is difficult to finish the edge next to the beam. Small quarter-round can be pre-stained and applied after the drywall is plastered and painted.

The use of purlins, though, doesn't limit the builder to finishing the ceiling with drywall. If a wood ceiling is desired, the space between the beams can be sheathed with anything from plywood to 1-inch thick tongue-and-groove. This nonstructural use of wood detracts from this roof system's economy. If a well-insulated, all-wood, no maintenance ceiling is desired, though, this roofing system makes it possible.

Building With an Attic

If an attic is desired, a roof can be conventionally framed with the attic floor joists serving to tie the structure together (Fig. 9-15). Still, collar ties every 4 feet are needed if a gable roof is used. The attic must be ventilated with approximately four square feet of louver. On a gabled house, a 12 × 24 inch vent on each side of the gable is typical. The size of the vent corresponds to the size of the attic space. Large attics must have larger vent openings.

The vents can occur as roof projections, as is needed on the hipped roof. It is wise to limit the number of roof

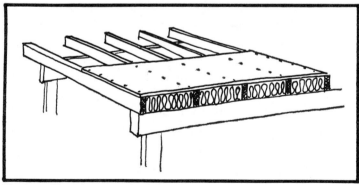

Fig. 9-14. The advantage of using purlins is that batt or fill insulation can be used between them. A well-insulated beamed ceiling results.

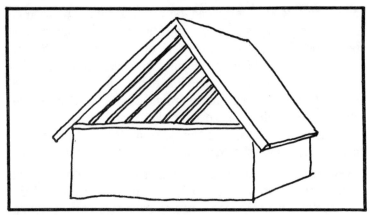
Fig. 9-15. Attics are good for storage and for secret meetings.

Projections since these areas are most likely to be the source of leaks. One form of common ventilation involves a continuous vent on the ridge of the roof. Because of its location at the very height of the roof where there would be the largest heat build-up, this type of vent is practical. Also, by being at the very top of the roof, it is not susceptible to leakage.

Although attics are not in vogue now, primarily because of the extra labor it takes to construct them, people always used this space well. In a house without a basement, unless an attic is constructed, you need special storage space. This means that the money you save by not building an attic goes towards making the house larger to allow for adequate storage space. If a flat ceiling is desired in the house, you might as well build an attic and have usable storage space.

The floor of the attic, especially if it is to be used to store heavy articles like furniture, should be well-constructed. Only the floor should be insulated, because if the roof were also insulated the attic would trap heat. Provisions should be made to supply light to this area. A large enough opening should be provided to allow accessibility of very large articles.

The Trussed Roof

In place of constructing roof joists and floor joists for an attic, trusses may be used (Fig. 9-16). There are many forms

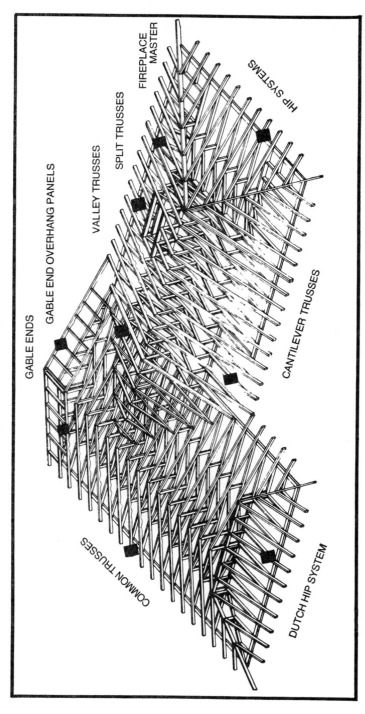

Fig. 9-16. Trusses can be arranged in an unlimited variety of ways but their use results in a limited amount of storage space. All of these structural components can be shop-fabricated for instant installation.

143

of trusses, several of which are shown below. These trusses can be arranged in many different ways so that practically any style roof can be constructed (Fig. 9-17).

The obvious advantage of working with trusses is that they are premanufactured, making roof and ceiling construction greatly simplified. The builder only has to set the trusses at 24 inches on center, brace and anchor them, and then the sheathing and drywall are ready to be installed. Since the trusses are made to span the entire area from outside wall to outside wall, no support wall is needed beneath them, which leads to greater versatility in arriving at an adequate floor plan. The major advantage, though, is that no cutting is necssary for building the roof and ceiling framework.

There are many disadvantages of building with trusses. Although much of the cutting has been eliminated, this is only because someone else has done it—and you have paid them well for their task. Trusses are expensive, running at about $1.50 per linear foot. Calculate this amount out for the average house, and the trusses alone will cost more than $1,000. This is the price for a standard truss.

If a less conforming roof is desired, it can be built with trusses, but it will cost you. The $1.50 a foot price is the minimum. All different sizes of trusses are needed for a hipped roof. There is much doubling up of the trusses to take the extra stresses. This "simplified" method of building becomes quite complex and very expensive.

Besides the initial expense of the trusses, the primary disadvantage is that they do not allow for storage space in the attic. A truss has been developed that allows for some space, but this space is relatively small compared to the space that could be considered usable. If usable attic space is desired, trusses generally should not be used.

The one inherent advantage of tusses—that they are capable of great spans—is generally not taken advantage of in residential homes. Usually a home's interior design will have a wall about in the middle of the floor plan regardless of whether the roof is trussed or not. Even if a wall is desired four feet off center, a conventional roof system can easily compensate for this. These walls may just as well be support

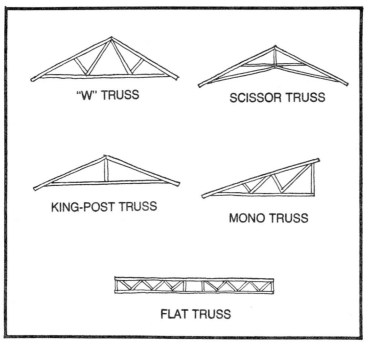

Fig. 9-17. The "W" truss is used extensively. For larger spans, more webs are incorporated into the design, making two or more "Ws." Trusses are tied together with bracing attached to the trusses' webs. Ridge boards are not needed.

walls as partitions; the only difference is that the studs will be 16 inches on center instead of 24 inches on center.

Professional builders use trusses because of the speed of erection. They can save money, too, if the builder is paying the crew union wages. For the owner-builder, though, trusses represent a waste of money and a tremendous waste of space.

OVERHANGS

All of the roof designs and construction methods mentioned in this chapter can and should incorporate overhangs into the design (Fig. 9-18). A large overhang protects a house from the elements and generally makes it more attractive. The area between the joists, purlins, or trusses must be ventilated from the overhang, which can be done in a variety of ways. Perforated aluminum offers a covering for

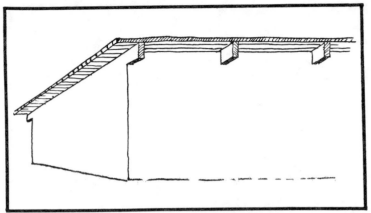

Fig. 9-18. All roof designs should use overhangs for protection and beautification.

the joists as well as the needed ventilation. A gutter system is now available that serves as the facia board and provides a channel for the perforated eave material. This type of no maintenance system generally costs no more than building with wood.

If aluminum finishing is not desired, there are two alternatives to choose from—either the joists may be covered with wood or they may be left exposed. It takes more material to fully cover the joists, producing a different effect. The primary advantage is the smooth surface is easier to stain or paint. The coating of the joists is more difficult because of the varied surface area; if the coating is going to be applied with a paint sprayer, this is not a major task. The simplest alternative is to leave the joists exposed and left natural. If the house's siding is also left natural, the joists and the siding will complement each other.

Joists or purlins exposed on the house's exterior produce a totally different effect from when they are covered. On some houses this exposure would not look right; for example, it would be difficult to find a colonial style house with this exposed structure. A primary consideration is whether or not the exposed structure will fit into the house's motif. If it will, they may as well be left exposed.

With exposed joists, all that has to be done is to "block" between the joists. This blocking must be ventilated to

146

eliminate moisture built-up in the roof. Generally, a pigeon-hole vent in every block is needed. These are easily set up before or after the installation of the blocking. In areas with high humidity, these vents must be increased in size.

The blocking is most easily installed as the joists are set into place. Instead of fitting the blocking between the joists, the blocking is installed as the joists are installed to insure accurate spacing of the joists. The blocking can be cut all at once to the specified length so its installation will not slow the setting of the joists. Because of the purpose it serves by providing accurate spacing of the joists, the blocking should speed the erection of the roof.

If you decide that the joists should be covered instead of using blocking between them, and if aluminum finishing is not desired, the ends of the joists are covered with a 1-inch thick facia board. The underside of the joists is usually covered with a high grade of exterior plywood, usually A-C. Typically, ⅜-inch plywood is used. The roof ventilation can be incorporated into this overhang in a variety of ways. The most economical method and the way that provides the cleanest

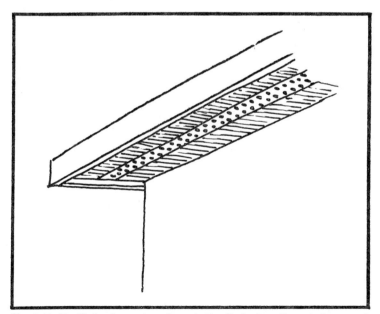

Fig. 9-19. Ventilation is most easily and attractively done through the use of continuous perforated vents.

appearance is through the use of a continuous vent, similar or identical to what would be used if the overhang were finished with aluminum. A 4-inch wide vent placed anywhere on the underside of the overhang, under most conditions, will produce adequate ventilation. Through the use of this continuous vent, which can be made of screening, less plywood is used and there is no extra cutting for the installation of the vents (Fig. 9-19).

In lieu of the continuous vent, square or round vents can be used. The square vents measure 6 × 9 inches and are placed about 8 feet apart. These vents look similar to heat register vents but are made of plastic. They are difficult to keep paint on and they usually warp. Because of these two reasons and the way they break up the smooth surface of the plywood, these vents leave much to be desired.

Round vents are easily installed by the boring of a hole and the pressing in of the vent. Since many of these vents are usually needed, their use may not be economical. These pigeon-hole vents are more predominant as auxiliary vents installed due to the lack of adequate ventilation. An overhang, without proper venilation, will build up moisture. If the overhang is painted, the paint will peel in large sheets. The plywood can warp not only on the overhang but also on the roof. If any of these problems are noticed, more vents should probably be installed. If a continuous vent is not being used, provisions should be made to vent the extra moisture in the kitchen and bathroom areas. By installing larger or extra vents the area above the kitchen and bathroom can adequately be ventilated.

CONCLUSION

Because of complexities, incredible standardization of roof design has resulted. This standardization has led to roofs that work well and generally look monotonous.

The roof is not only important as a functional item; the roof's lines are the most important visual element of a building's design. A roof must function properly—and this is paramount to its aesthetics—but this means more than just keeping out rain, and keeping heat inside during winter and outside during summer. These are only the minimum requirements.

Especially for an owner-builder's house, a roof should not be too complex. Simple designs are much easier to build and generally work better. Single-process roofs—those in which the ceiling is completed as the roof is built—are most easily and attractively built from planks and beams. The planks supply the structure between the beams as well as the finish treatment for the ceiling. This type of roof is simple to build, comparable in price, strong and attractive. Most of all, it saves a lot of work.

A good roof must do many things. It must keep the rain from coming inside and it must have adequate insulation value. It should also have overhangs to keep the outside of the house dry—this way one does not have to worry as much about leaks through other areas of the house. A roof should be attractive from both the outside and inside of the house. It should be economical and viable to build. And, to insure that these requirements are met throughout the years, all roof designs that could trap moisture should be adequately ventilated.

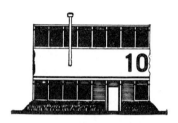

The Floors

A post-frame can be built with either a wood floor elevated above the ground level or with a concrete floor (Fig. 10-1). The advantages and disadvantages of both of these systems are numerous, being dependent on personal taste, climate, terrain, area lumber prices the builder's familiarity with working with concrete, and on the possibility of having transit concrete delivered.

THE CONCRETE FLOOR

Under most circumstances, the concrete slab floor is a less expensive floor system than the wood floor. A concrete floor can be both warm and dry; when a building site's variables are conducive to the building of a slab, generally it will be the least expensive and most satisfactory system.

Concrete can be obtained "transit-mixed," that is, delivered in a fluid state by a cement truck. This is the most viable way to obtain concrete. The concrete has been accurately measured, thoroughly mixed, and watered to a correct consistency. These three factors determine the strength of concrete; lacking any one of these three factors, concrete becomes weak. Correctly made, concrete is amazingly strong.

To insure yourself that strong concrete will be made, transit-mixed concrete should be ordered. The most difficult

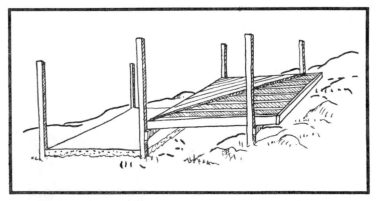

Fig. 10-1. Shown are a concrete floor at ground level and an elevated wood floor.

part of laying concrete is the mixing of the material. Transit-mixed concrete allows the builder to quickly lay the slab. And it costs little more.

Concrete is measured by the yard. A "yard" of concrete means a cubic yard. There are 27 cubic feet in one cubic yard. To calculate the amount of concrete needed to cover a given area, one uses the number 27. If, for example, a slab needed to be poured one foot thick, then a yard of concrete would cover only 27 square feet. Needless to say, this is rarely done. Often times, though, concrete is poured to a thickness of 6 inches. In this case, a yard of concrete would cover twice the area, or 54 square feet. Six-inch thick slabs are used for driveway approaches and streets. For a home's slab, ususally a four inch thickness is used. Since 4 inches is ⅓ of a foot, a 4-inch thick slab will cover three times the area that the foot thick slab covered; instead of covering 27 square feet, each yard of concrete will cover 81 square feet when poured to the 4-inch thickness. ($27 \times 3 = 81$). Three-inch thick slabs have also been used successfully for a home's floor. Especially when reinforced, a three-inch thick slab is sufficient. Since 3 inches is one-fourth of a foot, a yard of concrete will cover 108 ($27 \times 4 = 108$) square feet when poured to this thickness. By remembering that there are 27 cubic feet in a cubic yard and by determining at what fraction of a foot the slab will be poured, it is easy to calculate how many square feet a cubic yard will cover (Table 10-1).

Before the concrete is ordered, certain preparations are necessary. The slab area must be leveled and all topsoil must be scraped off. Organic materials, such as topsoil, cannot be built upon since these materials are constantly decomposing. Not only would the decomposition leave voids beneath the slab, the odor from the decomposition would permeate through the floor. To avoid these problems, the area must be scraped down to the inorganics—usually these are within a foot of the ground's surface.

Unless the inorganic soil is sand or gravel, a minimum of four inches of sand or gravel is required to be laid beneath the slab. This layer functions in four major ways: it can be easily leveled to provide a flat surface upon which to cast the slab; it provides padding as a safeguard against earth heaves or tremors—the sand or gravel cushions the force to keep the slab from breaking; it insulates the slab to keep it warm; and, by providing distance between the ground and slab, the slab will remain dry.

Sand or gravel both provide these four functions. But gravel is superior as an insulator and as a preventor of capillary action (the effect of water rising through the sand or gravel). Sand is superior to gravel as a substance that can be easily leveled. Both provide relatively equal amounts of cushion. The decision of which to use generally hinges on availability. Gravel is often much more expensive than sand, so usually sand is used. A 6-inch layer of sand provides essentially the same barriers as a 4-inch layer of gravel; in place of using gravel, a thicker layer of sand brings the same effect. It is not worth paying a lot of extra money for the

Table 10-1. The Table Shows the Number
of Square Feet Covered Per Cubic Yard of Concrete.

THICKNESS	Square feet covered
3″	108
4″	81
5″	67
6″	54

gravel. For the best possible system, though, a 4-inch layer of gravel is covered with a 4-inch (or thicker) layer of sand. With this two-layer system, the best of both components is utilized.

Before the slab is cast, a plastic membrane must be laid on top of the sand and/or gravel. Another advantage of using sand is the plastic is much less likely to puncture when walked upon if it is laid on sand. Gravel tends to poke through it. Since this plastic is meant to barricade moisture, caution must be taken to prevent its puncture. Although a few holes are inevitable, the less holes there are, the better it functions. By using this plastic membrane in conjunction with the sand and/or gravel fill, positive protection against the passage of moisture is assured.

To figure the cost of the slab floor system, suppose concrete is being ordered to pour a 4-inch thick slab for a house with a floor area of 1,280 square feet. Since each yard will cover 81 square feet, 81 must be divided into 1,280, which is 15.8. Sixteen yards of concrete, then, should be ordered (concrete is typically ordered in full yards). Order enough concrete to finish the job. If extra concrete is left over, it can be used to pour a porch slab or other optional area.

Sixteen yards of concrete will cost about $33 per yard, or about $544. This price is the cost of having the concrete delivered and, as all prices, will vary with area. Some cost savings will result if concrete is field mixed; the extra labor, though, makes this project absurd if transit mixed concrete is available.

To mix this much concrete, use a mixer. It can be mixed in a wheelbarrow, but it would take a long time. A slab should have at least a "five bag mix;" for every cubic yard of concrete, there should be five bags of cement. The cost of a bag of cement is around $4.00. Multiplied by five, this comes to $20.00 for cement alone. Added to this, we need a yard of 60-40, which is 60 percent sand and 40 percent gravel. This cost is around $4.00 to $5.00 per yard delivered, depending on locale and delivery charges. If delivery is not available, then you should figure in the cost of fuel to transport the

60-40 mix. You should also include the wear on the vehicle. If a mixer is rented, rental charges should be figured in, of course.

The materials alone will come to more than $25/yard. Once you figure in the labor it will take to mix this concrete, the transit mixed price of $33 is a good deal. You are much more assured of having a properly mixed slab. Concrete must be well-mixed with the proper amount of water and poured so that wet concrete is not poured next to concrete that is already setting. When all these factors are taken into consideration, ordering transit mixed concrete is sensible. It enables one to get the slab done in one day without holdup.

Working with the transit-mixed cost of $544 for the concrete, we need to add on $80 for twenty yards of fill sand delivered and $20 for a plastic vapor barrier to be laid between the sand and the concrete. Another $50 will be added on for the scraping away of the topsoil. The total cost figure for a 1,280 square foot slab comes to $694—about 55 cents per square foot.

THE WOOD FLOOR

Figuring the cost of a conventional wood floor is a little more difficult. Let us assume, though, that the design will be an all-wood system. The primary alternative is the use of a

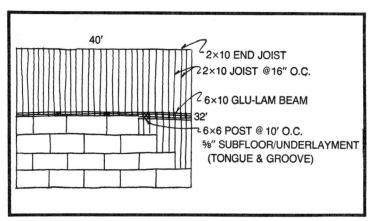

Fig. 10-2. An economical floor design using strong yellow pine joists and combination subfloor/underlayment plywood. Carpeting can be laid right over the plywood.

steel I-beam girder. The use of an I-beam, though, is not suggested since it is extremely heavy, expensive, and involves making one more connection—with a steel company. An economical floor design will look like Fig. 10-2.

With this design, there are (70) 2×10×16 foot for the joists (5) 2×10×16 foot for the end joists, and (8) 2×10×16 foot for the main beam. To support the main beam, (3) 6×6×8 foot posts are needed. Forty sheets of ⅝-inch plywood flooring provide the skin for this system. These materials add up to $1,572 (with $100 added for nails and glue) which calculates out to $1.23 per square foot for this wood floor system. This is more than twice the cost of the slab floor.

The floor joists, which are usually 2×8s, 2×10s, or 2×12s, are placed either 12, 16, or 24 inches on center. The size of the member and the spacing is determined by the span. Generally it is most economical to use larger joists and to space them further apart than to use many smaller members. With the use of fewer joists, there is less cutting and less nailing—resulting in saved time (Fig. 10-3).

It is sometimes more economical to use smaller lumber spaced closer together. When the alternative is between 2×10s spaced 16 inches on center or 2×12s spaced 24 inches on center, the 2×10 system may be less expensive. This is especially true when yellow pine joists are available. Yellow pine is usually much less expensive than fir except when large members are needed. Harvest time for yellow pine usually comes before the trees grow large enough to contain 2×12s; for this reason, yellow pine 2×12s are considerably more expensive than 2×10s. In this situation, using 2×10s at 16 inches on center may well be more economical even though more pieces are required. With a closer spacing of the joists, a thinner skin can be applied for the flooring. This alone can cut costs drastically. Before designing a floor system, the local lumber yards' prices should be procured; by knowing the dollar figures for the different materials, the price of each floor system can be tabulated.

With a post-frame, the clear span for a floor joist will generally be 9 inches less than the length of the joists. Six inches of each joist will be bolted onto the post and three

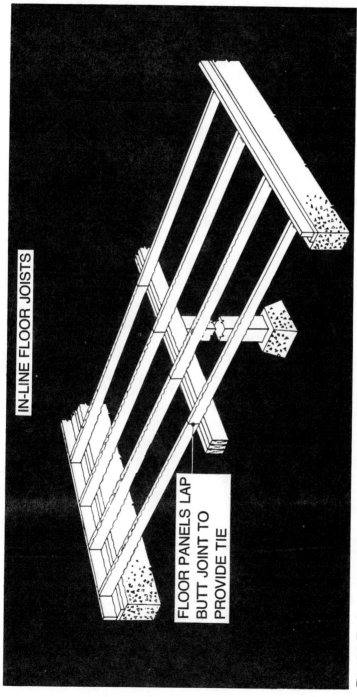

IN-LINE FLOOR JOISTS

FLOOR PANELS LAP
BUTT JOINT TO
PROVIDE TIE

Fig. 10-3. The floor joists here are 24 inches on center and are in line with each other. With in-line joists, each joist must be trimmed to the correct length, but the application of the plywood is sometimes easier.

157

inches of each joist will rest upon the center girder. A 16-foot joist would have a clear span of 15 feet 3 inches.

If we assume that the floor joists will be made from either #2 west coast douglas fir or yellow pine (both have the same strengths) to obtain a clear span of 15 feet 3 inches, we'd either need 2×10s placed 16 inches on center or 2×12s placed 24 inches on center. Two-by-tens at 16 inches on center will span 16 feet 9 inches. The 2×12s at 24 inches on center will span 17 feet 9 inches. Both allowable spans are above the needed span of 15 feet 3 inches. In this case, both allowable spans are quite a bit above the needed span, resulting in an extremely strong floor. Since the 2×12s at 24 inches on center have the greater capacity (17 feet 6 inches as opposed to 16 feet 9 inches) the 2×12s will result in the strongest floor.

The most economical wood floors use plywood combination subfloor/underlayment glued onto the floor joists with a continuous bead of construction adhesive. The combination subfloor/underlayment, as the name suggests, serves as both the subfloor and the underlayment. This is a one-process floor. Whereas usually thinner plywood is laid over the joists and then covered with particle board or finish flooring, thick plywood is all that is needed with this system.

The plywood must be tongue-and-groove. Tongue-and-groove plywood is manufactured simply by staggering the center two or three plys (dependent upon the total number of plys) so that a tongue is made on one side and a groove on the other side.

Some people are apprehensive about using the single process system; this apprehension is not warranted. When the tongue-and-groove plywood is glued and nailed onto the floor joists, the entire floor works together—much like a stressed-skin beam. Stressed-skin beams, made by applying plywood over a framework, are extremely strong. Properly designed, a stressed-skin beam can be made to fulfill functions that not even a solid or a laminated beam could fulfill. The glued floor system is remarkably similar to the stressed-skin beam; in fact, if one were to stand a glued and nailed floor system on its side, the floor system would be a stressed-skin beam. Plywood has remarkable strength, as does construction adhesive. When these two materials are combined over a framework, a very strong structure is made. The entire floor works together, dispersing load concentration.

The primary function of the glue is to eliminate any slippage. If this type of floor system were to be only nailed, there would be slight movements of the plywood over the floor joists at the areas between the nails. With a continuous bead of adhesive run along the top of the joist, no slippage will occur—resulting in a system that works as a single unit. Without the glue, the joist would work separately from the plywood; just the same, the plywood would work separately from the joist. The adhesive bonds the two together, creating a successful floor system.

Fig. 10-4. If construction adhesive would have been used in the past, wood floors would have fewer squeaks.

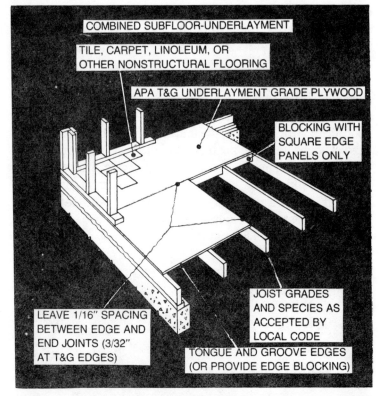

COMBINED SUBFLOOR-UNDERLAYMENT

TILE, CARPET, LINOLEUM, OR
OTHER NONSTRUCTURAL FLOORING

APA T&G UNDERLAYMENT GRADE PLYWOOD

BLOCKING WITH
SQUARE EDGE
PANELS ONLY

JOIST GRADES
AND SPECIES AS
ACCEPTED BY
LOCAL CODE

LEAVE 1/16" SPACING
BETWEEN EDGE AND
END JOINTS (3/32"
AT T&G EDGES)

TONGUE AND GROOVE EDGES
(OR PROVIDE EDGE BLOCKING)

Fig. 10-5. The single-process floor saves time and money—and it is just as good as the multi-layered floors of the past.

A strong adhesive is needed to fulfill this function. Construction adhesive comes in half-barrel tubes (11-ounce tubes that fit into a caulking gun with a half-barrel shape). This packaging allows for quick change-over when one tube is depleted; most importantly, the adhesive can be quickly, easily and neatly applied. The adhesive also comes in quartsized tubes which fit into a larger gun. The larger guns, which are much more expensive than the smaller ones, offset the slight cost savings realized by buying the larger tubes. Although you don't have to change tubes as frequently, the larger tubes and guns are much heavier and more awkward to use. If only one house is being built, 11 ounce tubes are fine. When bought by the case, a good price may be secured (Fig. 10-4).

Since the plywood tongue-and-groove serves as both the subfloor and the underlayment, carpeting can be laid directly over the plywood. Or the floor area can be covered with a vinyl floor covering or other desired finish. If ceramic tile is being used, ⅛th inch plywood should be applied before the tile. Because ceramic tile's grout can take no motion whatsoever without cracking, the area between the joists should be blocked every 24 inches (Fig. 10-5).

FLOOR TRUSSES

Another alternative in floor design is the use of wood floor trusses (Fig. 10-7). The primary advantage is the trusses can span the width of the building without the need for a central girder. This advantage is best utilized in conventional construction for a first floor being built over a

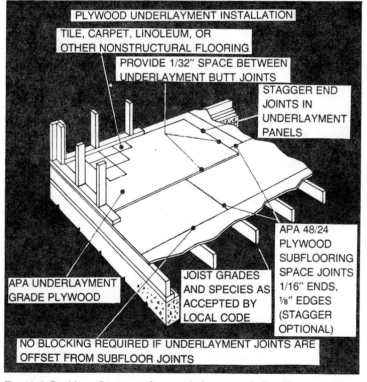

Fig. 10-6. Dual-layer floors are often used when ceramic tile will cover the floor. For the two layer system, thinner plywood is generally used. Particle board can be used for the top membrane.

basement. Without the central girder and accompanying posts, a basement becomes a much nicer area. All ductwork and wires can run either between or through the trusses—resulting in a ceiling that is free from projections. The ceiling can easily be finished with drywall or other appropriate covering. Since a post-frame can also be constructed with a basement, floor trusses could be used to great advantage for the first floor.

When any kind of house is built over a crawl space, the use of floor trusses makes little sense. With a crawl space there is no disadvantage to using the central girder/joist construction. The primary advantage is that joist construction is much less expensive than trusses.

For the floor of a second story, trusses offer the advantage of not needing interior support walls. Although there usually will be interior walls that can easily function as support walls, some interior plans use few walls. Above these "open floor plans," floor trusses are greatly utilized. Although a central beam, functioning much the same as the girder for the first floor, can make possible a floor plan without support walls, in some open plans a wide expanse of ceiling unbroken by beams is preferable.

Unfortunately, floor trusses are very expensive to buy. Plus, it is often against the building codes for a builder to field-fabricate trusses. Building codes disallow people from making their own trusses because of the highly engineered nature of a truss system. Trusses are designed to be made with precision cuts and specific gusset plates. They are rated according to species and grade of lumber used. Different types of lumber are usually used for the different parts of a truss. The bottom chord uses the highest grade lumber, the top chord uses the next highest grade lumber, and the webs are composed with lower quality wood. These types of specifications can be under strict quality control at the factory, but imagine a building inspector attempting to inspect every truss that is manufactured (Fig. 10-8).

It takes less lumber to truss a floor than it does to conventionally frame one. The nature of a truss is to convert compressive forces into tensile (or stretching) forces. Woods' tensile strength far surpasses its compressive

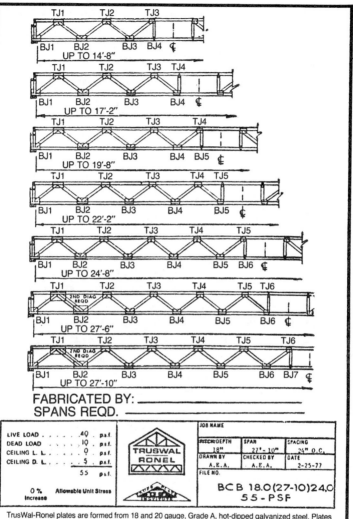

LIVE LOAD . . . . . .40 . p.s.f.
DEAD LOAD . . . . 10 . p.s.f.
CEILING L. L. . . . . 0 . p.s.f.
CEILING D. L. . . . . 5 . p.s.f.
55 p.s.f.

0 % Allowable Unit Stress
Increase

TRUSWAL
RONEL

JOB NAME		
PITCH/DEPTH	SPAN	SPACING
18"	27'- 10"	24" O.C.
DRAWN BY	CHECKED BY	DATE
A.E.A.	A.E.A.	2-25-77
FILE NO.		
BCB 18.0(27-10)24.0		
55-PSF		

TrusWal-Ronel plates are formed from 18 and 20 gauge, Grade A, hot-dipped galvanized steel. Plates shall be applied to both faces of truss at each joint. Where dimensions are not shown, piece plates symmetrically about joint. Where no sheathing is applied directly to top chords, they shall be braced at intervals not exceeding 3'-0". Where no rigid ceiling is applied directly to bottom chords, they shall be braced at intervals not exceeding 10'-0". All additional lateral bracing specified on truss is for bracing individual truss members only. All permanent bracing for the overall structure is to be provided by designer of complete structure. TrusWal-Ronel bears no responsibility for the erection of trusses. Persons erecting trusses are cautioned to seek professional advice regarding temporary erection bracing which is always required to prevent toppling and "dominoing". This truss has been designed to meet applicable provisions of the "National Design Specifications for Stress-Grade Lumber and its Fastenings" (NFPA) and "Design Specifications for Light-Torch Plate Connected Wood Trusses". (TPI). Cutting and fabrication shall be accomplished using equipment which will produce snug fitting joints and plates. Care should be exercised at all times to avoid damage through careless handling of trusses durilng unloading, storing and erection.

Fig. 10-7. Floor trusses are highly engineered. Here is a diagram of an 18-inch deep floor truss (courtesy Truswal Systems Incorporated)

strength. Think of how easily it is to break a wooden match. The bending force applied to it is compressive force—just the same as the force applied to a floor joist when it is stepped upon. Now take a match and try to pull it apart. If you can do that, you qualify for membership into the league of super-heroes. The webs of a truss take the compressive forces and, by their angled design, exert tensile forces upon the chords. Since the chords are in tension, the wood is used to its maximum efficiency.

When it is possible to field fabricate trusses, you need not buy all sorts of different grades of lumber; with construction grade wood, you can choose the best lumber for the bottom chord, the next best for the top chord, and the worst for the webs. Either metal gusset plates or pieces of plywood can be used to secure the joints. When plywood is glued and nailed to the areas where the webs meet the chords, a strong truss is made. The idea behind using metal gusset plates or plywood is to distribute stress over a greater area.

Another method of distributing this stress is through the use of split rings. A company called Teco makes "wedge-fit split rings" made especially for this purpose. A special tool is needed to cut a groove into the members receiving the split ring. The major advantage of this system is the truss members do not butt into each other. With the split ring system, the faces of the members are in contact. Because precision cuts are not needed and since these rings are manufactured particularly for making trusses, this type of system is the most likely to be accepted by your local building department.

The face-to-face contact method of building trusses is the best for owner-builders. Besides being easier because there is no need to make precision cuts, it can be done without plywood or metal gusset plates. It also can be done without the split rings. Since the only purpose of the split rings is to distribute stress, they can be eliminated if another way of distributing stress is used. Again, construction adhesive comes to the rescue—the primary factor which makes construction adhesive a great fastener is that it distributes stress. By building a truss with the face-to-face method, using nails and construction adhesive, a strong truss will be

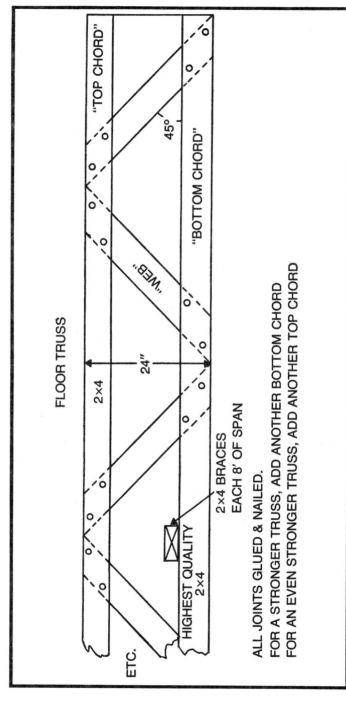

FLOOR TRUSS

"TOP CHORD"

"BOTTOM CHORD"

"WEB"

45°

24"

2×4

ETC.

HIGHEST QUALITY
2×4

2×4 BRACES
EACH 8' OF SPAN

ALL JOINTS GLUED & NAILED.
FOR A STRONGER TRUSS, ADD ANOTHER BOTTOM CHORD
FOR AN EVEN STRONGER TRUSS, ADD ANOTHER TOP CHORD

Fig. 10-8. The strength of floor trusses depends upon the type of wood used and the success of the connectors.

made. The primary function of the nails is to clamp the pieces together while the glue sets. Few nails are needed.

It must be remembered that most trusses are highly engineered. Don't gamble with guessing on how to design a truss. Besides finding a good way to fasten the pieces together and making sure that strong species of wood are used for different components of the truss, the truss must be engineered to make the span needed. The most important factor here is the depth of the truss. For large spans, a floor truss may be 24 or more inches in depth.

The drawing shows a truss fabricated with the face-to-face method. Notice that the chords are "on the edge" instead of on the flat. It is necessary to place them in this position for more surface-to-surface contact to assure a good bond. The chords—especially the bottom chord—should have a face grain, because this makes the lumber strong when placed in the "on edge" position.

With this arrangement, greater strength is obtained by the installation of a brace tying the bottom chords of the trusses together. This brace, running perpendicular to the trusses, can simply be nailed to the bottom chord of each truss. These braces, which prevent twisting, should be installed every 16 feet.

THE BEAMED FLOOR

Another method of floor construction involves using planks and beams (Fig. 10-9). Two-by-six tongue-and-groove planks can be placed over beams 6 feet on center or 3×6 planks with a double tongue-and-groove can be placed over beams eight feet on center. With the finished face down, these floors make nice ceilings for the rooms below.

Two and 3-inch thick tongue-and-groove boards are generally made from soft conifers like spruce. For this reason, the planks cannot serve forever as a finished floor since the wood easily dents. They can serve as a temporary floor; at a later time, the floor can be finished with carpet or other covering. Yellow pine can serve as the finish flooring.

The one disadvantage of this floor system is that since the structure is exposed, wires, plumbing, and heating

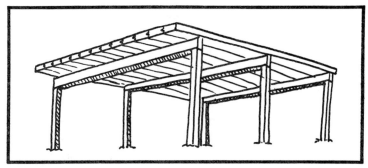
Fig. 10-9. The plank and beam floor is easily installed. Yellow pin planks can serve as the finish flooring.

ductwork must be left exposed if run beneath the floor. Generally alternative routes must be found, which means that more wire, plumbing, and ductwork must be used to weave their way around the opened floor structure. With wiring, this constitutes no great cost. Plumbing and ductwork, though, can become expensive.

Exposed ductwork does not have to look offensive. One form of architecture called brutalism works from the axiom that the inner workings of a building are never covered. Exposing the structure of the heating, wiring, and plumbing is analogized to exposing the beams in the ceiling. The acceptability of exposing the inner workings of a house is questionable. Although many buildings leave their ductwork exposed, a majority of homeowners like to see the mechanics of a building covered.

If the mechanical parts of a building are to be left exposed, nice workmanship must be done during installation. All exposed parts of the systems must be run in parallel and should bend at 90 degree angles in unison. The installer must make sure not to dent the heating ductwork, so it must be handled more carefully than if it were to be covered. These systems can be painted to blend them into their surroundings. They can be painted accent colors to make them stand out.

WOOD FLOORS VS. CONCRETE FLOORS

There are many factors to consider before deciding whether to build with a wood floor or a concrete floor. The final decision should be based upon which type of floor will be most inexpensive and desirable for the owner's personal taste. Personal taste, though, should not dictate the decision—prejudices against certain types of construction techniques only limit possibilities.

If a wooden floor is deemed preferable, all considerations should be pondered before deciding upon the use of girders and joists, trusses, or planks and beams. Generally speaking, a carpentry crew can erect pre-manufactured trusses the quickest, girder and joists the second quickest, planks and beams the third quickest, and field-fabricated trusses the least quickest. Inexperienced people can most easily build the plank and beam floor. Your personal situation determines the type of floor system which is best.

The primary advantage of the slab floor is its strength. You will be confident that the floor is strong enough to support an old piano, large bathtub or waterbed. The slab can endure these heavy weights indefinitely, whereas a wood floor's strength would be tested. The solidarity of the concrete floor gives a solidarity to the entire house. One will never walk upon a slab and hear it creak!

A slab must be used when the floor is to be below grade. Although a treated wood floor system could be worked out, the expense of this type of system (largely because of the treated plywood) is generally prohibitive. A concrete floor's largest assets are its ability to be placed below grade, its low cost, strength, the fact that the posts will not have to support it, and the bending resistance it gives to the posts.

The primary advantage of the wood floor is virtually no excavation has to be done. The ground below the house can remain in its natural state; in areas of rough terrain, this factor is a big plus. Especially when the ground is largely composed of boulders or other rock formation, it may necessitate leaving the home natural.

An important factor in determining whether to build with a wood floor or slab is the climate of the building site. In climates where temperatures reach below freezing, elevated wood floors will have to be insulated. This can be done in one of two ways. Either the side walls must be extended to the ground and fully insulated, or the bottom of the floor, all ductwork, and the plumbing must be insulated. With the first method, the building loses its lofty appearance. The ground underneath, which may have been attractive if left exposed, is obscured. Added to the cost of the wood floor is the expense of making the side wall extensions. By just insulating the floor and pipes, an effective compromise is reached. The ground beneath the house remains visible while the floor is adequately insulated.

In the cold climates, this expense of insulating the elevated floor must be calculated into the expense of the elevated wood floor. If the floor is more than a few feet above the ground, a rigid insulation board should be used in conjunction with batt or fill insulation. Without the rigid insulation, batts of insulation would have to be used—which should not be left exposed. Not only would it look bad, the insulation would be too susceptible to injury from wind, animals and people.

CONCLUSION

There are many considerations in deciding whether to build with a wood floor or a slab. Both have their advantages and disadvantages. The wood floor is best suited for the warmer climates. It is also ideal in damp areas and when the terrain is better left unexcavated. Because of their relative expense when compared to the slab's cost, wood floors are best used when they do not have to be insulated and when their use circumvents a potential problem. Because of the slab's economy and possession of many positive characteristics, its use promotes a low-cost design.

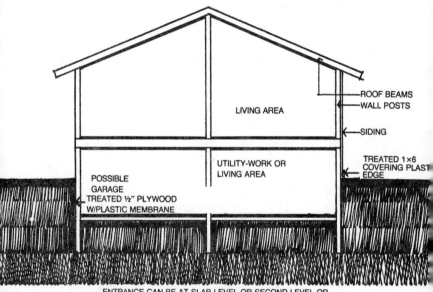

ROOF BEAMS
WALL POSTS

LIVING AREA

SIDING

UTILITY-WORK OR
LIVING AREA

TREATED 1×6
COVERING PLAST
EDGE

POSSIBLE
GARAGE
TREATED ½" PLYWOOD
W/PLASTIC MEMBRANE

ENTRANCE CAN BE AT SLAB LEVEL OR SECOND LEVEL OR
ENTRANCE CAN BE BETWEEN THESE LEVELS
WITH ½ STAIRWAY GOING TO EACH

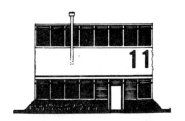

Exterior Design

Buildings are usable sculpture (Fig. 11-1). By being made attractive, a house is more than just a place to live—it becomes an expression of the builder. Every building has a certain "feel" to it. It can elicit feelings that make people feel at home, or it can feel stifling. The exterior design dictates these feelings. It determines, to an extent, the interior design of the home. Generally colonial style homes are furnished with colonial style furniture; modern homes have modern furniture. Certain congruencies are expected between the exterior and the interior of a home. The exterior design, then, has great significance.

I have drawn eight designs that hopefully will communicate some of the potentials of post design. These designs are intentionally basic and are meant to display forms rather than features. The wide variety of forms hopefully will display the unlimited arrangement post-frame homes are capable of possessing.

DESIGN NUMBER ONE

This first design is probably the most adaptive (Fig. 11-2). The typical gable roof makes its solar positioning unimportant. The majority of glass should face the approximate south-west direction, and could be placed on any side of this structure. Generally, though, this is not a solar design

Fig. 11-1. This beautiful home reflects the builder's tastes.

and is most readily adaptable for conventional window treatment.

By being two stories, this house can be placed on lots that slant in any direction without this geographic factor influencing any design change. Of course, it is just as well-suited for flat sites. If a steep site is encountered and this basic design is desired, by extending the treated plywood further up the side facing the hill, a higher grade can rest against the house.

Besides being very adaptable for different slopes, this design can be modified into many floor plans. A section of the

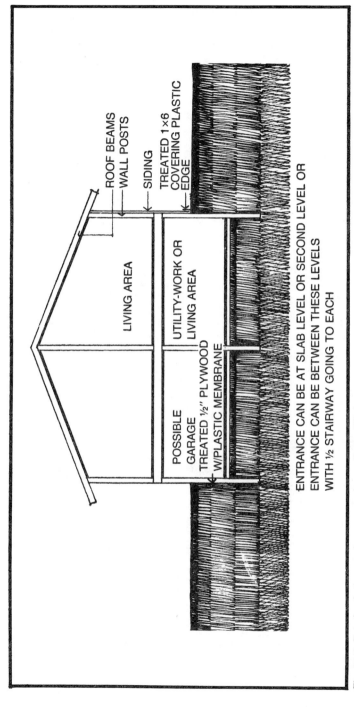

ROOF BEAMS
WALL POSTS
SIDING
TREATED 1×6 COVERING PLASTIC EDGE

LIVING AREA

UTILITY-WORK OR LIVING AREA

POSSIBLE GARAGE
TREATED ½" PLYWOOD W/PLASTIC MEMBRANE

ENTRANCE CAN BE AT SLAB LEVEL OR SECOND LEVEL OR ENTRANCE CAN BE BETWEEN THESE LEVELS WITH ½ STAIRWAY GOING TO EACH

Fig. 11-2. Exterior design number one can be easily modified.

first floor can serve as a garage, with the entrance on either the front or side of the house. The rest of the bottom floor can be a basement-utility area workshop, a living area, or a bedroom area. If the house is large, the upstairs can be entirely devoted to bedrooms. The design arrangements are endless.

This design has been drawn with a support wall holding up the peak of the roof. The ceiling follows the slant of the roof. If a support wall is not desired, the roof can be trussed. Or, if an attic is desired, a conventional roof may be constructed.

The first story support wall can be post-frame or post and beam. Another option is to have a framed support wall resting on the concrete slab, which should be made deeper beneath the wall for this circumstance. An 8-inch deep by 16-inch wide trench is filled with concrete to serve as this footing. If post and beam construction technique is used, the extra concrete only needs to be beneath the posts. When this support wall is needed before the slab can be poured, the 8 × 16-inch trench can be filled with crushed gravel. The gravel is well-tamped and leveled. A 2 × 8 that is treated serves as the footing. A treated 2 × 6 bottom plate acts as the base for a conventionally framed support wall. See Table 11-1 for minimum footing plate sizes.

DESIGN NUMBER TWO

Design #2 uses the same banked effect as design #1, allowing this design, too, to have much adaptability (Fig. 11-3). This design usually would be built without an attached garage, although one could be worked into the plan. It has a cantilevered roof that serves as a porch roof for the cantilevered deck. Through using the cantilever principle, decks can be made without too much extra trouble. And, a nice looking cantilevered deck adds a lot to a house.

Post-frames are very conducive to the use of cantilevers. As the word "cantilever" suggests, this system makes use of the simple teeter-toter principle of the lever. If downward pressure is exerted on one side of the fulcrum point, this pressure is transformed into upward pressure at

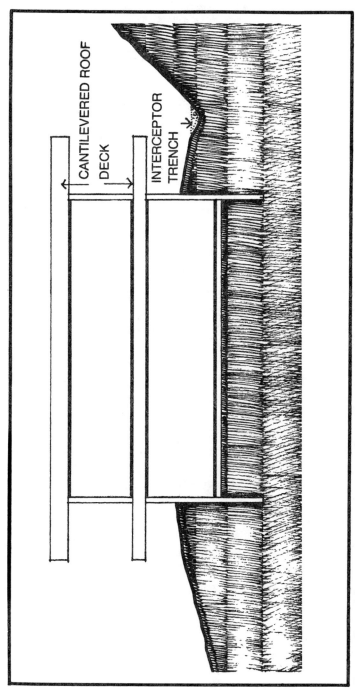

CANTILEVERED ROOF

DECK

INTERCEPTOR TRENCH

Fig. 11-3. For exterior design number two, this home's windows should face approximately southwest and be protected by an overhang.

Table 11-1. Use This Table for Minimum Footing Plate Sizes (Courtesy National Forest Products Association).

House width (feet)	Roof-40 psf live; 10 psf dead Ceiling-10 psf 1st floor-50 psf live & dead 2nd floor-50 psf live & dead		Roof-30 psf live; 10 psf dead Ceiling-10 psf 1st floor-50 psf live & dead 2nd floor-50 psf live & dead	
	2 stories	1 story	2 stories	1 story
32	2×10	2×8	2×10[3]	2×8
28	2×10	2×8	2×8	2×6
24	2×8	2×6	2×8	2×6

[1]Where width of footing plate is 4 inches or more wider than that of stud and bottom plate, use ¾ inch thick continuous treated plywood strips with face grain perpendicular to footing; minimum grade C-D (Exterior glue). Use plywood of same width as footing and fasten to footing with two 6d nails spaced 16 inches.

[2]This combination of house width and height may have 2×8 footing plate when second floor design load is 40 psf live and dead total load.

the other end. In a building, decks can project out from the exterior walls without visible support. The support comes from the cantilever effect. As long as there is downward pressure in the house on the cantilevered member, the deck will remain in position. The downward pressure comes from a natural gravitational effect and from the weight of the materials used inside the building. This type of structure actually results in a strengthening of the floor area. Since the deck is exerting upward pressure on the floor area, the floor can take greater loads.

The band of windows should face south-west to take advantage of the sun's heat. By having an overhang that projects over the windows, the sun will be blocked during the summer when it is high in the sky. With a solid band of windows, framing is simplified and a design is given harmony.

Since this design involves the door being below the rest of the grade, abutment walls must project from the sides of the doorway. These walls can be made of treated 2 × 6 tongue-and-groove nailed to posts sunk into the ground. The finished face should be left exposed. The tongue-and-groove should be nailed to the back of the posts for a more secure attachment.

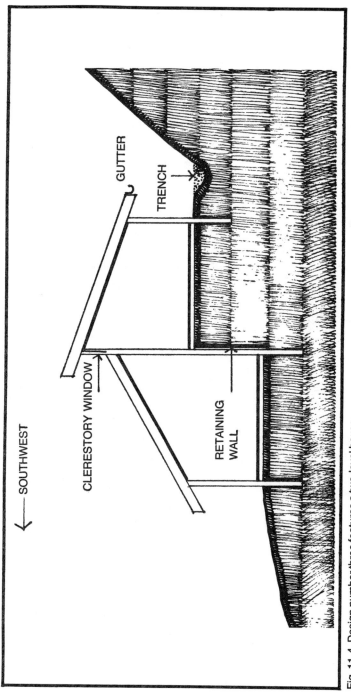

Fig. 11-4. Design number three features a two-level house.

177

The porch slab should be at least 6 inches below the level of the floor slab to prevent water from seeping into the house. The slab should be pitched away from the house to provide runoff. Since the posts next to this slab do not have banked protection on all sides, they must be deeper than the other posts to insure that they are both below the frost line and stable, where applicable.

DESIGN NUMBER THREE

Design number three is well-suited for a severely sloped site (Fig. 11-4). To take positive advantage of the slope, this house drops down the hillside, creating a duo-leveled structure. The lower level is ideally suited for a living , dining, bath and utility area. By consolidating these areas at the first level, the other levels are free for other activities.

Since the higher roof slopes toward the hillside, there must be a gutter at the eave to keep water from accumulating next to the house. The downspout should be carefully placed so that the runoff does not cause erosive action. Ideally, the downspout should lead directly into an underground pipe that goes to a storm sewer or drywell. Water should at least be channeled to an area that is somewhat level and away from the house. It is extremely important that the hillside be protected from erosive activity since the hill is supporting the house. As has been the case in some flood areas, entire hillsides have lost hold of their footing, resulting in the house sliding down the hill. Whenever possible, the vegetation on severe slopes should remain untouched because it protects the hillside. If the vegetation is excavated, it should be replaced immediately. Severe erosion can occur during a rainstorm.

The hillside may have to be sculptured to direct the water flow away from the house. The bank should not slope only toward the house—it should slope toward one side so that some water will run down the side of the slope away from the house. Excavated areas can be quickly covered with ground cover to protect the ground. Grass is one of the best covers and is readily available. If it is put on a severe slope, it should be staked in place until it takes root.

The retainer wall shown toward the center of the drawing must project out from the side of the house to protect the slope. This retainer wall's size is dependent upon the incline of the terrain. It should project out from the house a distance equal to its height. In this instance, that distance would be approximately 6 feet.

The construction of this wall is most easily accomplished with treated 2 × 6 tongue-and-groove boards nailed onto

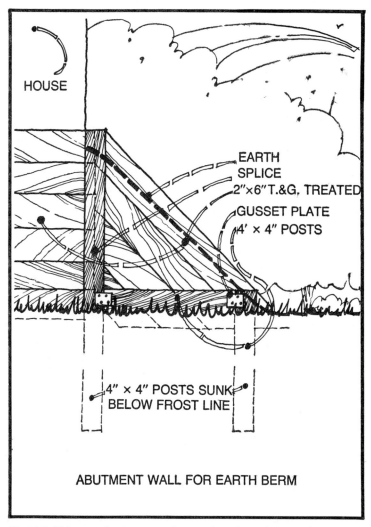

HOUSE

EARTH
SPLICE
2"×6" T.&G, TREATED
GUSSET PLATE
4' × 4" POSTS

4" × 4" POSTS SUNK
BELOW FROST LINE

ABUTMENT WALL FOR EARTH BERM

Fig. 11-5. Make sure the tongue-and-groove boards are fastened horizontally.

posts sunk into the ground. Because of the force exerted upon the wall, these posts should be as deep as the other ones.

There are several methods of construction for this type of wall. Since the wall protects a slope, the least expensive and most attractive design applies the 2 × 6 boards at an angle that approximately matches the angle of the slope the wall protects. In this manner, no extra wood is used far above grade where it has absolutely no benefit.

The retainer wall exposed from the inside of the lower level should have the tongue-and-groove applied horizontally (Fig. 11-5). The boards should always be applied to the back of the posts so the dirt presses them against the post instead of away from it. This retainer wall should project at least a few inches below the slab level so there will be no seepage from under the wall. It is a good idea to protect the wood with a plastic membrane before the area is backfilled. Not only does this help the wood to retain its vigor, it prevents the possibility of seepage from between the boards. With the finished side of the boards left exposed, these retainer walls serve an important purpose in an attractive manner.

DESIGN NUMBER FOUR

For severe grades that are better left untouched, it is wiser to build with wood floors that are elevated above the ground (Fig. 11-6). In this manner, very little of the slope needs to be disturbed. With this design, the lowest floor shown could be changed to wood construction. Obviously, if the lowest level's floor is of wood, it would not be used as a garage. With elevated wood floors, though, often there is room beneath a floor for a carport.

The advantage of building with elevated wood floors is that the hillside remains naturally intact. Virtually no excavation needs to be done—only for the posts and the plumbing. Any other type of construction makes huge disturbances in the hillside which can be potentially disastrous. With a post-frame, the vegetation is left beneath the house and there is no harm with water running down the hill and under the house. The steeper the hillside, the greater the amount of caution you must take. Steep hillsides exert a forward

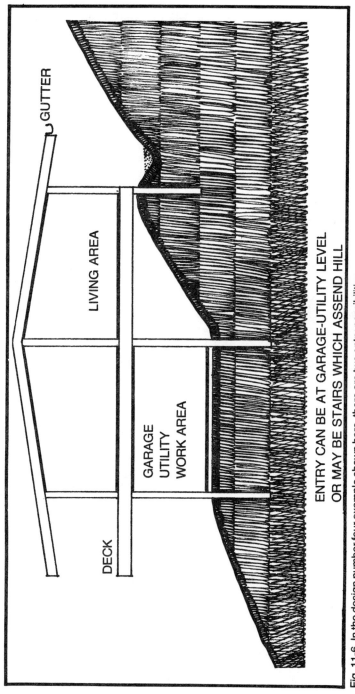

GUTTER

DECK

LIVING AREA

GARAGE
UTILITY
WORK AREA

ENTRY CAN BE AT GARAGE-UTILITY LEVEL
OR MAY BE STAIRS WHICH ASSEND HILL

Fig. 11-6. In the design number four example shown here, there are two entry possibilities.

motion on the posts on the higher part of the hill. These posts must be deeper. The dimension of the lumber, too, should be enlarged. And steep hillsides should be tested for the soil's stability before one decides to build.

This design needs only a small retainer wall by the garage. The same procedure should be used in constructing this wall as was mentioned for design #3. Other similarities include the necessity of a gutter to prevent erosion and the use of a pea gravel interceptor trench to stop water from building up near the house.

DESIGN NUMBER FIVE

Design #5 is best suited for a smaller place. This design incorporates a retainer wall that provides much of the wall structure for the house (Fig. 11-7). This retainer wall extends from the side of the house to compose a sunken patio. The slab for the patio must be sunk at least 6 inches below the level of the house's slab as protection against water runnning into the house. This patio can extend the entire distance across the southwest side of the house, serving as a nice-sized patio and as a retainer wall to keep the grade away from the house. Since this wall faces the sun, the wall is allowed to absorb the sun's heat if you keep the dirt away. By installing a doorwall on that side, the house should heat itself in the winter. Light colored drapes or shades shelter the windows from the summer sun.

By following the roof's pitch with the retainer wall, the siding can be installed at a 90-degree angle to both—which will simplify application. Also, there will be very little cutting required.

The advantage of this design is that a single story house can be built on a steep slope without burying the house too far into the slope, thereby freeing the south-west side for the patio and added glass. Especially when the slope is in the direction as shown in the drawing, there is little advantage to burying the house. If the slope was in the opposite direction, the southwest side would be naturally exposed and the northern side could be bermed for the insulating effect. This

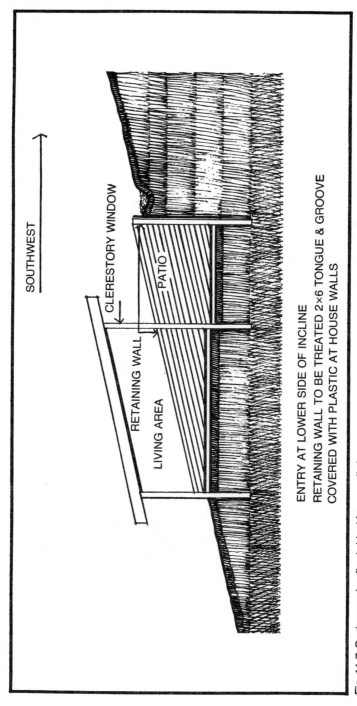

SOUTHWEST →

CLERESTORY WINDOW

PATIO

RETAINING WALL

LIVING AREA

ENTRY AT LOWER SIDE OF INCLINE
RETAINING WALL TO BE TREATED 2×6 TONGUE & GROOVE
COVERED WITH PLASTIC AT HOUSE WALLS

Fig. 11-7. Design number five is ideal for a small place.

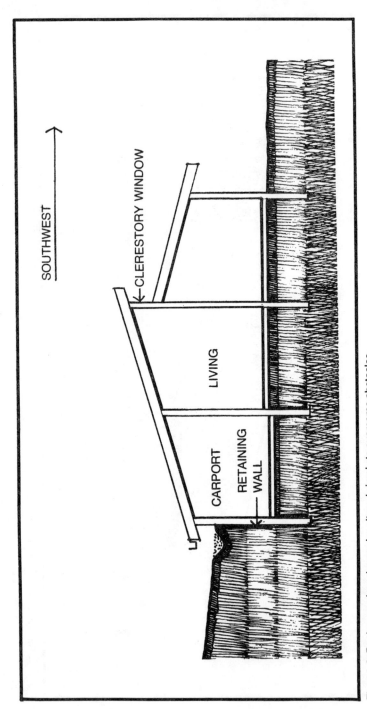

Fig. 11-8. Design number six may be altered simply to overcome obstacles.

design is especially well-suited for a slope in this direction when a single story house is desired. The design is one of the easiest to build and offers excellent drainage. The simplicity of the design makes it attractive.

DESIGN NUMBER SIX

If the slope does come from the other direction, the next design becomes very practical (Fig. 11-8). This design has a retainer wall that runs parallel to the back of the house. By retaining the bank out from the house, an entrance is provided for use of this area as a carport. The area can also be used for a patio like the one in the last design.

By keeping the slope away from the house, no treated wood needs to be used for the house's studs or siding. Construction is simplified by being able to use the same material throughout the exterior of the house. However, this house could be bermed to keep the slab warm or for aesthetics. There is much versatility with this plan. If a steeper roof pitch was added, the high part of the house would be conducive to taking an extra story.

DESIGN NUMBER SEVEN

This next plan is suitable for a slope in any direction, or for a flat site (Fig. 11-9). There are many different ceiling

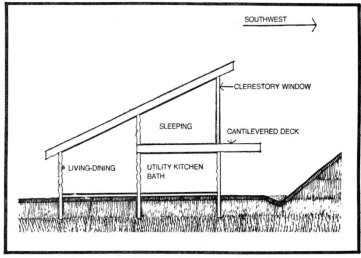

Fig. 11-9. Design number seven is fine for both level and hilly areas .

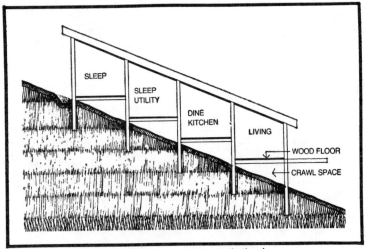

Fig. 11-10. This unique design is easy on your pocketbook

heights—each is best suited for specific rooms; the roof pitch is the critical factor because too steep a roof would make an exceedingly high ceiling in the lower part of the house. Too slight of a pitch would not give the second story sufficient height. If you are worried about losing too much heat due to the 12-foot height of the living areas's ceiling, heat channels could be installed through the closet into the sleeping areas. The heat would rise and would be transmitted into the other rooms.

If the sides of this house are bermed, the area behind the berm must be treated accordingly. Any grade sloping toward the house should have the pea gravel interceptor trenches.

DESIGN NUMBER EIGHT

This last design is for those who like something different (Fig. 11-10). It is an all-wood house well-suited only for dramatic slopes. As can be seen by the cut-away drawing, there are four levels. Approximately three steps connect the levels together, depending on the slope of the hill. The roof follows the hill's slope. All posts can be of equal length and a certain amount of standardization is possible. This design should prove easy to build and economical. Because of the wood floors, little excavation need be done, which obscures the possibility of erosive activity.

A central hallway aids cross-ventilation and lends itself to an effective floor design. By having the living area at the downhill portion of this plan, this design is fit for placement at a water's edge. A doorwall at the front of the house is receptive for nice views and gives the living area a more expensive effect. This effect is emphasized through the incorporation of the doorwall and the cantilevered deck.

CONCLUSION

The plans presented are hypothetical and can be adapted to various situations. Many of the elements of certain designs were inherent elements in other designs; yet each plan was composed around dissimilar criteria—mainly, land form. The other major criterion was building size.

Because each plot of land has individual characteristics, as people do, each house that is built should be designed to satisfy the geograpical needs of the structure. Only then will the physical and psychological needs of the inhabitants be fulfilled. After taking into consideration the geographical elements of the building site, the designer can incorporate the elements of perhaps several designs outlined in the chapter. By adding one's individual requirements (specific areas like darkrooms, number of bedrooms, etc.) a proper building design is likely to result.

Interior Design

The insides of a home should emulate a well-designed machine—each part should function as a separate unit and synchronic with the other parts. As an example, the kitchen unit should be engineered to enable you to efficiently prepare meals; it should also be in alignment with the eating area, for obvious reasons. Good floor plans incorporate a sensible arrangement of rooms within a limited amount of space. Like large engines and four-barrel carburetors, huge homes will soon be a thing of the past. The disadvantages of large homes outweigh the advantages. Family members need sufficient room to work, play and entertain. We do not need extra rooms for each individual action. Dual purpose rooms help keep the initial cost of building and operating expenses down. The attempt is to work within a limited amount of space. But the division of that space should be appropriate for all present and future residents. The design should also insure that mechanical functions of the house will work with optimum efficiency.

There are few actual specifications that must be followed. The minimum size of a house is 750 square feet. An area of this size can contain one bedroom comfortably and two bedrooms rather uncomfortably. Besides being the minimum legal size, it is the minimum practical size.

The ceiling height must be at least 7½ feet for any habitable room, laundry room, or storage room. Hallways and bathrooms can have 7-foot ceilings. No habitable room other than a kitchen can be less than 7 feet in any direction. Each house must have at least one room 150 square feet. Typical ceilings range from 7 feet to 8 feet high.

The door height must be 6 feet 8 inches high for all doors. There must be two 36-inch wide doors that offer outside exits. This requirement is for fire safety. If one exit is blocked, the other one may be open. This 36-inch width is a minimum; doors can be as wide as desired. A sliding glass door-wall can substitute for one of the exit doors. Without two doors in a house, it would be mighty inconvenient having to walk around the house every time one wanted to reach the backyard. Interior doors are generally 30 inches wide. Wider doors are sometimes desired if large furniture is to be moved into the house. A 30-inch wide door, especially if it is around a turn, will stop a lot of furniture.

For ventilation, each room must have at least 5 per cent window opening. A 12×15 foot room, which is 180 square feet, must have 9 square feet of window opening. Assuming that only half the window area can be opened, two 3×3 windows would provide adequate ventilation. If the bathroom is in the interior of the home, which would prohibit a window opening other than a skylight, a ventilation fan must be installed. The water closet compartment cannot be less than 30 inches wide and must provide at least 24 inches in front of the toilet.

So far, only the legal requirements for design have been mentioned. These can be looked at as the game's rules. The "game" is to arrange the space in an attractive and functional way. It should look nice and fulfill the needs of the occupants. In some cases, the walls must provide support for the building. Often enough, economics plays an important role, too. With these factors in interplay, a design evolves.

Usually there must be a support wall inside the house. Unless the roof is trussed, it generally will need support either at its center or at two points off center. The first instance divides the house into two; the latter divides it into three. Obviously, these walls provide the basis for the design. The exterior walls provide the boundries for the design. I usually start with a rectangle with each side's length being a multiple of 4 feet, which simplifies construction and saves materials. The rectangle shape is used because it is the easiest to build and uses materials economically. Cyclic and multi-sided structures use less materials to enclose the same amount of space, but both present problems with feasible interior designs and construction. Square designs also use less material for side-wall construction, but they often use more material to build the roof due to the increased spans unless an extra support wall is added. The construction of a rectangle is simple, it uses material efficiently, and is receptive to good interior layout. It will be used for the following design considerations.

Within the rectangle shape, which we will assume will be divided by at least one support wall, the rooms must be strategically placed. For designs that make the most of the potential open space, the living area and eating area should be in alignment. The space is thus opened up, making one large room. The table in the eating area is always available for any project that needs a clean surface.

The living area should be placed approximately in the southwest direction to take advantage of the evening sunlight. Less electricity is used because the lights will not have to be turned on as soon. Besides, natural light is nicer for living. Since the living area is generally used more in the evening, the placement to receive evening light makes sense.

Part of cutting down building and construction costs involves the consolidation of the living room and family room. Unless one has a large family and is willing to use both rooms constantly (the living room is often a taboo place except for special occasions), it doesn't make too much sense to have two separate rooms. Also, there is no reason to have two eating areas if the "dining room" goes unused. Instead of being cramped in the "eating nook" six days a week, while saving the dining room for Sunday dinners, it makes more sense to make a nice eating area that can be used daily.

The kitchen, which should be next to the eating area, is best suited, like the bathroom, for the eastern side of the house since these rooms are used extensively in the morning. The two rooms should be close to each other, preferably, so that the plumbing is simplified. The utility area, which also needs plumbing, should be near both these rooms. This placement simplifies plumbing and makes the system work better. Through the close placement of the hot water heater, you do not have to wait for the hot water to reach the tap. In some houses, it takes thirty seconds for the water to become hot. It is wasteful because the hot water heater is heating up water that is remaining in many feet of line and cooling down after the tap is closed.

If the utility area is to contain the furnace, it should be rather centrally located for greater efficiency. By having the ductwork radiate from a centrally located furnace, a house is more evenly heated and less ductwork is used. With the furnace and water heater next to each other, both can share a roof vent.

The kitchen, utility room, and bathroom all require few windows. Fewer windows in the kitchen and utility room mean more space for cupboards and cabinets. Bathroom windows usually remain covered, negating any need for large amounts of glass. By having these rooms to the east, it frees the west and south for more glass. By having glass in these directions, it will help heat the house in the winter. Glass in the other directions represents only heat loss.

The kitchen is an ideal place for a skylight. They eliminate the need for a large window and supply a much light. By being able to work in adequate natural light, chores become more pleasant when working in adequate light.

The master bedroom can be placed in the east if you like to wake up with the sun. Most importantly, the bedroom should either have a private bath or be connected to the main bathroom.

You can see how the floor plan begins to take shape. There is somewhat of a string of rooms, from the living area to the eating area to the kitchen, utility area, bathroom, master bedroom, and finally the other bedrooms, if any. It must be assured, though, that each area has sufficient space—living and storage space.

There should be closets by each exterior door for coats. Each bedroom should have sufficient closet space for clothes

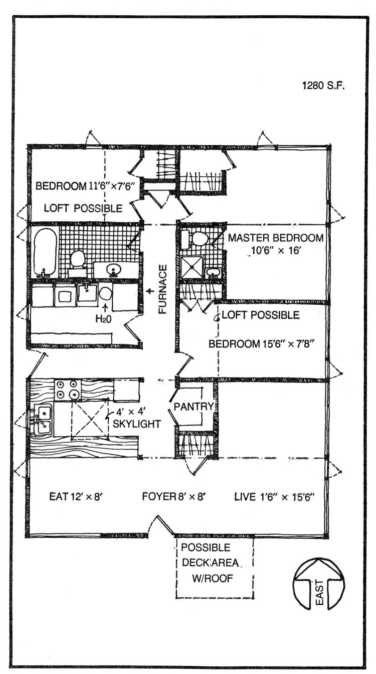

1280 S.F.

BEDROOM 11'6" ×7'6"

LOFT POSSIBLE

MASTER BEDROOM
10'6" × 16'

FURNACE

H₂0

LOFT POSSIBLE

BEDROOM 15'6" × 7'8"

4' × 4'
SKYLIGHT

PANTRY

EAT 12' × 8'   FOYER 8' × 8'   LIVE 1'6" × 15'6"

POSSIBLE
DECK AREA
W/ROOF

EAST

Fig. 12-1. This plan offers plenty of room for all family members. Plan 1
post-frame w/ interior posts 40' × 32' cathedral ceiling.

and other articles. There should be a linen closet for the bathroom(s), the kitchen must have food, dish, cooking gear, cleaner, and garbage storage areas, and there should be at least one storage closet for occasionally used articles. Closet placement can provide sound barriers between rooms. The closets work into a floor plan best when they are either back-to-back or side-to-side.

Storage areas are important to eliminate clutter and provide easy access to things. If a design does not include a basement, liberal storage space is a must. Walk-in closets provide a lot of space without taking up much room. Since only one door is used on the walk-in closet, it provides more freedom in room design. And it is less expensive to build.

One of the largest problems of interior planning involves door placement. If doors open into each other, it is bothersome and hard on the doors. Sliding doors can be used, especially on closets where the doors can overlap. Sliding doors on closets present no extra construction problems and are often less expensive to install—only tracks and handles are needed instead of hinges, knobs, and latches. Their one disadvantage is because the doors overlap, only half the closet is in view at once. Regardless, sliding doors on closets can be used effectively.

Room entrance doors that slide into a pocket in the wall are especially well-suited in areas where the door is infrequently used. If it is left open, the door is completely out of the way. Sliding doors are also used effectively in areas where a swinging door would get in the way. In other areas, though, the sliding door can be undesirable because it complicates wall framing and is more difficult to open and close.

Doors which are frequently closed and used should not be sliding because they are more difficult to use. Frequently used sliding doors are more prone to break than swinging doors.

The doors and windows should be placed to enhance cross-ventilation. Through aiding the natural flow of air, a more pleasant environment will result. Doors should be placed across from each other whenever possible; windows, too, should be placed across from doors or other windows.

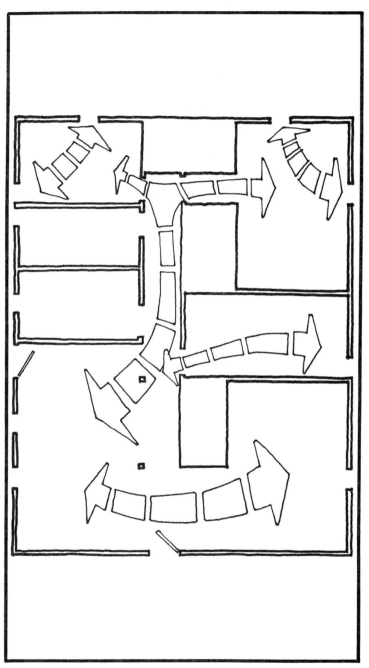

Fig. 12-2. The illustration shows proper ventilation for a home using floor plan number one. Ventilation Plan 1.

Some windows and doors should be located towards the direction of prevalent weather, since this is the wind direction. The placement of opening windows is important. As long as the locale of the openings is well-planned, many windows will not have to open.

Non-opening windows are much less expensive, easier to install and lose less heat. They are better looking and nicer to look out. Wherever a window is desired, but not needed for ventilation, a non-opening window should be installed.

The following three designs have been created especially for use with post-type structures. Plan #1, which has 1,280 square feet of floor area, has two post support walls helping to support the roof. The interior of this plan has an exposed plank and beam ceiling, with the beams 8 feet on center. Because of the beamed ceiling, most interior partitions exist directly beneath the beams. The partitions are built to the bottom of the beams.

The roof is pitched at 3/12 with the ceiling following the pitch of the roof. The interior ceiling ranges in height from 7 feet at the eaves to 11 feet at the ridge, which is directly between the two rows of supporting posts. A sloped ceiling gives the interior of a house a slightly dynamic effect. By having a natural wood ceiling becomes interesting.

The added ceiling height, by giving the interior a new dimension, makes the rooms feel larger. By giving the eye more space to roam, the occupant does not feel contained. Through not building all partitions up to the ceiling (thereby not curtailing the line of sight), this effect is accentuated. In, plan #1, for example, the pantry area can be built up to an 8 foot height, which is about the limit of accessibility anyway. The ceiling of the pantry can serve as a display area and the space above, by being left open, does not limit one's line of sight.

FLOOR PLAN NUMBER ONE

The interior floor design is an open one (Figs. 12-1 and 12-2). The large living room set against a large foyer and in line with the eating area gives the house an immense feeling. From the living room to the eating area is 32 feet of open area. Combined with the open ceiling, this design is spacious.

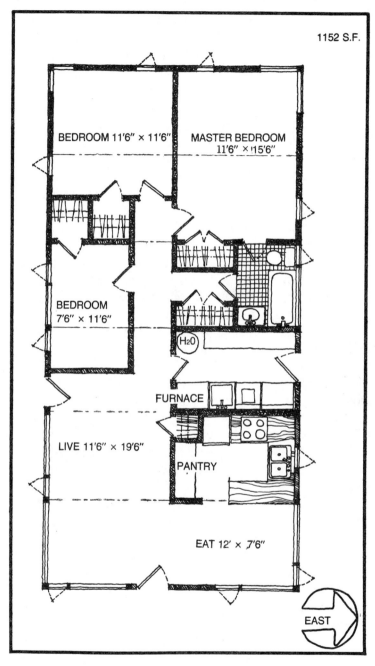

1152 S.F.

BEDROOM 11'6" × 11'6"

MASTER BEDROOM
11'6" × 15'6"

BEDROOM
7'6" × 11'6"

H₂0

FURNACE

LIVE 11'6" × 19'6"

PANTRY

EAT 12' × 7'6"

EAST

Fig. 12-3. Use floor plan number two if you are building on a narrow lot . Plan 2
48' × 24 post-frame.

All the rooms are large. Although the total floor area is only 1,280 sf (square feet), three bedrooms, two baths, and a utility room are fit in comfortably. There is plenty of storage space. Notice the large pantry adjacent to the kitchen, the walk-in closets for two bedrooms, and the storage space in the utility room.

The open ceiling permits the use of lofts in all the bedrooms. With a 7-foot ceiling on the master bathroom and a 7-foot high loft in bedroom #2, there is still up to 4 feet of headroom in the lofts. The loft in bedroom #3 would have a maximum of 3 feet of headroom, sufficient for a youngster. Through the use of these lofts, the floor area can be used for other things besides beds.

Modifications can easily be made upon this plan. For economy's sake, the master bedroom's bathroom can be eliminated—giving this bedroom an extra 32 square feet of living area. This area could also be made into a closet area, if extra storage space was desired. If a closet were built instead of a bathroom, this room could still have the option of having a loft. Instead of building two separate closets, the entire bathroom area could be moved over against the other closet, resulting in one huge closet. The entrance door to the room would open against the wall that separates bedroom #1 and #2.

Another change that can easily be made involves the side entrance. Some people like to have an entrance into a mudroom. If this is your case, the wall of the utility room can be moved to back up against the kitchen. The entrance door then would open between these closets and the laundry tub. The utility room thus serves the dual function as a mudroom.

Simple changes might involve a double bowl sink in the main bathroom and a door between the toilet and sink in the main bathroom and a door between the toilet and sink areas for maximum privacy. If the master bedroom's bathroom is eliminated from the plan, the separation of the main bathroom into units is advised, as is the installation of double sinks.

In this plan, the kitchen does not have cupboards above the countertop because of the large pantry and extreme length of the counter top. There is plenty of cupboard space. Many people like as much cupboard space as possible. If this

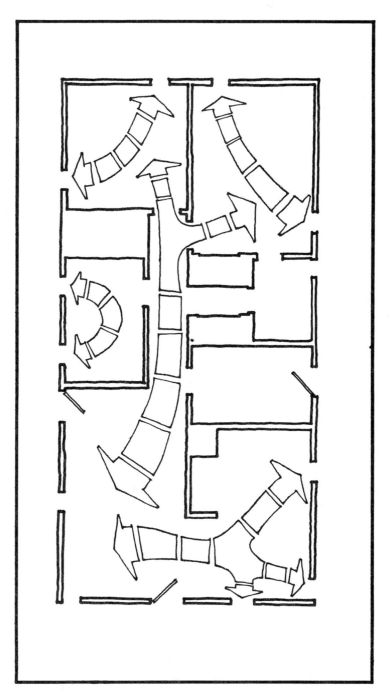

Fig. 12-4. This venilation diagram is used with floor plan number two.

is your case, cupboards above this countertop can easily be installed. They should open from both sides. Dishes can be put into the cupboards from the kitchen side and taken out of the cupboard from the dining area side. The cupboards below the countertop can open from both sides if desired.

Another feature of this plan is it easily can be cut down in size. If only two bedrooms are needed, this plan can be built so it ends where the bathrooms are. The last 8 feet can be eliminated. Bedroom #2 and the master bedroom would be combined, making a room that is 16×12 plus the ell under the proposed loft. The total area, would be 32×32, or 1024 sf.

FLOOR PLAN NUMBER TWO

This next floor plan is ideally suited for a skinny lot (Figs. 12-3 and 12-4). Although it can be situated so that the wide side faces the street, it is also capable of being placed longwise on a lot. This can be advantageous in circumstances where very little building room is available. The door on the designated west side can be eliminated and the front door can be located on the designated south side, opening between the living area and the dining area.

The plan features a large living and eating area, varied sizes in bedrooms, a secondary entrance through the utility room, and direct access into the bathroom from the master bedroom.

FLOOR PLAN NUMBER THREE

Plan #3, which incorporates only 768 square feet, offers the builder with a limited budget a very tolerable and livable two bedroom, two bathroom home (Figs. 12-5 and 12-6). Because of its limited size, storage space in large walk-in closets is a big advantage. Additional storage space is offered in the utility room. Besides the closet, shelving could be installed above the washer, dryer and tub.

The majority of the walls are 8 feet on center—allowing for a beamed ceiling with the beams 8 feet on center. The walls are built up to the height of the beams. This building method allows for simplified interior wall construction—especially if glulam beams with a level bottom and fabricated with a pitch are used. The construction of this type of beam

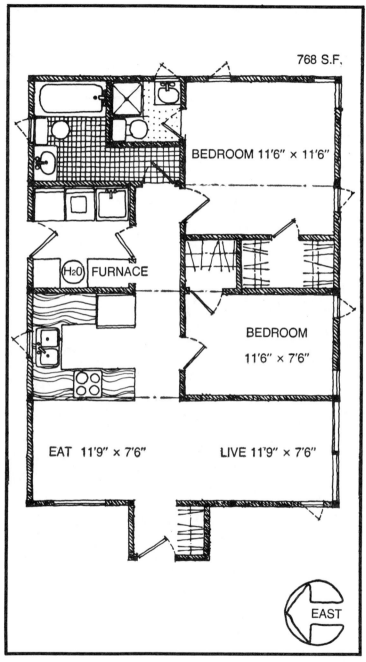

768 S.F.

BEDROOM 11'6" × 11'6"

H₂O FURNACE

BEDROOM

11'6" × 7'6"

EAT 11'9" × 7'6"

LIVE 11'9" × 7'6"

EAST

Fig. 12-5. Floor plan number three is nice for a small family. Plan 3 post-frame 32' × 24'.

201

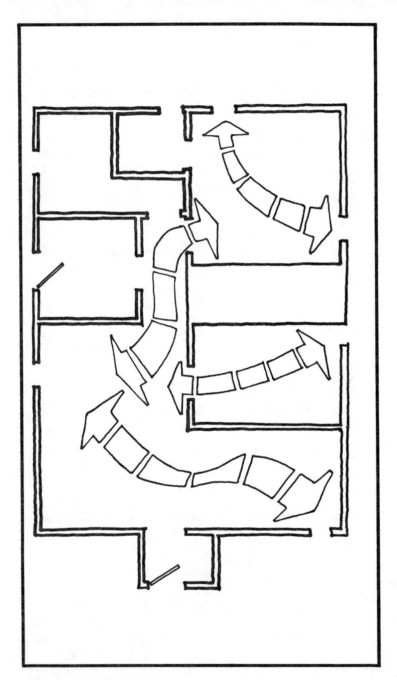

Fig. 12-6. Follow this drawing when determining ventilation for a home with floor plan number three . Ventilation Plan 3.

will be presented later in the survival cabin chapter. This floor plan is readily adaptable for that cabin.

A nice improvement on this plan would be the addition of a wood deck on the west side of this house. With the deck in

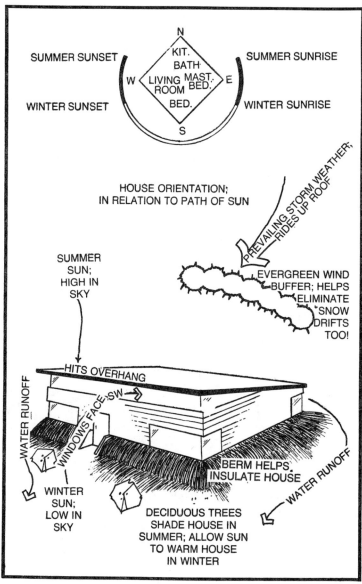

Fig. 12-7. Weather factors are important considerations when planning a home's design.

that location, the small porch could be eliminated. Part of the deck could be screened in off from the eating area to serve as an outdoor eating location. If the deck were to extend the entire width of the house, the portion off from the living area would extend the living area to the outside. By installing a doorwall on the living area's west side, the living room would seem much larger than it is.

The designs presented in this chapter intentionally do not have such frills. It is always easier to add to a plan than to subtract from it. So the plans have stuck to the basics. This way, people can add as much to a plan as they want or can afford. If such additions are not desired or cannot be afforded, these plans are autonomous as they stand.

Much of the owner-building that occurs involves creating a structure and then modifying it as the years go by. It is a good approach because it enables people to erect a shelter more quickly—then they can recoup. At a later time improvements like decks can be made. By waiting, a person realizes exactly what is needed, is more likely to have the money to complete the project, and can build the improvement at a more leisurely pace.

CONCLUSION

In this chapter, the essentials of interior planning have been discussed. Through following the suggestions, a more livable and economical floor plan will result.

Each family unit has specific, individual needs and desires. And each building site has its own individuality. By creating a floor plan with both of these factors as prime considerations, a good floor plan will be conceived. For example, if a building site contains a beautiful area for a rear yard and if the builder enjoys spending a lot of time outside, a floor plan may well evolve around these factors. If one likes to eat outside after preparing the food inside, the kitchen should have direct access to the rear yard. If these are the crucial factors, the floor plan should begin by planning how these details will be worked out. Less critical factors can then be incorporated into the plan by working around the crucial factors.

For a successful floor plan, you must be able to accurately assess your needs. You must know, first of all, where your values lie. And, if the house is being built for a family, the entire family's needs and values must be assessed—not only for the present. Wise planning involves accurate extrapolation so that a house is not soon outgrown (Fig. 12-7).

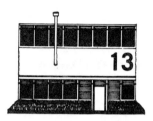

Insulation

We've all heard too much about energy shortages, black-outs, brownouts and the like (Fig. 13-1). Most likely, we've all received from one of our energy companies a bill that we thought was outrageous. For those of you who don't mind a little work in exchange for independence, I urge the possession of a wood stove. There is wood waiting to be claimed almost everywhere; after the wood stove, chimney, and chain saw have been bought, there's little more to spend. For the work (or exercise) of hauling wood, you've got free heat. Even if you would rather buy wood, the heat from a cord of wood will reduce the utility bill by more than you paid for the cord, assuming that it is burned in an efficient wood stove and not a fireplace or Franklin stove. Benjamin invented many fine things, but his wood stove is not one of them.

Maybe there isn't much wood where you plan to live. Maybe you don't fancy having to keep a place for a good sized woodpile. Justifiably, maybe you don't want to have to bring in logs from outside and through the house. It's a lot of work. We all know what we are willing to do—and what we aren't willing to do. A decision must be made, though, on how you will heat your home. The way you will insulate it is contingent upon the heating method.

Heat is expensive. So is insulation. One could easily spend $3,000 insulating a house, not counting insulating glass. If your choice of heating fuel is expensive, it is well worth spending as much as you can to fully insulate the house. If you can spend an extra $2,000 to give your house a super insulating job, it is worth it if you will save $2,000 in heating bills during the next ten years. From an investor's point of view, if it takes ten years to get an even return on your $2,000 investment, that investment is paying off at the rate of 10 percent per year, which is a respectable investment. Furthermore, if you plan on living in the house for more than 10 years, from that point on your investment is paid off and you're on "Easy Street." Besides, if you ever sell the house, the insulation job will be a selling point, and it will raise the home's value. From the viewpoint of insulation installers it is one investment the homeowner can make that will result in an immediate financial return. This is fine, but not everyone has an extra few thousand dollars needed to make this kind of investment. Does this mean you shouldn't build? No.

The added expense of insulation comes at the worst possible time—when there are hundreds of other things for which the money is needed. For this reason, I've come up with a design that provides adequate insulation for a low price. At a later time, after one recovers from all the expenses it took to build the home, the place can be better insulated. And, it won't cost much more than it would have if done when the house was under construction. This design will be covered later in the chapter.

Getting away from the crass economic part of the world for a moment, the essential nature of insulation is to provide increased comfort. No one likes feeling too warm or too cool. Insulation helps modify temperature. When the materials of our homes are cold, these materials tug at our body heat. Our bodies, then, begin to warm the house when this is something that our furnace should be doing.

Insulation is more than an economic investment—it contributes to our comfort. Insulation also helps conserve energy. "Heat loss" and "energy loss" are congruous. Every little bit of heat that our home keeps inside means a little less energy the world must provide.

Heat loss can occur in many different ways. Heat can migrate through the walls, windows, floors, and roof. These

Fig. 13-1. This fellow is getting ready for winter.

materials conduct the heat. When heat is lost this way, it is called conductive heat loss. Heat waves can also zoom right through the walls. This heat is called reflective heat. And, when there are voids through which the heat passes, this constitutes infiltrative heat loss. Voids occur around doors and windows, through electrical outlets and fixtures, and between joints.

In conventional housing, the solid part of the wall—the studs—is the weaker part of the insulation system. In other words, the studs, inch for inch, conduct more heat than the hollow areas between the studs. The reason is the studs are in direct contact with both the interior and exterior surfaces. With some designs of the post-frame (those which use girts applied to the inner and outer face of the posts), there is a minimum amount of material which is in direct contact with the inside and outside. Because of this, these wall systems have little conductive heat loss. Post-frames are also easily built with thick wall areas. When this entire wall area is filled with insulation, an extremely well-insulated wall is created.

With some of the other wall systems, especially wall system #4, a lot of wall area is in contact with both the inside and outside wall surfaces. For these systems, the entire outer wall surface can be sheathed with sheets of foam. When foam sheets are used, the heat transmitted through the solid wall structure is brought down to a minimum.

Reflective heat loss is curtailed through the application of reflective surfaces. The best way to get a reflective surface is to purchase batts of insulation with a foil facing. The foil reflects back heat. Drywall can also be obtained with a foil facing on the back. Although the foil surface is more continuous than that of the insulation, it does not work as well because ideally there should be an air space between the foil and the wall surface. Insulation can be installed this way, whereas the foil is directly against the drywall's surface. Sheets of foil can also be used and, when properly installed, can work better than either of the above two systems. More on this comes later.

Infiltrative heat loss can be curtailed by building with tight joints. The doors and windows should be installed with precision. Joints can be caulked and insulation can be shoved in small spaces under windows and behind electrical outlets. Large sheets of plastic can be applied over the wall surface prior to installing the drywall or paneling. Besides working as a moisture barrier, the plastic seals all areas of the walls. Plastic can also be applied before the ceiling finishing materials.

MOISTURE BARRIERS

A moisture barrier is important for three major reasons: it keeps moisture from rotting out the house; it helps the insulation to work properly; and it helps keep the people inside warm. Lacking a moisture barrier, water migrates through the walls of a house. In the winter, when the water meets with the cold exterior wall surfaces, it condenses. The condensation occurs because warm air holds more humidity than cold air. The condensed water either drips down into the fill insulation or freezes first, then later drips into the insulation. Besides rotting out the wall structure, the moisture-laden insulation cannot work properly. It must be dry to work effectively since water conducts heat. Without a moisture barrier, the walls rot while losing more heat. Of course, with rotted walls, heat loss is the least of your worries.

The moisture barrier helps keep people warm not only by cutting down on infiltrative heat loss. By prohibiting the migration of moisture, the inside air retains more of its natural moisture. We are all aware of the fact that it seems hotter outside when the day is also humid. This same effect occurs inside a home. If the air is more humid, we feel warmer. The thermostat can be turned down and the building's occupants will feel just as warm as when the air was hotter and dryer. A moisture barrier helps keep us warm.

Since the moisture barrier's primary function is to keep interior moisture from going through the wall, it must be applied just behind the interior wall surface. And there should be only one moisture barrier. If there is more than one, they must be back-to-back and functioning as one moisture barrier. This can occur when plastic and foil-faced insulation are both placed directly behind the interior wall surface. If two moisture barriers are used and not applied back-to-back, the inside of the wall *must* be ventilated. If it is not ventilated, moisture will be trapped inside the wall. Two moisture barriers are sometimes used when foil-faced sheathing is used on the outer wall surface. An interior moisture barrier is still needed to keep the water from migrating from the building's inside through the wall to this second moisture barrier. Ventilation is usually achieved through the use of corrugated plastic strips which are nailed to the outer wall

Table 13-1. The Chart Gives Insulating Values of Rigid Materials.

MATERIAL	"R"/INCH	¢/S.F/INCH	¢/"R"/S.F.	PROVIDES STRUCTURAL PURPOSE	PROVIDES NAILBASE
plywood	1.26	54	43	X	X
fiberboard	2.38	16	7	X	
softwood	3.23	56	17	X	X
styrofoam	5.40	25	5	X	
uretane panels	6.67	45	7	X	X

Table 13-2. Use This Table to Find Insulating Values of Fill Materials.

MATERIAL	"R"/INCH	¢/S.F./INCH	¢/"R"/S.F.	CAN BE USED IN WALLS	CAN BE USED IN CEILINGS
cellulose	3.7	4	1	X	X
fiberglass batts	3.17	4	1	X	X
fiberglass fill	2.2	5	2	X	X
Urea-formaldehyde (foam)	4.8	14*	3*	X	

*INSTALLED PRICE

surface before the sheathing. These strips are about 1-⅜ inches wide and are usually nailed 2 feet on center. Wide strips must cover all plates. The sheathing is then nailed over the strips. This constitutes extra work and expense for a nominal cause. And, if the vents ever become clogged, the wall would rot out. For these reasons, dual moisture barriers are not recommended unless they are applied back-to-back so the interior of the wall does not have to be ventilated.

Vapor barriers can be overdone. Some vapor must be allowed to escape or else a dehumidifier must be used. Vapor can condense on the ceiling of the home if excessive vapor is in the air. If the insulation has a vapor barrier facing, a continuous plastic membrane usually would not be needed. If it is used, the second vapor barrier is often slashed.

Home ceilings are often left without a vapor barrier. It is figured that the attic will be ventilated so the insulation will not become damp. But you can't forget that moisture barriers provide other functions. With a vapor barrier, an attic needs less ventilation—1 square foot of ventilation for every 300 square feet of attic area. Without a vapor barrier, this size vent covers only half the area.

"R" VALUE

Before we discuss different types of insulations, we need a basic for comparison. Fortunately, there are many different ways to compare these materials. The easiest to understand method used to compare materials' insulating properties is by how well each resists heat transfer. This resistance is abbreviated "R." Materials are mentioned as having an "R" value of, say, 11. When used to compare

212

different materials, the "R" value is easily understood. The greater the "R," the better the material insulates. Since the purchase of a material must take into consideration the "R" value, the following chart has broken materials down into their "R" value per inch of thickness. And, since the buyer is, essentially, buying "Rs," I have calculated how many cents per "R" each material costs. In this manner, each material can be judged according to its insulating value per inch thickness, its cost per inch, and its cost per "R." See Tables 13-1 through 13-3.

As can easily be seen, the non-structural insulators generally cost less per "R" than insulators which can be used for structural purposes. This is understandable since the structural insulators serve other purposes besides merely insulating. For example, fiberboard is extensively used as sheathing. It insulates and provides the needed surface for the exterior finishing materials.

THE FILL INSULATIONS

Conversely, the fill insulators are generally cheaper, but they need a structure to fill. Now then, if one builds a stud wall, the wall has a built-in cavity which can be filled with insulation. Dead air space, alone, has little insulating value. It has some, or else we wouldn't make double pane windows. But, compared to an area filled with insulation, a vacant air space has relatively no insulating value. Since most walls will have a cavity, the fill insulators are almost always used.

Fiberglass

There are many popular types of fill insulation; spun fiberglass is the most widely used. Fiberglass insulation

Table 13-3. Here Are Installed Prices of Fill Insulation Materials.

MATERIAL	¢/S.F./INCH	¢/"R"/S.F.
cellulose	14	4
fiberglass batts	7	2
fiberglass fill	14	6
urea-formaldehyde (foam)	14	3

comes packaged in four different ways: as loose fill, in unfaced batts, in batts faced with kraft paper, and in batts faced with foil. Loose fill is blown into place with expensive machinery. It is generally used in attics, especially for the re-insulation of older homes. Unless the area to be insulated is inaccessible, there is little sense to using blown fiberglass. The reasons are an installer must be hired to do the job because of the machinery needed, the material itself is more expensive, and it cannot be made as compact as batt fiberglass so it doesn't have the same insulating value per inch as the fiberglass batts.

The best type of fiberglass insulation combines a fiberglass batt with a foil facing. The foil facing serves three functions: it functions as a moisture barrier; the reflective surface reduces reflective heat loss; and the facing provides tabs with which to secure the insulation batts to the wall. For many applications, this foil-faced fiberglass insulation is the best. It can be used in both the ceiling and the walls and is easily installed. This insulation serves three functions at once: insulating, reflecting, and providing the moisture barrier. And it doesn't cost much.

The 3½-inch batts, which fit into the typical thickness of a wall, provide an "R" value of eleven, which is acceptable. The foil facing can add as much as two more "Rs" to its insulation value, giving it the potential of 13 "Rs." A 6-inch batt has an "R" value of 19; this is often used in the thicker walls. An "R" of 19 is even acceptable for the roofs in some areas.

The foil facing eliminates the need for other moisture barriers. During installation, care should be taken not to tear this vapor barrier. If it becomes torn, the rip should be taped closed. The foil facing, which should always point toward the interior of the house, works best if there is a ¾ inch air space between it and the interior wall surface. This is no problem if the insulation is correctly installed. The fastening tabs should always be secured to the sides of the girts or studs—not to their faces. In this manner, the foil facing is inset from the wall surface. A staple gun is used to fasten the tabs to the sides of the girts or studs. These guns have a tendency to puncture through the facing, so a little trick to prevent this is to tape the end of the gun with masking tape.

Fiberglass batts also come with a kraft paper facing which serves as a moisture barrier but does not reflect. Unless foil-faced insulation is not available, there's no advantage to using the kraft-faced insulation. Except if you are afraid of having microwaves or color television waves bounced back into the room, why not use foil-faced insulation? These waves shouldn't be zipping around anyway.

Unfaced batts of fiberglass can also be obtained, and they are the easiest to install. Instead of having to staple them in place, these batts are friction-fit or merely shoved into place. Insulating walls or attics with these batts is quick work. They should be used when another vapor barrier is planned into the wall system or when no vapor barrier is desired.

Whenever installing batt insulation, care should to taken to fully insulate the wall. This means making accurate cuts so that the entire void is filled. A sharp utility knife is used to cut insulation. Instead of cramming insulation around electrical wires, it helps to partially sever the insulation to make a chase for the wire. And, instead of bending the insulation around electrical boxes, part of the insulation should be cut out and worked behind the box. It is also important not to insulate water pipes from the house's heat by applying the insulation over the pipes. Again, the insulation should be severed so that the pipe is encased in it. Or, if this is too much work, at least shove the insulation behind the pipe so that the house keeps the pipe warm.

The unfaced batts combine especially well with rolls of foil. Builder's foil can be obtained in 4-foot wide rolls which can be applied over the unfaced batts of insulation to provide an unbroken moisture barrier and a continuous reflective surface. As with the foil-faced insulation, the builder's foil should be applied so that a slight air gap exists between it and the wall finishing material. The foil should not be applied taut; it should be allowed to be concave between the walls' supporting members.

Of all the fill insulations, fiberglass batts are the most versatile and the most reliable. They can be installed in both the walls and the roof, whether the roof has a closed joist system or an attic. It takes no special material, equipment, or intelligence to do a proper installation. And, since both the roof and walls can be insulated with the same material, the insulation of the house is simplified. It must be remembered, though, that *all* of the wall area must be insulated; leave no voids around electrical wires, boxes, bridging, or pipework.

Fiberglass batts come as thick as 12 inches. If 9½ inches were needed, a 3½ and a 6-inch thick batt could be used together. Remember, though, that only one moisture barrier should be used. The top batt, then, should be unfaced. It is also imperative to leave an air space for ventilation above the insulation in a closed joist system. The air space need not be large; ½ inch above all the insulation is plenty. With a 2 × 8 roof, then, two 3½-inch batts would be just right (since 2 × 8s are actually only 7¼ to 7½ inches). By buying thick batts or through the combination of different thicknesses of batts, a correct thickness can usually be found. If the correct thickness cannot be found, though, part of the top batt can be peeled away to provide an air channel. Although this is extra work, it is better than skimping on insulation to get an air space. Remember that insulation works best when it is dry. An air space helps insulation work better, so be sure to provide one.

Although the roof must be ventilated, the walls do not need ventilation. No air space is required. If an air space were to exist on both sides of the insulation, the insulation would not function correctly. Convective air currents (caused by the natural rise of hot air) would tend to encircle the insulation. In this situation, the insulation provides no block—the air moves around it.

As an example of this, imagine a wall with girts on both sides of the posts. If the area between the posts was insulated but not the areas next to the walls, air would flow around the girts in convective currents. Although the wall had a lot of insulation material, it would be poorly insulated.

To circumvent this, the entire wall cavity must be insulated. The areas beneath and behind the girts must be filled. To do this with wall design #2, with girts attached to both faces of the posts, the insulation is secured to the edges of the girts and attached (if a vapor barrier is used) from the inside of the house. Strips of insulation must be cut to fit into the areas behind the girts. The entire cavity is thus filled. With this type of wall system it is much easier to blow in the insulation. Although not as high of an "R" value can be obtained, this wall is thick enough that blown-in insulation will work fine. The major advantage of blown-in insulation is it fills in all cavities in a wall which is irregular or has many obstructions.

Foam

There are two types of spray foams that have been used extensively. One is a urethane foam and the other is a urea-formaldehyde resin. Either of these foams can be used in the side walls of a home; neither can be used in the ceiling or attic. The major advantage of the spray foams is that they have excellent, unparalleled "R" values. Especially when a limited amount of space is available, the spray foams can give adequate insulation. The other advantage is that they can be used for existing construction. The foams offer easy installation when a home's exterior is brick. A small (⅝-inch) hole is drilled into the mortar joint between the brick; a nozzle is then introduced through the hole to fill the wall cavity. Foam insulation is generally not used for roof insulation because it can collect moisture.

UREA-FORMALDEHYDE

Urea-formaldehyde insulation is composed from urea and formaldehyde. Urea is a compound in urine; formaldehyde is a water-soluble gas, mainly used as an aqueous solution for preservation purposes. Biological specimen companies typically pack frogs, baby pigs, and other specimens in formaldehyde solutions to ship them for dissecting purposes. High school biology class may have introduced you to formaldehyde—it possesses a very vile odor. The components of this foam border on being esoteric.

Great caution must be taken with the use of foams. Being introduced into the wall in a liquid state, they can bow the drywall and the exterior siding because of the pressure under which they are pumped. One friend of mine was sitting in his family room while the garage wall behind him was being foamed. The family room's paneling was nailed directly onto the wall's studs, and, under the pressure popped loose—covering my friend with foam.

The liquid-state foams take three days to cure. During this time, the wall structure is subjected to this moisture. Since wood expands with moisture, the studs or girts in the wall will enlarge when in contact with the wet foam. When the foam dries, the studs shrink, which can create gaps between the foam and the studs or girts. Although this decreases the insulation value, it helps the wall ventilate.

Foam can also be troweled onto the wall surface before the interior drywall is applied. In this situation the foam dries out too fast, making it brittle. The wall can quickly be covered with plastic, which helps alleviate this effect. Still, there may be some problems. The drywall should be applied the very next day.

There are many different types of foam, all of which are differently composed. Some are diluted by adding water. Since each locale has different chemicals in the water, little consistency can be obtained. If foam is being considered, pay attention to who makes it and to who installs it. Don't accept a guarantee from the installer—the longevity of foam insulation installers is short. They go out of business as frequently as old cars break down. Get a guarantee from the manufacturers. Some foams may be fine to use; the obvious advantage is that an inch of foam has an "R" value of almost 5. In a limited space, this is important. Insulation must function well throughout the years to be a good deal.

The best systems use a two-part composition, consisting of combining the urea-formaldehyde resin to the foaming agent. No other materials are added. These materials must be combined to the correct proportions for a good product to result. Generally the resin comprises from 1.1 to 1.5 parts of the system to one part of the catalyst. Since the resin is the more expensive component, it is sometimes diluted with too much catalyst.

A proper amount of air, too, must be calibrated into this system. The air gives the foam its bulk. If the foam does not have the correct amount of air, a proper product will not result. Before a wall cavity is injected with foam, a field test should be made to insure that the foam is correctly made. The foam can be shaped into a beehive form to make sure it doesn't slump. More importantly, it should be weighed. The Borden company, which makes a product called Insulspray, has a test where the foam is injected into a 1-gallon plastic bag. A chart is then examined to make sure that the foam has the correct weight for the proportions of resin and catalyst.

Poorly mixed foam insulation can smell, bleed through the wall during the drying process, fall apart, and not have adequate insulating value. When mixed and installed correctly, it can work very well. The Borden company seems to have some of the highest quality control over its product. It licenses the installers and does periodic check-ups to insure that the foam is being correctly installed. Since the preparation and installation of the foam are the crucial factors determining the success of the product, this type of watchdog approach is good to see.

After installation, the foam must be allowed to ventilate for proper curing. In most instances, this means leaving open the hole though which the foam was injected. By allowing the foam to ventilate, the chances of bleeding through the drywall and stinking are decreased.

A moisture barrier should be used in conjunction with foam insulation. A moisture barrier is not absolutely necessary—or else foam could not be used for existing construction. For new construction a moisture barrier should be used. Either plastic or sheets of foil are recommended.

The urea-formaldehyde foams are non-flammable. They contribute no fuel to a fire. For this reason, their use is recommended instead of the urethane foam.

Urethane

Urethane is the best insulating material around: it gives as much as 8 "Rs" per inch, far surpassing any other insulating material. It has been used extensively in the past and, for some purposes, it works fine. For underground water storage tanks, urethane can be sprayed on and then the tank can be backfilled with dirt applied directly over the urethane. Urethane can expand with moisture, but it generally gives many years of good service.

The major problem with urethane is that it is extremely flammable and emits toxic fumes when it burns. A fire hazard is created. Most of the deaths that occur in fires, though, are not from flame or heat exposure; smoke inhalation constitutes the major cause of death and injury in fires. So deadly urethane fumes in the air would slighten one's chances of survival in a fire. For this reason, urethane should be avoided.

Like urea-formaldehyde foam, urethane is used in the walls of a dwelling. It does have excellent insulating value. It should not be used in ceilings because of its inability to pass moisture. If your choice for wall insulation is urethane, make sure to cover it with low fire hazard materials. The inside of the wall can have ⅝-inch drywall which produces a one-hour fire barrier. The exterior sheathing can be made from a fire-resistant fiberboard or the siding can be fire-retardant treated lumber.

Cellulose

The largest advantage of cellulose is that it is fireproof. It has a class A fire rating, making it the best insulation against fire. In some cases, cellulose has been credited not only for thwarting the spread of fire, but also for smothering it.

Cellulose is made from recycled newsprint. The paper is treated with fire-retardant chemicals to make it fireproof. It has excellent insulating properties, about 3.7 "Rs" per inch. It can be blown into existing walls as easily as foam and does not need a large cavity for entrance.

Cellulose can also be installed in attics by merely dumping the contents of the bags between the joists. It is one of the easiest to install and is better for one's health than installing fiberglass. Still, though, caution should be taken during installation because of the chemicals with which cellulose is treated. The hands should be washed after working with this material.

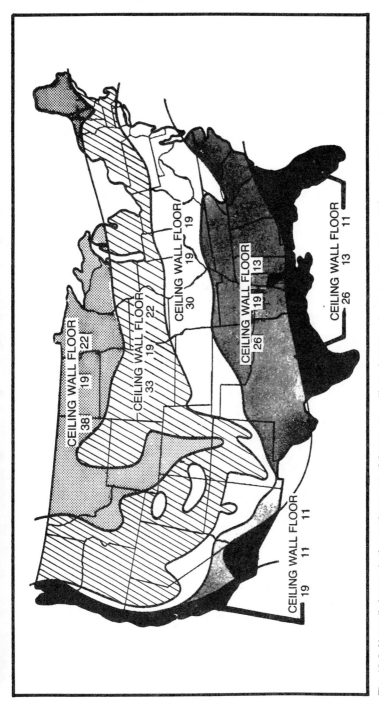

CEILING WALL FLOOR
38 | 19 | 22

CEILING WALL FLOOR
33 | 19 | 22

CEILING WALL FLOOR
30 | 19 | 19

CEILING WALL FLOOR
26 | 19 | 13

CEILING WALL FLOOR
26 | 13 | 11

CEILING WALL FLOOR
19 | 11 | 11

Fig. 13-2. Naturally homes in the northern part of the country will require more insulation. Install the right amount for your home.

221

There is some controversy about the usage of cellulose. Although the manufacturers recommend it for both ceiling and wall cavities, many people feel it should not be used in the walls. Since it is a loose fill, cellulose may have a tendency to settle. There are possibilities of the material collecting moisture. Some people say cellulose should not be used in the ceiling, since much of the moisture that exists in our homes exits though the ceiling.

Cellulose has many positive characteristics, namely that it is lightweight, can be easily installed, is competitively priced, has the greatest "R" value of the non-foam fill insulations, is fireproof, and is made from recycled material. The manufacturers also boast that it takes less energy to create cellulose insulation than other insulations. It should be used with caution, though, because of some of its dubious qualities; it may settle and it may collect moisture. If it does settle in the walls, the high part of the wall—where you most need insulation because of the rising heat—is left unprotected and uninsulated.

There are many manufacturers of cellulose. Although their products all have the same base, the treatments of the wood fiber may be very different from each other. If cellulose insulation is desired, choose a company who will back their product. If the settling problem is one's only worry, a guarantee can help remedy the problem: the company will have to come out and fill the wall back up. If it is installed by the building's owner, though, settling will be blamed on the installer, negating any benefit of the guarantee. Moisture problems, though, are not easily remedied. Be cautious with the use of cellulose and use moisture barriers whenever it is used (Fig. 13-2).

THE RIGID INSULATIONS

Rigid boards of styrofoam seem to be about the best form of rigid insulation. Styrofoam is a polystyrene foam, as are many other brands of rigid foam. The difference between styrofoam and the other types of polystyrene is that styrofoam is pressed out by having it forced through a die. This manufacturing technique increases its compressive strength because it is formed through compression. Other than increasing its compressive strength, it also makes it more resistant to moisture. Styrofoam SM is often used for the insulation of sidewall construction. Styrofoam RM is used on roofs. The RM is a little more resistant to moisture, which is important for roofing materials. Both have exactly the same thermo properties.

Styrofoam

Some of the Styrofoam panels come with a tongue-and-groove design. This offers continuous protection for the sidewalls or roof of a structure. Often times the Styrofoam SM tongue-and-groove is applied directly over the studs of a home. The finished siding is then applied directly over the styrofoam. The advantage of using a rigid board insulation on the outside of the studs or girts of a post-frame is that the entire wall is completely insulated. Infra-red tests, which show the amount of heat transmission, prove that the supporting members of a structure will conduct more heat, inch for inch, than the insulated voids within a wall. By sheathing the outside of the wall with styrofoam, this heat loss is curtailed.

Styrofoam RM helps to insulate plank and beam roof structures. The foam panels are laid directly over the planking and are usually covered with a sheet of plywood. This type of insulation system is usually prohibitively expensive. As will be shown later, it is less expensive to create a void to insulate with batt insulation.

Molded Polystyrene

There are many manufacturers of molded polystyrene. Molded polystyrenes generally have about the same "R" value as Styrofoam, but have much greater water absorption properties and about a third of styrofoam's compressive strength. The polystyrenes generally have a greater capacity to pass water, which is not good for roofs but is really better for walls.

Since only one vapor barrier is desired for a wall, styrofoam can be undesirable since it composes somewhat of a vapor barrier (.6 perm). It need not be avoided, under most circumstances, since it can pass enough water so moisture will not be dangerously trapped. The molded polystyrenes, since they do have greater permeability (2.0 perm), can be deemed more desirable for exterior sheathing under many conditions. If the builder is building in a damp area, for example, the molded polystyrenes may work much better.

Their lack of compressive strength means only one thing. If polystyrenes are used for a roof, care should be taken to cover them with plywood before they get trampled. Besides, all of the polystyrenes, including styrofoam, deteriorate with sunlight. Sunlight causes a dusting of the surface which inhibits a good bonding with other materials. If the surface does become dusty, it must be brushed off before applying mastic.

The molded polystyrenes are not as good on roofs as styrofoam because of greater water absorption properties and their lack of compressive strength. Many of the molded products may be superior to styrofoam for wall sheathing since they possess a greater ability to pass water. Greater care must be taken during installation since the polysterenes, lesser compressive strength means that more denting during installation is possible. If the panels are to be well-secured, it is advised to adhere them to the wall structure with special foam adhesive. Ordinary construction adhesive will melt any of the polystyrenes.

Urethane

Urethane, also called polyurethane, has the best "R" value per inch of any of the insulations, whether rigid or fill. Although an inch of urethane can give as much as 8 "Rs," this insulation value can deteriorate with age. Urethane has its best uses when you need a rigid insulation board which must resist solvents. The polystyrenes will melt, whereas urethane can endure exposure to many solvents. As was mentioned earlier, urethane also has wide usage underground because it has good water resistance. Being underground, it is protected against fire. Urethane is so flammable that when it burns, it emits toxic fumes.

Regardless of this fact, many of the insulation/sheathing panels that are coming out on the market use urethane for their structure. Most are covered on both sides with either a laminated cardboard or a foil coating. Their use is not recommended unless they can be immediately covered with a flame resistant material, such as drywall. Great care must be taken if this material is used. The plumbers, for example, must be forewarned that the material is extremely flammable so they are careful while using torches. Urethane, too, must be protected from ultraviolet light. Since most of the urethane panels are covered with foil or other vapor-blocking material, these panels must be applied over vent strips. Without these vent strips, moisture would be trapped inside the wall.

INSULATION CONCERNS

If the builder is trying to achieve a well-insulated house, the answer is not in rigid insulation. It simply is too expensive for what it does. If the builder wants the roof to have an "R" value of thirty or more, some kind of fill insulation must be used. The best insulated ceiling you would need would be built out of 2×12s placed 24-inches on center and filled with the cellulose insulation. A house with a floor area of 32×40 or 1,280 sf would probably have a roof area of 1368 sf. To figure out the price for insulating this area, we multiply $1,368 \times .04$ cents/sf $\times 11.5$ inches. This comes to $630. The "R" rating would be an effective 42. The plywood, felt paper, and drywall would bring it up to an excellent 43.

Even more insulation could be stuffed in a trussed attic if access to that attic was not desired. A type of truss has been developed that has a raised bottom chord to enable better insulating conditions. Trussed houses built without this feature generally loose much heat right by the eave. An R rating over 40, though, is not really needed. It must be remembered that a house likes to breathe a little bit, too.

There are many insulating products on the market. New products are arriving constantly. Price influxes from time to time determine to a large extent which insulation will be most practical to use. During the early winter months, for example, there lately have been some insulation shortages (what next?) which drives the price up drastically. And, when the work demand is high, people charge more because they don't need the work.

Great care should be taken to insure oneself that the product is a good one. Some foams may well be satisfactory for use in a ceiling cavity. Some celluloses may be good for walls. Some of these products haven't been on the market long enough to really know how they will work out. They still are used because no one is sure if anything else is better. If there was a wonder product, it would be so expensive no one could afford it anyway. One type of panel costs $25 for 16 square feet. Even with a flat roof, $1.60 would be added onto the cost of the building per square foot.

The people that really must think intelligently about insulation are those who live in cold climates and use an expensive form of heat, such as oil or electricity. If heat like this is being used, a well-insulated house could save you $400 a year—which would pay for your insulation job in just a few years. For homes like these, the entire house must be designed around heat loss charts, sad as that may seem. Other designs are not practical. Window area, especially, should be avoided, particularly in high areas of the house. High ceilings should be avoided altogether in these cases. It can get to the point where you feel insulated from the world.

All of this is so unfortunate. Windows let in sunlight and fill the house with warmth. Even on cold days, if the sun shines and is allowed to enter the house, the house will stay warm. Combined with a wood stove, proper window place-ment will warm the house naturally. I would rather haul wood and tend a fire than live in a house with no windows, low ceilings and a high heating bill. Clerestory windows and skylights enable you to keep tabs on the clouds. These windows and lights lose heat at night, but let it in during the day.

Insulation concern, really, should not totally dominate architecture. If heat in certain areas is extremely expensive, a wood stove will save money. One wood stove can heat a small house with little effort. A stove capable of being closed tight and of accepting huge logs (about 3 feet) will provide warmth and slash the heat bill.

We can fight with nature and totally insulate ourselves from her, or we can design to take advantage of her positive properties by opening ourselves up to her. Both approaches are logical. A house that is well-insulated will not heat up too much in the summer. But when the sun goes down, it will take a long time for the house to cool down. A poorly insulated house will heat up somewhat more during the day, but will quickly lose heat at dusk. High windows facing southwest will lose heat at night. If a winter day is sunny, these windows will heat the house during the day. High ceilings steal heat in the winter, but in the summer they let hot air rise. All of these designs have definite functions.

A smart builder will choose the areas to insulate with care. All the outside walls of a home do not need to be insulated to the same extent. For example, if a wood stove is against an outside wall, the wall behind the wood stove should be insulated as well as possible. The walls facing the direction of prevailing bad weather and the northern wall should also be insulated better. Other walls may not need as much insulation.

Human beings and animals need warmth. One design function that directly affects a building's occupants is its temperature. A good design takes into consideration the construction methods, forms of insulation, the natural elements we want to block, and the ones that we want to enter our homes.

Glass

A single pane of glass has virtually no "R" value. Its "R" is rated at only .1! By installing double-pane windows, this resistance rating can be brought up to 1.44. In other words, the second layer of glass increases a window's resistance by over 14 times. Triple-pane windows are also sometimes used but, because of their expense, they have not gained wide usage. Triple pane windows are fine for clerestory windows in high parts of the house. It is in these parts that windows could constitute large amounts of heat loss. Triple pane windows have an "R" value of about 2.1.

One of the added advantages of having thermopane windows is that they will not condense under most conditions. Single panes of glass are likely to frost on the inside during cold nights and then drip during the early part of the day. The water can stain wood window frames and it often deteriorates drywall if the drywall rests on the window sill.

If single pane windows are used, drywall should not be used next to the glass. And, to prevent water stains on the surrounding woodwork, it should not be left natural. If sealed with a good wood sealer, wood will not become stained. Plastic laminates adhered to particle board can make attractive, worry-free window sills. For single pane windows, plastic laminates or solid marble or slate seem to work the best.

Because of the condensation problem, single pane skylights are not recommended. They constitute a lot of heat loss by being in the ceiling. Single pane skylights will condense and then drip. This dripping would be most uncomfortable if the skylight were over your bed.

Some people have made their own double pane skylights, and I've seen some excellent systems. For best results, the skylight should be made on a very dry day when there is little humidity. Any humidity in the air will be trapped between the panes once the skylight is sealed. When the humidity in the air becomes lower than that which is trapped inside, the skylight would condense. Skylights made under the right conditions seem to work fine.

Thermopane windows, besides being made under highly controlled conditions, have a desiccant incorporated within their seal. The desiccant, or drying agent, absorbs moisture. Rice in a salt shaker is a desiccant. I don't recommend making thermopane windows, simply because so many made under rigid factory conditions fail. Once the seal is broken, the windows fog.

If only single panes can be afforded, they can be insulated with draperies. Foam-backed fabric can add as much as two "Rs" to a window. Any drapery will help insulate a window, but the foam-backed drapes work the best. If they can be made to fit tightly, drapes will function better than triple-pane windows. Conventional-looking drapes can function well if the pleats on the bottom almost rest upon a wide window sill. With this arrangement, little air will creep beneath the pleats. Another drapery system that works well involves running either the top and bottom of the drapes or both sides on a track. The track insures a tight fit. Through any of these systems, windows will not create heavy amounts of heat loss.

The Two Step Roof

In circumstances when a builder needs to erect a shelter but cannot afford to insulate it fully during the time of construction, the following system offers adequate temporary insulation. At a later time the system can be improved. By using the one-process roof, made with 2-inch thick tongue-and-groove applied over beams, a builder has a finished ceiling, a roof structure and marginal insulation. As can be seen by the insulation chart, 1½ inches of softwood have an "R" factor of over 4-½. This alone is plenty of insulation for the warmer climates. There are many homes and buildings with only 2 × 6 decking on the roofs. It is a common roof structure and has been used all over the United States—including the cold climates. Obviously, a better insulated roof is preferable; but this system will get anyone through at least a few winters.

When this system is used with plans to revamp it someday, the least expensive roofing material should be used—roll roofing. The roll roofing is the only expendable item. When the roof is revamped, the roll roofing can remain in place and the new roof can be applied directly over it.

There are two different approaches to revamping this kind of roof. A rigid insulation can be applied, followed by sheathing—if the rigid insulation does not already have a nail-base sheathing attached. The roofing material is then installed over the sheathing. Or, the rooftop can be framed with lumber, creating a place to fill with insulation. Once insulated, either plywood sheathing and shingles can be installed or metal roofing can be applied directly over the joists. Although metal roofing is used extensively on commercial and farm buildings, it is fine for home rooftops, too. It is inexpensive, easy to install and durable.

At first it may seem silly to frame the top of a roof merely to create a void to fill with insulation. But it is more economical to avoid rigid insulation. I've done a cost comparison on a roof that is 36 × 32 feet, which is 1152 square feet. To lay up 2 × 10 joists, insulate between the joists with fiberglass and then sheath and shingle this structure. We're talking about $1,700 for an "R" value of about 34.

For the same roof, insulated with 4 inches of rigid foam for an "R" value of 32, sheathed and shingled it would cost $2,900. As can be seen, if a well-insulated roof is desired, it is more economical to frame up the roof and use batt (or fill) insulation.

To frame up a 2-inch tongue-and-groove roof, 2 × 12s are used around the perimeter, being nailed onto the butt ends of the tongue-and-groove. Two-by-tens are then laid on top of the roof. The 2 × 12s are nailed on to the tongue-and-groove at the same height as the top of the 2 × 10s so that a level roof results. Since these members serve no structural purpose other than holding up plywood sheathing, they can be placed as far as 4 feet apart for ¾-inch plywood tongue-and-groove sheathing—the same as can be applied to floor joists spaced 24 inches apart. If ⅝-inch sheathing is used, the members must be 32 inches on center.

It is best to try to keep this secondary roof structure as light as possible, since this is a dead load that will constantly be exerting weight on the beams. The dead weight of this system (about 10 psf) should be tabulated into the load when figuring out the sizes of the beams to use when building the primary roof structure.

Because of the $1,700 cost for building this roof system, it is often advantageous to hold off a while until after the rest of the house is built to fully insulate the roof. It is something that should be done well and, if a better job can be done after one recoups from spending a lot of money on the original structure, then why not wait? Although an inch of foam could be put on the roof during construction to get nominal insulation value, it is better economics to wait a while, expend some roll roofing, and then insulate the roof when your financial situation is in balance.

If money is not an object, this same type of secondary roof structure can be done during original construction. It is the best way to insulate a plank and beam roof because it's the easiest to do, the least expensive, and the most satisfactory. There aren't many things in the world that fall into all three of these categories!

There is one other advantage to waiting until a later date to insulate the roof. The United States Government has all sorts of tax deductions and grants eligible to people who improve the insulation of their *existing* homes. If the home is already built, then you become eligible. At this point in time, the maximum deduction is $2,200. The $1,700 roof job would be totally tax deductible!

If insulation cannot be afforded for the wall area, provisions can be made for easy future insulation. For masonry walls, tubes can be inserted in the brick's mortar joints. Many types of wall construction are just as easily insulated a year after construction as to insulate them during construction. Attics can be insulated at any time.

CONCLUSION

Insulation keeps the home's residents warm. It also helps keep a house from deteriorating by limiting the amount of freezing and re-freezing of the water on a house's roof, eaves, and in its gutters. By incorporating vapor barriers, insulation helps keep condensation out of walls.

Besides keeping people warm and helping keep the building together, insulation conserves energy. We cannot drain the earth of its gas and oil, for these are two vital fluids. Just as importantly, we cannot gather up all the dead wood laying around, for this is the forests' fertilizer and the home of many animals. It is important to conserve energy, regardless of its form. If we don't, then we become leeches. Make an intelligent assessment of how much insulation is practical for your particular situation and either build that insulation into your home or plan on doing it. It's something you can do for your own comfort, for the world, and for your pocketbook.

Planning

Every aspect of building centers around good planning (Fig. 14-1). A well-planned approach is needed to locate a satisfactory building site. And you must map out the strategies of building a house. By using a correct schedule of building activity and good timing, the builder will create a good house.

The order of building activity depends upon many factors. How many people will be building the house? Will it be a full-time project or will other things have to be done? Will some of the work be sub-contracted out to professionals? Will the house be built during cold or rainy weather? Is there a large possibility of theft or vandalism? How much money is available? These factors will influence the directions you take.

If the weather is cold, you will probably want to erect a shell as fast as possible. Trenches should be backfilled during rainy weather as soon as possible. No two houses will be built exactly the same. What must be established, though, is a general procedure. Once this procedure is mapped out, you can make deviations from this schedule to fulfill the individual requirements of either the building or the builder.

If a shelter must be established quickly, the heating, driveway, and sidewalk (where needed) could be postponed until a shell is built. And if money is tight, the street tap (because of its expense) could be postponed until needed.

SUBCONTRACTING

The mechanical aspects of the house should be subcontracted out if it can be afforded. Heating, plumbing, and electrical systems are complex to install. Regulations on these systems change so quickly that people retired only two years are often in possession of archaic knowledge. A professional can complete the task quickly. Almost invariably, he will complete it more competently, too. A professional can often complete in a day a job that would take two weeks for an amateur to do. At this rate, one doesn't save much money because so much time is spent doing the job.

When jobs are planned on being subcontracted out, the builder can receive bids from three or more contractors for each job. Typically, the lowest bidder gets the job; although if someone else seems like a better choice, then a higher bidder can be chosen. Jobs other than mechanical ones with subcontracting possibilities are drywall work, possibly the concrete work, and rough framing. Excavation should always be done by someone with the equipment. If you desire, the entire house can be built by other people with the owner acting as the contractor. It just depends on how much money is available and how you feel about doing physical labor.

Primarily there are two methods of building a house. Either you handle all the tasks yourself or you work with professionals. If professionals are involved, the project should center around them. By making the conditions as ideal as possible—especially if the professional is being paid hourly—the best possible job at the least amount of money will be done.

The workman who is granted the contract should be kept informed on the progress of construction so he knows the approximate date he will be needed. When that date nears, he should be given notice of about three days. A confirmation should be made the day before he is to arrive. In this way, no misunderstanding will occur.

234

TODAY

1/ FINISH HANGING WINDOWS
2/HANG EXTERIOR DOORS
3/LOCATE AREAS FOR INTERIOR WALLS
4/CALL HEATMAN: Y. BEACOLD
5/CALL PLUMBER: JOHN LEEKS
6/CALL ELECTRICIAN: HARRY WYRES

Fig. 14-1. Sample schedules like this one are a "must" for home builders.

Give some leeway to the professional. Most jobs—like the heating—can be done while other things are being done. In this manner, there will be no holdup if there is a delay in the heating installation. It is wise to allow the professional to enter the job as soon as possible. If he is late, it is of little consequence. Tight scheduling rarely works out. There is always some delay (lack of parts, bad weather, sickness, breakdowns, labor problems, etc.) that will throw off a tight schedule. By working around the professionals, adequate leeway is given to thwart scheduling delays.

There will be two different procedures that might be taken. If professionals are helping, the job centers around their work. But if you are doing all the work yourself, one job should be completed before another is begun. Instead of having the heating system work started as soon as possible, if you are doing the work, begin after the roof and sides are completed. A shelter has then been established and safe storage of the heating system parts is possible.

The following checklist is centered around having a professional do the heating, plumbing and electrical work. The order of drywall and plastering work is unaffected by who does the work. The following order is figuring on the construction of the walls before the slab is poured, thus eliminating the splashboard. For other designs where the slab is poured before the wall (which enables the builder to build the wall on top of the slab), splashboards will have to be added. In this case, the heating work should definitely begin as soon as the posts are aligned and braced. The slab can be poured as soon as the roof decking and wall framing are secured.

Figure 14-2 outlines the general procedure that the construction of a post-frame will assume when some mechanical tasks are done by professionals. Besides allowing the professionals access to the job quickly, this procedure allows for as much as possible to be done by each professional each time he is on the job site.

Thorough explanations of these steps will be presented later. At this point, though, a brief explanation of the logic behind this order of events is necessary.

WORK IN A LOGICAL ORDER

The site is first flattened out by an excavator. Most excavators have dump trucks capable of carrying enough sand in one or two trips to provide a base of the concrete slab. While the truck is there, this sand base should be installed. The excavator's bulldozer can spread the sand quickly. While he is there, the sewer lines in the street should be tapped. (If the house is being built in the country, the septic system can be installed at this point.) While this is being done, you can locate the corners of the house to designate the areas of excavation. The excavation can then be done immediately. When this is done, all the plumbing drains from inside the house down to the street (or septic tank) can be completed and backfilled. The perimeter excavation must be dug first since the excavation equipment would not be able to work around the rough plumbing drains. The work done so far will take only two days. After these two days, all the plumbing drains are completed, the street is tapped (or the septic tank is installed), the site is leveled and has a sand base, and the footing excavation is done. By doing this work at once, the plumbing can all be backfilled so no trenches will have to be worked around. The immediate backfilling also allows for the settling of these areas; most settling will occur well before the finished grade is obtained.

As soon as the next five steps are done (these will be explained fully later), the heating contractor can do the rough heating work that must be completed before the slab is

PROCEDURE WITH PROFESSIONAL AID

1. FLATTEN SITE
2. LAY 12" SAND BASE
3. TAP STREET OR INSTALL SEPTIC
4. LOCATE HOUSE CORNERS
5. DETERMINE HOLE LOCATIONS
6. DIG HOLES
7. LAY ALL BELOW-GRADE ROUGH PLUMBING
8. BACKFILL ROUGH PLUMBING
9. INSTALL FOOTINGS
10. ALLIGN POSTS & BRACE
11. PARTIALLY BACKFILL POSTS
12. HANG BEAMS
13. COMPLETE BACKFILL
14. BELOW-GRADE ROUGH HEATING
15. ROOF DECKING
16. ROOF INSULATION
17. ROOFING
18. WALL FRAMEWORK & WIND BRACING
19. POUR SLAB (SIDEWALK & DRIVEWAY, TOO, IF NEEDED)
20. SIDING
21. WINDOWS
22. DOORS
23. INTERIOR PARTITIONS
24. ABOVE SLAB ROUGH HEATING
25. ABOVE SLAB ROUGH PLUMBING (GAS LINE, IF NEEDED)
26. ROUGH ELECTRICAL
27. WALL INSULATION
28. DRYWALL & PLASTER
29. PAINT INSIDE & OUTSIDE
30. CABINETS
31. FINISH HEATING
32. FINISH PLUMBING
33. FINISH ELECTRICAL
34. INTERIOR DOORS
35. INTERIOR MOLDING & TRIM
36. FINISH GRADE
37. LAY CARPET

Fig. 14-2. This procedure may be followed when professionals are helping with mechanical jobs.

poured. While this work is being done, work can continue on the framing of the house. The roof decking, insulation, and roofing can all be completed. The walls can be framed and braced. As soon as this is finished, the concrete contractor can pour the slab (and the sidewalk and driveway, if desired). The siding, windows, and doors can then be installed. If there is a delay with the concrete work, the siding, windows and doors can be installed before the slab is poured. The interior partitions can then be framed. If the heating ductwork must be fed through the walls—as is the case with two story structures—this work is done at this time. The heating work precedes the plumbing and electrical because the ducts can be worked around; it would be much more difficult to install the ductwork after the plumbing and electrical work has been done. For this same reason, the plumbing is installed before the electrical lines, since it is easy to run wires around the plumbing and heating. The order is 1) heating, 2) plumbing, and 3) electrical.

After these things are finished, the wall insulation can be installed. The drywall is then applied. Painting is most easily done with an airless sprayer (which can be rented). The entire inside and outside can be sprayed in one day. For people unaccustomed to spray guns, it is helpful to have someone handy with a roller to catch runs and sags. This painting should be completed inside before the cabinets are installed.

After the painting is finished and the cabinets are installed, the finish heating, plumbing, and electrical tasks can be done. The interior doors can be hung while these tasks are being completed. Molding and trim can be applied, as well as any other finish carpentry. The finish grade can then be established and the yard can be seeded or sodded. The carpet is done last.

With good organization and reliable professionals, all this work can be completed in two months. Through the use of professionals, the time it takes to finish the house is cut down drastically. It will take six months at the minimum for one to complete the house by doing all the work aided only with a helper. It may take much longer. The professionals know all the regulations, have all the tools, know the exact procedure,

PROCEDURE WITHOUT PROFESSIONAL AID

1. FLATTEN SITE
2. LAY 12" SAND BASE
3. LOCATE HOUSE CORNERS
4. LOCATE HOLES
5. DIG HOLES
6. INSTALL FOOTINGS
7. ALLIGN POSTS & BRACE
8. PARTIALLY BACKFILL POSTS
9. HANG BEAMS
10. COMPLETE BACKFILL
11. ROOF DECKING
12. ROOF INSULATION
13. ROOFING
14. WALL FRAMEWORK & BRACING
15. SIDING
16. WINDOWS
17. DOORS
18. BELOW GRADE ROUGH PLUMBING
19. BELOW-GRADE ROUGH HEATING
20. LAY SLAB
21. INTERIOR PARTITIONS
22. ABOVE SLAB ROUGH HEATING
23. ABOVE SLAB ROUGH PLUMBING (GAS LINE, IF NEEDED)
24. ROUGH ELECTRICAL
25. WALL INSULATION
26. DRYWALL & PLASTER
27. PAINT INSIDE & OUTSIDE
28. CABINETS
29. FINISH HEATING
30. FINISH PLUMBING
31. FINISH ELECTRICAL
32. INTERIOR DOORS
33. INTERIOR MOLDING & TRIM
34. FINISH GRADE
35. CARPET

Fig. 14-3. Use this list when you are doing all the tasks.

and are accustomed to doing their job. A person unfamiliar with the tasks will make many mistakes and will have to do many jobs two, three or more times before everything is correct. Professionals will save the builder enough time that it is worthwhile to hire them. The time saved can be spent earning the extra money it cost to have the professional do the job for you.

Sometimes the money just isn't available to hire out these tasks. When the owner must complete all tasks himself, Fig. 14-3 shows the altered procedure:

This procedural order seeks first to establish a shelter without doing tasks first that don't necessarily need to be done. If a shelter is needed, it can be established. A secondary benefit is that the enclosure provides a safe place to store tools and materials. Besides, the heating and plumbing work can then be worked on under a shelter. Inclement weather will not cause delays.

The procedure merely flattens out the site first, spreads the sand base, and does the footing excavation. The excavator is then done and can leave. Building can then proceed until the structure is a finished enclosure. The rough plumbing and heating are then done inside the finished structure prior to the slab being poured. The rest of the procedure is the same. The street tap or septic tank can be completed after everything else is done, just before having the area finish graded. Or it can be done when the other plumbing work is completed.

You can modify the order of events to your immediate situation. The important aspect of these models is that certain things *must* be done before others or else there is great confusion. If, for example, the sand base was not spread until the rough structure were up, the sand would have to be dumped outside the perimeter of the house and then wheelbarrowed inside. Extra work and a poorer job are the results. By dumping the sand directly inside the house's perimeter, there is less possibility of mixing dirt in with the sand. By having the bulldozer spread the sand, it is compacted in the same process.

For reasons already mentioned, certain orders should be followed when doing the heating, plumbing, and electrical work. The only time this order is interrupted is when rough plumbing drains are installed. Since the plumbing drains are set deeper than the rough heating ductwork, the plumbing is done first. Once covered with sand, the heating ductwork can be done. The reversal of these jobs would result in having to tunnel beneath the ductwork to lay the plumbing.

It is wise to complete most painting before the cabinets, doors, and carpeting are installed. The danger of mishaps is then reduced. Especially if the trim is to be stained, the walls should be painted first. The trim should be stained before it is applied—resulting in a neater job and one that takes less time.

By following a logical sequence, much time will be saved and the work is better. Because of individuality, no two procedures will be the same. The builder must map out a procedure that meets his needs and simplifies the building process.

In the following chapter, the essentials of building a post-frame will be covered. Because of limitations in space, the mechanical tasks will not be covered. Other sources must be consulted if the builder is going to complete these tasks himself. Excluding these mechanical tasks, though, each aspect of building a post-frame will be covered in detail.

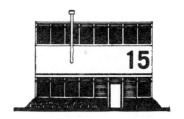

The Procedure

The purpose of this chapter is two-fold (Fig. 15-1). First, it is meant to show how the separate divisions of a building (i.e., the footings, foundation, posts, wall structure, and roof system) are brought together in a logical sequence to form one entity. Secondly, by having the construction of an entire building explained in detail, you are more able to conceptualize how everything fits together.

This building uses variations of the designs which have been covered in previous chapters. It uses a plank and beam gable roof capable of becoming the well-insulated "two-step roof" described in the insulation chapter. The wall structure is that of design #8 of the wall chapter, where a studded framework fills in the space between the posts. The footings are composed of poured concrete and their design has been slightly modified to suit all potential codes to which this structure could be subjected. The foundation system is a variation of foundation system #2. The interior floor plan is design #1 of the interior design chapter.

The above components were selected for many rea-sons. Most importantly, this house is suitable for virtually any climate; therefore it is one of the more universal designs. The floor plan is extremely livable but can be altered by eliminating the last 8 feet of the house—as was described in the interior design chapter. It can be erected quickly and economically. It is not a complex building; yet it has some very attractive features, namely, the all-wood plank and beam cathedral ceiling, an unconfining floor plan, lofts, and large expanses of glass. Importantly, the glass in this house has proper solar orientation. The band of windows faces south to take advantage of the winter sunlight and the west side has plenty of glass to catch the evening sunlight. The other two sides have limited amounts of windows since those on the north and east constitute large amounts of heat loss.

The use of this design for this chapter accentuates the major concepts of this book—ease of erection, economy, solar orientation, functionality and lasting beauty. As for planning, I've opted to take the easier route—building with professional help to take care of the mechanical tasks. There simply isn't room enough to cover everything in detail. I've devoted most of this chapter to the portions of building which are exclusively post-frame features, since this information is available nowhere else. Some skimping has been done on those particulars of building which are the same for both post-frames and conventional housing. Some of these are the drywall work, the painting, cabinets and the carpeting. There are many other sources for the information which applies to conventional housing. A few tips, though, will be dropped on these subjects. Here is the house which will be discussed (Figs. 15-2 through 15-8).

DETERMINING THE BUILDING'S LOCATION

Once the building site has been bought, a building permit obtained, and the land boundries plotted, you are ready to begin the building process (Fig. 15-9).

The first thing that must be done is to determine where the building is to be built. You should first determine where will be the front line of the building. Then roughly stake out the front corners of the proposed building. Once these front two points have been plotted, roughly determine the other two corners. At this point, you don't have to be too accurate. The entire area is going to be bulldozed anyway, and the stakes will have to be removed.

THE PROCEDURE

1. DETERMINE PROPERTY LINES
2. DETERMINE BUILDING'S PERIMETER
3. FLATTEN SITE
4. LAY 12 INCH SAND BASE
5. TAP STREET OR INSTALL SEPTIC
6. DETERMINE BUILDING PERIMETER
7. DETERMINE INTERIOR HOLE LOCATIONS
8. TRENCH FOR PERIMETER FOOTING
9. LAY ALL BELOW-GRADE PLUMBING
10. BACKFILL ROUGH PLUMBING
11. DIG INTERIOR HOLES
12. INSTALL FOOTINGS
13. SET POSTS & BRACE
14. ¾ (INCH) FOAM
15. PLASTIC MOISTURE BARRIER
16. 1 x 8 SPLASHBOARD
17. 2 INCH GRAVEL FILL FOR DRAINS
18. INSTALL STORM DRAINS
19. SAND & GRAVEL BACKFILL
20. HANG BEAMS & BRACE
21. BELOW-GRADE ROUGH HEATING
22. PLANK ROOF, SHINGLE
23. LAY SLAB
24. ATTACH WALL FRAMEWORK
25. WINDOWS
26. 30 # FELT
27. 1 x 8 SIDING
28. DOORS
29. INTERIOR WALLS
30. ABOVE SLAB HEATING
31. ABOVE SLAB PLUMBING
32. ABOVE SLAB ELECTRICAL
33. INSULATE WALLS
34. DRYWALL & PLASTER
35. PAINT INSIDE & OUTSIDE
36. CABINETS
37. FINISH HEATING
38. FINISH PLUMBING
39. FINISH ELECTRICAL
40. INTERIOR DOORS
41. INTERIOR MOLDING & TRIM
42. FINISH GRADE
43. CARPET

Fig. 15-1. This list gives the order for tasks involved in building a post-frame home.

Once the four corners of the building have been determined, pound in long stakes (old broom and shovel handles work fine) about 2 feet outside from the corners of the proposed house. These four stakes mark the extent of excavation. The length of the stakes insures the bulldozer operator of the boundries without having him fret about running over the stakes and ruining his tires. The entire excavation will leave 2 feet on each side of the building as working room (Fig. 15-10).

Before the bulldozer arrives, decide exactly where all the scraped off topsoil should go (Fig. 15-11). Have it scraped in the general area that it will be used. If there will not be any immediate use for it, remove the top soil. By deciding beforehand where the topsoil will go, the bulldozer will spend less time at the site.

LEVELING THE SITE

All topsoil must be removed since any organic substance will gradually decompose. Understandably, you don't want to build on a material that is decomposing. It would be more than "just" unstable; the smell of decomposition can penetrate a concrete slab, making for an unsuitable living environment.

Don't try to simply "eyeball" the leveling procedure. Any time there is uneven land behind the area being leveled, it will work to create an optical illusion—the area in front of higher ground will appear level with the area in front of the lower ground. As it turns out, the area in front of the higher ground will actually be higher, although it looks level.

To insure yourself that an adequately level area is obtained, a transit can be used. Through the use of a transit, leveling can easily occur within ¼ inch. Although exactness is not necessary at this point, there's nothing wrong with it. In place of a transit, though, you can easily achieve a level area through the use of a long straight board with a level on top, a brick, and a concrete block. After a rough grade is achieved, the board can be pivoted from the block which occupies a spot near the middle of the excavated area (Fig. 15-12).

Fig. 15-2. This beautiful home is located in an attractive setting.

An 8-inch brick is set under the extended board; if the level shows that the area is level, then you can quickly examine the area beneath the board to insure that it, too, is basically level. This procedure should then be repeated every 8 feet or so by simply pivoting the 2×4 on the block. Getting within ½-inch off level from the block to the end of the 16 foot 2×4 is good enough. This discrepancy will later be made up when the area is filled with sand.

SPREADING THE SAND

The sand can be spread over the entire area when you know the site is acceptably level. Spreading is best done at this point for several reasons. First of all, the person doing the excavation probably will have a truck capable of carrying enough sand in a few loads to cover the area to the depth needed. By using his truck, one can save extra delivery charges. Secondly, as long as the bulldozer is there, it might as well spread the sand for you. The dozer can do it more quickly and easily. Thirdly, by having the sand down, it is gradually compacted when it is walked upon. By the time the slab is ready to be poured, the sand will be adequtely compacted. Fourthly, the sand is generally easier and safer to walk on than uneven ground. Fifthly, if it rains, the sand will absorb the water. Lastly, by knowing the exact height of the sand, there can be no mistake when determining the height of splatter boards, which consequently determines the beam height. If heating ductwork is to be run under the slab, a 12 inch base of sand is needed. You should attempt to replace the amount of dirt excavated with sand so that the slab is slightly above grade. If 15 inches of top soil was removed, 15 inches of sand would bring the bottom of the slab up to grade. When the finish grade is established for the ground around the house, it is desirous to slope the grade away from the house by at least 1 foot for every 30 feet. To do this, obviously the house will have to be slightly higher than the surrounding ground. For this reason, one should replace the excavated topsoil with sand. This insures against any threat of flooding and helps keep a comfortably dry slab. If the site has a gentle slope, making it impossible to slope

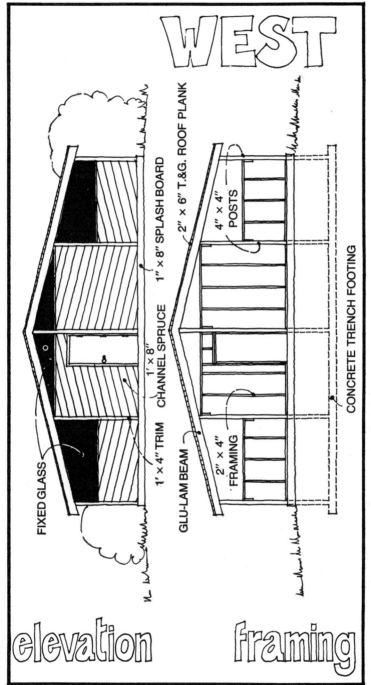

WEST

FIXED GLASS

1' × 4" TRIM

1' × 8" CHANNEL SPRUCE

1" × 8" SPLASH BOARD

2" × 6" T.&G. ROOF PLANK

4" × 4" POSTS

GLU-LAM BEAM

2" × 4" FRAMING

CONCRETE TRENCH FOOTING

elevation

framing

Fig. 15-3. The drawing illustrates the home's west side elevation and framing.

the grade away from the house on all sides, it will be necessary to route water runoff around the house by installing interceptor trenches. Installation can be done at this time to reduce the chance of flooding.

THE SANITARY HOOK-UPS

When the excavator is finished leveling the sand, the work on the sanitary hook-ups can begin. Do this work when the excavator is there. While the excavation for the pipes is being done, you can be determining the building's perimeter. Then, when you have completed your determinations, he can immediately excavate for the building's foundation.

DETERMINING THE EXACT PERIMETER OF THE BUILDING

Once the sand is somewhat leveled, the perimeter of the building can be determined. At this point, you shouldn't have to worry too much about the exact level of the sand. It's going to get disturbed anyway. Simply get a rough level established.

Like before, it is best to first establish the front line. Stake #1 is sunk at one corner. An 8d nail is pounded into the stake, leaving at least ½ inch of the nail protruding from the stake. A tape measure (at least 50 feet) is then attached to the nail on the stake and unwound until the desired measurement for the front line is reached. At this point stake #2 is driven. Tie a string onto the nails of these two front line stakes and pull it taut. The front line is now established.

To determine the side line, the Pythagorean Theorum for determining a right triangle is again used. Pound stake #3 30 feet down from the front line from the first stake which was pounded. Again, sink a nail in the end of the stake, making sure that the nail's head is exactly at 30 feet. Attach a tape measure onto this nail and unwind it to 50 feet. Attach another tape measure onto stake #1 and measure down 40 feet. Drive stake #4 at the intersection of these two points. Once the stake is firmly in the ground, the tapes should again be brought together to detemine the exact spot where the marks meet. At this point, a nail is hammered into the stake. Since the sideline is 40 feet, it has been established (Fig. 15-13).

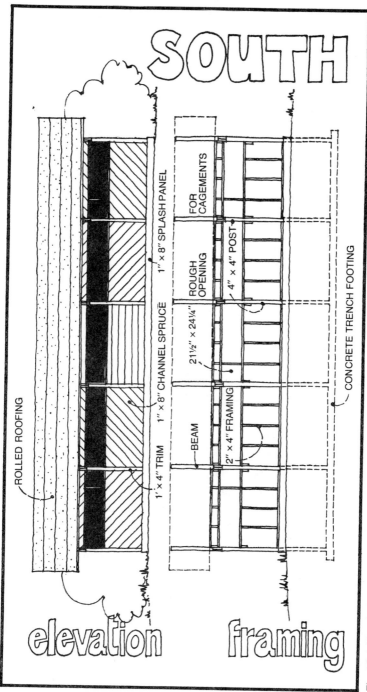

SOUTH

elevation

ROLLED ROOFING

1" × 4" TRIM   1" × 8" CHANNEL SPRUCE   1" × 8" SPLASH PANEL

framing

FOR CAGEMENTS

ROUGH OPENING

4" × 4" POST

21½" × 24¼"

BEAM

2" × 4" FRAMING

CONCRETE TRENCH FOOTING

Fig. 15-4. Here is the home's south side elevation and framing.

251

The most simple way to determine the other two sides is to hook one tape on stake #4 and unwind it the 32-foot distance of the back line. The other tape measure is hooked to stake #2 and unwound the 40-foot distance of the side line. The point where the two measurements meet is the point where the last stake is to be driven.

Check to see how accurately the four corner stakes have been placed. Measure diagonally from right front to left rear and from left front to right rear. If the measurements are within ½ inch, you've done great. If there is less than an inch discrepancy, this is tolerable. There will be room for adjustment once the trench is dug.

If there is more than an inch difference between these two measurements, some adjustment should be made. Make sure, first of all, that each side is of the desired length. If each side has been accurately measured, then adjustment must be made to make 90 degree angles. A discrepancy between the two measurements means that you have laid out a parallelogram. Correction involves moving the two stakes of larger measurement inward and moving the stakes of smaller measurement outward. It does not take much movement to make slight corrections (Fig. 15-14). The stakes can be knocked sideways to make the corrections.

THE INTERIOR HOLES

After the perimeter of the building has been exactly determined, the locations for the interior posts can be assessed. This is done simply by measuring in 8-foot increments down each 40-foot line. At the 8-foot points, the string can be marked with a felt-tipped marker. The 32-foot lines are marked at the points 12 feet from each corner. At all of these points, stakes are driven into the ground. An 8d nail is hammered into the top of each stake. Lines can then be strung to connect the stakes opposite one another. At the intersections of the lines are the interior post locations (Fig. 15-15).

Exact measurements must be made. Incorrect determinations only cause a lot of extra work. Check and re-check your measurements to insure yourself that everything is in

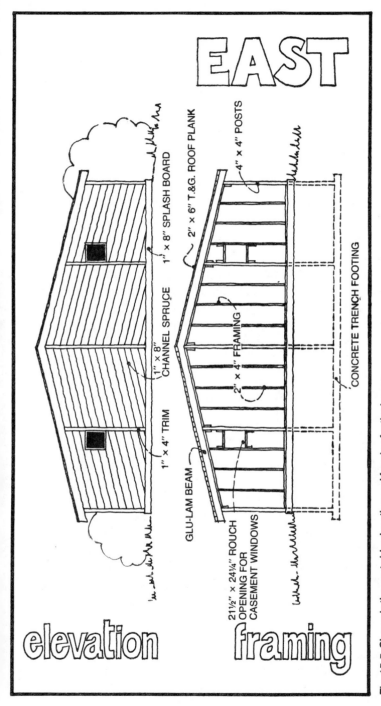

EAST

elevation

framing

4" × 4" POSTS

2" × 6" T.&G. ROOF PLANK

1" × 8" SPLASH BOARD

1" × 8" CHANNEL SPRUCE

1" × 4" TRIM

2" × 4" FRAMING

CONCRETE TRENCH FOOTING

GLU-LAM BEAM

21½" × 24¼" ROUCH OPENING FOR CASEMENT WINDOWS

Fig. 15-5. Shown is the east side elevation and framing for the house.

order. Once it has been determined that the correct locations have been made, stakes can be driven at the ascertained points. When the stakes are fixed, all strings can be taken down. The stakes should be left in the ground, though, to serve as a guide for the perimeter excavation.

The perimeter excavation can now be done, but first a little more on the interior holes. These holes, since they are inside the building, do not have to be below the frost line. The building will keep the ground from freezing beneath the posts. All that has to be done is to remove the sand from the area where the post is to stand. Generally there will be at least 6 inches of sand fill. For most diameters of footings, a 6-inch thick footing is sufficient. In these cases, the sand should be dampened and then carved out to make a mold for the footing. By dampening the sand, it is easy to shape; hopefully you've had some experience making sandcastles.

The holes can be carved out square with plumb sides. Nothing fancy is needed here. Remember to calculate out the proper size for these footings according to the weight of the structure and the soil type. If the footings need to be thicker than the sand depth, the ground is going to have to be dug down some. The bottoms of the holes must be made flat and must be firm ground.

This work can directly precede the making of (or delivery of) the concrete. It is best to cast concrete into a wet mold so that the sand doesn't suck the concrete dry quickly.

The thickness of the concrete slab floor should not necessarily enter into the calculation of the footings' thickness, since the slab will later be poured around the posts. Be sure that the footings are thick enough alone, without the slab's help. The slab may help some, though, because large spikes can be pounded into the posts at the point where the concrete slab will encase them, thus entering the concrete slab·into the footing. When this is done, the slab can be calculated to add about 2 inches onto the depth of the footings. This technique is useful in achieving more bearing surface for the footing. On especially poor soils, by spreading the footing onto the slab it is given a crutch.

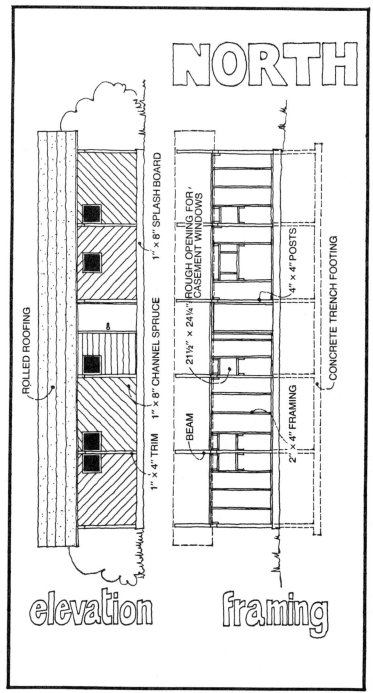

NORTH

elevation

ROLLED ROOFING

1" × 4" TRIM

1" × 8" CHANNEL SPRUCE

1" × 8" SPLASH BOARD

framing

BEAM

ROUGH OPENING FOR CASEMENT WINDOWS

21½" × 24¼"

2" × 4" FRAMING

4" × 4" POSTS

CONCRETE TRENCH FOOTING

Fig. 15-6. North side elevation and framing is pictured here.

255

The footings should not be too thin or too thick. It is best to get a full thickness of slab poured over the footings. The slab is then not weakened in the area around the footings. Also, by making the footings only as thick as is necessary, it limits the possibility of the footing being too high and sticking above the floor level. As long as the excavation job is level, this could never happen. By determining the average thickness of the sand base and by making sure that the footing does not rise above that limit, the footing will not impinge upon the slab thickness at all. Just don't get carried away trying to make super-strong footings because it isn't necessary. They can be made only as thick as is needed. Any added thickness is waste and may weaken the slab.

As was mentioned before, this work should be done just prior to the casting of the concrete. As soon as the locations of the holes have been determined, the next major operation should get under way—the excavation of the trench around the perimeter of the house.

DIGGING THE PERIMETER TRENCH

For this design, a trench is dug around the perimeter of the building so that an adequate frost barrier can be constructed. In areas where no frost barrier is needed, post holes replace the trench. As mentioned in the chapter on foundations, the warmer climates permit easier construction. Since the designs using frost barriers are more universal, this house utilizes a frost barrier.

The foundation system this house uses is different from those presented in the foundation chapter. This system uses styrofoam and gravel for the frost barrier. To give moisture protection, the styrofoam is covered with plastic. A treated 1×8 serves as both protection for the plastic's edge and as a splashboard. It also serves as a starting point for the house's visible structure.

To provide this foundation, a trench is dug around the perimeter of the house. The bottom of this trench must be below the area's frost line. It also should be at least 3½ feet deep. This trench really does not have to be any wider than a foot—if it is dug accurately. It is better, though, to give some extra leeway; a 16-inch wide trench is a typical width and should be used for this building. If the trench is a couple of inches off, it's not going to cause much trouble.

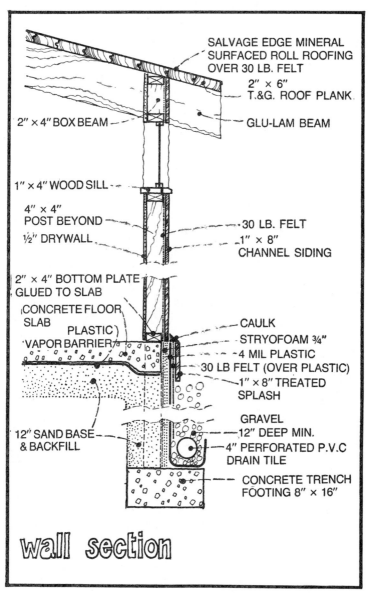

SALVAGE EDGE MINERAL SURFACED ROLL ROOFING OVER 30 LB. FELT

2" × 6" T.&G. ROOF PLANK

2" × 4" BOX BEAM

GLU-LAM BEAM

1" × 4" WOOD SILL

4" × 4" POST BEYOND

½" DRYWALL

30 LB. FELT

1" × 8" CHANNEL SIDING

2" × 4" BOTTOM PLATE GLUED TO SLAB

CONCRETE FLOOR SLAB

PLASTIC VAPOR BARRIER

CAULK

STRYOFOAM ¾"

4 MIL PLASTIC

30 LB FELT (OVER PLASTIC)

1" × 8" TREATED SPLASH

12" SAND BASE & BACKFILL

GRAVEL 12" DEEP MIN.

4" PERFORATED P.V.C DRAIN TILE

CONCRETE TRENCH FOOTING 8" × 16"

wall section

Fig. 15-7. Much effort is required in constructing the home's wall sections.

An accurate digging is needed so that everything will fit into the trench. Room must be provided for the posts and for storm drains that will surround the house. The trench is dug right down the middle of the stakes which define the perimeter of the building. If anything, have it dug a little towards the outside of the building since this is where room must be provided for the storm drains. Ideally it should be dug 1 inch off-center from the stakes toward the outside of the building. This gives equal tolerance on both sides of the posts. We may be getting a bit too accurate, though. If you can get the trench dug straight down the center of the stakes defining the building's perimeter, you will be in good shape (Fig. 15-16).

There are many machines for digging narrow trenches. The "ditch witch" is probably the most popular. Backhoes, too, are capable of digging narrow trenches. They can be fit with a 16 inch wide bucket. It takes a lot of work to hand-dig trenches, especially one all the way around the house. It is worthwhile to hire a machine to do a neat job.

The sides of the trench should be straight and reasonably plumb. The bottom of the trench should reach inorganic, undisturbed soil. And, to insure a good bearing surface, the bottom of the trench should be flat and free of loose dirt.

There are two ways to compose footings in this trench: either the entire trench can receive a layer of concrete, making a continuous footing; or a separate footing can be cast for each post. The continuous footing is sometimes used for two reasons. First of all, it is easier to do if the concrete is being delivered—the trench is simply filled with 6 inches of concrete. You don't have to worry about where the posts will go to make sure the footings are in the right places. Secondly, the continuous footing can be stronger than separate footings. The continuous footing spreads the building's weight around the entire structure. On poor soils, this can be a great asset.

If you are mixing your own concrete, and if the soil is good enough that it doesn't need a continuous footing, separate footings should be made. These can be made in one

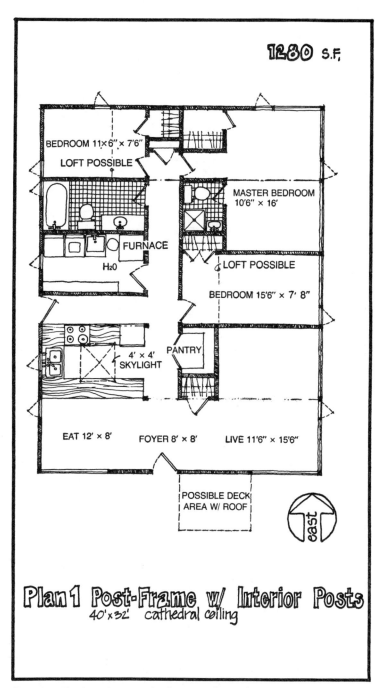

1280 S.F.

BEDROOM 11×6″ × 7′6″
LOFT POSSIBLE

MASTER BEDROOM
10′6″ × 16′

FURNACE

H₂O

LOFT POSSIBLE

BEDROOM 15′6″ × 7′ 8″

4′ × 4′
SKYLIGHT

PANTRY

EAT 12′ × 8′   FOYER 8′ × 8′   LIVE 11′6″ × 15′6″

POSSIBLE DECK
AREA W/ ROOF

east

Plan 1 Post-Frame w/ Interior Posts
40′×32′ cathedral ceiling

Fig. 15-8. The home's room plan features plenty of space.

of two ways. Either holes can be dug in the bottom of the trench and footings cast in these holes; or formwork can be made to frame up the footing. If holes are dug in the bottom of the trench, the trench does not have to be excavated as deeply with the backhoe. Only the bottom of the footings must be below the frost line—not the entire trench. This method is preferable for casting individual footings because the plastic moisture barrier and the foam will reach the bottom of the trench, thereby creating a very good moisture

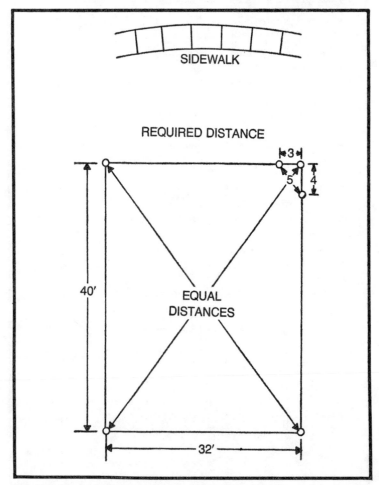

Fig. 15-9. The preliminary staking out of the building must consider the setback requirements. The building must be set back the required distance from the property line .

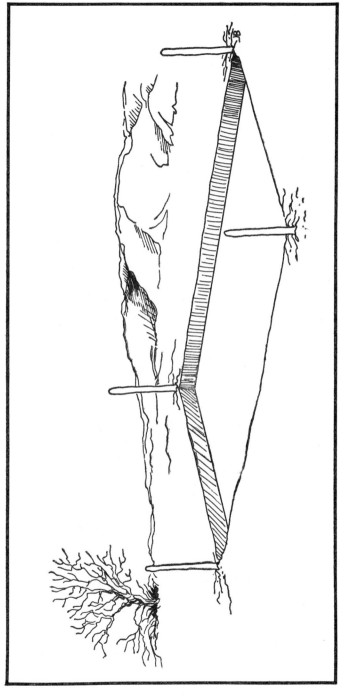

Fig. 15-10. Old broomsticks work fine as stakes to designate the extent of the preliminary excavation. Precise measurements are not needed at this stage of building .

261

barrier. Plus, there is less excavated soil to deal with and less backfill to buy and install.

If you can't deal with getting down into the trench to dig some holes and you want to do individual footings, then plywood can be cut the width of the trench, inserted into it, and adjusted to the proper width. The concrete can then be poured into the plywood framework.

Maybe it costs more for having the concrete delivered, but for this house I'm going to opt for the continuous footing—it's easier and better. This way, too, the interior posts' footings can be made at the same time and finished in about two hours. After it's done, let the footings sit overnight.

THE ROUGH PLUMBING

As soon as the perimeter trench is dug, work on the rough plumbing can begin. This work can wait until a bit later. If a plumber is helping the excavator with the lines going out to the septic system or city sewer, though, he might as well lay the drain lines inside the house's perimeter, too. By doing as much as possible during each visit by the professional, expenses are cut down. Besides, everything will soon be ready for the rough heating work to be done. The rough plumbing must be done first.

The only obstacles that must be observed are the interior posts' footings and the areas where the perimeter posts will stand. Make sure that the plumbing will not interfere with either of these areas.

SETTING UP THE POSTS

Once the footings are installed and have been allowed to set at least overnight, work can begin on setting up the posts. The corner posts are done first. Use the straightest ones for these corner posts, since all other posts will be aligned with them. When the corner posts are crooked, everything else will be off.

The first corner post is stood up, plumbed and braced. Two-by-fours are usually used for the braces. They are lightly nailed onto the post at about a 5-foot height from the grade. These boards angle down and are nailed onto stakes

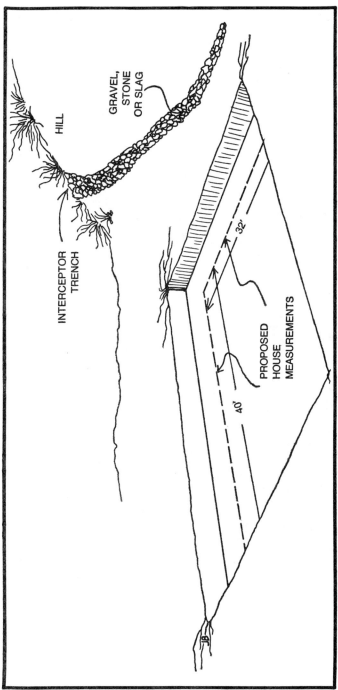

Fig. 15-11. The excavation should leave approximately two feet on each side of the proposed building as working room. If a hill descends towards the excavated area, an interceptor trench should be installed.

Fig. 15-12. In lieu of using an expensive transit, a cinder block, brick, a straight 16 foot 2x4 and a level may be used. The 2x4 is pivoted on the cinder block, resting the extended end of the 2x4 on the brick. If the 2x4 is level, so is the excavation.

driven into the ground. The corner posts will usually receive two braces. Material for girts can be used for the braces (Fig. 15-17).

When placing these corner posts, care must be taken to leave sufficient room for the styrofoam and drains running by the outside face of the posts below grade. If the trench has been accurately dug, this will automatically occur.

Once this first corner post is braced and is plumb, the second corner post is next. Attach a 100 foot measure to a nail driven into the first aligned post. The nail should be on the outside of the post, since the measurements will be taken from outside to outside. Measure down 32 feet to the other front corner post. Adjust the post so that the outside of this post is at the 32 foot mark and is plumb. Brace this post so it is exactly in the right place.

The alignment of the third post involves making sure that the building is square. Again, use the Pythagorean Theorem. The distance along the side of the house is measured to be sure the post is the correct distance by again using the tape attached to a nail driven in post #2. This third post can then be braced (Fig. 15-18).

To set the fourth post, measure from post #3 along the back of the house the 40 foot distance of the back line. Then measure with another tape from post #1 the distance of the side line. These two tapes intersection is the outside location of post #4.

After all corner posts are properly braced, measure the diagonals to make sure that the building is square. Re-

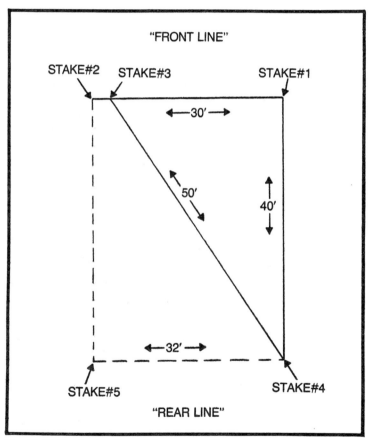

Fig. 15-13. Precise locations of the proposed house corners is established by the 3-4-5 method of squaring a corner. By using the measurements 30 feet, 40 feet, and 50 feet, the 40 foot stake locates the third corner immediately. Then, by measuring 40 feet from stake #2 and 32 feet from stake #4, the last corner is established .

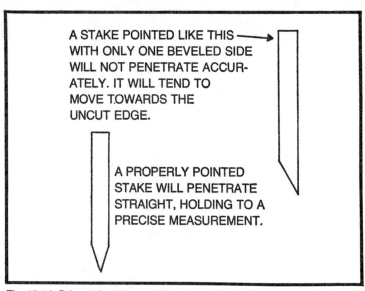

A STAKE POINTED LIKE THIS ⟶
WITH ONLY ONE BEVELED SIDE
WILL NOT PENETRATE ACCUR-
ATELY. IT WILL TEND TO
MOVE TOWARDS THE
UNCUT EDGE.

A PROPERLY POINTED
STAKE WILL PENETRATE
STRAIGHT, HOLDING TO A
PRECISE MEASUREMENT.

Fig. 15-14. Drive stakes in correctly to insure precise measurements. Be sure the stakes are pointed properly .

member that these diagonals should be equal to each other. If the measurement is within ½ inch, this is good (Fig. 15-19).

Remeasure all walls so that all dimensions are accurate. If all dimensions are correct, then you are ready to stand up the side posts.

With the corner posts securely braced, place a line around the perimeter of the posts. A line around the tops of the posts and a second line around the bottom of the posts will simplify matters greatly. With those two lines taut, the posts for the sides are merely stood up so that their outside edge touches both these lines. The post should now be plumb. Measure the distance from the corner post and make any adjustments to get an exact 8 foot on center measurement. Plumb the side of the post and brace it.

This process is done around the entire building until all posts are properly braced and aligned. When this is done, 2×4s should be nailed to the posts to tie them together (Fig. 15-20).

Lines can now be strung across the house to establish the exact location of the interior posts. They are set, braced, and backfilled just like the perimeter posts.

Continue this process until all interior posts are properly aligned and braced. At this point, all posts are properly aligned, the building is square, and the posts are all plumb and securely braced.

INSTALLING THE FOAM

The next step is to install the ¾-inch styrofoam. The builder must be sure that no further adjustment of the perimeter posts will be needed; it is advised, then, to check and re-check every measurement. Make sure, too, that the posts are plumb in both directions. Everything must be in ship-shape before the foam is applied, since any adjustment made after the foam is installed would partially or wholly break it.

If everything is in order, the foam can be applied. The top of the foam will be on the same plane as the floor area. Make an accurate determination for the foam's height. Remembering that we need a 4-inch thick slab, the foam must be applied 4 inches above the level of the sand base inside the perimeter of the house. This measurement can be

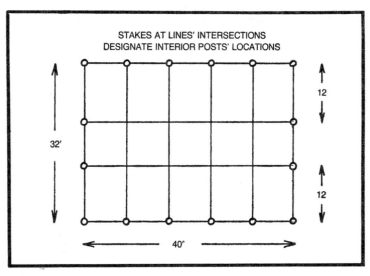

Fig. 15-15. Stakes are secured around the perimeter of the proposed house. On the 40 foot sides, the stakes are 8 feet apart; on the 32 foot sides they are 12 feet from each corner. Lines strung to connect opposing stakes locate the interior post locations at the lines' intersections .

assessed easily by stringing a line across the sand base from opposite posts. A line level is attached to the string so that the line is level. When the distance beneath the line is 4 inches, the proper height has been determined. It is worthwhile to string up a few lines to make sure that an accurate assessment has been made. Once this has been done, the posts can all be marked at the proper height.

To mark the posts, a straight board, a good level, and a felt tipped pen are used. One post can be marked at the point to where the top of the slab will come. Then, with the top of the board on this mark, the level is placed atop the board and placed against the face of the next post. When the board is level, that post can be marked. This continues around the perimeter of the house (Fig. 15-21).

It is helpful to have three people helping with this task—one to hold the board on the mark, one to check the level and adjust the board, and one to make the marks. If insufficient people are around, a nail can be driven into the posts on which to rest the straight board. This task could now be completed with only one person.

Once all posts are marked, the foam can be applied to the posts. The foam's top edge should end right on the marks. To secure the foam to the posts, a bead of foam adhesive should be applied to the foam at points where it will touch the posts. The foam can also be nailed onto the posts.

THE PLASTIC

Plastic (which should be four mils thick or thicker) is applied over the face of the foam to form a moisture barrier. The top of the plastic should be glued onto the foam with a continuous bead of foam adhesive. The rest of the plastic need not be adhered to the foam; it can merely rest against it.

The bottom of the plastic should form a "U" shape at the bottom of the trench—as is shown in the drawing. This way water is less likely to seep beneath the plastic. The drain then fits into this "U" shape.

Plastic can be obtained in rolls which are 100 feet long. It would be conceivable to have only two breaks in the plastic water barrier. The fewer breaks, the better it will work.

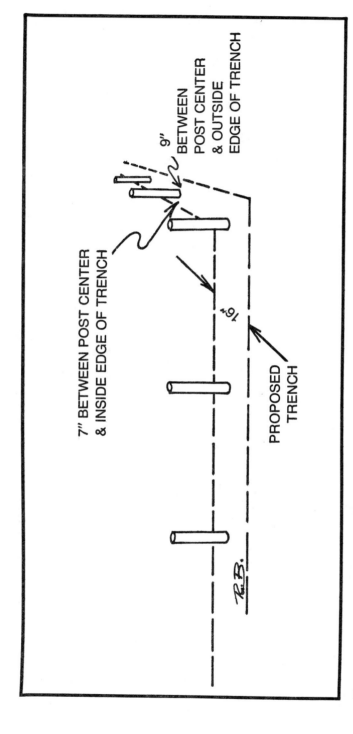

7" BETWEEN POST CENTER
& INSIDE EDGE OF TRENCH

9" BETWEEN POST CENTER
& OUTSIDE EDGE OF TRENCH

16"±

PROPOSED TRENCH

Fig. 15-16. The perimeter stakes are left in the ground to designate the proposed trench location. The trench is dug 16 inches wide, the outer extent of excavation being 9 inches from the center of the stakes. This leaves 7 inches from the center of the stakes to the inside of the trench.

269

Where one sheet of plastic ends, the next sheet should overlap at least 1 foot. At this point, it should be determined which way the water will run through those drains sitting at the bottom of the trench. The overlaps should occur so the water will not sweep beneath the laps. The top sheets should be in the direction from which the water is coming.

THE 1 × 8 SPLASHBOARD

In this design, a 1×8 serves as both a splashboard and protector for the plastic's edge. This board is secured at the same height as the foam. Its level has already been deter-

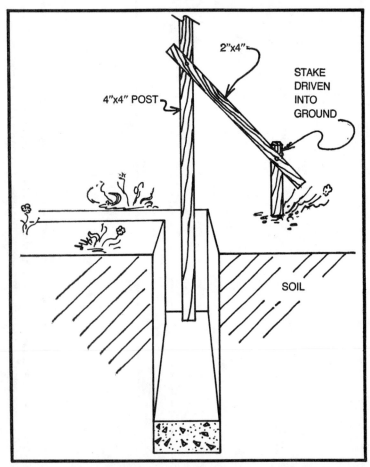

Fig. 15-17. The corner posts are set up first, being braced with only one brace until it is assured that the building is square.

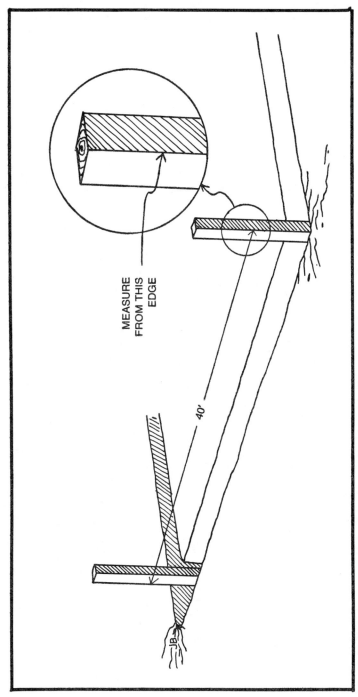

MEASURE FROM THIS EDGE

40'

JB

Fig. 15-18. Measurements are taken from the outside edge of the corner posts when squaring the building .

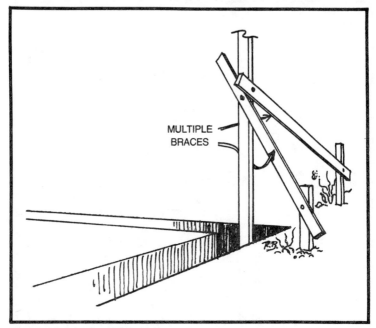

Fig. 15-19. Once the building is properly square, the corner posts are securely braced. The stakes the braces attach to should be at least 18 inch 2x2s.

mined. The ends of the splashboard should terminate on the posts. Since the posts are 8 feet on center, 16-foot long splashboards are ideal. 16d nails are used to secure the splashboards since the nails must penetrate through the foam and into the posts. Attaching these splashboards is quick work.

THE DRAINS

After the splashboard is applied, a 4-inch perforated plastic drain is installed at the bottom of the trench. This drain must rest on about 2 inches of pea gravel. The pea gravel is thrown in first.

The drain should gradually slope downhill towards its outlet. The slight amount of pea gravel can be adjusted to make this slope. After this preliminary amount of pea gravel is installed, the drain can be dropped into place.

The easiest type of plastic drain to install is bought in long rolls instead of in 10-foot sections. The long rolls permit installation with a minimum of joints. Elbows are bought to

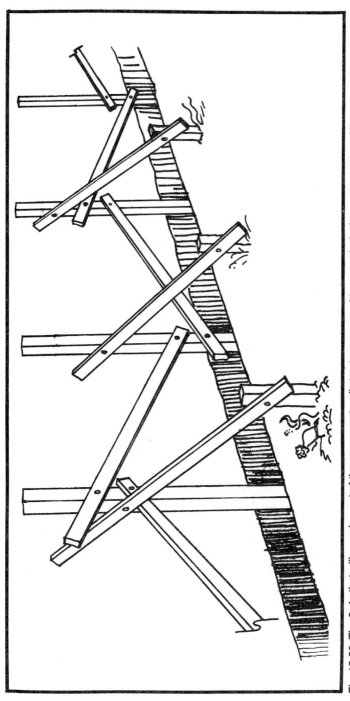

Fig. 15-20. The 2x4s that will soon be part of the permanent wall structure are used to securely tie the posts together. All posts must be plumb. The nails used to secure the braces should not be hammered in all the way. By leaving a little of the nail protruding, it will be easy to pull it out when the time comes.

make the bends at the corners of the building, and a "wye" (shaped like a "Y") is used to feed the ends at the point where the drain leads to the storm sewer. A continuous loop of drain surrounds the house.

After this drain is installed, it can be covered with at least 8 inches of pea gravel. Make sure that the plastic moisture barrier does not cover the top of the storm drain, since this would render the drains ineffective.

THE BACKFILL

The pea gravel set over the drains can be installed at the same time the sand fill is placed behind the foam. In this manner, the fill will not bow the styrofoam. By having two people working—one on each side of the foam—the backfilling can go quickly.

The sand fill, especially, should be tamped to inhibit settling. It need not be excessively tamped, as this could injure the foam if not done carefully. It can be tamped in 6-inch layers with a 4×4 as the trench is filled. As the fill reaches the surface, it can be stepped on instead of using the 4×4.

Notice in the cutaway drawing that the slab is thickened to give it more strength next to the posts. The sand fill should not quite reach the level of the rest of the sand base. The slab should be thickened to about 6 inches around the perimeter of the building—especially in the area next to the posts. It doesn't hurt to surround the posts with a little more concrete; so a 12-inch depth surrounding the posts would be all right, although it does not have to be done. Thickening of the slab will thwart movement of the posts by wind. The wind velocity in the locale is the largest determining factor of how much concrete should surround the posts.

If ratwalls are required in your area, the pea gravel fill can be substituted with concrete. The drains still need an 8-inch layer of pea gravel over them; above this, though, can be poured concrete. Ratwalls are generally made only 24 inches deep, so plenty of room will be available for the necessary pea gravel.

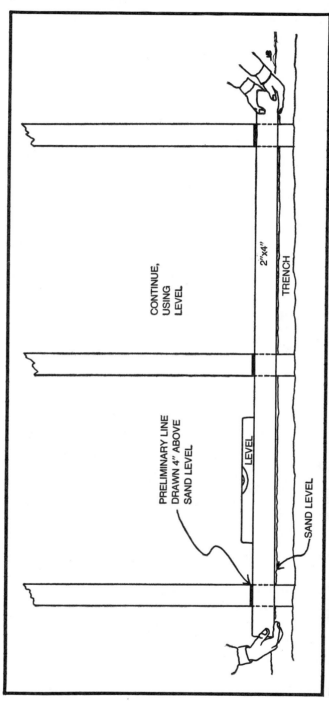

Fig. 15-21. A straight 2x4 and a level are used to transfer the preliminary line designating the top of the splashboard. These marks must be accurately made to determine the floor level. Many measurements will be made from the splashboard. When the splashboard is attached level, the rest of the house will be straight and easy to build.

When poured concrete ratwalls are to be made, the sand fill should be installed first, providing a backing for the foam when the concrete is poured. After the concrete is poured, the sand can be firmly tamped. One way to compact sand is to flood it with water.

MAKING THE BEAMS

When available, solid wood beams can be used for the roof's structure. If douglas fir beams can be obtained, the builder will be purchasing strong, good-looking, and easy to work with beams. If available, (12) 4×10s will be needed. Trim the beams' ends at the proper angle.

In many areas, solid wood beams are either not available or are very expensive. A description follows on how to fabricate your own beams. We'll be making beams from (2) 2×10s and ½-linch plywood. By using the plywood in combination with the 2×10s, a stronger beam is made and one that is the exact same width as the posts. The beam is thus easily and more neatly attached. Although the beam could be simply nailed together, a stronger beam is made through the use of construction adhesive—it eliminates slippage between the nails.

The plywood can be cut into 8 inch wide strips. Some leeway is given at the top of the beam so the plywood never sticks above the 2×10s. By making the plywood strip a lesser dimension than the 2×10s, it will not show from the inside of the house. It should be inset approximately an inch. The edge that points toward the inside of the house can be painted black so it is unnoticeable. This painting should be done before the beam is fabricated. It is most easily done with a paint roller.

With the plywood strips cut and painted, they can be applied to the first 2×10. Construction adhesive is applied to the first 2×10 before the plywood is set into place. A few small nails will temporarily secure the plywood to the 2×10. The adhesive is then applied to the other face of the plywood and the second 2×10 is set into place. All three laminations are clamped together with 16d nails (Fig. 15-22).

It is best to allow the beams to sit overnight before they are handled. The ends of the beams can be trimmed at this

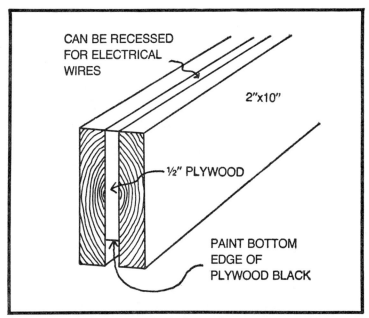

CAN BE RECESSED
FOR ELECTRICAL
WIRES

2"x10"

½" PLYWOOD

PAINT BOTTOM
EDGE OF
PLYWOOD BLACK

Fig. 15-22. The glulam beam with ½-inch plywood sandwiched between two 2x10s is strong and exactly the same width as the posts. With the plywood recessed and painted black, it is totally unobtrusive. The plywood at the top of the beam can also be recessed for wires if lights or fans are desired to be hung from the beams.

point to a 3/12 angle on both ends. If the beams are going to be stained, now is the time. Simply get out the paint roller and the staining will go fast. Staining is difficult to do when you must be very careful not to get the stain on surrounding areas—such as roof planks. It is especially difficult when the stainer must reach upward to reach the surface to be stained. The stain tends to run down the bristles of the brush. For a good staining job, usually the stain is rubbed out with a cloth. Make sure you don't let one place dry before going over it again. Lap marks look tacky.

While the glue is curing and the stain is drying, the posts can be marked and trimmed.

TRIMMING THE POSTS

With all the posts completely backfilled and the beams made, it is time to trim the posts. First, the perimeter posts on the sides of the house are marked. Since the wall height is

6 feet to the bottom of the beams, this measurement can be taken from the splashboard. Most simply, a 6 foot 2×4 is stood up on the splashboard and the post is marked at the top of the 2×4. A bevel is then used to mark the proper angle into the posts.

To set your bevel at the 3/12 angle, you must first mark the angle on a 1×8. One-inch lumber should be used since it does not have rounded edges like 2-inch lumber. By having sharp edges, an absolutely accurate angle can be made. A 3/12 angle is transferred to the board by a carpenter's square. By placing the square as the following diagram shows, a 3/12 angle is made (Fig. 15-23).

After the angle has been marked onto the 1×8, your bevel can be adjusted to the 3/12 angle. The bevel is used to determine the angle at which the post will be cut.

Next, the gable end posts are marked. Since the roof rises 3 feet for every 12, the posts 8 feet from the corner will be marked at the 8-foot level. This height should again be taken from the splashboard. The posts which reach the peak will be marked at the 10-foot level. Since the beams meet on the gable end posts, the 3/12 angle will have to be made in both directions on these posts (Fig. 15-24).

The interior posts can now be marked. Since all measurements have been taken from the splashboards, the interior measurements should also be taken from them. Lines can be strung across the house to determine this height. A small block of wood can be nailed onto the post at the string's height to insure an accurate measurement. These posts will be marked at 9 feet, so a 9-foot 2×4 can be rested on the block to make this mark.

When all of the posts are marked, they should be double and triple-checked so that all marks are at the proper height and in the proper direction. Lines can be strung across the rows of posts to make sure that all marks are "on the money." Your roof will be as straight as your marks are accurate. Adjustments should be made if discrepancies are apparent.

With all of the marks made and scrutinized for accuracy, the posts can be trimmed. A circular saw adjusted at the

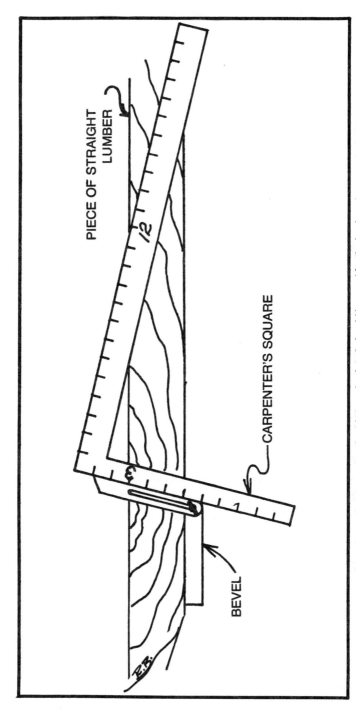

Fig. 15-23. A carpenter's square is used to determine the 3/12 angle. A 1x8 should be used for the lumber since one-inch thick boards have sharp edges, resulting in a most accurate determination. The bevel is set according to the square.

279

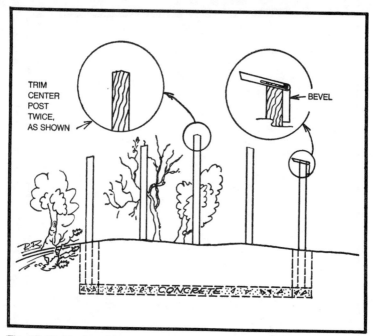

TRIM CENTER POST TWICE, AS SHOWN

BEVEL

Fig. 15-24. The bevel is used to determine the trim angle on the posts. All marks should be made before the posts are cut so that a re-check can be done to insure the builder that all marks are correct.

proper angle can make most of the cut. From there, a hand saw can complete the cut.

HANGING THE BEAMS

The beams are secured to the posts with construction adhesive and gusset plates (Fig. 15-25). A gusset plate should be nailed onto each side of the post and beam arrangement. The adhesive is applied to the top of the post; although it is not necessarily needed, it does give added strength.

The beams at the ends of the house are secured first. Care must be taken to insure that they are exactly in the right place. The peak must occur exactly in the middle of the house. With the gable ends' beams in the proper place, a line can be strung between the two gable ends. The interior beams can then be butted up to this string. A straight roof will result.

Gusset plates are used to secure opposing beams **to** each other at the peak. When this is done, the roof structure is all in place. Before the planking is applied, though, a few braces should be installed on top of the beams to hold the beams at exact 8-foot centers. When this is done, the roof is ready to be planked.

THE ROUGH HEATING

While the roof is being planked, a professional can do the rough heating. Everything is all ready for him and the roof work can be done without interfering with his work. And his work can be done without interfering with your work.

THE ROOF PLANKING

Roof planking is easily installed. It should be procured in 16-foot, 10-foot and 18-foot lengths so that no visible splices

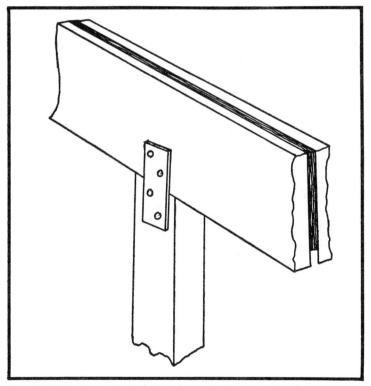

Fig. 15-25. The beam is attached to the post with a gusset plate.

will occur. The 18-foot and 10-foot lengths are used to create overhangs on the home's sides. Two-by-six spruce planking is generally available and is usually the most attractive and most economical planking.

To apply the planking, you begin at the lower end of the roof. The first plank is usually ripped so that the groove is taken off. It is then applied with the tongue pointing towards the peak. Each plank should be secured with two 16d nails at each point where it meets a beam.

To get a full plank at the peak of the roof, you measure down the roof and begin the first plank on a measurement that is a multiple of five. Each plank takes up 5 inches of a beam. Figure 15-26 shows a strong order for the planks.

Planks which have slight warps can be coerced into place if several people are around when the roof is being constructed. One person can lay on the beam and kick the plank into place while a person on each side of the beam pulls at it. The nail should be started. When the plank comes into place, someone can finish pounding in the nail.

As soon as the planking is completed, the roofing should be applied. The salvage-edge roll roofing is easy to install and works nicely. It comes in a variety of colors. Apply 30# felt to the planks before the roofing. Remember to install the felt absolutely parallel to the planking so that the white lines on the felt can serve as designators for laying the roll roofing. Explicit directions come with the roofing material.

LAYING THE SLAB FLOOR

By the time the roof and roofing are completed, the work on the heating system should be done. As long as all the rough plumbing is done, you are ready to lay the slab.

The sand must be evened out to provide a level and smooth surface upon which to cast the slab. Sand can be raked out and then rolled with a lawn roller to tamp it down. After the sand is all evened out, the plastic moisture barrier can be laid. It is best to do this no more than a day before the concrete arrives to keep it from being punctured. Seams in the plastic should be overlapped by at least 6 inches.

Formwork must be constructed so that the concrete can be properly placed. This process involves running a 2-inch

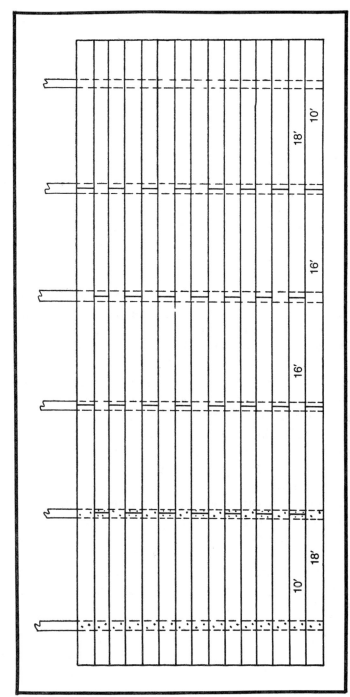

Fig. 15-26. The roof planks tie the beams together. By staggering the splices, a strong roof results. Each board also ends over a beam—making for a most attractive ceiling.

283

thick plank on top of the formwork to provide a level floor surface. The formwork can be attached directly to the interior and exterior posts—negating the need to fasten it to stakes. Staking formwork accurately is sometimes difficult, but more importantly, punctures are made in the vapor barrier. With this design, then, it is possible to construct a slab without puncturing the moisture barrier.

With this design, the slab can be smoothed in eight foot wide strips. The more narrow the strip, the easier it will be to screed. Also, with this design, section number two and four can be done in the morning and the other three in the afternoon. All of the concrete does not have to be done at once, simplifying the work. When the truck returns, the first two sections will be hard enough to walk on.

If 1×4s are used for the formwork, they may simply be left in the slab, providing expansion joints (Fig. 15-27). If you don't want to do this, they must be replaced with tar expansion joints. No expansion joints are needed around the perimeter of the building since the foam serves this purpose.

Concrete is usually finished by screeding it twice, going over it with a wooden or metal trowel attached to a long handle, and then finishing the surface with a metal trowel. This can be done simply enough. A wooden trowel can be fashioned out of a 10-foot 2×4 with a 1×8 (slightly warped, hopefully, and cupped in the up position) nailed onto it. The person handling the metal trowel generally uses a piece of plywood to kneel on while troweling so his knees don't sink into the concrete.

Concrete smoothing is done best three or four times with a 2×6. One person is at each end of it. The plank is moved back and forth, rhythmically (we hope) with a sawing motion. Another person handles getting the concrete approximately in place, moving the truck's chute back and forth to disperse the concrete evenly. A rake, shovel, and hoe are useful to move the fluid material. A fourth person takes care of keeping just the right amount of concrete in front of the screedboard. By using a rake, pockets can be filled in and excessive concrete can be moved away from the screedboard. If more people are available, a second screedboard

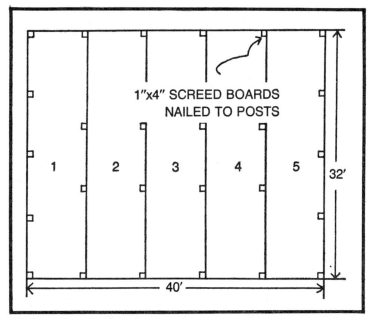

Fig. 15-27. Screed boards are nailed to the sides of the posts. No stakes will have to be pounded through the plastic moisture barrier. When treated 2x4s are used for the screed boards, they can be left in the slab, providing the needed expansion joints. The 1x4s can be braced from the posts to make them stay straight when the concrete is poured against them.

can follow the first. One person can also be available to take care of evening the concrete around the posts and taking care of other small, yet important details. The more people available, the better the concrete job will turn out. If a troweled surface is desired, extra people should be available to do this work.

Make sure that there is a path so that the concrete truck can get close so the concrete will not have to be wheelbarrowed around. This makes it much easier.

THE WALL STRUCTURE

The wall structure for this building is wall structure #8, which uses vertical studs between the posts. The studs are placed on 2-foot centers. This wall system is extremely easy to build and is easily insulated. Since it closely resembles a typical home's wall structure, the professionals doing the mechanical tasks will feel more comfortable than they would with some of the other wall systems. Major deviations from the norm tend to disturb some people.

Starting with the north elevation of the house, a top plate and a bottom plate are cut to fit between the posts. The studs are then secured to these plates with 16d nails. Two nails should secure each end. A few globs of construction adhesive are applied to the bottom plate and then the wall is tipped into place. The bottom plate can be toe-nailed into the posts to secure it until the adhesive hardens. With this done, the wall can be plumbed and anchored into the roof planks.

The window size that has been selected for all opening windows is 21½ inches wide by 23 13/16 inches high. This size is made by several of the leading window companies, including Anderson Windows. Although this is a small window, it is a casement window. The entire window opens by being cranked out, thereby giving plenty of ventilation. It should open toward the direction of prevailing wind, when possible, to catch the breeze. The advantage of using this small sized window is that it fits right between the post and the stud perfectly! The walls can be made for this entire side and then the windows can be framed in. Trimmings from the studs and plates are used as blocks to support the window framing. Since this wall is non-loadbearing and the window is small, only one 2×4 is needed at the top and bottom of the frame. The support blocks are nailed onto the post, beam and stud. Then the plates are secured to the blocks. The top framing member (the lintel) can be nailed and glued to the blocks.

For the windows which are not next to a post, an extra 2×4 on one side of the window opening narrows the opening to the proper dimension. This situation is only with the kitchen window.

The same procedure is used to frame in the east wall. It is a bit more complex since this wall has a gable. Measurements or calculations must be made to determine the correct lengths for the studs. Since the back is symmetrical, the measurements or calculations taken for one side will apply to the other.

The other gable end has windows which make the framing-in easier. Walls are simply built up to the height of the window level. For this side, the top plate for the wall is nailed onto blocks which are secured to the posts. The door needs a double 2×4 on both the side and the top. The top two 2×4s rest on the end of one of the vertical 2×4s. A strong door frame is made.

The framing for the south side beneath the band of windows is done exactly the same way as the windows were done for the last side—the top plate is secured to blocks to stabilize the wall. Above the band of windows, a modification of this system is used. Although a typical header could be composed out of two 2×10s with ½-inch plywood spacers (to make the header the same width as the posts), a more economical header can easily be made. A box beam is made out of 2×4s; the box beam is made 9¼ inches in height and long enough to fit between the posts. The top 2×4 of this box beam is then nailed into the roofing; the sides of it are secured to the beams.

The advantages of using a box beam for the header is that it is more economical, it is more easily made, it provides a channel in which to run wires, and it can be insulated. The header composed of 2×10s would constitute a bit of heat loss. The box beam header's better. Since drapery rods will often be attached to this part of the wall, the vertical webs of the beam should be accurately spaced. They will be easier to find when it comes time to hang drapes. Some drapery rods will be inset from the sides of the beam to allow the drapery material to pleat around the sides of the traverse rod. If this type of system will be used, an extra block can be glued into place after the box beam is hung. (An extra block added before the beam is hung would complicate the beam's attachment.) After the beam is hung, the extra blocks can be added at the correct locations.

With this done, the exterior wall framing is complete. The windows can be done next.

THE WINDOWS

Most casement windows are installed before the exterior siding is applied. As long as the openings have been accurately made, the windows are very easily installed. Most windows are simply nailed into place from the outside. The siding then covers up the nails.

The fixed windows can either be installed now or you can wait until later. The most economically fixed thermopane windows do not come with a frame; they consist only of two panes of glass with the aluminum spacer. These windows can be simply set upon the top plate of the wall and then encased with a frame. It is best to set the glass back only as far as is necessary so that the inside of the house has room for a window sill. A beveled drip edge is usually used on the outside of the window at the bottom to provide for water runoff. These drip edges are typically 1¼ inches wide and in this case should cover the edge of the siding. Room is left on the inside of the house to have a 1×3 for a sill. When a trim board is used beneath the entire band of windows, the drip edge can be moved out another ¾ inch to cover this edge. A 1×4 could then be used for the inside windowsill.

These details are mainly determined by what kind of casement windows are bought and if unframed fixed windows are to be used. The most simple window installation comes from purchasing fixed windows with frames that are compatible with the casement windows. This is an expensive way to go.

For some of the fixed window installations, it is best to wait until the siding is installed. Then the glass is not in danger of being broken. The only advantage of installing the fixed windows before the siding is that the builder is assured that they fit properly. If adjustments would have to be made after the siding was installed, it would be difficult.

THE NUMBER 30 FELT

At this pont the felt can be applied. It is fastened to the outer face of the wall framework with a staple gun. Run the felt horizontally, beginning at the bottom of the wall and working upward. An overlap of 3 inches is adequate.

THE SIDING

This house was designed so that it could take either 1×8 channel siding applied either horizontally or diagonally or 4×8 sheets of plywood siding. The diagonal application of the 1×8 siding is more than aesthetic—it gives great rigidity to the structure. Each piece acts like a brace.

Using the 4×8 sheets of plywood siding is the easiest and least expensive way. It is extensively used, but I doubt it will take the test of time. Within twenty years, most of the siding will need replacing. The interior glue that was used in the past was much better than the exterior glue that is used today. I've left used sheets of interior plywood outside all winter without it delaminating; the exterior grade plywood bought today will begin to delaminate tomorrow. In three days it can swell to twice its original thickness. The siding plywood that is grooved seems to hold up better, but I doubt that it will look good for 10 years.

For this house, then, 1×8 channel siding will be used. Apply it diagonally for the bracing effect. The ends of the siding must terminate on a wall member unless the entire structure is sheathed with ½-inch plywood. When plywood is used as sheathing, it simplifies the application of the diagonal design since splices can occur at any point. Some codes specify that solid sheathing must be used. If this is true for your area, plywood sheathing should be applied before the 1×8 is fastened diagonally. Without the plywood, splices most easily occur on the posts since there is more surface.

With the siding applied in the pattern shown in the elevations' drawings, all splices can occur on the posts. A 1×4 applied vertically over the splices function to cover the splices. This permits the siding to be installed without the making of precision cuts for the spliced areas. The 1×4 also functions to seal the spliced area. Since the splices all occur over the posts, the 1×4 also accentuates the post design of this structure.

Siding and trim should be secured with 8d galvanized nails. Galvanized nails don't rust; if ordinary nails were to be used, the siding would soon become streaked with rust stains. Aluminum nails can also be used, but they are more expensive and bend easily.

The doors can now be hung. For the easiest installation, pre-hung doors are usually used. The types of doors should be decided on early so that accurate rough openings are made. With the openings correctly made, these pre-hung items are easily installed.

THE INTERIOR WALLS

At this point, the concrete slab has cured enough so the interior walls may be built. These walls are most easily made in the conventional frame-wall mode. If an area between the posts is to be closed in up to the ceiling, a wall with a single top plate and a single bottom plate (with the studs either 16 inches or 24 inches on center) is nailed together. Two 16d nails are used to go through the plates and into the studs. This wall is then glued down to the floor and nailed into the ceiling. 12d nails should be used to fasten the top plate to the ceiling. The end studs are nailed into the posts they rest against. By building and anchoring a wall in this manner, a strong wall results.

The decision of whether to use a 16-inch or a 24-inch spacing for the studs is based on only one object—the drywall. One-half inch drywall goes on a bit more even when it only has to span 16 inches.

These walls can be built either 16 or 24 inches on center. Since the posts will be covered with drywall, these "on center" measurements should come from the center of the posts when they enter into the wall structure.

When walls do not go all the way up to the ceiling, a continuous top plate is needed to give the wall rigidity. If this is not possible, the wall should be made in two sections with studs backing up to each other at the break. When the studs are glued and nailed together, the wall becomes almost as rigid as when a continuous top plate is used (Fig. 15-28).

Closet and bathroom ceilings are made by attaching 2×6s to the studs of the wall. They are nailed to the face of the stud. When this occurs over the header of a doorway, the header should be made with a piece of ½ inch plywood sandwiched between two 2×6s. The ceiling joist can then hang from the header with a joist hanger. The advantage in this plan of lowering ceiling levels for some closets and bathroms is that loft space above is created. Besides expanding the living area, this loft space is good for storage.

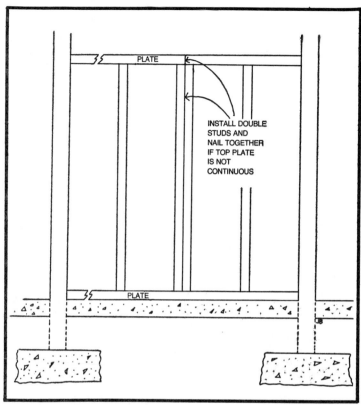

PLATE

INSTALL DOUBLE
STUDS AND
NAIL TOGETHER
IF TOP PLATE
IS NOT
CONTINUOUS

PLATE

Fig. 15-28. When a continuous top plate is not possible, studs applied back-to-back will result in a strong partition. They can be nailed and/or glued together.

THE ROUGH HEATING, PLUMBING, AND ELECTRICAL

With the interior walls framed up, the rough heating and plumbing work can be finished. And the rough electrical work can be started. Remember that the heating is done first, the plumbing second, and the electrical work third. Once this work is done, it's time to insulate.

THE INSULATION

With this exterior wall design, the best insulation is foil-faced fiberglass batts obtained in 24-inch wide strips. When possible, full-length strips should be used. The leftover trimmings can be used for some of the interior walls for soundproofing.

It is good to soundproof the wall between the living room and bedroom if a youngster will occupy the bedroom. This way, everything will not have to be "hush-hush" after he goes to bed. The bathroom walls, too, can be insulated for privacy. Sometimes it's not a bad idea to insulate the walls dividing bedrooms.

THE DRYWALL

With all of the rough heating, electrical, and plumbing done, the walls can be drywalled. Before the drywall is installed, though, is there anything else that you'd like to have in the walls? Telephone lines can be run inside walls, as can speaker and intercom wire. How about the antenna for the TV? There should be a wire for the thermostat and for burglar and fire alrms. If all of the lifelines for the building are installed, it's drywall time.

When the drywall is installed nicely, it greatly simplifies the taping and plastering of its surface. Drywall work is hard to do, so if there's any extra money around, you should consider getting a professional to do it for you. You won't be missing anything. There's a lot of sanding to do and it's very dusty work.

If you would like to do it yourself, use construction adhesive to glue the panels to the wall. This way, less fasteners need to be used. For ½ inch drywall, 1⅜-inch nails are used. For ⅝-inch drywall, 1½-inch nails are needed. With construction adhesive, only two nails are needed in the middle of the panel. Three nails on each edge are usually sufficient to hold the panel. These nails simply act as clamps until the glue hardens. The fewer nails that are used, the fewer nails there are to plaster and to make nail pops. Go as lightly as possible with the nails.

Without construction adhesive, nails are patterned in twos. Sets of two nails spaced 18 inches on center are used on each stud or girt. Around the edges, the nails do not need to be patterned in twos. The benefit of patterning the nails in twos, for areas other than the edges, is the drywall is less likely to pull away from two nails than only one nail. Although single nails could successfully hold on the drywall if spotted every 9 inches or so, this would complicate plastering. Two nails together can be plastered as fast as one.

The following system works well for drywalling the inside corners. Ordinarily, two extra 2×4s would be placed at this corner to give backing for the drywall. Instead, this system finishes one wall with drywall, using the corner post for the backer. After the drywall is applied, a 1×2 is nailed onto the drywall, being hammered into the post. The 1×2 serves as the backer for the other sheets of drywall. This system is more economical in its use of wood; also, with fewer solid members connecting the inside to the outside, less heat loss will occur (Fig. 15-29).

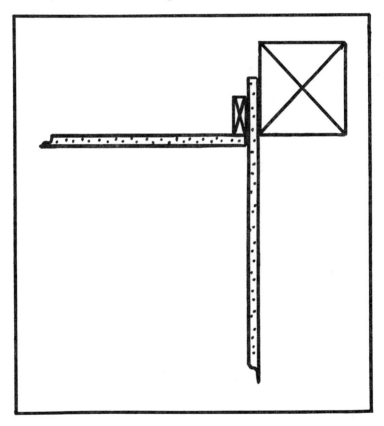

Fig. 15-29. Typically, 2x4s would be nailed to both faces of the post to give backing for the drywall. Instead, the drywall for one wall can be applied using the post as backing. A 1x2 is then nailed into the post through the drywall. The 1x2 serves as backing for the other sheet of drywall.

After the drywall is in place, a layer of joint compound is applied to the seams. Joint compound can be obtained ready-mixed. It is cheap and easy to use. Immediately after the joint compound is applied, drywall tape is used over the compound. The compound must be put on thick enough so it entirely covers the area that is to be taped. If some drywall is not covered with the compound, the tape will not stick to it in that place—it will bubble up. Don't put the compound on too thick since this would make a bulge in the wall. It is best to experiment a little in a closet before attempting a wall that will be out in the open.

The tape must be put on smoothly. It can be gone over with a wide taping knife and more taping compound to smooth it out. After it dries, it is gone over with topping compound, which also is obtained ready-mixed. Usually two coats of topping are needed, with sanding between all coats. The preliminary sandings should only take off the high spots. Shallow spots will be filled in with the next coat. A vibration sander is used for this work. Try not to fuzz up the tape or the drywall during these sandings. Only take off as much plaster as is needed to smooth out the area. Excessive sanding is bad and only means that more topping must be re-applied.

PAINTING

Everything is now ready to paint. The drywall must be primed with a latex-based wall primer. It can then be finish-coated. If you can get your hands on an airless paint sprayer, the painting will go fast. The wood ceiling will have to be masked off, as will the windows. Everything else can be painted. If you're concerned about it, the floor can be covered with sheets of plywood to protect it from overspray. For the finish coat of interior paint, a latex-based paint will work fine. Buy a high-quality paint that is washable.

For the exterior siding, either an oil-based or a latex-based stain may be used. The latex stain is easier to use, but the oil stain can produce better results. Especially if a semi-transparent stain is desired, oil must be used. The semi-transparent stains show more of the wood's grain.

THE CABINETS

With the painting done, the cabinets can be installed. If pre-made cabinets are bought, they can be easily inserted. They just slide into place. Rows of cabinets are bolted together, and the only major factor is if they are level. Shims can be put on the floor to make everything level.

Pre-made laminated plastic countertops can be purchased for less money than it costs to make them. The countertops are not a bad deal at all. They fit over the cupboards, resting on top of them.

If a nicer countertop is desired, one can be made from ceramic tile. The advantage of tile is that hot pans can be set directly on it. It is hard and scratch-resistant, too. Tile is a little more difficult to do since its base must be exterior-grade plywood sitting on a 2×4 framework but, once done, it is there to stay. The grout on a ceramic countertop should be colored so that it doesn't show stains.

The countertop must be cut to take a sink so that the plumber merely drops the sink into the hole. The hole for the sink is usually cut 1½ inches smaller than the sink, although different sinks' specifications vary. Sinks generally come with detailed instructions of the installation procedure.

FINISH HEATING, PLUMBING, AND ELECTRICAL

With the cupboards sitting in place, the finish work on the heating, plumbing, and electrical work can be done. These things can all be done at once at this point, but it is worthwhile to make sure that the different trades don't get in each other's way. This finish work usually takes only a day per trade, so it really doesn't hurt to schedule people for different days. While this work is going on, there are a few other things that you have to do.

THE INTERIOR DOORS

The interiors doors must be hung. These doors, like the exterior doors, can be obtained pre-hung. Generally, though, the pre-hung interior doors are hollow-core doors. If solid doors are desired, you must hang them yourself. It is tricky to hang a door properly, but it can be done with a lot of

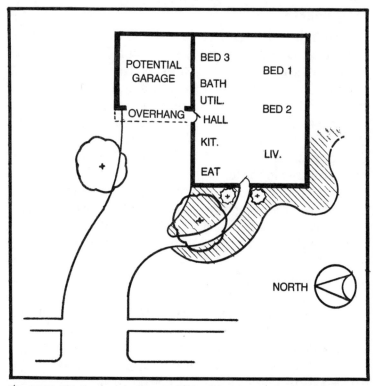

Fig. 15-30. This house can sit on a lot three different ways. Because of the solar orientation, the bedroom/living room side should always point either south or southwest. Naturally, with an attached garage, certain window details will have to be modified.

patience. My recommendation, though, is to get the pre-hung doors. There are a lot of components to a door—which you find out by the time you finish hanging one.

THE INTERIOR TRIM AND MOLDING

If pre-hung doors are used, they already have the door casing installed. The interior trim involves mostly baseboard and window molding. If the molding is to be stained, stain it before it is installed.

Tear molding is the most reasonably-priced molding. It is easily installed and most people think it looks fine. One-by-threes can also be used to trim around the windows and for base molding. If the doors have a tear molding (most do), then this should also be used for the windows. A house lacks a sense of congruity if several types of molding are used.

THE FINISH GRADE

With all the above things accomplished, it is time to finish grade. This is best done before the carpet is laid, for obvious reasons. If possible, the yard should be sodded—it quickly eliminates a muddy and unfinished-looking situation. Sod can prevent erosion if the grade is steep. When the finish grade is done, make sure it is sculptured so that water is not retained near the house. Channels should be made so that water is kept clear of the house entirely.

THE CARPETING

The last thing to be done is to lay the carpet. Fiber pads offer greater durability and insulation value than the foam

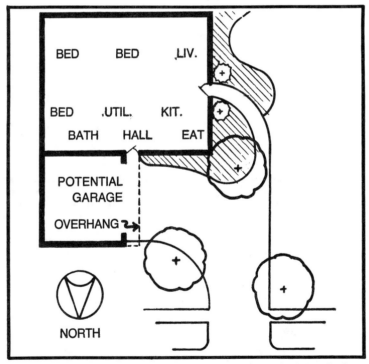

Fig. 15-31. Through the layout of the walkway, people can be led to the front door. A projecting overhang from a potential garage can provide a roof for the side door.

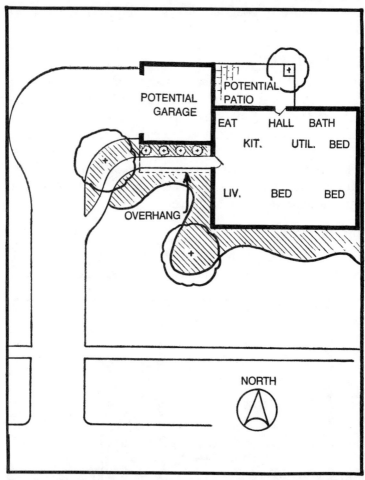

Fig. 15-32. Plantings, such as scrubs, can help define the front entrance to the house. With this plan, a doorwall off from the eating area can provide access onto the patio as well as an accent for the eating area and a view of the backyard from the living room. The patio is in a perfect location for those who like to eat outside. It is readily accessible from both the kitchen and eating area and is sheltered from the strong evening sun by the garage.

pads, so their use is suggested. On the concrete slab, a thick carpet pad is preferable since it offers good insulation value and a decent amount of cushion underfoot.

Carpeting should be laid so there are a minimum of seams. Seams are hard to construct so that they don't show. Generally they don't wear as well as the rest of the carpet. Wide rolls of carpeting should be obtained.

With the carpeting laid and everything else done, you're ready to move into your own little palace. It's time to lay back, look around, and enjoy what you've done! Figures 15-30 through 15-32 represent possible room layouts for homes.

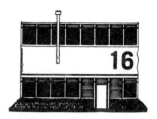

The 1980s Survival Cabin

Establishing even a simple shelter can be extremely costly in terms of both time and money, especially if aesthetics are a consideration (See Table 16-1 and Fig. 16-1). This design was planned around the following criteria in response to the needs of multitudes of people who want to build a low-cost shelter. It is a dwelling that can be built for about $2,000 and is adequate in size, is attractive from the outside and inside, is permanent, has fair insulation value, can be built easily by unskilled labor in about two weeks, can be built with only hand tools in areas without electricity, and can be improved easily at later dates. Yet it meets all applicable codes for the erection of a shell.

As unbelievable as it may seem, a person can still build a shelter for $2,000—and it will be attractive. Through the combining of several forms of construction, this 80's survival cabin may well be called a new form of architecture. It is an all-wood, post-frame, post and laminated beam, berm house. Outside of the glue-laminated beams, it is built entirely from treated wood, which guarantees longevity. It never needs painting or staining.

This type of building can serve many purposes besides providing basic shelter. It can be the basis for a weekend cabin or permanent shelter. This $2,000 unit can serve as a studio, workshop, garage, storage area, or as a combination of these things.

Before building one's permanent home, it is helpful to be aware of changes the land endures throughout the year. These changes include the varying position of the sun from winter to summer, the direction of prevailing weather, the direction of storm weather, the predominant wind velocity, the amount of rainfall, the direction and extent of drainage, and the locations of drifting snow and amount of snow build-up in colder climates. By building a cabin on the land that will hold your permanent home, you can observe and record these phenomena to achieve an efficient home design. While living in this cabin, you are more able to accumulate the needed money to build the eventual house since you have no rent payments.

This house is built out of natural materials and uses nature to its advantage by sensible solar and weather orientation and by using earth berms (mounds of dirt piled against the side of the house) to keep the floor warm. It is meant to be heated by a wood stove located near the building's center.

The design of this cabin was based around the following ideas: wood is the least expensive building material which offers an adequate amount of insulating value; the 2 × 6 tongue-and-groove is used because of its structural value, attractive appearance, and its easiness to use. By using treated wood, a more permanent structure is built for less money than through the use of untreated wood. Although this is not universally true, treated wood generally uses a less expensive species—resulting in a less expensive building material. And treated wood never needs painting. Through the use of laminated beams, the roof pitch can be built into the beams. In most areas, you can fabricate laminated beams for less money than solid beams would cost. By using the post-frame method, the posts provide the foundation and wall support for the structure, as well as holding up the laminated beams—meaning a simplified method of building and one in which no masonry foundation is required. By building a berm, the floor stays warm without the use of artificial and expen-

Table 16-1. Use this list when acquiring materials for building a survival cabin.

3,872 Board feet treated yellow pine 2×6 t&g @ $307/m (This equals 242 16' planks)	1,188
14 12 foot 4×4 treated posts @ 354/m	80
1 50# carton 16d coated nails	18
6 cases (60 tubes total) ½ barrel tubes Rely-on caulk @ .50/tube	30
13 yards fill sand delivered @ $4.00/yard	52
1 roll 10×100 foot 4 mil plastic	14
8 yards concrete delivered @ $33/yard	264
6 24 foot 2×10 fir @ 354/m	101
6 12 foot 2×10 yellow pine / $6.08/piece	37
2 12 foot 2×10 treated yellow pine @ $354/m	14
3 gusset plates	2
4 8 foot × 15¼ inch plate glass @ $3.00/square foot	120
1 ½ barrel tube silicone: clear	5
5 ½ barrel tubes construction adhesive	8
3 432 square foot rolls 15# felt	30
10 rolls 108 square feet roll roofing (65#)	100
1 5-gallon bucket plastic roof cement	10
1 50# carton 1 inch galvanized roofing nails	27
4 ⅜-inch diameter × 3 inch lag bolts	1
12 ¾ inch diameter × 8 inch hex-head bolts	12
1 power post-hole digger, rental	15
2 pounds 10d nails	1
6 pounds 50d spikes	4
	$2,133

sive materials. Besides, the berm uses leftover dirt that otherwise would have to be carried further; by using it against the structure, the dirt also promotes drainage.

The dimensions of this building are 24 feet by 31 feet 5½ inches. The floor area is approximately 750 square feet, which is the minimum allowable size for a home in most areas. The odd measurement 31 feet 5½ inches enables this entire structure to be built without trimming a single piece of tongue-and-groove—reducing waste and labor.

Location of this building should be where the ground is not too damp. The band of windows should face approximately southwest; the door should face the direction of prevailing weather. In this way, with the second door built in the adjacent wall and both doors open, there will be plenty of ventilation.

DETERMINE LOCATION

The approximate location of the building should be determined. The topsoil within the proposed building's perimeter should be scraped away. This soil can be placed just outside the building's perimeter, making its displacement relatively easy. For a building this small, the work may be done by hand, although a bulldozer is better if available.

A 13-yard load of sand serves as backfill for the posts, as both insulation for the slab and for leveling the area in

```
                          TOOLS

HANDSAW
½ BARREL CAULK GUN
CLAW HAMMER
(2) 50 FOOT TAPE MEASURES
MASONS' LINE
KNIFE
KEY-HOLE SAW
SHOVEL
LEVEL
POST-HOLE DIGGER (PREFERABLY GAS-POWERED)
METAL TROWEL
```

Fig. 16-1. These tools are needed for building the cabin.

preparation for the slab, and for helping build the berm. If a dozer is available, it can spread the sand within the building's perimeter.

After the sand is approximately leveled, the building's perimeter can be defined. It is imperative that exact measurements be made so that no trimming of the tongue-and-groove boards is needed. The front line of the building should be staked out. By pounding stakes into the ground and then hammering a nail into the butt end of the stake, the nail gives a place to attach a 50-foot tape measure. The third corner stake must be placed accurately to get a 90 degree angle. To do this, measure 24 feet down the side line and measure 39 feet 9/16 inches diagonally from the other front corner stake. At the point where these two measurements intersect, the third stake is placed. This same technique is used to locate the fourth corner stake.

With the tape measure attached to the nails in the stakes, the perimeter and diagonal measurements should be checked for exactness. The side post locations are then determined as specified by Fig. 16-2. Stakes should mark the locations.

Once the stakes are all secured, the holes can be dug. This process can easily be done by a rental gas-powered post hole digger, although soft ground may permit the use of a hand digger. The post depth should be at least 3 feet, preferably 3½ feet. The depth must be beneath the frost line (the berm counts as frost protection, too) and must reach firm soil capable of carrying the load which the building will impose upon it. The 3-foot depth, with the addition of the 18-inch berm is well below most areas' frost line.

The posts should have a footing to distribute the building's weight. This footing can consist of 6-inch deep poured concrete, a large flat stone, or a chunk of broken concrete. Whichever is most available should be used. The bottom of the hole must be smooth and clean of loose dirt. If the soil is not firm, the bottom of the hole should be belled out to allow for a larger footing. The builder should wait a day to set the posts if poured concrete is used.

The corner posts are first placed in the holes and braced to insure that the building is properly square. Slight adjust-

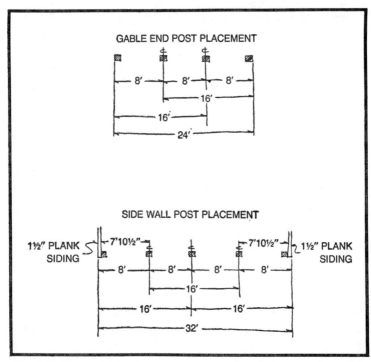

Fig. 16-2. The posts' locations are programmed so that no trimming of the 16-foot planks will have to occur.

ments are possible at this point and should be made if needed. These corner posts can be partially backfilled with sand once they are straight and plumb. The side posts can then be aligned and partially backfilled. Then tamp the sand fill into place with a 2 × 4. Once it is determined that the building is square and all posts are correctly positioned and plumb, the posts can be completely backfilled.

The sand is now finish-leveled inside the house and the area prepared for the slab. The first row of planking serves as the formwork for the concrete slab. It should be applied 3½ inches above the sand level. Make sure that this first row is applied level—so that the floor is level and the entire house will not be thrown off. Aside from the aesthetic disadvantage, this would complicate further construction.

A plastic membrane is spread out, forming the moisture barrier for the floor. A row of formwork must be set down the middle of the house. This height can be set by stringing a

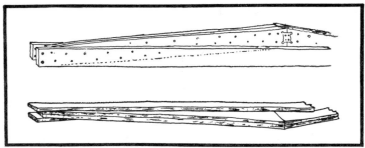

Fig. 16-3. This glulam beam has a built-in pitch. All four laminations are glued and nailed together. A gusset plate is used at its center.

line from the side planking. A screed board is used to level the concrete by riding it on the formwork "rails."

The slab should be allowed to cure at least a day, preferably two or three days. Since concrete does not gain total strength for 28 days, it should not be pounded upon for at least a week. While the slab is curing, though, the beams can be made. Figures 16-3 and 16-4 show the beam construction. Follow details such as the use of construction adhesive and the nailing scheme since these factors greatly increase the strength of the beam. Although the slab offers a great surface on which to fabricate the beams, it should not be used because it is not cured. The builder will have to find another

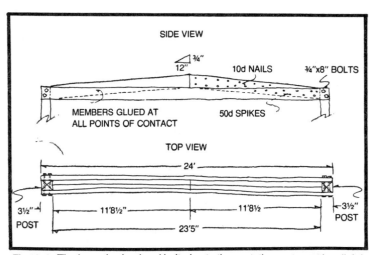

Fig.16-4 . The beam is glued and bolted onto the post; the post must be slightly notched to take the beam. If desired, a pronged gusset plate can be hidden between the two center laminations.

307

place to make the beams; besides, it is good to water down the slab every few hours, if convenient, to help it cure harder.

Once the beams are made and the slab has been given a chance to begin its cure, work can begin on the ends of the building, which should be sided first. Two 16d nails are used at each place a plank meets a post. The builder must make sure to seal between the planks by running a bead of caulk on the outerside of the plank's tongue. This caulk helps to seal the boards against the entrance of moisture and air. Although this cabin could be made without the caulk, it takes little material to properly seal the building. If you want to, a little extra caulk can be used and allowed to squeeze out the crack between the planks for the visual effect.

The building is dimensioned to enable the builder to install the planks without having any splices between the posts. The ends of each plank, then, will end on the posts. Apply the planks in a staggered pattern to tie the entire building together.

In the doors locations, which should hinge next to a post, instead of caulking the planks the area should receive a generous bead of construction adhesive. The doors are cut into the sides after the planking is completed. Through the use of a rip saw and a keyhole saw, the door can easily be cut. The bottom plank of the door should be cut before it is applied to create a starting point into which the saw can be inserted. After the hinge side of the door is cut, it can be hinged to the planking by the post. Door stops can be applied to the inside of the door casing. The 4-foot width for the door is to insure good ventilation.

When each gable end is completed to the height of the eave, the treated 2 × 10s are cut diagonally and set on top of the tongue-and-groove. The tongue must first be removed. These triangle pieces are bolted to the posts using lag bolts. The gable ends are then completed.

Strings tied between these gables locate the beam height. The posts must be marked at the proper height and notched to take the beams. The notch on each side of the post must only be ¼ inch deep. It can be done with a hand saw. The beams can now be bolted into place by using ¾-inch diameter bolts. Make sure that each side of the roof lies in one plane. Any adjustments should be made at this point before the beams are fully bolted. One bolt at each end of the beam will secure it while the straightness of the roof is being checked; it should then be glued and bolted securely.

The other sides can now receive the planking. Be sure to allow for the windows. The bottom plank, on which the window will rest, must be beveled (to provide a drip edge) before installation. This bevel, which can be done during the period the slab is curing, can be made with a saw, plane or knife. The sides are then completed to the height of the eaves.

If the posts protrude above the roof height, they should be cut flush with the top of the beams. The roof planking is then applied, starting at the point 145 inches from the roof ridge. This will allow for a 1 inch overhang while leaving the builder with a full board at the ridge of the roof. The roof's other side is then completed in the same way.

Once the roof planking is complete, it should be covered with felt. This quantity of felt can be overlapped more than 1 foot (to leave no waste) and should be started at the bottom of the roof pitch. The roll roofing is then applied over the felt; roofing adhesive is applied with a large stiff brush or paint roller where the roofing overlaps. With the 10 rolls of roofing material, this allows for a 9-inch overlap. The rolls of roofing material are 36 feet long, but the extra length need not be

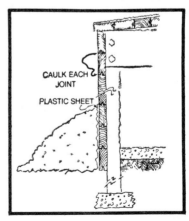

Fig. 16-5. A cut-away of the survival cabin. The plastic sheet's edge is secured in between two pieces of tongue-and-groove. An earth berm keeps the slab warm.

CAULK EACH JOINT

PLASTIC SHEET

used. Piecing roofing material is unwise since leaks are most likely to occur at spliced areas. The extra 4 feet is waste. At least one piece might be saved, though, in case it is needed for repair or alteration.

At all the seams and around the perimeter of the roof, a nail is used every 2 inches. Great care should be taken when hammering so as to not injure the roofing material. After all the nailing has been completed, the nails are covered with the remainder of the adhesive. Hot, dry days are excellent for working with this tar-based adhesive. Warm days allow for rapid and thin spreading of this material; the absence of moisture assures a good bond.

The seam where the roof boards meet the siding should now be caulked, as well as around the gable end. The windows can be set into place. Small nails can be bent to hold the window into place until the silicone sets. Run the silicone around the entire pane of glass (Fig. 16-5).

The berm can now be made. Ideally, there should be either sand or gravel next to the wood to keep it dry. As the berm is built, some sand or gravel can be secured next to the wood. The berm should be planted with a ground-cover to retain it. By the doors, rocks set on the berm will keep the dirt from washing away until the ground cover roots.

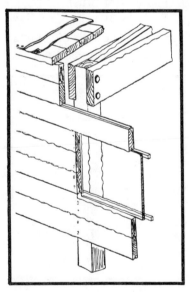

Fig. 16-6. Nice workmanship results in a nice cabin, and one that is easy to build. The plate glass fits into the groove above, with the plank it rests upon being beveled to provide water runoff. Small strips of wood can help secure the window when necessary. The removed tongue of the board at the top of the wall can serve this purpose .

Fig. 16-7. The completed cabin is cute and comfortable.

READY TO LIVE IN

The house is now ready to be occupied. Before winter begins, coat the roof with a tar-based roof coating. A paint roller works fine for this job. This will help the roof last longer and will prevent leaks. A wood stove will need to be installed; if money is scarce a stove can be made from a 55-gallon drum. A double-wall pipe should be used next to the roof to insulate the roof decking from the intense heat. These pipes can be easily made by combining different diameter pipes.

The floor can be insulated with used carpeting—much of which can be obtained through carpet installers. By using three layers of carpet, the slab floor is made as warm as a wood floor.

There are numerous improvements that can be added to this shelter. Primarily, though, it is intended to protect people from the elements. It is sufficient for keeping people warm and dry for a minimum amount of work and money. The simplicity of the structure makes it ideal for improvements, which can be done whenever you feel like it. The importance is not in the improvements that can be made; rather, the importance lies in lack of extraneous detail. You discover that we need little to survive (Figs. 16-6and 16-7).

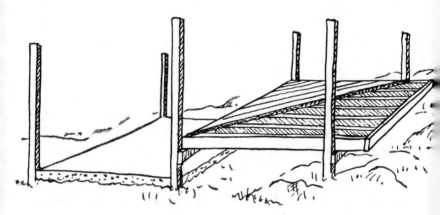

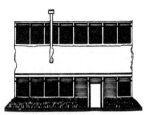

Charts & Tables

Table 17-1. This chart gives working stresses for joists and rafters. (Continued on pages 314-318.)

These "F_b" values are for use where repetitive members are spaced not more than 24 inches. For wider spacing, the "F_b" values should be reduced 13 percent.

Values for surfaced dry or surfaced green lumber apply at 19 percent maximum moisture content in use.

SPECIES AND GRADE	SIZE	ALLOWABLE UNIT STRESS IN BENDING "F_b"			MODULUS OF ELASTICITY "E" 1x10⁶ psi
		FLOOR MEMBERS	ROOF MEMBERS		
			SNOW LOADING	NO SNOW LOADING	
BALSAM FIR (Surfaced dry or surfaced green)					
Construction	2x4	800	920	1000	.9
Standard		450	520	560	.9
Utility		200	230	250	.9
Studs		600	690	750	.9
No. 1 & Appearance	2x6 and wider	1150	1320	1440	1.2
No. 2		950	1090	1190	1.1
No. 3		550	630	690	.9
CALIFORNIA REDWOOD (Surfaced dry or surfaced green)					
Construction	2x4	950	1090	1190	.9
Standard		550	630	690	.9
Utility		250	290	310	.9
Studs		700	800	880	.9
No. 1	2x6 and wider	1700	1960	2120	1.4
No. 1, Open grain		1350	1550	1690	1.1
No. 2		1400	1610	1750	1.3
No. 2, Open grain		1100	1260	1370	1.0
No. 3		800	920	1000	1.1
No. 3, Open grain		650	750	810	.9
DOUGLAS FIR—LARCH (Surfaced dry or surfaced green)					
Construction	2x4	1200	1380	1500	1.5
Standard		675	780	840	1.5
Utility		325	370	410	1.5
Studs		925	1060	1160	1.5
No. 1 & Appearance	2x6 and wider	1750	2010	2190	1.8
Dense No. 2		1700	1960	2120	1.7
No. 2		1450	1670	1810	1.7
No. 3		850	980	1060	1.5
DOUGLAS FIR SOUTH (Surfaced dry or surfaced green)					
Construction	2x4	1150	1320	1440	1.1
Standard		650	750	810	1.1
Utility		300	340	380	1.1
Studs		875	1010	1090	1.1
No. 1 & Appearance	2x6 and wider	1650	1900	2060	1.4
No. 2		1350	1550	1690	1.3
No. 3		800	920	1000	1.1
EASTERN HEMLOCK—TAMARACK (Surfaced dry or surfaced green)					
Construction	2x4	1050	1210	1310	1.0
Standard		575	660	720	1.0
Utility		275	320	340	1.0
Studs		800	920	1000	1.0
No. 1 & Appearance	2x6 and wider	1500	1720	1880	1.3
No. 2		1200	1380	1500	1.1
No. 3		725	830	910	1.0

Table 17-1. Working stresses for joists and rafters (continued).

| SPECIES AND GRADE | SIZE | ALLOWABLE UNIT STRESS IN BENDING "F_b" | | | MODULUS OF ELASTICITY "E" 1×10^6 psi |
| | | FLOOR MEMBERS | ROOF MEMBERS | | |
			SNOW LOADING	NO SNOW LOADING	
EASTERN SPRUCE (Surfaced dry or surfaced green)					
Construction		875	1010	1090	1.1
Standard	2x4	500	580	620	1.1
Utility		225	260	280	1.1
Studs		675	780	840	1.1
No. 1 & Appearance	2x6	1250	1440	1560	1.4
No. 2	and	1000	1150	1250	1.2
No. 3	wider	600	690	750	1.1
EASTERN WHITE PINE (Surfaced dry or surfaced green)					
Construction		800	920	1000	1.0
Standard	2x4	450	520	560	1.0
Utility		200	230	250	1.0
Studs		600	690	750	1.0
ENGELMANN SPRUCE (ENGELMANN SPRUCE—LODGEPOLE PINE) (Surfaced dry or surfaced green)					
Construction		775	890	970	1.0
Standard	2x4	425	490	530	1.0
Utility		200	230	250	1.0
Studs		600	690	750	1.0
No. 1 & Appearance	2x6	1150	1320	1440	1.2
No. 2	and	925	1060	1160	1.1
No. 3	wider	550	630	690	1.0
HEM—FIR (Surfaced dry or surfaced green)					
Construction		975	1120	1220	1.2
Standard	2x4	525	600	660	1.2
Utility		250	290	310	1.2
Studs		725	830	910	1.2
No. 1 & Appearance	2x6	1400	1610	1750	1.5
No. 2	and	1150	1320	1440	1.4
No. 3	wider	675	780	840	1.2
IDAHO WHITE PINE (Surfaced dry or surfaced green)					
Construction		850	980	1060	1.1
Standard	2x4	475	550	590	1.1
Utility		225	260	280	1.1
Studs		650	750	810	1.1
No. 1 & Appearance	2x6	1200	1380	1500	1.4
No. 2	and	1000	1150	1250	1.3
No. 3	wider	575	660	720	1.1
LODGEPOLE PINE (Surfaced dry or surfaced green)					
Construction		875	1010	1090	1.0
Standard	2x4	500	580	620	1.0
Utility		225	260	280	1.0
Studs		675	780	840	1.0
Select Structural	2x6	1500	1720	1880	1.3
No. 1 & Appearance	and	1300	1500	1620	1.3
No. 2	wider	1050	1210	1310	1.2
No. 3		625	720	780	1.0

Table 17-1. Working stresses for joists and rafters (continued).

SPECIES AND GRADE	SIZE	ALLOWABLE UNIT STRESS IN BENDING "F_b"			MODULUS OF ELASTICITY "E" 1x10⁶ psi
		FLOOR MEMBERS	ROOF MEMBERS		
			SNOW LOADING	NO SNOW LOADING	
MOUNTAIN HEMLOCK (Surfaced dry or surfaced green)					
Construction	2x4	1000	1150	1250	1.0
Standard		575	660	720	1.0
Utility		275	320	340	1.0
Studs		775	890	970	1.0
No. 1 & Appearance	2x6	1450	1670	1810	1.3
No. 2	and	1200	1380	1500	1.1
No. 3	wider	700	800	880	1.0
MOUNTAIN HEMLOCK—HEM—FIR (Surfaced dry or surfaced green)					
Construction	2x4	975	1120	1220	1.0
Standard		550	630	690	1.0
Utility		250	290	310	1.0
Studs		750	860	940	1.0
No. 1 & Appearance	2x6	1400	1610	1750	1.3
No. 2	and	1150	1320	1440	1.1
No. 3	wider	675	780	840	1.0
NORTHERN PINE (Surfaced dry or surfaced green)					
Construction	2x4	950	1090	1190	1.1
Standard		525	600	660	1.1
Utility		250	290	310	1.1
Studs		725	830	910	1.1
No. 1 & Appearance	2x6	1400	1610	1750	1.4
No. 2	and	1100	1260	1380	1.3
No. 3	wider	650	750	810	1.1
NORTHERN WHITE CEDAR (Surfaced dry or surfaced green)					
Construction	2x4	675	780	840	.6
Standard		375	430	470	.6
Utility		175	200	220	.6
Studs		525	600	660	.6
No. 1 & Appearance	2x6	1000	1150	1250	.8
No. 2	and	825	950	1030	.7
No. 3	wider	475	550	590	.6
PONDEROSA PINE—SUGAR PINE (PONDEROSA PINE—LODGEPOLE PINE) (Surfaced dry or surfaced green)					
Construction	2x4	825	950	1030	1.0
Standard		450	520	560	1.0
Utility		225	260	280	1.0
Studs		625	720	780	1.0
No. 1 & Appearance	2x6	1200	1380	1500	1.2
No. 2	and	975	1120	1220	1.1
No. 3	wider	575	660	720	1.0
SITKA SPRUCE (Surfaced dry or surfaced green)					
Construction	2x4	925	1060	1160	1.2
Standard		500	580	620	1.2
Utility		250	290	310	1.2
Studs		700	800	880	1.2

Table 17-1. Working stresses for joists and rafters (continued).

SPECIES AND GRADE	SIZE	ALLOWABLE UNIT STRESS IN BENDING "F_b"			MODULUS OF ELASTICITY "E" 1x10⁶ psi
		FLOOR MEMBERS	ROOF MEMBERS		
			SNOW LOADING	NO SNOW LOADING	
SITKA SPRUCE (Surfaced dry or surfaced green) Con't.					
No. 1 & Appearance	2x6	1300	1500	1620	1.5
No. 2	and	1050	1210	1310	1.3
No. 3	wider	600	690	750	1.2
SOUTHERN PINE (Surfaced dry)					
Construction		1200	1380	1500	1.4
Standard	2x4	700	800	880	1.4
Utility		325	375	410	1.4
Studs		950	1090	1190	1.4
No. 1		1750	2010	2190	1.8
No. 1 Dense		2050	2380	2590	1.9
No. 2	2x6	1200	1380	1500	1.4
No. 2 MG	and	1450	1670	1810	1.6
No. 2 Dense	wider	1650	1900	2060	1.7
No. 3		825	950	1030	1.4
No. 3 Dense		975	1120	1220	1.5
SUBALPINE FIR (WHITE WOODS) (WESTERN WOODS) (Surfaced dry or surfaced green)					
Construction		725	830	910	.8
Standard	2x4	400	460	500	.8
Utility		200	230	250	.8
Studs		550	630	690	.8
No. 1 & Appearance	2x6	1050	1210	1310	.9
No. 2	and	850	980	1060	.9
No. 3	wider	500	580	620	.8
WESTERN CEDARS (Surfaced dry or surfaced green)					
Construction		850	960	1060	.9
Standard	2x4	475	550	590	.9
Utility		225	260	280	.9
Studs		650	750	810	.9
No. 1 & Appearance	2x6	1250	1440	1560	1.1
No. 2	and	1000	1150	1250	1.0
No. 3	wider	600	690	750	.9
COAST SITKA SPRUCE (Surfaced dry or surfaced green)					
Construction		875	1010	1090	1.3
Standard	2x4	500	580	630	1.3
Utility		225	260	280	1.3
Stud		675	780	840	1.3
No. 1	2x6	1250	1440	1560	1.7
No. 2	and	1050	1210	1310	1.5
No. 3	wider	600	690	750	1.3
Appearance		1250	1440	1560	1.7
DOUGLAS FIR—LARCH (NORTH) (Surfaced dry or surfaced green)					
Construction		1200	1380	1500	1.5
Standard	2x4	675	780	840	1.5
Utility		325	370	410	1.5
Stud		925	1060	1160	1.5

Table 17-1. Working stresses for joists and rafters (continued).

SPECIES AND GRADE	SIZE	ALLOWABLE UNIT STRESS IN BENDING "F$_b$"			MODULUS OF ELASTICITY "E" 1x10^6 psi
		FLOOR MEMBERS	ROOF MEMBERS		
			SNOW LOADING	NO SNOW LOADING	
DOUGLAS FIR—LARCH (NORTH) (Surfaced dry or surfaced green) Con't.					
Dense No. 1		2050	2360	2560	1.9
No. 1	2x6	1750	2010	2190	1.8
Dense No. 2	and	1700	1960	2120	1.7
No. 2	wider	1450	1670	1810	1.7
No. 3		850	980	1060	1.5
Appearance		1750	2010	2190	1.8
EASTERN HEMLOCK—TAMARACK (NORTH) (Surfaced dry or surfaced green)					
Construction		1050	1210	1310	1.0
Standard	2x4	575	660	720	1.0
Utility		275	320	340	1.0
Stud		800	920	1000	1.0
No. 1	2x6	1500	1720	1880	1.3
No. 2	and	1200	1380	1500	1.1
No. 3	wider	725	830	910	1.0
Appearance		1500	1720	1880	1.3
EASTERN WHITE PINE (NORTH) (Surfaced dry or surfaced green)					
Construction		800	920	1000	1.0
Standard	2x4	450	520	560	1.0
Utility		200	230	250	1.0
Stud		600	690	750	1.0
HEM—FIR (NORTH) (Surfaced dry or surfaced green)					
Construction		950	1090	1190	1.2
Standard	2x4	525	600	660	1.2
Utility		250	290	310	1.2
Stud		725	830	910	1.2
No. 1	2x6	1400	1610	1750	1.5
No. 2	and	1150	1320	1440	1.4
No. 3	wider	675	780	840	1.2
Appearance		1400	1610	1750	1.5
PONDEROSA PINE (Surfaced dry or surfaced green)					
Construction		825	950	1030	1.0
Standard	2x4	450	520	560	1.0
Utility		225	260	280	1.0
Stud		625	720	780	1.0
No. 1	2x6	1200	1380	1500	1.2
No. 2	and	975	1120	1220	1.1
No. 3	wider	575	660	720	1.0
Appearance		1200	1380	1500	1.2
RED PINE (Surfaced dry or surfaced green)					
Construction		800	920	1000	1.0
Standard	2x4	450	520	560	1.0
Utility		225	260	280	1.0
Stud		625	720	780	1.0
No. 1	2x6	1150	1320	1440	1.3
No. 2	and	950	1090	1190	1.2
No. 3	wider	550	630	690	1.0
Appearance		1150	1320	1440	· 1.3

Table 17-1. Working stresses for joists and rafters (continued).

SPECIES AND GRADE	SIZE	ALLOWABLE UNIT STRESS IN BENDING "F_b"			MODULUS OF ELASTICITY "E" 1×10^6 psi
		FLOOR MEMBERS	ROOF MEMBERS		
			SNOW LOADING	NO SNOW LOADING	
SPRUCE—PINE—FIR (Surfaced dry or surfaced green)					
Construction	2x4	850	980	1060	1.2
Standard		475	550	590	1.2
Utility		225	260	280	1.2
Stud		650	750	810	1.2
No. 1	2x6 and wider	1200	1380	1500	1.5
No. 2		1000	1150	1250	1.3
No. 3		575	660	720	1.2
Appearance		1200	1380	1500	1.5
WESTERN CEDARS (NORTH) (Surfaced dry or surfaced green)					
Construction	2x4	850	980	1060	.9
Standard		475	550	590	.9
Utility		225	260	280	.9
Stud		650	750	810	.9
No. 1	2x6 and wider	1250	1440	1560	1.1
No. 2		1000	1150	1250	1.0
No. 3		600	690	750	.9
Appearance		1250	1440	1560	1.1
WESTERN WHITE PINE (Surfaced dry or surfaced green)					
Construction	2x4	775	890	970	1.2
Standard		425	490	530	1.2
Utility		200	230	250	1.2
Stud		600	690	750	1.2
No. 1	2x6 and wider	1150	1320	1440	1.4
No. 2		925	1060	1160	1.3
No. 3		550	630	690	1.2
Appearance		1150	1320	1440	1.4

Tables 17-1 through 17-11 are courtesy of the International Conference of Building Officials.

Table 17-2. Use this table to find allowable spans for floor joists at 40 pounds per square foot live load.

DESIGN CRITERIA: Deflection - For 40 lbs. per sq. ft. live load. Limited to span in inches divided by 360. Strength - Live load of 40 lbs. per sq. ft. plus dead load of 10 lbs. per sq. ft. determines the required fiber stress value.

JOIST SIZE	SPACING (IN)	Modulus of Elasticity, "E", in 1,000,000 psi													
		0.8	0.9	1.0	1.1	1.2	1.3	1.4	1.5	1.6	1.7	1.8	1.9	2.0	2.2
2x6	12.0	8-6 720	8-10 780	9-2 830	9-6 880	9-9 940	10-0 990	10-3 1040	10-6 1090	10-9 1140	10-11 1190	11-2 1230	11-4 1280	11-7 1320	11-11 1410
	16.0	7-9 790	8-0 860	8-4 920	8-7 980	8-10 1040	9-1 1090	9-4 1150	9-6 1200	9-9 1250	9-11 1310	10-2 1360	10-4 1410	10-6 1460	10-10 1550
	24.0	6-9 900	7-0 980	7-3 1050	7-6 1120	7-9 1190	7-11 1250	8-2 1310	8-4 1380	8-6 1440	8-8 1500	8-10 1550	9-0 1610	9-2 1670	9-6 1780
2x8	12.0	11-3 720	11-8 780	12-1 830	12-6 890	12-10 940	13-2 990	13-6 1040	13-10 1090	14-2 1140	14-5 1190	14-8 1230	15-0 1280	15-3 1320	15-9 1410
	16.0	10-2 790	10-7 850	11-0 920	11-4 980	11-8 1040	12-0 1090	12-3 1150	12-7 1200	12-10 1250	13-1 1310	13-4 1360	13-7 1410	13-10 1460	14-3 1550
	24.0	8-11 900	9-3 980	9-7 1050	9-11 1120	10-2 1190	10-6 1250	10-9 1310	11-0 1380	11-3 1440	11-5 1500	11-8 1550	11-11 1610	12-1 1670	12-6 1780
2x10	12.0	14-4 720	14-11 780	15-5 830	15-11 890	16-5 940	16-10 990	17-3 1040	17-8 1090	18-0 1140	18-5 1190	18-9 1230	19-1 1280	19-5 1320	20-1 1410
	16.0	13-0 790	13-6 850	14-0 920	14-6 980	14-11 1040	15-3 1090	15-8 1150	16-0 1200	16-5 1250	16-9 1310	17-0 1360	17-4 1410	17-8 1460	18-3 1550
	24.0	11-4 900	11-10 980	12-3 1050	12-8 1120	13-0 1190	13-4 1250	13-8 1310	14-0 1380	14-4 1440	14-7 1500	14-11 1550	15-2 1610	15-5 1670	15-11 1780
2x12	12.0	17-5 720	18-1 780	18-9 830	19-4 890	19-11 940	20-6 990	21-0 1040	21-6 1090	21-11 1140	22-5 1190	22-10 1230	23-3 1280	23-7 1320	24-5 1410
	16.0	15-10 790	16-5 860	17-0 920	17-7 980	18-1 1040	18-7 1090	19-1 1150	19-6 1200	19-11 1250	20-4 1310	20-9 1360	21-1 1410	21-6 1460	22-2 1550
	24.0	13-10 900	14-4 980	14-11 1050	15-4 1120	15-10 1190	16-3 1250	16-8 1310	17-0 1380	17-5 1440	17-9 1500	18-1 1550	18-5 1610	18-9 1670	19-4 1780

[1] The required extreme fiber stress in bending, F_b, in pounds per square inch is shown below each span.

[2] Use single or repetitive member bending stress values (F_b) and modules of elasticity values (E), from Table No. 25-A-1.

[3] For more comprehensive tables covering a broader range of bending stress values (F_b) and Modulus of Elasticity values (E), other spacing of members, and other conditions of loading, see the Uniform Building Code.

[4] The spans in these tables are intended 'or use in covered structures or where moisture content in use does not exceed 19 percent.

319

Table 17-3. Shown are allowable spans for ceiling joists at 10 pound per square foot live load.

DESIGN CRITERIA: Deflection - For 10 lbs. per sq. ft. live load. Limited to span in inches divided by 240. Strength - Live load of 10 lbs. per sq. ft. plus dead load of 5 lbs. per sq. ft. determines required fiber stress value.

JOIST SIZE (IN)	SPACING (IN)	Modulus of Elasticity, "E", in 1,000,000 psi													
		0.8	0.9	1.0	1.1	1.2	1.3	1.4	1.5	1.6	1.7	1.8	1.9	2.0	2.2
2x4	12.0	9-10 / 710	10-3 / 770	10-7 / 830	10-11 / 880	11-3 / 930	11-7 / 980	11-10 / 1030	12-2 / 1080	12-5 / 1130	12-8 / 1180	12-11 / 1220	13-2 / 1270	13-4 / 1310	13-9 / 1400
	16.0	8-11 / 780	9-4 / 850	9-8 / 910	9-11 / 970	10-3 / 1030	10-6 / 1080	10-9 / 1140	11-0 / 1190	11-3 / 1240	11-6 / 1290	11-9 / 1340	11-11 / 1390	12-2 / 1440	12-6 / 1540
	24.0	7-10 / 900	8-1 / 970	8-5 / 1040	8-8 / 1110	8-11 / 1170	9-2 / 1240	9-5 / 1300	9-8 / 1360	9-10 / 1420	10-0 / 1480	10-3 / 1540	10-5 / 1600	10-7 / 1650	10-11 / 1760
2x6	12.0	15-6 / 710	16-1 / 770	16-8 / 830	17-2 / 880	17-8 / 930	18-2 / 980	18-8 / 1030	19-1 / 1080	19-6 / 1130	19-11 / 1180	20-3 / 1220	20-8 / 1270	21-0 / 1310	21-8 / 1400
	16.0	14-1 / 780	14-7 / 850	15-2 / 910	15-7 / 970	16-1 / 1030	16-6 / 1080	16-11 / 1140	17-4 / 1190	17-8 / 1240	18-1 / 1290	18-5 / 1340	18-9 / 1390	19-1 / 1440	19-8 / 1540
	24.0	12-3 / 900	12-9 / 970	13-3 / 1040	13-8 / 1110	14-1 / 1170	14-5 / 1240	14-9 / 1300	15-2 / 1360	15-6 / 1420	15-9 / 1480	16-1 / 1540	16-4 / 1600	16-8 / 1650	17-2 / 1760
2x8	12.0	20-5 / 710	21-2 / 770	21-11 / 830	22-8 / 880	23-4 / 930	24-0 / 980	24-7 / 1030	25-2 / 1080	25-8 / 1130	26-2 / 1180	26-9 / 1220	27-2 / 1270	27-8 / 1310	28-7 / 1400
	16.0	18-6 / 780	19-3 / 850	19-11 / 910	20-7 / 970	21-2 / 1030	21-9 / 1080	22-4 / 1140	22-10 / 1190	23-4 / 1240	23-10 / 1290	24-3 / 1340	24-8 / 1390	25-2 / 1440	25-11 / 1540
	24.0	16-2 / 900	16-10 / 970	17-5 / 1040	18-0 / 1110	18-6 / 1170	19-0 / 1240	19-6 / 1300	19-11 / 1360	20-5 / 1420	20-10 / 1480	21-2 / 1540	21-7 / 1600	21-11 / 1650	22-8 / 1760
2x10	12.0	26-0 / 710	27-1 / 770	28-0 / 830	28-11 / 880	29-9 / 930	30-7 / 980	31-4 / 1030	32-1 / 1080	32-9 / 1130	33-5 / 1180	34-1 / 1220	34-8 / 1270	35-4 / 1310	36-5 / 1400
	16.0	23-8 / 780	24-7 / 850	25-5 / 910	26-3 / 970	27-1 / 1030	27-9 / 1080	28-6 / 1140	29-2 / 1190	29-9 / 1240	30-5 / 1290	31-0 / 1340	31-6 / 1390	32-1 / 1440	33-1 / 1540
	24.0	20-8 / 900	21-6 / 970	22-3 / 1040	22-11 / 1110	23-8 / 1170	24-3 / 1240	24-10 / 1300	25-5 / 1360	26-0 / 1420	26-6 / 1480	27-1 / 1540	27-6 / 1600	28-0 / 1650	28-11 / 1760

[1]The required extreme fiber stress in bending, F_b, in pounds per square inch is shown below each span.

[2]Use single or repetitive member bending stress values (F_b) and modulus of elasticity values (E), from Table No. 25-A-1.

[3]For more comprehensive tables covering a broader range of bending stress values (F_b) and Modulus of Elasticity values (E), other spacing of members and other conditions of loading, see the Uniform Building Code.

[4]The spans in these tables are intended for use in covered structures or where moisture content in use does not exceed 19 percent.

Table 17-4. The table lists allowable spans for low or high slope rafters at 20 pounds per square foot live load.

DESIGN CRITERIA: Strength - 15 lbs. per sq. ft. dead load plus 20 lbs. per sq. ft. live load determines required fiber stress. Deflection - For 20 lbs. per sq. ft. live load. Limited to span in inches divided by 240. RAFTERS: Spans are measured along the horizontal projection and loads are considered as applied on the horizontal projection.

Allowable Extreme Fiber Stress in Bending, "F_b" (psi).

Each cell lists allowable span (feet–inches) over required modulus of elasticity E (in $1{,}000{,}000$ psi).

Rafter Size (in)	Spacing (in)	500	600	700	800	900	1000	1100	1200	1300	1400	1500	1600	1700	1800	1900
2x6	12.0	8-6 / 0.26	9-4 / 0.35	10-0 / 0.44	10-9 / 0.54	11-5 / 0.64	12-0 / 0.75	12-7 / 0.86	13-2 / 0.98	13-8 / 1.11	14-2 / 1.24	14-8 / 1.37	15-2 / 1.51	15-8 / 1.66	16-1 / 1.81	16-7 / 1.96
2x6	16.0	7-4 / 0.23	8-1 / 0.30	8-8 / 0.38	9-4 / 0.46	9-10 / 0.55	10-5 / 0.65	10-11 / 0.75	11-5 / 0.85	11-10 / 0.97	12-4 / 1.07	12-9 / 1.19	13-2 / 1.31	13-7 / 1.44	13-11 / 1.56	14-4 / 1.70
2x6	24.0	6-0 / 0.19	6-7 / 0.25	7-1 / 0.31	7-7 / 0.38	8-1 / 0.45	8-6 / 0.53	8-11 / 0.61	9-4 / 0.70	9-8 / 0.78	10-0 / 0.88	10-5 / 0.97	10-9 / 1.07	11-1 / 1.17	11-5 / 1.28	11-8 / 1.39
2x8	12.0	11-2 / 0.26	12-3 / 0.35	13-3 / 0.44	14-2 / 0.54	15-0 / 0.64	15-10 / 0.75	16-7 / 0.86	17-4 / 0.98	18-0 / 1.11	18-9 / 1.24	19-5 / 1.37	20-0 / 1.51	20-8 / 1.66	21-3 / 1.81	21-10 / 1.96
2x8	16.0	9-8 / 0.23	10-7 / 0.30	11-6 / 0.38	12-3 / 0.46	13-0 / 0.55	13-8 / 0.65	14-4 / 0.75	15-0 / 0.85	15-7 / 0.96	16-3 / 1.07	16-9 / 1.19	17-4 / 1.31	17-10 / 1.44	18-5 / 1.56	18-11 / 1.70
2x8	24.0	7-11 / 0.19	8-8 / 0.25	9-4 / 0.31	10-0 / 0.38	10-7 / 0.45	11-2 / 0.53	11-9 / 0.61	12-3 / 0.70	12-9 / 0.78	13-3 / 0.88	13-8 / 0.97	14-2 / 1.07	14-7 / 1.17	15-0 / 1.28	15-5 / 1.39
2x10	12.0	14-3 / 0.26	15-8 / 0.35	16-11 / 0.44	18-1 / 0.54	19-2 / 0.64	20-2 / 0.75	21-2 / 0.86	22-1 / 0.98	23-0 / 1.11	23-11 / 1.24	24-9 / 1.37	25-6 / 1.51	26-4 / 1.66	27-1 / 1.81	27-10 / 1.96
2x10	16.0	12-4 / 0.23	13-6 / 0.30	14-8 / 0.38	15-8 / 0.46	16-7 / 0.55	17-6 / 0.65	18-4 / 0.75	19-2 / 0.85	19-11 / 0.96	20-8 / 1.07	21-5 / 1.19	22-1 / 1.31	22-10 / 1.44	23-5 / 1.56	24-1 / 1.70
2x10	24.0	10-1 / 0.19	11-1 / 0.25	11-11 / 0.31	12-9 / 0.38	13-6 / 0.45	14-3 / 0.53	15-0 / 0.61	15-8 / 0.70	16-3 / 0.78	16-11 / 0.88	17-6 / 0.97	18-1 / 1.07	18-7 / 1.17	19-2 / 1.28	19-8 / 1.39
2x12	12.0	17-4 / 0.26	19-0 / 0.35	20-6 / 0.44	21-11 / 0.54	23-3 / 0.64	24-7 / 0.75	25-9 / 0.86	26-11 / 0.98	28-0 / 1.11	29-1 / 1.24	30-1 / 1.37	31-1 / 1.51	32-0 / 1.66	32-11 / 1.81	33-10 / 1.96
2x12	16.0	15-0 / 0.23	16-6 / 0.30	17-9 / 0.38	19-0 / 0.46	20-2 / 0.55	21-3 / 0.65	22-4 / 0.75	23-3 / 0.85	24-3 / 0.97	25-2 / 1.07	26-0 / 1.19	26-11 / 1.31	27-9 / 1.44	28-6 / 1.56	29-4 / 1.70
2x12	24.0	12-3 / 0.19	13-5 / 0.25	14-6 / 0.31	15-6 / 0.38	16-6 / 0.45	17-4 / 0.53	18-2 / 0.61	19-0 / 0.70	19-10 / 0.78	20-6 / 0.88	21-3 / 0.97	21-11 / 1.07	22-8 / 1.17	23-3 / 1.28	23-11 / 1.39

[1] The required modulus of elasticity, E, in $1{,}000{,}000$ pounds per square inch is shown below each span.

[2] Use single or repetitive member bending stress values (F_b) and modulus of elasticity values (E), from Table No. 25-A-1.

[3] For more comprehensive tables covering a broader range of bending stress values (F_b) and Modulus of Elasticity values (E), other spacing of members and other conditions of loading, see the Uniform Building Code.

[4] The spans in these tables are intended for use in covered structures or where moisture content in use does not exceed 19 percent.

321

Table 17-5. Here are more allowable spans for low or high slope rafters at 30 pounds per square foot live load.

DESIGN CRITERIA: Strength - 15 lbs. per sq. ft. dead load plus 30 lbs. per sq. ft. live load determines required fiber stress. Deflection - For 30 lbs. per sq. ft. live load. Limited to span in inches divided by 240. RAFTERS: Spans are measured along the horizontal projection and loads are considered as applied on the horizontal projection.

RAFTER SIZE (IN)	SPACING (IN)	Allowable Extreme Fiber Stress in Bending, "F_b" (psi)														
		500	600	700	800	900	1000	1100	1200	1300	1400	1500	1600	1700	1800	1900
2x6	12.0	7-6 / 0.27	8-2 / 0.36	8-10 / 0.45	9-6 / 0.55	10-0 / 0.66	10-7 / 0.77	11-1 / 0.89	11-7 / 1.01	12-1 / 1.14	12-6 / 1.28	13-0 / 1.41	13-5 / 1.56	13-10 / 1.71	14-2 / 1.86	14-7 / 2.02
	16.0	6-6 / 0.24	7-1 / 0.31	7-8 / 0.39	8-2 / 0.48	8-8 / 0.57	9-2 / 0.67	9-7 / 0.77	10-0 / 0.88	10-5 / 0.99	10-10 / 1.10	11-3 / 1.22	11-7 / 1.35	11-11 / 1.48	12-4 / 1.61	12-8 / 1.75
	24.0	5-4 / 0.19	5-10 / 0.25	6-3 / 0.32	6-8 / 0.39	7-1 / 0.46	7-6 / 0.54	7-10 / 0.63	8-2 / 0.72	8-6 / 0.81	8-10 / 0.90	9-2 / 1.00	9-6 / 1.10	9-9 / 1.21	10-0 / 1.31	10-4 / 1.43
2x8	12.0	9-10 / 0.27	10-10 / 0.36	11-8 / 0.45	12-6 / 0.55	13-3 / 0.66	13-11 / 0.77	14-8 / 0.89	15-3 / 1.01	15-11 / 1.14	16-6 / 1.28	17-1 / 1.41	17-8 / 1.56	18-2 / 1.71	18-9 / 1.86	19-3 / 2.02
	16.0	8-7 / 0.24	9-4 / 0.31	10-1 / 0.39	10-10 / 0.48	11-6 / 0.57	12-1 / 0.67	12-8 / 0.77	13-3 / 0.88	13-9 / 0.99	14-4 / 1.10	14-10 / 1.22	15-3 / 1.35	15-9 / 1.48	16-3 / 1.61	16-8 / 1.75
	24.0	7-0 / 0.19	7-8 / 0.25	8-3 / 0.32	8-10 / 0.39	9-4 / 0.46	9-10 / 0.54	10-4 / 0.63	10-10 / 0.72	11-3 / 0.81	11-8 / 0.90	12-1 / 1.00	12-6 / 1.10	12-10 / 1.21	13-3 / 1.31	13-7 / 1.43
2x10	12.0	12-7 / 0.27	13-9 / 0.36	14-11 / 0.45	15-11 / 0.55	16-11 / 0.66	17-10 / 0.77	18-8 / 0.89	19-6 / 1.01	20-4 / 1.14	21-1 / 1.28	21-10 / 1.41	22-6 / 1.56	23-3 / 1.71	23-11 / 1.86	24-6 / 2.02
	16.0	10-11 / 0.24	11-11 / 0.31	12-11 / 0.39	13-9 / 0.48	14-8 / 0.57	15-5 / 0.67	16-2 / 0.77	16-11 / 0.88	17-7 / 0.99	18-3 / 1.10	18-11 / 1.22	19-6 / 1.35	20-1 / 1.48	20-8 / 1.61	21-3 / 1.75
	24.0	8-11 / 0.19	9-9 / 0.25	10-6 / 0.32	11-3 / 0.39	11-11 / 0.46	12-7 / 0.54	13-2 / 0.63	13-9 / 0.72	14-4 / 0.81	14-11 / 0.90	15-5 / 1.00	15-11 / 1.10	16-5 / 1.21	16-11 / 1.31	17-4 / 1.43
2x12	12.0	15-4 / 0.27	16-9 / 0.36	18-1 / 0.45	19-4 / 0.55	20-6 / 0.66	21-8 / 0.77	22-8 / 0.89	23-9 / 1.01	24-8 / 1.14	25-7 / 1.28	26-6 / 1.41	27-5 / 1.56	28-3 / 1.71	29-1 / 1.86	29-10 / 2.02
	16.0	13-3 / 0.24	14-6 / 0.31	15-8 / 0.39	16-9 / 0.48	17-9 / 0.57	18-9 / 0.67	19-8 / 0.77	20-6 / 0.88	21-5 / 0.99	22-2 / 1.10	23-0 / 1.22	23-9 / 1.35	24-5 / 1.48	25-2 / 1.61	25-10 / 1.75
	24.0	10-10 / 0.19	11-10 / 0.25	12-10 / 0.32	13-8 / 0.39	14-6 / 0.46	15-4 / 0.54	16-1 / 0.63	16-9 / 0.72	17-5 / 0.81	18-1 / 0.90	18-9 / 1.00	19-4 / 1.10	20-0 / 1.21	20-6 / 1.31	21-1 / 1.43

[1] The required modulus of elasticity, E, in 1,000,000 pounds per square inch is shown below each span.

[2] Use single or repetitive member bending stress values (F_b) and modulus of elasticity values (E), from Table No. 25-A-1.

[3] For more comprehensive tables covering a broader range of bending stress values (F_b) and Modulus of Elasticity values (E), other spacing of members and other conditions of loading, see the Uniform Building Code.

[4] The spans in these tables are intended for use in covered structures or where moisture content in use does not exceed 19 percent.

Table 17-6. The chart gives allowable spans for low slope rafters with a slope 3 in 12 or less at 30 pounds per square foot live load.

DESIGN CRITERIA: Strength - 10 lbs. per sq. ft. dead load plus 20 lbs. per sq. ft. live load determines required fiber stress. Deflection - For 20 lbs. per sq. ft. live load. Limited to span in inches divided by 240. RAFTERS: Spans are measured along the horizontal projection and loads are considered as applied on the horizontal projection.

Allowable Extreme Fiber Stress in Bending, "F_b" (psi).

RAFTER SIZE (IN)	SPACING (IN)	500	600	700	800	900	1000	1100	1200	1300	1400	1500	1600	1700	1800	1900
2x6	12.0	9-2 / 0.33	10-0 / 0.44	10-10 / 0.55	11-7 / 0.67	12-4 / 0.80	13-0 / 0.94	13-7 / 1.09	14-2 / 1.24	14-9 / 1.40	15-4 / 1.56	15-11 / 1.73	16-5 / 1.91	16-11 / 2.09	17-5 / 2.28	17-10 / 2.47
	16.0	7-11 / 0.29	8-8 / 0.38	9-5 / 0.48	10-0 / 0.58	10-8 / 0.70	11-3 / 0.82	11-9 / 0.94	12-4 / 1.07	12-10 / 1.21	13-3 / 1.35	13-9 / 1.50	14-2 / 1.65	14-8 / 1.81	15-1 / 1.97	15-6 / 2.14
	24.0	6-6 / 0.24	7-1 / 0.31	7-8 / 0.39	8-2 / 0.48	8-8 / 0.57	9-2 / 0.67	9-7 / 0.77	10-0 / 0.88	10-5 / 0.99	10-10 / 1.10	11-3 / 1.22	11-7 / 1.35	11-11 / 1.48	12-4 / 1.61	12-8 / 1.75
2x8	12.0	12-1 / 0.33	13-3 / 0.44	14-4 / 0.55	15-3 / 0.67	16-3 / 0.80	17-1 / 0.94	17-11 / 1.09	18-9 / 1.24	19-6 / 1.40	20-3 / 1.56	21-0 / 1.73	21-7 / 1.91	22-3 / 2.09	22-11 / 2.28	23-7 / 2.47
	16.0	10-6 / 0.29	11-6 / 0.38	12-5 / 0.48	13-3 / 0.58	14-0 / 0.70	14-10 / 0.82	15-6 / 0.94	16-3 / 1.07	16-10 / 1.21	17-6 / 1.35	18-2 / 1.50	18-9 / 1.65	19-4 / 1.81	19-10 / 1.97	20-5 / 2.14
	24.0	8-7 / 0.24	9-4 / 0.31	10-1 / 0.39	10-10 / 0.48	11-6 / 0.57	12-1 / 0.67	12-8 / 0.77	13-3 / 0.88	13-9 / 0.99	14-4 / 1.10	14-10 / 1.22	15-3 / 1.35	15-9 / 1.48	16-3 / 1.61	16-8 / 1.75
2x10	12.0	15-5 / 0.33	16-11 / 0.44	18-3 / 0.55	19-6 / 0.67	20-8 / 0.80	21-10 / 0.94	22-10 / 1.09	23-11 / 1.24	24-10 / 1.40	25-10 / 1.56	26-8 / 1.73	27-7 / 1.91	28-5 / 2.09	29-3 / 2.28	30-1 / 2.47
	16.0	13-4 / 0.29	14-8 / 0.38	15-10 / 0.48	16-11 / 0.58	17-11 / 0.70	18-11 / 0.82	19-10 / 0.94	20-8 / 1.07	21-6 / 1.21	22-4 / 1.35	23-2 / 1.50	23-11 / 1.65	24-7 / 1.81	25-4 / 1.97	26-0 / 2.14
	24.0	10-11 / 0.24	11-11 / 0.31	12-11 / 0.39	13-9 / 0.48	14-8 / 0.57	15-5 / 0.67	16-2 / 0.77	16-11 / 0.88	17-7 / 0.99	18-3 / 1.10	18-11 / 1.22	19-6 / 1.35	20-1 / 1.48	20-8 / 1.61	21-3 / 1.75
2x12	12.0	18-9 / 0.33	20-6 / 0.44	22-2 / 0.55	23-9 / 0.67	25-2 / 0.80	26-6 / 0.94	27-10 / 1.09	29-1 / 1.24	30-3 / 1.40	31-4 / 1.56	32-6 / 1.73	33-6 / 1.91	34-7 / 2.09	35-7 / 2.28	36-7 / 2.47
	16.0	16-3 / 0.29	17-9 / 0.38	19-3 / 0.48	20-6 / 0.58	21-9 / 0.70	23-0 / 0.82	24-1 / 0.94	25-2 / 1.07	26-2 / 1.21	27-2 / 1.35	28-2 / 1.50	29-1 / 1.65	29-11 / 1.81	30-10 / 1.97	31-8 / 2.14
	24.0	13-3 / 0.24	14-6 / 0.31	15-8 / 0.39	16-9 / 0.48	17-9 / 0.57	18-9 / 0.67	19-8 / 0.77	20-6 / 0.88	21-5 / 0.99	22-2 / 1.10	23-0 / 1.22	23-9 / 1.35	24-5 / 1.48	25-2 / 1.61	25-10 / 1.75

[1] The required modulus of elasticity, E, in 1,000,000 pounds per square inch is shown below each span.

[2] Use single or repetitive member bending stress values (F_b) and modulus of elasticity values (E), from Table No. 25-A-1.

[3] For more comprehensive tables covering a broader range of bending stress values (F_b) and Modulus of Elasticity values (E), other spacing of members and other conditions of loading, see the Uniform Building Code.

[4] The spans in these tables are intended for use in covered structures or where moisture content in use does not exceed 19 percent.

Table 17-7. Shown are allowable spans for low slope rafters with a slope 3 in 12 or less at 30 pounds per square foot live load.

DESIGN CRITERIA: Strength - 10 lbs. per sq. ft. dead load plus 30 lbs. per sq. ft. live load determines required fiber stress. Deflection - For 30 lbs. per sq. ft. live load. Limited to span in inches divided by 240. RAFTERS: Spans are measured along the horizontal projection and loads are considered as applied on the horizontal projection.

RAFTER SIZE (IN)	SPACING (IN)	Allowable Extreme Fiber Stress in Bending, "F_b" (psi).														
		500	600	700	800	900	1000	1100	1200	1300	1400	1500	1600	1700	1800	1900
2x6	12.0	7-11 0.32	8-8 0.43	9-5 0.54	10-0 0.66	10-8 0.78	11-3 0.92	11-9 1.06	12-4 1.21	12-10 1.36	13-3 1.52	13-9 1.69	14-2 1.86	14-8 2.04	15-1 2.22	15-6 2.41
2x6	16.0	6-11 0.28	7-6 0.37	8-2 0.47	8-8 0.57	9-3 0.68	9-9 0.80	10-2 0.92	10-8 1.05	11-1 1.18	11-6 1.32	11-11 1.46	12-4 1.61	12-8 1.76	13-1 1.92	13-5 2.08
2x6	24.0	5-7 0.23	6-2 0.30	6-8 0.38	7-1 0.46	7-6 0.55	7-11 0.65	8-4 0.75	8-8 0.85	9-1 0.96	9-5 1.08	9-9 1.19	10-0 1.31	10-4 1.44	10-8 1.57	10-11 1.70
2x8	12.0	10-6 0.32	11-6 0.43	12-5 0.54	13-3 0.66	14-0 0.78	14-10 0.92	15-6 1.06	16-3 1.21	16-10 1.36	17-6 1.52	18-2 1.69	18-9 1.86	19-4 2.04	19-10 2.22	20-5 2.41
2x8	16.0	9-1 0.28	9-11 0.37	10-9 0.47	11-6 0.57	12-2 0.68	12-10 0.80	13-5 0.92	14-0 1.05	14-7 1.18	15-2 1.32	15-8 1.46	16-3 1.61	16-9 1.76	17-2 1.92	17-8 2.08
2x8	24.0	7-5 0.23	8-1 0.30	8-9 0.38	9-4 0.46	9-11 0.55	10-6 0.65	11-0 0.75	11-6 0.85	11-11 0.96	12-5 1.08	12-10 1.19	13-3 1.31	13-8 1.44	14-0 1.57	14-5 1.70
2x10	12.0	13-4 0.32	14-8 0.43	15-10 0.54	16-11 0.66	17-11 0.78	18-11 0.92	19-10 1.06	20-8 1.21	21-6 1.36	22-4 1.52	23-2 1.69	23-11 1.86	24-7 2.04	25-4 2.22	26-0 2.41
2x10	16.0	11-7 0.28	12-8 0.37	13-8 0.47	14-8 0.57	15-6 0.68	16-4 0.80	17-2 0.92	17-11 1.05	18-8 1.18	19-4 1.32	20-0 1.46	20-8 1.61	21-4 1.76	21-11 1.92	22-6 2.08
2x10	24.0	9-5 0.23	10-4 0.30	11-2 0.38	11-11 0.46	12-8 0.55	13-4 0.65	14-0 0.75	14-8 0.85	15-3 0.96	15-10 1.08	16-4 1.19	16-11 1.31	17-5 1.44	17-11 1.57	18-5 1.70
2x12	12.0	16-3 0.32	17-9 0.43	19-3 0.54	20-6 0.66	21-9 0.78	23-0 0.92	24-1 1.06	25-2 1.21	26-2 1.36	27-2 1.52	28-2 1.69	29-1 1.86	29-11 2.04	30-10 2.22	31-8 2.41
2x12	16.0	14-1 0.28	15-5 0.37	16-8 0.47	17-9 0.57	18-10 0.68	19-11 0.80	20-10 0.92	21-9 1.05	22-8 1.18	23-6 1.32	24-4 1.46	25-2 1.61	25-11 1.76	26-8 1.92	27-5 2.08
2x12	24.0	11-6 0.23	12-7 0.30	13-7 0.38	14-6 0.46	15-5 0.55	16-3 0.65	17-0 0.75	17-9 0.85	18-6 0.96	19-3 1.08	19-11 1.19	20-6 1.31	21-2 1.44	21-9 1.57	22-5 1.70

[1] The required modulus of elasticity, E, in 1,000,000 pounds per square inch is shown below each span.

[2] Use single or repetitive member bending stress values (F_b) and modulus of elasticity values (E), from Table No. 25-A-1.

[3] For more comprehensive tables covering a broader range of bending stress values (F_b) and Modulus of Elasticity values (E), other spacing of members and other conditions of loading, see the Uniform Building Code.

[4] The spans in these tables are intended for use in covered structures or where moisture content in use does not exceed 19 percent.

Table 17-8. Use this chart to find allowable spans for high slope rafters with a slope over 3. These figures are based on 12-20 pounds per square foot live load.

DESIGN CRITERIA: Strength - 15 lbs. per sq. ft. dead load plus 20 lbs. per sq. ft. live load determines required fiber stress. Deflection - For 20 lbs. per sq. ft. live load. Limited to span in inches divided by 180. RAFTERS: Spans are measured along the horizontal projection and loads are considered as applied on the horizontal projection.

RAFTER SIZE (in)	SPACING (in)	Allowable Extreme Fiber Stress in Bending, "Fb" (psi)														
		500	600	700	800	900	1000	1100	1200	1300	1400	1500	1600	1700	1800	1900
2x4	12.0	5-5 0.20	5-11 0.26	6-5 0.33	6-10 0.40	7-3 0.48	7-8 0.56	8-0 0.65	8-4 0.74	8-8 0.83	9-0 0.93	9-4 1.03	9-8 1.14	9-11 1.24	10-3 1.36	10-6 1.47
	16.0	4-8 0.17	5-1 0.23	5-6 0.28	5-11 0.35	6-3 0.41	6-7 0.49	6-11 0.56	7-3 0.64	7-6 0.72	7-10 0.80	8-1 0.89	8-4 0.98	8-7 1.08	8-10 1.17	9-1 1.27
	24.0	3-10 0.14	4-2 0.18	4-6 0.23	4-10 0.28	5-1 0.34	5-5 0.40	5-8 0.46	5-11 0.52	6-2 0.59	6-5 0.66	6-7 0.73	6-10 0.80	7-0 0.88	7-3 0.96	7-5 1.04
2x6	12.0	8-6 0.20	9-4 0.26	10-0 0.33	10-9 0.40	11-5 0.48	12-0 0.56	12-7 0.65	13-2 0.74	13-8 0.83	14-2 0.93	14-8 1.03	15-2 1.14	15-8 1.24	16-1 1.36	16-7 1.47
	16.0	7-4 0.17	8-1 0.23	8-8 0.28	9-4 0.35	9-10 0.41	10-5 0.49	10-11 0.56	11-5 0.64	11-10 0.72	12-4 0.80	12-9 0.89	13-2 0.98	13-7 1.08	13-11 1.17	14-4 1.27
	24.0	6-0 0.14	6-7 0.18	7-1 0.23	7-7 0.28	8-1 0.34	8-6 0.40	8-11 0.46	9-4 0.52	9-8 0.59	10-0 0.66	10-5 0.73	10-9 0.80	11-1 0.88	11-5 0.96	11-8 1.04
2x8	12.0	11-2 0.20	12-3 0.26	13-3 0.33	14-2 0.40	15-0 0.48	15-10 0.56	16-7 0.65	17-4 0.74	18-0 0.83	18-9 0.93	19-5 1.03	20-0 1.14	20-8 1.24	21-3 1.36	21-10 1.47
	16.0	9-8 0.17	10-7 0.23	11-6 0.28	12-3 0.35	13-0 0.41	13-8 0.49	14-4 0.56	15-0 0.64	15-7 0.72	16-3 0.80	16-9 0.89	17-4 0.98	17-10 1.08	18-5 1.17	18-11 1.27
	24.0	7-11 0.14	8-8 0.18	9-4 0.23	10-0 0.28	10-7 0.34	11-2 0.40	11-9 0.46	12-3 0.52	12-9 0.59	13-3 0.66	13-8 0.73	14-2 0.80	14-7 0.88	15-0 0.96	15-5 1.04
2x10	12.0	14-3 0.20	15-8 0.26	16-11 0.33	18-1 0.40	19-2 0.48	20-2 0.56	21-2 0.65	22-1 0.74	23-0 0.83	23-11 0.93	24-9 1.03	25-6 1.14	26-4 1.24	27-1 1.36	27-10 1.47
	16.0	12-4 0.17	13-6 0.23	14-8 0.28	15-8 0.35	16-7 0.41	17-6 0.49	18-4 0.56	19-2 0.64	19-11 0.72	20-8 0.80	21-5 0.89	22-1 0.98	22-10 1.08	23-5 1.17	24-1 1.27
	24.0	10-1 0.14	11-1 0.18	11-11 0.23	12-9 0.28	13-6 0.34	14-3 0.40	15-0 0.46	15-8 0.52	16-3 0.59	16-11 0.66	17-6 0.73	18-1 0.80	18-7 0.88	19-2 0.96	19-8 1.04

[1] The required modulus of elasticity, E, in 1,000 pounds per square inch is shown below each span.

[2] Use single or repetitive member bending stress values (F_b) and modulus of elasticity values (E), from Table No. 25-A-1.

[3] For more comprehensive tables covering a broader range of bending stress values (F_b) and Modulus of Elasticity values (E), other spacing of members and other conditions of loading, see the Uniform Building Code.

[4] The spans in these tables are intended for use in covered structures or where moisture content in use does not exceed 19 percent.

Table 17-9. Here are allowable spans for high slope rafters with a slope over 3 at 12-30 pounds per square foot live load.

DESIGN CRITERIA: Strength - 15 lbs. per sq. ft. dead load plus 30 lbs. per sq. ft. live load determines required fiber stress. Deflection - For 30 lbs. per sq. ft. live load. Limited to span in inches divided by 180. RAFTERS: Spans are measured along the horizontal projection and loads are considered as applied on the horizontal projection.

RAFTER SIZE (IN)	SPACING (IN)	Allowable Extreme Fiber Stress in Bending, "F$_b$" (psi).														
		500	600	700	800	900	1000	1100	1200	1300	1400	1500	1600	1700	1800	1900
2x4	12.0	4-9 / 0.20	5-3 / 0.27	5-8 / 0.34	6-0 / 0.41	6-5 / 0.49	6-9 / 0.58	7-1 / 0.67	7-5 / 0.76	7-8 / 0.86	8-0 / 0.96	8-3 / 1.06	8-6 / 1.17	8-9 / 1.28	9-0 / 1.39	9-3 / 1.51
	16.0	4-1 / 0.18	4-6 / 0.23	4-11 / 0.29	5-3 / 0.36	5-6 / 0.43	5-10 / 0.50	6-1 / 0.58	6-5 / 0.66	6-8 / 0.74	6-11 / 0.83	7-2 / 0.92	7-5 / 1.01	7-7 / 1.11	7-10 / 1.21	8-0 / 1.31
	24.0	3-4 / 0.14	3-8 / 0.19	4-0 / 0.24	4-3 / 0.29	4-6 / 0.35	4-9 / 0.41	5-0 / 0.47	5-3 / 0.54	5-5 / 0.61	5-8 / 0.68	5-10 / 0.75	6-0 / 0.83	6-3 / 0.90	6-5 / 0.99	6-7 / 1.07
2x6	12.0	7-6 / 0.20	8-2 / 0.27	8-10 / 0.34	9-6 / 0.41	10-0 / 0.49	10-7 / 0.58	11-1 / 0.67	11-7 / 0.76	12-1 / 0.86	12-6 / 0.96	13-0 / 1.06	13-5 / 1.17	13-10 / 1.28	14-2 / 1.39	14-7 / 1.51
	16.0	6-6 / 0.18	7-1 / 0.23	7-8 / 0.29	8-2 / 0.36	8-8 / 0.43	9-2 / 0.50	9-7 / 0.58	10-0 / 0.66	10-5 / 0.74	10-10 / 0.83	11-3 / 0.92	11-7 / 1.01	11-11 / 1.11	12-4 / 1.21	12-8 / 1.31
	24.0	5-4 / 0.14	5-10 / 0.19	6-3 / 0.24	6-8 / 0.29	7-1 / 0.35	7-6 / 0.41	7-10 / 0.47	8-2 / 0.54	8-6 / 0.61	8-10 / 0.68	9-2 / 0.75	9-6 / 0.83	9-9 / 0.90	10-0 / 0.99	10-4 / 1.07
2x8	12.0	9-10 / 0.20	10-10 / 0.27	11-8 / 0.34	12-6 / 0.41	13-3 / 0.49	13-11 / 0.58	14-8 / 0.67	15-3 / 0.76	15-11 / 0.86	16-6 / 0.96	17-1 / 1.06	17-8 / 1.17	18-2 / 1.28	18-9 / 1.39	19-3 / 1.51
	16.0	8-7 / 0.18	9-4 / 0.23	10-1 / 0.29	10-10 / 0.36	11-6 / 0.43	12-1 / 0.50	12-8 / 0.58	13-3 / 0.66	13-9 / 0.74	14-4 / 0.83	14-10 / 0.92	15-3 / 1.01	15-9 / 1.11	16-3 / 1.21	16-8 / 1.31
	24.0	7-0 / 0.14	7-8 / 0.19	8-3 / 0.24	8-10 / 0.29	9-4 / 0.35	9-10 / 0.41	10-4 / 0.47	10-10 / 0.54	11-3 / 0.61	11-8 / 0.68	12-1 / 0.75	12-6 / 0.83	12-10 / 0.90	13-3 / 0.99	13-7 / 1.07
2x10	12.0	12-7 / 0.20	13-9 / 0.27	14-11 / 0.34	15-11 / 0.41	16-11 / 0.49	17-10 / 0.58	18-8 / 0.67	19-6 / 0.76	20-4 / 0.86	21-1 / 0.96	21-10 / 1.06	22-6 / 1.17	23-3 / 1.28	23-11 / 1.39	24-6 / 1.51
	16.0	10-11 / 0.18	11-11 / 0.23	12-11 / 0.29	13-9 / 0.36	14-8 / 0.43	15-5 / 0.50	16-2 / 0.58	16-11 / 0.66	17-7 / 0.74	18-3 / 0.83	18-11 / 0.92	19-6 / 1.01	20-1 / 1.11	20-8 / 1.21	21-3 / 1.31
	24.0	8-11 / 0.14	9-9 / 0.19	10-6 / 0.24	11-3 / 0.29	11-11 / 0.35	12-7 / 0.41	13-2 / 0.47	13-9 / 0.54	14-4 / 0.61	14-11 / 0.68	15-5 / 0.75	15-11 / 0.83	16-5 / 0.90	16-11 / 0.99	17-4 / 1.07

[1]The required modulus of elasticity, E, in 1,000,000 pounds per square inch is shown below each span.

[2]Use single or repetitive member bending stress values (F$_b$) and modulus of elasticity values (E), from Table No. 25-A-1.

[3]For more comprehensive tables covering a broader range of bending stress values (F$_b$) and Modulus of Elasticity values (E), other spacing of members and other conditions of loading, see the Uniform Building Code.

[4]The spans in these tables are intended for use in covered structures or where moisture content in use does not exceed 19 percent.

Table 17-10. The chart lists allowable spans for high slope rafters with a slope over 3 at 12-20 pounds per square foot live load.

DESIGN CRITERIA: Strength - 7 lbs. per sq. ft. dead load plus 20 lbs. per sq. ft. live load determines required fiber stress. Deflection - For 20 lbs. per sq. ft. live load. Limited to span in inches divided by 180. RAFTERS: Spans are measured along the horizontal projection and loads are considered as applied on the horizontal projection.

Allowable Extreme Fiber Stress in Bending, "F_b" (psi).

RAFTER SIZE (IN)	SPACING (IN)	500	600	700	800	900	1000	1100	1200	1300	1400	1500	1600	1700	1800	1900
2x4	12.0	6-2 / 0.29	6-9 / 0.38	7-3 / 0.49	7-9 / 0.59	8-3 / 0.71	8-8 / 0.83	9-1 / 0.96	9-6 / 1.09	9-11 / 1.23	10-3 / 1.37	10-8 / 1.52	11-0 / 1.68	11-4 / 1.84	11-8 / 2.00	12-0 / 2.17
	16.0	5-4 / 0.25	5-10 / 0.33	6-4 / 0.42	6-9 / 0.51	7-2 / 0.61	7-6 / 0.72	7-11 / 0.83	8-3 / 0.94	8-7 / 1.06	8-11 / 1.19	9-3 / 1.32	9-6 / 1.45	9-10 / 1.59	10-1 / 1.73	10-5 / 1.88
	24.0	4-4 / 0.21	4-9 / 0.27	5-2 / 0.34	5-6 / 0.42	5-10 / 0.50	6-2 / 0.59	6-5 / 0.68	6-9 / 0.77	7-0 / 0.87	7-3 / 0.97	7-6 / 1.08	7-9 / 1.19	8-0 / 1.30	8-3 / 1.41	8-6 / 1.53
2x6	12.0	9-8 / 0.29	10-7 / 0.38	11-5 / 0.49	12-3 / 0.59	13-0 / 0.71	13-8 / 0.83	14-4 / 0.96	15-0 / 1.09	15-7 / 1.23	16-2 / 1.37	16-9 / 1.52	17-3 / 1.68	17-10 / 1.84	18-4 / 2.00	18-10 / 2.17
	16.0	8-4 / 0.25	9-2 / 0.33	9-11 / 0.42	10-7 / 0.51	11-3 / 0.61	11-10 / 0.72	12-5 / 0.83	13-0 / 0.94	13-6 / 1.06	14-0 / 1.19	14-6 / 1.32	15-0 / 1.45	15-5 / 1.59	15-11 / 1.73	16-4 / 1.88
	24.0	6-10 / 0.21	7-6 / 0.27	8-1 / 0.34	8-8 / 0.42	9-2 / 0.50	9-8 / 0.59	10-2 / 0.68	10-7 / 0.77	11-0 / 0.87	11-5 / 0.97	11-10 / 1.08	12-3 / 1.19	12-7 / 1.30	13-0 / 1.41	13-4 / 1.53
2x8	12.0	12-9 / 0.29	13-11 / 0.38	15-1 / 0.49	16-1 / 0.59	17-1 / 0.71	18-0 / 0.83	18-11 / 0.96	19-9 / 1.09	20-6 / 1.23	21-4 / 1.37	22-1 / 1.52	22-9 / 1.68	23-6 / 1.84	24-2 / 2.00	24-10 / 2.17
	16.0	11-0 / 0.25	12-1 / 0.33	13-1 / 0.42	13-11 / 0.51	14-10 / 0.61	15-7 / 0.72	16-4 / 0.83	17-1 / 0.94	17-9 / 1.06	18-5 / 1.19	19-1 / 1.32	19-9 / 1.45	20-4 / 1.59	20-11 / 1.73	21-6 / 1.88
	24.0	9-0 / 0.21	9-10 / 0.27	10-8 / 0.34	11-5 / 0.42	12-1 / 0.50	12-9 / 0.59	13-4 / 0.68	13-11 / 0.77	14-6 / 0.87	15-1 / 0.97	15-7 / 1.08	16-1 / 1.19	16-7 / 1.30	17-1 / 1.41	17-7 / 1.53
2x10	12.0	16-3 / 0.29	17-10 / 0.38	19-3 / 0.49	20-7 / 0.59	21-10 / 0.71	23-0 / 0.83	24-1 / 0.96	25-2 / 1.09	26-2 / 1.23	27-2 / 1.37	28-2 / 1.52	29-1 / 1.68	30-0 / 1.84	30-10 / 2.00	31-8 / 2.17
	16.0	14-1 / 0.25	15-5 / 0.33	16-8 / 0.42	17-10 / 0.51	18-11 / 0.61	19-11 / 0.72	20-10 / 0.83	21-10 / 0.94	22-8 / 1.06	23-7 / 1.19	24-5 / 1.32	25-2 / 1.45	25-11 / 1.59	26-8 / 1.73	27-5 / 1.88
	24.0	11-6 / 0.21	12-7 / 0.27	13-7 / 0.34	14-6 / 0.42	15-5 / 0.50	16-3 / 0.59	17-1 / 0.68	17-10 / 0.77	18-6 / 0.87	19-3 / 0.97	19-11 / 1.08	20-7 / 1.19	21-2 / 1.30	21-10 / 1.41	22-5 / 1.53

[1] The required modulus of elasticity, E, in 1,000,000 pounds per square inch is shown below each span.

[2] Use single or repetitive member bending stress values (F_b) and modulus of elasticity values (E), from Table No. 25-A-1.

[3] For more comprehensive tables covering a broader range of bending stress values (F_b) and Modulus of Elasticity values (E), other spacing of members and other conditions of loading, see the Uniform Building Code.

[4] The spans in these tables are intended for use in covered structures or where moisture content in use does not exceed 19 percent.

Table 17-11. Listed are allowable spans for high slope rafters with a slope over 3 at 12-30 pounds per square foot live load.

DESIGN CRITERIA: Strength - 7 lbs. per. sq. ft. dead load plus 30 lbs. per sq. ft. live load determines required fiber stress. Deflection - For 30 lbs. per sq. ft. live load. Limited to span in inches divided by 180. RAFTERS: Spans are measured along the horizontal projection and loads are considered as applied on the horizontal projection.

RAFTER SIZE (IN)	SPACING (IN)	Allowable Extreme Fiber Stress in Bending, "F_b" (psi)														
		500	600	700	800	900	1000	1100	1200	1300	1400	1500	1600	1700	1800	1900
2x4	12.0	5-3 / 0.27	5-9 / 0.36	6-3 / 0.45	6-8 / 0.55	7-1 / 0.66	7-5 / 0.77	7-9 / 0.89	8-2 / 1.02	8-6 / 1.15	8-9 / 1.28	9-1 / 1.42	9-5 / 1.57	9-8 / 1.72	10-0 / 1.87	10-3 / 2.03
2x4	16.0	4-7 / 0.24	5-0 / 0.31	5-5 / 0.39	5-9 / 0.48	6-1 / 0.57	6-5 / 0.67	6-9 / 0.77	7-1 / 0.88	7-4 / 0.99	7-7 / 1.11	7-11 / 1.23	8-2 / 1.36	8-5 / 1.49	8-8 / 1.62	8-10 / 1.76
2x4	24.0	3-9 / 0.19	4-1 / 0.25	4-5 / 0.32	4-8 / 0.39	5-0 / 0.47	5-3 / 0.55	5-6 / 0.63	5-9 / 0.72	6-0 / 0.81	6-3 / 0.91	6-5 / 1.01	6-8 / 1.11	6-10 / 1.21	7-1 / 1.32	7-3 / 1.43
2x6	12.0	8-3 / 0.27	9-1 / 0.36	9-9 / 0.45	10-5 / 0.55	11-1 / 0.66	11-8 / 0.77	12-3 / 0.89	12-9 / 1.02	13-4 / 1.15	13-10 / 1.28	14-4 / 1.42	14-9 / 1.57	15-3 / 1.72	15-8 / 1.87	16-1 / 2.03
2x6	16.0	7-2 / 0.24	7-10 / 0.31	8-5 / 0.39	9-1 / 0.48	9-7 / 0.57	10-1 / 0.67	10-7 / 0.77	11-1 / 0.88	11-6 / 0.99	12-0 / 1.11	12-5 / 1.23	12-9 / 1.36	13-2 / 1.49	13-7 / 1.62	13-11 / 1.76
2x6	24.0	5-10 / 0.19	6-5 / 0.25	6-11 / 0.32	7-5 / 0.39	7-10 / 0.47	8-3 / 0.55	8-8 / 0.63	9-1 / 0.72	9-5 / 0.81	9-9 / 0.91	10-1 / 1.01	10-5 / 1.11	10-9 / 1.21	11-1 / 1.32	11-5 / 1.43
2x8	12.0	10-11 / 0.27	11-11 / 0.36	12-10 / 0.45	13-9 / 0.55	14-7 / 0.66	15-5 / 0.77	16-2 / 0.89	16-10 / 1.02	17-7 / 1.15	18-2 / 1.28	18-10 / 1.42	19-6 / 1.57	20-1 / 1.72	20-8 / 1.87	21-3 / 2.03
2x8	16.0	9-5 / 0.24	10-4 / 0.31	11-2 / 0.39	11-11 / 0.48	12-8 / 0.57	13-4 / 0.67	14-0 / 0.77	14-7 / 0.88	15-2 / 0.99	15-9 / 1.11	16-4 / 1.23	16-10 / 1.36	17-4 / 1.49	17-11 / 1.62	18-4 / 1.76
2x8	24.0	7-8 / 0.19	8-5 / 0.25	9-1 / 0.32	9-9 / 0.39	10-4 / 0.47	10-11 / 0.55	11-5 / 0.63	11-11 / 0.72	12-5 / 0.81	12-10 / 0.91	13-4 / 1.01	13-9 / 1.11	14-2 / 1.21	14-7 / 1.32	15-0 / 1.43
2x10	12.0	13-11 / 0.27	15-2 / 0.36	16-5 / 0.45	17-7 / 0.55	18-7 / 0.66	19-8 / 0.77	20-7 / 0.89	21-6 / 1.02	22-5 / 1.15	23-3 / 1.28	24-1 / 1.42	24-10 / 1.57	25-7 / 1.72	26-4 / 1.87	27-1 / 2.03
2x10	16.0	12-0 / 0.26	13-2 / 0.34	14-3 / 0.43	15-2 / 0.53	16-2 / 0.63	17-0 / 0.74	17-10 / 0.85	18-7 / 0.97	19-5 / 1.09	20-1 / 1.22	20-10 / 1.35	21-6 / 1.49	22-2 / 1.63	22-10 / 1.78	23-5 / 1.93
2x10	24.0	9-10 / 0.19	10-9 / 0.25	11-7 / 0.32	12-5 / 0.39	13-2 / 0.47	13-11 / 0.55	14-7 / 0.63	15-2 / 0.72	15-10 / 0.81	16-5 / 0.91	17-0 / 1.01	17-7 / 1.11	18-1 / 1.21	18-7 / 1.32	19-2 / 1.43

[1] The required modulus of elasticity, E, in 1,000,000 pounds per square inch is shown below each span.

[2] Use single or repetitive member bending stress values (F_b) and modulus of elasticity values (E), from Table No. 25-A-1.

[3] For more comprehensive tables covering a broader range of bending stress values (F_b) and Modulus of Elasticity values (E), other spacing of members and other conditions of loading, see the Uniform Building Code.

[4] The spans in these tables are intended for use in covered structures or where moisture content in use does not exceed 19 percent.

Table17-12. This table gives spacing of Doublas fir or southern pine posts for wind loads on gable roofed buildings. The design bending strength is 1500 pounds per square inch (courtesy Northeast Regional Agricultural Engineering Service).

Post Size in × in[b]	Wind Load psf[c]	Wind Speed mph	Effective Building Height[a], feet					
			9.0	10.5	12.0	13.5	15.0	19.0
			Maximum Spacing[d], feet					
5.5×9.5	10	62	X	X	38.3	30.3	24.5	15.3
	12	68	X	X	31.9	25.2	20.4	12.8
	15	76	X	X	25.5	20.2	16.3	10.2
7.5×7.5	10	62	X	X	32.5	25.7	20.8	13.0
	12	68	X	35.4	27.1	21.4	17.4	10.8
	15	76	38.6	28.3	21.7	17.1	13.9	8.7
6.0×8.0	10	62	X	38.7	29.6	23.4	19.0	11.8
	12	68	X	32.3	24.7	19.5	15.8	9.8
	15	76	35.1	25.8	19.7	15.6	12.6	7.9
5.5×7.5[e]	10	62	X	31.2	23.9	18.9	15.3	9.5
	12	68	35.4	26.0	19.9	15.7	12.7	7.9
	15	76	28.3	20.8	15.9	12.6	10.2	6.3
6.0×6.0	10	62	29.6	21.8	16.7	13.2	10.7	6.6
	12	68	24.7	18.1	13.9	11.0	8.9	5.5
	15	76	19.7	14.5	11.1	8.8	7.1	4.4
5.5×5.5[e]	10	62	22.8	16.8	12.8	10.1	8.2	5.1
	12	68	19.0	14.0	10.7	8.4	6.8	4.3
	15	76	15.2	11.2	8.5	6.8	5.5	3.4
4.0×6.0	10	62	19.7	14.5	11.1	8.8	7.1	4.4
	12	68	16.5	12.1	9.3	7.3	5.9	3.7
	15	76	13.2	9.7	7.4	5.8	4.7	2.9
3.5×5.5[e]	10	62	14.5	10.7	8.2	6.5	5.2	3.3
	12	68	12.1	8.9	6.8	5.4	4.4	2.7
	15	76	9.7	5.4	5.4	4.3	3.5	2.2
4.0×4.0	10	62	8.8	6.4	4.9	3.9	3.2	2.0
	12	68	7.3	5.4	4.1	3.2	2.6	1.6
	15	76	5.8	4.3	3.2	2.6	2.1	1.3

[a]For roof slopes 4 in 12 or less the effective height is the vertical distance from grade level to the eave. For roof slopes greater than 4 in 12 the effective building height is the vertical distance from grade level to eave height plus half the roof height.

[b]The larger post dimension is in the same direction as the wind or parallel to the building width.

[c]In areas with 20 lb/sq. ft. (psf) wind loads (88 mph) use half the 10 psf spacing.

[d]Spacing greater than 20' not recommended.

[e]These sizes are commonly available in most areas.

329

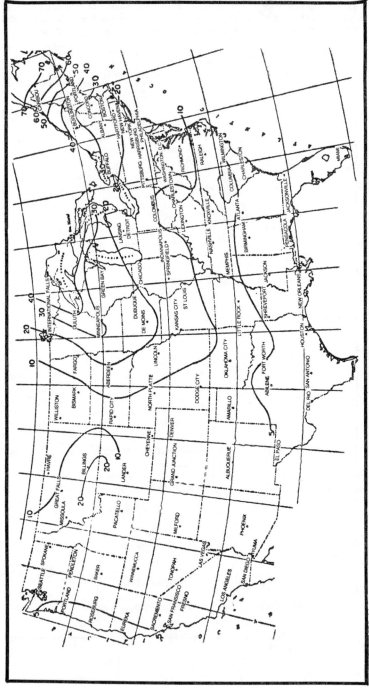

Fig. 17-1. The map shows snow loads in pound-force per square foot on the ground, at a 25-year mean recurrence interval.

Table 17-13. Shown are allowable spans for plywood and roof sheathing continuous over two or more spans and face grain perpendicular to supports (span in inches).

Panel identification index[2] Roof span, roof/floor span	Thickness (inches)	Roof				Floor
		Maximum Span (Inches)		Load (psf)		Maximum span[5] (Inches)
		Edges blocked[3]	Edges unblocked	Total load	Live load	
12/0	5/16	12	12	130	100	0
16/0	5/16, 3/8	16	16	75	55	0
20/0	5/16, 3/8	20	20	55	45	0
24/0	3/8, 1/2	24[6]	24	60	45	0
30/12	5/8	30	26	55	40	12[7]
32/16	1/2, 5/8	32	28	50[4]	40	16[8]
36/16	3/4	36	30	50[4]	35[4]	16[8]
42/20	5/8, 3/4, 7/8	43[9]	32	45[4]	35[4]	20[8]
48/24	3/4, 7/8	48	36	40[4]	40	24

Note 1. These values apply for Structural I and II, Standard Sheathing and C-C grades only. Spans shall be limited to values shown because of possible effect of concentrated loads.

Note 2. Identification index appears on all panels in the construction grades listed in footnote (1).

Note 3. Edges may be blocked with lumber or other approved type of edge support.

Note 4. For roof live load of forty (40) psf or total load of fifty-five (55) psf, decrease spans by thirteen (13) per cent or use panel with next greater identification index.

Note 5. Plywood edges shall have approved tongue-and-groove joints or shall be supported with blocking, unless one-fourth (1/4) inch minimum thickness underlayment is installed, or finish floor is twenty-five thirty-seconds (25/32) inch wood strip. Allowable uniform load based on deflection of one three-sixtieth (1/360) of space is one hundred sixty-five (165) psf.

Note 6. Plywood roof sheathing continuous over two or more spans may be placed with face grain parallel to supports spaced not over twenty-four (24) inches on center if all panel edges are blocked or other approved type edge support is provided, and if live loads do not exceed twenty-five (25) psf for one-half (1/2) inch Structural 1 (4-ply) and one-half (1/2) inch 5-ply in other grades, or forty (40) psf for one-half (1/2) inch Structural 1 (5-ply) and five-eights (5/8) inch 5-ply in other grades.

Note 7. May be sixteen (16) inches, if twenty-five thirty-seconds (25/32) inch wood strip flooring is installed at right angles to joists.

Note 8. May be twenty-four (24) inches if twenty-five thirty-seconds (25/32) inch wood strip flooring is installed at right angles to joists.

Note 9. For joists spaced twenty-four (24) inches on center plywood sheathing with Identification Index Numbers 42/20 or greater can be used for subfloors when supporting one and one-half (1½) inches of lightweight concrete.

Table 17-14. To use this chart and tables 15-22, first determine the span, the live load to be supported and the deflection limitation. For nominal 2-inch planks, here are required values for fiber stress in bending (f) and modulus of elasticity (E) to safely support a live load of 20, 30 or 40 pounds per square foot within a deflection limitation of l/240, l/300 or l/360 (courtesy National Forest Products Association). (Continued on page 333).

PLANK SPAN IN FEET	LIVE LOAD psf	DEFLECTION LIMITATION	TYPE A		TYPE B		TYPE C		TYPE D	
			f psi	E psi	f psi	E psi	f psi	E psi	f psi	E psi
6'	20	$\frac{l}{240}$	360	576000	360	239000	288	305000	360	408000
		$\frac{l}{300}$	360	720000	360	299000	288	381000	360	509000
		$\frac{l}{360}$	360	864000	360	359000	288	457000	360	611000
	30	$\frac{l}{240}$	480	864000	480	359000	384	457000	480	611000
		$\frac{l}{300}$	480	1080000	480	448000	384	571000	480	764000
		$\frac{l}{360}$	480	1296000	480	538000	384	685000	480	917000
	40	$\frac{l}{240}$	600	1152000	600	478000	480	609000	600	815000
		$\frac{l}{300}$	600	1440000	600	598000	480	762000	600	1019000
		$\frac{l}{360}$	600	1728000	600	717000	480	914000	600	1223000

PLANK SPAN IN FEET	LIVE LOAD psf	DEFLECTION LIMITATION	f psi	E psi	f psi	E psi	f psi	E psi	f psi	E psi
7'	20	$\frac{l}{240}$	490	915000	490	380000	392	484000	490	647000
		$\frac{l}{300}$	490	1143000	490	475000	392	605000	490	809000
		$\frac{l}{360}$	490	1372000	490	570000	392	726000	490	971000
	30	$\frac{l}{240}$	653	1372000	653	570000	522	726000	653	971000
		$\frac{l}{300}$	653	1715000	653	712000	522	907000	653	1213000
		$\frac{l}{360}$	653	2058000	653	854000	522	1088000	653	1456000
	40	$\frac{l}{240}$	817	1829000	817	759000	653	968000	817	1294000
		$\frac{l}{300}$	817	2287000	817	949000	653	1209000	817	1618000
		$\frac{l}{360}$	817	2744000	817	1139000	653	1451000	817	1941000
8'	20	$\frac{l}{240}$	640	1365000	640	567000	512	722000	640	966000
		$\frac{l}{300}$	640	1707000	640	708000	512	903000	640	1208000
		$\frac{l}{360}$	640	20480C*	640	850000	512	1083000	640	1449000
	30	$\frac{l}{240}$	853	2048000	853	850000	682	1083000	853	1449000
		$\frac{l}{300}$	853	2560000	853	1063000	682	1354000	853	1811000
		$\frac{l}{360}$	853	3072000	853	1275000	682	1625000	853	2174000
	40	$\frac{l}{240}$	1067	2731000	1067	1134000	853	1444000	1067	1932000
		$\frac{l}{300}$	1067	3413000	1067	1417000	853	1805000	1067	2415000
		$\frac{l}{360}$	1067	4096000	1067	1700000	853	2166000	1067	2898000

333

Table 17-15. Regarding floor and roof beams, the chart gives required values for fiber stress in bending (f) and modulus of elasticity (E) for the sizes shown to support a live load of 20 pounds per square foot within a deflection limitation of I/240 (courtesy National Forest Products Association). (continued on page 335).

SPAN OF BEAM	NOMINAL SIZE OF BEAM	MINIMUM "f" & "E" IN psi FOR BEAMS SPACED:					
		6'-0" f	6'-0" E	7'-0" f	7'-0" E	8'-0" f	8'-0" E
10'	2-3x6	1070	780000	1250	910000	1430	1040000
	1-3x8	1235	680000	1440	794000	1645	906000
	2-2x8	1030	570000	1200	665000	1370	760000
	1-4x8	880	485000	1030	566000	1175	646000
	3-2x8	685	380000	800	443000	915	506000
	2-3x8	615	340000	720	397000	820	453000
	2-2x10	630	273000	735	319000	840	364000
11'	2-3x6	1295	1037000	1510	1210000	1730	1382000
	1-3x8	1490	905000	1740	1056000	1990	1206000
	2-2x8	1245	754000	1450	880000	1660	1005000
	1-4x8	1065	647000	1245	755000	1420	862000
	3-2x8	830	503000	970	587000	1105	670000
	2-3x8	745	453000	870	529000	995	604000
	2-2x10	765	363000	890	424000	1020	484000
12'	2-3x6	1545	1346000	1800	1571000	2060	1794000
	1-3x8	1775	1175000	2070	1371000	2370	1566000
	2-2x8	1480	980000	1725	1144000	1970	1306000
	1-4x8	1270	840000	1480	980000	1690	1120000
	3-2x8	985	653000	1150	762000	1315	870000
	2-3x8	890	588000	1035	686000	1185	784000
	1-6x8	755	483000	880	564000	1005	644000
	2-2x10	910	477000	1060	551000	1210	629000
	1-3x10	1090	566000	1275	660000	1455	754000
13'	2-3x6	1815	1711000	2110	1997000	2415	2281000
	1-3x8	2085	1494000	2430	1743000	2780	1991000
	2-2x8	1740	1245000	2025	1453000	2315	1660000
	1-4x8	1490	1067000	1735	1245000	1985	1422000
	3-2x8	1160	830000	1350	969000	1545	1106000
	2-3x8	1045	747000	1215	872000	1390	996000
	1-6x8	885	614000	1040	716000	1185	818000
	2-2x10	1070	600000	1245	700000	1420	800000
	1-3x10	1280	719000	1495	839000	1710	958000
17' contd.	2-3x10	1095	804000	1280	938000	1460	1072000
	1-6x10	945	675000	1100	788000	1260	900000
	4-2x10	910	670000	1065	782000	1215	894000
	1-8x10	690	495000	805	578000	910	660000
	1-3x12	1480	894000	1725	1043000	1975	1192000
	2-2x12	1060	639000	1230	746000	1645	993000
	1-4x12	820	497000	960	580000	1410	852000
	3-2x12					1095	663000
18'	2-2x10	2045	1592000	2385	1858000	2725	2123000
	1-4x10	1755	1364000	2045	1592000	2340	1819000
	3-2x10	1365	1061000	1590	1238000	1815	1415000
	1-6x10	1270	955000	1480	1114000	1695	1273000
	2-3x10	1060	801000	1235	935000	1415	1068000
	4-2x10	1020	796000	1195	929000	1365	1062000
	1-8x10	780	588000	910	686000	1040	784000
	1-3x12	1660	1062000	1935	1239000	2210	1416000
	2-2x12	1380	885000	1615	1033000	1845	1180000
	1-4x12	1185	758000	1385	885000	1580	1011000
	3-2x12	920	590000	1075	688000	1230	786000
	2-3x12	830	531000	970	620000	1105	708000
19'	3-2x10	1520	1248000	1775	1456000	2025	1664000
	2-3x10	1365	1123000	1595	1310000	1825	1497000
	1-6x10	1170	943000	1365	1100000	1560	1248000
	4-2x10	1140	936000	1330	1092000	1520	1257000
	1-8x10	975	802000	1140	936000	1300	1070000
	1-3x12	1850	1249000	2155	1457000	2465	1665000
	2-2x12	1540	1041000	1800	1215000	2055	1388000
	1-4x12	1320	892000	1540	1041000	1760	1190000
	3-2x12	1025	694000	1200	810000	1370	926000
	2-3x12	925	624000	1080	728000	1230	832000
	1-6x12	805	531000	940	620000	1070	708000

MINIMUM "f" & "E" IN psi FOR BEAMS SPACED:

SPAN OF BEAM	NOMINAL SIZE OF BEAM	6'-0" f	6'-0" E	7'-0" f	7'-0" E	8'-0" f	8'-0" E
14'	2-2x8	2015	1555000	2350	1815000	2685	2073000
	3-2x8	1340	1037000	1570	1210000	1790	1382000
	2-3x8	1210	933000	1410	1089000	1610	1244000
	1-6x8	1025	766000	1200	894000	1370	1021000
	1-3x10	1485	899000	1730	1049000	1980	1198000
	2-2x10	1235	749000	1445	874000	1650	998000
	1-4x10	1060	642000	1240	749000	1415	856000
	3-2x10	825	499000	965	582000	1100	665000
	2-3x10	740	449000	865	524000	990	598000
15'	3-2x8	1540	1275000	1800	1488000	2055	1699000
	2-3x8	1390	1148000	1620	1340000	1850	1530000
	1-6x8	1180	943000	1375	1100000	1570	1257000
	1-3x10	1705	1105000	1990	1289000	2270	1473000
	2-2x10	1420	921000	1660	1075000	1895	1228000
	1-4x10	1220	789000	1420	921000	1625	1052000
	3-2x10	950	614000	1105	717000	1265	818000
	2-3x10	850	553000	995	645000	1135	737000
	1-6x10	735	464000	855	541000	980	618000
	4-2x10	710	461000	830	538000	945	614000
	2-2x12	960	512000	1120	597000	1280	682000
16'	3-2x8	1755	1548000	2045	1806000	2340	2063000
	2-3x8	1580	1393000	1840	1626000	2105	1857000
	1-4x10	1615	1118000	1890	1305000	2155	1490000
	3-2x10	1385	958000	1615	1118000	1845	1277000
	1-6x10	1075	745000	1260	869000	1435	993000
	2-3x10	970	671000	1130	783000	1290	894000
	4-2x10	835	563000	975	657000	1130	750000
	1-8x10	810	559000	945	652000	1080	745000
	1-3x12	615	413000	715	482000	815	550000
	2-2x12	1310	746000	1530	871000	1750	994000
	2-2x12	1090	621000	1275	725000	1455	828000
17'	2-2x10	1825	1341000	2125	1565000	2430	1787000
	1-4x10	1565	1149000	1825	1341000	2085	1532000
	3-2x10	1215	894000	1420	1043000	1620	1192000

MINIMUM "f" & "E" IN psi FOR BEAMS SPACED:

SPAN OF BEAM	NOMINAL SIZE OF BEAM	6'-0" f	6'-0" E	7'-0" f	7'-0" E	8'-0" f	8'-0" E
20'	3-2x10	1685	1456000	1965	1699000	2245	1942000
	2-3x10	1515	1310000	1770	1529000	2020	1747000
	1-6x10	1300	1099000	1515	1282000	1735	1465000
	4-2x10	1260	1092000	1475	1274000	1685	1456000
	2-4x10	1080	936000	1265	1092000	1445	1248000
	1-8x10	960	806000	1120	941000	1280	1075000
	2-2x12	1705	1214000	1990	1417000	2275	1619000
	1-4x12	1465	1040000	1710	1214000	1950	1387000
	3-2x12	1140	809000	1330	944000	1520	1079000
	2-3x12	1025	728000	1195	850000	1365	971000
	1-6x12	970	620000	1130	723000	1295	826000
	2-4x12	730	520000	855	607000	975	694000
21'	3-2x10	1855	1685000	2165	1966000	2475	2247000
	2-3x10	1670	1516000	1950	1827000	2225	2088000
	1-6x10	1430	1273000	1670	1485000	1905	1697000
	4-2x10	1390	1264000	1625	1475000	1855	1686000
	2-4x10	1195	1083000	1390	1264000	1590	1444000
	1-8x10	1050	933000	1225	1089000	1400	1244000
	2-2x12	1880	1405000	2195	1640000	2510	1874000
	1-4x12	1615	1204000	1880	1405000	2150	1606000
	3-2x12	1255	937000	1465	1093000	1670	1249000
	2-3x12	1130	843000	1320	984000	1505	1124000
	1-6x12	970	717000	1130	837000	1295	956000
	2-4x12	805	602000	940	702000	1075	802000
22'	1-6x10	1580	1463000	1845	1707000	2105	1951000
	4-2x10	1525	1453000	1780	1696000	2035	1938000
	2-4x10	1310	1245000	1530	1453000	1745	1660000
	1-8x10	1160	1073000	1355	1252000	1545	1431000
	1-4x12	1770	1384000	2065	1615000	2360	1846000
	3-2x12	1375	1077000	1605	1257000	1835	1436000
	2-3x12	1240	969000	1445	1130000	1655	1291000
	1-6x12	1080	825000	1260	963000	1440	1100000
	2-4x12	885	692000	1035	807000	1180	922000
	4-2x12	1035	808000	1205	943000	1375	1078000
	5-2x12	825	646000	965	754000	1105	862000
	3-3x12	825	639000	965	746000	1105	852000

Table 17-16. Shown are fiber stress in bending and modulus of elasticity values for the beam sizes shown to adequately support a live load of 20 pounds per square foot within a deflection limitation of 1/300 (courtesy National Forest Products Associaton). (Continued on page 337).

SPAN OF BEAM	NOMINAL SIZE OF BEAM	MINIMUM "f" & "E" IN psi FOR BEAMS SPACED:					
		6'-0"		**7'-0"**		**8'-0"**	
		f	E	f	E	f	E
10'	2-3x6	1020	925000	1190	1080000	1360	1240000
	1-3x8	1100	730000	1280	855000	1460	970000
	2-2x8	890	590000	1030	690000	1180	790000
	1-4x8	790	530000	920	620000	1050	705000
	3-2x8	590	395000	690	460000	790	525000
	2-3x8	550	365000	640	425000	730	485000
	2-2x10	550	290000	640	340000	730	390000
11'	2-3x6	1230	1130000	1440	1440000	1640	1650000
	1-3x8	1320	970000	1540	1140000	1760	1300000
	2-2x8	1070	785000	1250	920000	1430	1050000
	1-4x8	960	705000	1120	825000	1270	940000
	3-2x8	710	525000	830	615000	950	700000
	2-3x8	660	485000	780	565000	880	650000
	2-2x10	660	390000	780	455000	880	520000
12'	2-3x6	1470	1600000	1840	1470000	1700	1360000
	1-3x8	1580	1260000	1490	1190000	1510	1220000
	2-2x8	1270	1020000	1330	1070000	1130	910000
	1-4x8	1140	915000	990	795000	1050	840000
	3-2x8	850	680000	920	735000	1000	805000
	2-3x8	790	630000	880	705000	1050	670000
	1-6x8	750	605000				
	2-2x10	790	505000	920	590000		
13'	1-3x8	1850	1600000	1740	1440000	1990	1730000
	2-2x8	1500	1300000	1550	1280000	1780	1550000
	1-4x8	1340	1160000	1160	960000	1330	1160000
	3-2x8	990	865000	1080	885000	1230	1070000
	2-3x8	920	800000	1030	850000	1180	1020000
	1-6x8	880	770000	1080	705000	1230	850000
	2-2x10	920	640000				
	1-3x10	1150	790000	1350	875000	1540	1050000
	1-4x10	830	570000	970	630000	1110	760000

SPAN OF BEAM	NOMINAL SIZE OF BEAM	MINIMUM "f" & "E" IN psi FOR BEAMS SPACED:					
		6'-0"		**7'-0"**		**8'-0"**	
		f	E	f	E	f	E
17'	2-2x10	1590	1430000	1860	1670000	1900	1710000
	1-4x10	1430	1280000	1670	1490000	1410	1270000
	3-2x10	1060	955000	1240	1110000	1310	1180000
	2-3x10	990	885000	1150	1030000	1250	1120000
	1-6x10	940	845000	1100	980000	1060	955000
	4-2x10	790	715000	930	835000	920	825000
	1-8x10	690	620000	810	720000		
	1-3x12	1350	1000000	1580	1160000	1800	1330000
	2-2x12	1090	805000	1280	940000	1450	1080000
	1-4x12	980	720000	1140	840000	1300	960000
	3-2x12	730	535000	850	625000	970	715000
	2-3x12	680	500000	790	580000	900	665000
18'	1-4x10	1600	1520000	1870	1780000	1570	1510000
	3-2x10	1190	1130000	1370	1320000	1480	1400000
	2-3x10	1110	1050000	1300	1230000	1410	1340000
	1-6x10	1060	1000000	1230	1170000	1190	1130000
	4-2x10	890	850000	1040	995000	1030	980000
	1-8x10	780	735000	910	860000		
	1-3x12	1520	1190000	1780	1380000	2020	1580000
	2-2x12	1230	960000	1430	1120000	1630	1280000
	1-4x12	1100	855000	1280	1000000	1460	1140000
	3-2x12	820	640000	960	745000	1090	850000
	2-3x12	760	595000	890	690000	1010	790000
	1-6x12	720	570000	840	660000	960	750000
19'	3-2x10	1320	1340000	1550	1560000	1760	1780000
	2-3x10	1230	1240000	1440	1440000	1650	1650000
	1-6x10	1170	1180000	1370	1370000	1570	1570000
	4-2x10	990	1000000	1160	1170000	1320	1340000
	1-8x10	860	900000	1040	1040000	1190	1190000
	1-3x12	1680	1400000	1970	1630000	1150	1160000
	2-2x12	1360	1130000	1590	1320000	1820	1510000
	1-4x12	1220	1010000	1430	1180000	1630	1350000
	3-2x12	910	755000	1060	825000	1210	1000000
	2-3x12	840	700000	980	815000	1130	1860000

MINIMUM "f" & "E" IN psi FOR BEAMS SPACED:

Spans 14', 15', 16'

SPAN OF BEAM	NOMINAL SIZE OF BEAM	6'-0" f	6'-0" E	7'-0" f	7'-0" E	8'-0" f	8'-0" E
14'	3-2x8	1150	1080000	1350	1260000	1540	1440000
	2-3x8	1070	1000000	1250	1170000	1430	1340000
	1-6x8	1030	960000	1200	1120000	1370	1280000
	1-3x10	1340	990000	1570	1150000	1780	1320000
	2-2x10	1070	810000	1260	935000	1430	1070000
	1-4x10	970	715000	1130	835000	1290	955000
	3-2x10	670	525000	840	625000	960	710000
	2-3x10	670	495000	780	575000	890	660000
	1-6x10	640	470000	750	550000	850	630000
	4-2x10	540	405000	630	417000	720	535000
	2-2x12	740	450000	870	525000	990	600000
15'	3-2x8	1320	1330000	1550	1540000	1770	1770000
	2-3x8	1230	1230000	1440	1430000	1640	1640000
	1-6x8	1180	1170000	1370	1370000	1570	1570000
	1-3x10	1540	1210000	1800	1410000	2050	1610000
	2-2x10	1230	1020000	1440	1140000	1640	1310000
	1-4x10	1110	875000	1300	1020000	1480	1170000
	3-2x10	820	655000	960	761000	700	872000
	2-3x10	770	605000	860	705000	1030	805000
	1-6x10	740	580000	860	675000	980	770000
	2-2x12	620	510000	725	570000	830	655000
	4-2x10	850	553000	990	645000	1140	737000
	1-4x12	760	495000	890	576000	1020	660000
16'	2-3x8	1410	1490000	1650	1740000	1880	1590000
	2-2x10	1410	1190000	1650	1390000	1680	1420000
	1-4x10	1260	1070000	1470	1240000	1250	1060000
	3-2x10	940	795000	1100	930000	1170	985000
	2-3x10	880	740000	1020	860000	1110	935000
	1-6x10	840	705000	970	820000	940	795000
	4-2x10	770	595000	820	695000	810	690000
	1-8x10	610	515000	710	600000		
	1-3x12	1200	830000	1400	970000	1600	1110000
	2-2x12	870	670000	1130	785000	1290	895000
	1-4x12	870	600000	1010	705000	1150	805000
	3-2x12	650	448000	750	522000	860	597000

Spans 20', 21', 22'

SPAN OF BEAM	NOMINAL SIZE OF BEAM	6'-0" f	6'-0" E	7'-0" f	7'-0" E	8'-0" f	8'-0" E
20'	3-2x10	1470	1550000	1600	1680000		
	2-3x10	1370	1440000	1520	1600000		
	1-6x10	1300	1370000	1280	1360000	1470	1550000
	4-2x10	1100	1160000	1150	1220000	1320	1390000
	1-4x10	990	1040000	1120	1180000	1280	1340000
	1-8x10	960	1010000	1770	1530000	2020	1750000
	2-2x12	1510	1310000	1580	1370000	1800	1570000
	1-4x12	1010	1170000	1180	1020000	1350	1160000
	3-2x12	1350	873000	1090	950000	1250	1080000
	2-3x12	1010	810000	1040	905000	1190	1030000
	1-6x12	940	775000		765000		875000
	4-2x12	890	655000				
21'	2-3x10	1500	1670000	1680	1850000	1450	1610000
	1-6x10	1430	1590000	1420	1570000	1400	1550000
	4-2x10	1210	1350000	1270	1410000		
	2-4x10	1090	1210000	1230	1360000		
	1-8x10	1050	1170000	1950	1770000	1990	1810000
	2-2x12	1660	1520000	1740	1580000	1480	1350000
	1-4x12	1490	1360000	1300	1180000	1380	1250000
	3-2x12	1110	1010000	1200	1100000	1310	1200000
	2-3x12	1030	940000	1130	1050000	1110	1010000
	1-6x12	970	895000	970	885000	990	907000
	4-2x12	830	740000	870	795000		
	2-4x12	750	680000				
22'	4-2x10	1330	1550000	1400	1620000	1550	1790000
	2-4x10	1200	1380000	1350	1570000		
	1-8x10	1160	1350000				
	1-4x12	1640	1560000	1420	1360000	1630	1550000
	3-2x12	1220	1160000	1320	1260000	1520	1440000
	2-3x12	1130	1080000	1260	1210000	1450	1370000
	1-6x12	1080	1030000	1070	1020000	1230	1160000
	4-2x12	920	870000	960	915000	1100	1040000
	5-2x12	820	785000	880	840000	980	930000
	3-3x12	750	720000			1010	960000

337

Table 17-17. The table gives fiber stress in bending and modulus of elasticity values for beam sizes shown to support a live load of 20 pounds per square foot within a deflection limitation of I/360 (courtesy National Forest Products Association). (Continued on page 339).

SPAN OF BEAM	NOMINAL SIZE OF BEAM	MINIMUM "f" & "E" IN psi FOR BEAMS SPACED:					
		6'-0"		7'-0"		8'-0"	
		f	E	f	E	f	E
10'	2-3x6	1020	1110000	1190	1300000	1360	1480000
	1-3x8	1100	875000	1280	1020000	1460	1170000
	2-2x8	890	710000	1030	825000	1180	940000
	1-4x8	790	635000	920	740000	1050	845000
	3-2x8	590	475000	690	550000	790	630000
	2-3x8	550	440000	640	510000	730	585000
	1-6x8	520	520000	610	490000	700	560000
11'	2-3x6	1230	1480000	1440	1730000	1760	1550000
	1-3x8	1320	1170000	1540	1360000	1430	1260000
	2-2x8	1070	945000	1250	1100000	1270	1130000
	1-4x8	960	845000	1120	985000	950	840000
	3-2x8	710	630000	830	735000	880	775000
	2-3x8	660	585000	780	680000	840	745000
	1-6x8	630	560000	740	650000		
12'	1-3x8	1580	1510000	1840	1760000	1700	1640000
	2-2x8	1270	1220000	1490	1430000	1510	1460000
	1-4x8	1140	1100000	1330	1280000	1130	1090000
	3-2x8	850	815000	990	955000	1050	1010000
	2-3x8	790	755000	920	882000	1000	965000
	1-6x8	750	720000	880	845000	1060	805000
	2-2x10	790	600000	920	705000	1310	995000
	1-3x10	980	745000	1150	870000		
13'	2-2x8	1500	1560000	1740	1820000		
	1-4x8	1340	1400000	1550	1630000	1330	1400000
	3-2x8	990	1040000	1160	1220000	1230	1290000
	1-6x8	880	925000	1030	1130000	1180	1130000
	2-2x10	930	770000	1080	900000	1240	1030000
	1-3x10	1150	950000	1350	1110000	1540	1270000
	1-4x10	830	690000	970	805000	1110	920000

SPAN OF BEAM	NOMINAL SIZE OF BEAM	MINIMUM "f" & "E" IN psi FOR BEAMS SPACED:					
		6'-0"		7'-0"		8'-0"	
		f	E	f	E	f	E
17'	2-2x10	1590	1720000	1670	1790000	1410	1530000
	1-4x10	1430	1530000	1240	1330000	1310	1410000
	3-2x10	1060	1140000	1150	1240000	1250	1350000
	2-3x10	990	1060000	1100	1180000	1060	1140000
	1-6x10	940	1010000	930	1000000	920	990000
	4-2x10	790	860000	810	865000		
	1-8x10	690	740000				
	1-3x12	1350	1200000	1580	1400000	1800	1600000
	2-2x12	1090	970000	1280	1130000	1450	1290000
	1-4x12	980	865000	1140	1010000	1300	1150000
	3-2x12	730	645000	850	740000	970	858000
	2-3x12	680	600000	790	700000	900	800000
18'	3-2x10	1190	1360000	1370	1590000	1480	1680000
	2-3x10	1110	1260000	1300	1470000	1410	1600000
	1-6x10	1060	1200000	1230	1400000	1190	1360000
	4-2x10	890	1020000	1040	1190000	1030	1180000
	1-8x10	780	840000	910	1030000		
	1-3x12	1520	1420000	1780	1660000	1630	1530000
	2-2x12	1230	1150000	1430	1340000	1460	1370000
	1-4x12	1100	1030000	1280	1200000	1090	1020000
	3-2x12	820	765000	960	895000	1010	950000
	2-3x12	760	710000	890	830000	960	900000
	1-6x12	720	680000	840	790000	820	765000
	4-2x12	620	575000	720	676000		
19'	3-2x10	1320	1600000	1440	1730000	1320	1600000
	2-3x10	1230	1480000	1370	1650000	1190	1430000
	1-6x10	1170	1410000	1160	1400000	1150	1380000
	4-2x10	990	1200000	1040	1250000		
	2-4x10	890	1070000	1010	1210000		
	1-8x10	860	1040000				
	2-2x12	1360	1350000	1590	1580000	1630	1610000
	1-4x12	1220	1210000	1430	1410000	1210	1200000
	3-2x12	910	900000	1060	1050000	1130	1110000
	2-3x12	840	835000	980	980000	1070	1060000
	1-6x12	800	800000	940	930000		

MINIMUM "f" & "E" IN psi FOR BEAMS SPACED: (spans 20', 21', 22')

SPAN OF BEAM	NOMINAL SIZE OF BEAM	6'-0" f	6'-0" E	7'-0" f	7'-0" E	8'-0" f	8'-0" E
20'	2-3x10	1370	1730000	1280	1630000	1320	1660000
	1-6x10	1300	1650000	1150	1460000	1280	1610000
	4-2x10	1100	1400000	1120	1410000		
	2-4x10	990	1250000				
	1-8x10	960	1210000				
	2-2x12	1510	1580000	1580	1640000	1350	1400000
	1-4x12	1350	1410000	1180	1220000	1250	1300000
	3-2x12	1010	1050000	1090	1140000	1190	1240000
	2-3x12	940	975000	1040	1090000	1010	1050000
	1-6x12	890	930000	880	920000	900	940000
	4-2x12	760	790000	790	820000		
	2-4x12	680	705000				
21'	4-2x10	1210	1620000	1270	1690000	1480	1620000
	2-4x10	1090	1450000	1230	1630000	1380	1500000
	1-8x10	1050	1400000			1310	1430000
	1-4x12	1490	1630000	1300	1420000	1110	1210000
	3-2x12	1110	1210000	1200	1320000	990	1090000
	2-3x12	1030	1130000	1130	1060000	920	1000000
	1-6x12	970	1070000	970	950000	960	1050000
	4-2x12	830	910000	870	875000	750	826000
	2-4x12	750	815000	800	920000		
	3-3x12	690	750000	840	725000		
	1-8x12	720	790000	660			
	1-10x12	580	620000				
22'	2-4x10	1200	1670000	1420	1630000	1520	1730000
	1-8x10	1160	1610000	1320	1510000	1450	1650000
	3-2x12	1220	1400000	1260	1450000	1230	1400000
	2-3x12	1130	1300000	1070	1230000	1100	1250000
	1-6x12	1080	1240000	960	1090000	980	1120000
	4-2x12	920	1050000	880	980000	1010	1160000
	2-4x12	820	940000	920	1010000	1060	1210000
	5-2x12	730	840000	730	1060000	830	955000
	3-3x12	750	865000		835000		
	1-8x12	790	910000				
	1-10x12	620	715000				

MINIMUM "f" & "E" IN psi FOR BEAMS SPACED: (spans 14', 15', 16')

SPAN OF BEAM	NOMINAL SIZE OF BEAM	6'-0" f	6'-0" E	7'-0" f	7'-0" E	8'-0" f	8'-0" E
14'	3-2x8	1150	1300000	1350	1510000	1540	1730000
	2-3x8	1070	1200000	1250	1400000	1430	1600000
	1-6x8	1030	1150000	1200	1340000	1370	1530000
	1-3x10	1340	1180000	1570	1380000	1780	1580000
	2-2x10	1080	960000	1260	1120000	1440	1280000
	1-4x10	970	860000	1130	1000000	1290	1140000
	3-2x10	720	640000	840	745000	960	855000
	2-3x10	670	590000	780	690000	890	790000
	1-6x10	640	565000	750	660000	850	755000
	4-2x10	540	480000	630	560000	720	640000
	2-2x12	740	540000	870	630000	990	720000
15'	3-2x8	1320	1590000	1440	1720000	1650	1570000
	2-3x8	1230	1480000	1370	1650000	1480	1400000
	1-6x8	1180	1410000	1800	1700000	1100	970000
	1-3x10	1540	1460000	1450	1380000	1030	1050000
	2-2x10	1240	1180000	1300	1230000	980	925000
	1-4x10	1110	1050000	960	918000	830	785000
	3-2x10	820	786000	900	850000	1140	885000
	2-3x10	770	730000	860	810000	1020	792000
	1-6x10	740	695000	720	690000		
	4-2x10	620	590000	990	775000		
	2-2x12	850	665000	890	695000		
	1-4x12	760	594000				
16'	2-2x10	1410	1440000	1650	1670000	1680	1710000
	1-4x10	1260	1280000	1470	1490000	1250	1270000
	3-2x10	940	960000	1100	1110000	1170	1180000
	2-3x10	880	886000	1020	1030000	1110	1130000
	1-6x10	840	845000	970	985000	940	955000
	4-2x10	700	720000	820	835000	810	830000
	1-8x10	610	620000	710	725000	1600	1330000
	1-3x12	1200	1000000	1400	1177000	1290	1080000
	2-2x12	970	810000	1130	940000	1150	965000
	1-4x12	870	725000	1010	845000	860	720000
	3-2x12	650	540000	750	630000	800	665000
	2-3x12	600	500000	700	588000		

Table 17-18. Fiber stress and elasticity values for these beam sizes will support a live load of 30 pounds per square foot within a deflection limitation of 1/240 (courtesy National Forest Products Association). (Continued on page 341).

(Continued on page 341).

MINIMUM "F" & "E" IN psi FOR BEAMS SPACED:

SPAN OF BEAM	NOMINAL SIZE OF BEAM	6'-0" f	6'-0" E	7'-0" f	7'-0" E	8'-0" f	8'-0" E
10'	2-3x6	1360	1110000	1590	1290000	1810	1480000
	1-3x8	1460	877000	1700	1020000	1950	1160000
	1-4x8	1050	635000	1220	740000	1400	845000
	3-2x8	790	475000	920	550000	1050	630000
	2-3x8	730	440000	850	510000	970	580000
	2-4x8	530	320000	610	370000	700	425000
	2-2x10	740	350000	860	405000	980	465000
11'	2-3x6	1640	1480000	1920	1730000		
	1-3x8	1770	1160000	2060	1360000		
	1-4x8	1270	845000	1490	985000	1700	1130000
	3-2x8	950	630000	1110	735000	1270	840000
	2-3x8	880	580000	1030	680000	1180	775000
	2-4x8	640	425000	750	495000	850	565000
	2-2x10	890	465000	1040	545000	1180	620000
12'	1-4x8	1510	1100000	1770	1280000	2020	1460000
	3-2x8	1130	820000	1320	955000	1510	1090000
	2-3x8	1050	760000	1230	880000	1400	1010000
	2-4x8	760	550000	880	640000	1010	730000
	1-6x8	1000	725000	1170	845000	1340	965000
	2-2x10	1060	605000	1230	705000	1410	805000
	2-3x10	660	370000	760	435000	880	500000
13'	1-4x8	1780	1400000				
	3-2x8	1330	1040000	1550	1220000	1770	1390000
	2-3x8	1230	960000	1440	1120000	1650	1280000
	2-4x8	890	700000	1040	815000	1190	930000
	1-6x8	1180	920000	1370	1070000	1570	1230000
	2-2x10	1240	770000	1450	895000	1650	1030000
	3-2x10	830	515000	970	600000	1100	680000
	2-3x10	770	475000	900	555000	1030	630000

MINIMUM "F" & "E" IN psi FOR BEAMS SPACED:

SPAN OF BEAM	NOMINAL SIZE OF BEAM	6'-0" f	6'-0" E	7'-0" f	7'-0" E	8'-0" f	8'-0" E
17'	3-2x10	1420	1140000	1650	1340000	1900	1530000
	2-3x10	1320	1060000	1540	1240000	1760	1410000
	1-4x10	1900	1530000				
	1-6x10	1260	1010000	1470	1180000	1680	1350000
	2-4x10	950	770000	1110	895000	1270	1020000
	4-2x10	1060	855000	1240	1000000	1420	1140000
	1-8x10	920	740000	1080	865000	1230	990000
	2-2x12	1460	965000	1700	1130000	1950	1290000
	1-4x12	1310	865000	1520	1010000	1750	1150000
	3-2x12	970	640000	1140	750000	1300	860000
	2-3x12	900	600000	1060	700000	1210	800000
	4-2x12	730	485000	850	565000	970	645000
18'	2-3x10	1480	1240000	1730	1470000	1970	1680000
	1-6x10	1410	1180000	1650	1400000	1880	1600000
	2-4x10	1070	895000	1250	1060000	1430	1210000
	4-2x10	1190	1000000	1390	1190000	1590	1360000
	1-8x10	1040	865000	1210	1030000	1380	1170000
	2-2x12	1640	1130000	1910	1340000	2180	1530000
	1-4x12	1470	1030000	1710	1200000	1950	1370000
	3-2x12	1090	750000	1270	890000	1460	1020000
	2-3x12	1010	700000	1180	840000	1350	950000
	4-2x12	820	565000	960	670000	1090	760000
	5-2x12	660	450000	770	540000	880	610000
19'	2-4x10	1190	1070000	1390	1260000	1590	1450000
	4-2x10	1330	1200000	1550	1400000	1770	1600000
	1-8x10	1150	1040000	1340	1210000	1540	1380000
	1-4x12	1220	1210000	1420	1410000	1620	1610000
	3-2x12	1140	900000	1320	1050000	1500	1200000
	4-2x12	910	835000	1060	985000	1210	1110000
	2-4x12	820	605000	950	705000	1090	805000
	5-2x12	730	540000	850	630000	970	720000
	1-6x12	1070	795000	1250	925000	1430	1050000
	3-3x12	750	555000	880	650000	1000	740000

Left section

OF BEAM	SIZE OF BEAM	6'-0" f	6'-0" E	7'-0" f	7'-0" E	8'-0" f	8'-0" E
14'	3-2x8	1540	1300000	1800	1520000	1910	1600000
	2-3x8	1430	1200000	1670	1400000	1380	1160000
	2-4x8	1030	875000	1210	1020000	1830	1160000
	1-6x8	1370	1150000	1600	1340000	1930	1530000
	2-2x10	1490	960000	1680	1120000	1280	1280000
	2-3x10	960	670000	1120	750000	1200	855000
	1-4x10	890	595000	1050	695000	1720	790000
	1-6x10	1290	860000	1510	1000000	1140	1150000
	1-8x10	850	565000	1000	660000	860	755000
	2-4x10	650	430000	750	510000		580000
15'	2-4x8	1190	1070000	1380	1250000	1580	1430000
	1-6x8	1570	1410000	1830	1650000		
	2-2x10	1650	1180000	1930	1380000	2200	1570000
	3-2x10	1100	785000	1280	920000	1470	1050000
	2-3x10	1030	730000	1200	850000	1370	970000
	1-4x10	1480	1060000	1730	1230000	1970	1400000
	1-6x10	980	695000	1140	810000	1300	925000
	2-4x10	740	525000	865	615000	990	700000
	4-2x10	830	590000	960	690000	1100	785000
	1-8x10	720	510000	840	595000	960	680000
	2-2x12	1040	665000	1330	775000	1510	885000
	1-4x12	1020	595000	1190	695000	1350	790000
16'	2-2x10	1880	1430000	2200	1610000	1670	1270000
	3-2x10	1250	955000	1460	1110000	1550	1180000
	2-3x10	1170	850000	1360	1030000	1480	1120000
	1-4x10	1690	1280000	1970	1500000	1120	855000
	1-6x10	1110	840000	1300	985000	1250	955000
	2-4x10	840	640000	980	745000	1090	825000
	4-2x10	940	715000	1100	835000	1720	1080000
	1-8x10	830	620000	950	720000	1540	960000
	2-2x12	1290	805000	1510	940000	1150	715000
	1-4x12	1160	720000	1350	845000	1070	665000
	3-2x12	860	535000	1000	625000		
	2-3x12	800	500000	930	580000		

Right section (…RING SPACING)

OF BEAM	SIZE OF BEAM	6'-0" f	6'-0" E	7'-0" f	7'-0" E	8'-0" f	8'-0" E
20'	4-2x10	1460	1400000	1720	1630000	1530	1610000
	1-8x10	1150	1210000	1340	1410000	1620	1400000
	3-2x12	1210	1050000	1410	1220000	1500	1300000
	2-3x12	1120	975000	1310	1140000	1210	1050000
	4-2x12	910	790000	1060	920000	1090	945000
	2-4x12	810	705000	950	825000	970	840000
	5-2x12	730	630000	850	735000	1430	1240000
	1-6x12	1070	650000	1250	1080000	1000	865000
	3-3x12	750	680000	880	755000	1050	910000
	1-8x12	790	730000	920	750000	830	830000
	1-10x12	620	535000	720	625000	920	750000
	4-3x12	560	490000	660	570000	750	650000
21'	1-8x10	1410	1400000	1640	1630000	1980	1620000
	3-2x12	1490	1210000	1730	1410000	1830	1500000
	2-3x12	1380	1130000	1600	1310000	1480	1210000
	4-2x12	1110	910000	1300	1060000	1330	1090000
	2-4x12	1000	820000	1160	955000	1190	970000
	5-2x12	890	730000	1040	850000	1750	1430000
	1-6x12	1310	1070000	1530	1250000	1220	1000000
	3-3x12	920	750000	1070	875000	990	1050000
	1-8x12	970	790000	1020	920000	1010	830000
	1-10x12	760	620000	880	725000	920	750000
	4-3x12	690	565000	800	660000	1330	930000
	2-3x14	1000	700000	1160	815000		
22'	2-3x12	1510	1300000	1760	1510000	2020	1750000
	4-2x12	1220	1050000	1420	1220000	1630	1400000
	2-4x12	1090	940000	1280	1090000	1460	1260000
	5-2x12	1430	1240000	1680	1440000	1920	1650000
	1-6x12	1010	860000	1180	1010000	1340	1150000
	3-3x12	830	715000	970	835000	1410	1210000
	1-8x12	750	650000	880	760000	1110	950000
	1-10x12	1090	808000	1280	940000	1010	865000
	4-3x12	1040	765000	1220	895000	1460	1070000
	2-3x14	730	535000	850	625000	1390	1020000
	1-6x14	860	580000	920	680000	970	715000
	3-3x14					1060	775000

Table 17-19. The stress and elasticity values for shown beam sizes will support a live load of 30 pounds per square foot within a deflection limitation of 1/300 (courtesy National Forest Products Association). (Continued on page 343).

SPAN OF BEAM	NOMINAL SIZE OF BEAM	MINIMUM "f" & "E" IN psi FOR BEAMS SPACED:					
		6'-0" f	6'-0" E	7'-0" f	7'-0" E	8'-0" f	8'-0" E
10'	2-3x6	1360	1390000	1590	1620000	1950	1460000
	1-3x8	1460	1090000	1700	1280000	1400	1060000
	1-4x8	1050	795000	1220	925000	1050	790000
	3-2x8	790	590000	920	690000	970	730000
	2-3x8	730	545000	850	640000	700	530000
	2-4x8	530	400000	610	465000	980	585000
	2-2x10	740	435000	860	515000		
11'	1-3x8	1770	1460000	2060	1690000	1700	1410000
	1-4x8	1270	1060000	1490	1240000	1270	1050000
	3-2x8	950	790000	1110	920000	1180	970000
	2-3x8	880	730000	1030	850000	850	710000
	2-4x8	640	530000	750	620000	1180	780000
	2-2x10	890	585000	1040	680000	1480	960000
	1-3x10	1100	720000	1290	840000		
12'	1-4x8	1510	1370000	1770	1600000	1510	1360000
	2-2x8	1130	1?90000	1320	1190000	1400	1260000
	2-3x8	105C	945000	1230	1100000	1010	915000
	2-4x8	760	685000	880	800000	1340	1210000
	1-6x8	1000	905000	1170	1050000	1410	1010000
	2-2x10	1060	755000	1230	880000	940	675000
	3-2x10	750	505000	820	590000	880	620000
	2-3x10	660	465000	760	545000		
13'	1-4x8	1780	1750000	1550	1520000	1770	1740000
	3-2x8	1330	1300000	1440	1400000	1650	1600000
	2-3x8	1230	1210000	1040	1020000	1190	1170000
	2-4x8	890	875000	1370	1350000	1570	1540000
	1-6x8	1180	105?000	1450	1120000	1650	1280000
	2-2x10	1240	965000	970	750000	1100	855000
	3-2x10	830	640000	900	695000	1030	790000
	2-3x10	770	595000	1300	1000000	1480	1150000
	1-3x12	11?0	860000				

SPAN OF BEAM	NOMINAL SIZE OF BEAM	MINIMUM "f" & "E" IN psi FOR BEAMS SPACED:					
		6'-0" f	6'-0" E	7'-0" f	7'-0" E	8'-0" f	8'-0" E
17'	3-2x10	1420	1430000	1650	1670000	1760	1770000
	2-3x10	1320	1330000	1540	1550000	1680	1690000
	1-6x10	1260	1260000	1470	1480000	1270	1280000
	2-4x10	950	960000	1110	1120000	1420	1430000
	4-2x10	1060	1070000	1240	1250000	1230	1240000
	1-8x10	920	930000	1080	1080000	1950	1610000
	2-2x12	1460	1210000	1700	1410000	1750	1440000
	1-4x12	1310	1080000	1520	1260000	1300	1070000
	3-2x12	970	805000	1140	1080000	1210	1000000
	2-3x12	900	750000	1060	870000	970	805000
	4-2x12	730	605000	850	705000	870	725000
	2-4x12	650	545000	760	635000		
18'	2-3x10	1480	1580000	1650	1760000	1430	1520000
	1-6x10	1410	1510000	1250	1330000	1590	1700000
	2-4x10	1070	1140000	1390	1490000	1380	1470000
	4-2x10	1190	1280000	1210	1290000	1950	1710000
	1-8x10	1040	1100000	1910	1680000	1460	1280000
	2-2x12	1640	1440000	1710	1500000	1350	1190000
	1-4x12	1470	1290000	1270	1120000	1090	960000
	3-2x12	1090	960000	1180	1040000	980	860000
	2-3x12	1010	890000	960	840000	870	765000
	4-2x12	820	720000	860	755000		
	5-2x12	660	575000	770	670000		
19'	1-6x10	1570	1770000	1390	1560000	1590	1780000
	2-4x10	1190	1340000	1550	1750000	1540	1720000
	4-2x10	1330	1500000	1340	1510000		
	1-4x12	1630	1510000	1900	1760000	1620	1500000
	3-2x12	1220	1120000	1420	1310000	1500	1390000
	2-3x12	1140	1040000	1320	1220000	1210	1120000
	4-2x12	910	845000	1060	980000	1090	1010000
	2-4x12	820	760000	950	885000	970	900000
	5-2x12	730	675000	850	785000	1430	1330000
	1-6x12	1070	995000	1250	1160000		

MINIMUM "f" & "E" IN psi FOR BEAMS SPACED (Spans 14′–16′)

SPAN OF BEAM	NOMINAL SIZE OF BEAM	6′-0″ f	6′-0″ E	7′-0″ f	7′-0″ E	8′-0″ f	8′-0″ E
14′	3-2x8	1540	1620000	1670	1750000		
	2-3x8	1430	1500000	1210	1280000		
	2-4x8	1030	1090000	1600	1680000	1380	1450000
	1-6x8	1370	1440000	1680	1400000		
	2-2x10	1490	1200000	1120	935000	1930	1600000
	3-2x10	960	800000	1050	865000	1280	1070000
	2-3x10	890	740000	1510	1250000	1200	980000
	1-4x10	1290	1070000	1000	825000	1720	1430000
	1-6x10	850	710000	750	625000	1140	940000
	2-4x10	650	535000			860	715000
15′	2-4x8	1190	1340000	1380	1560000	1580	1780000
	1-6x8	1570	1770000	1930	1720000	1470	1310000
	2-2x10	1650	1480000	1280	1150000	1370	1220000
	3-2x10	1100	985000	1200	1060000	1970	1760000
	2-3x10	1030	910000	1730	1540000	1300	1060000
	1-4x10	1480	1320000	1140	1020000	990	880000
	1-6x10	980	870000	865	770000	1100	980000
	2-4x10	740	660000	960	860000	960	850000
	1-8x10	830	740000	840	745000	1510	1110000
	2-2x12	720	640000	1330	970000	1350	990000
	1-4x12	1040	830000	1190	870000		
	2-3x12	1020	745000				
16′	2-2x10	1880	1780000	1460	1390000	1670	1590000
	3-2x10	1250	1190000	1360	1290000	1550	1470000
	2-3x10	1170	1100000	1300	1230000	1480	1410000
	1-4x10	1690	1600000	980	950000	1120	1070000
	1-6x10	1110	1050000	1100	1040000	1250	1190000
	2-4x10	840	810000	950	905000	1090	1030000
	4-2x10	940	895000	1510	1180000	1720	1340000
	1-8x10	830	720000	1350	1050000	1540	1050000
	2-2x12	1290	1010000	1000	785000	1150	895000
	1-4x12	1160	900000	930	730000	1070	830000
	3-2x12	860	670000				
	2-3x12	800	620000				

MINIMUM "f" & "E" IN psi FOR BEAMS SPACED (Spans 20′–22′)

SPAN OF BEAM	NOMINAL SIZE OF BEAM	6′-0″ f	6′-0″ E	7′-0″ f	7′-0″ E	8′-0″ f	8′-0″ E
20′	1-8x10	1150	1510000	1340	1760000	1620	1750000
	3-2x12	1210	1310000	1410	1530000	1500	1630000
	2-3x12	1120	1220000	1310	1420000	1210	1310000
	4-2x12	910	1090000	1060	1090000	1090	1180000
	2-4x12	810	885000	950	1030000	970	1050000
	5-2x12	730	790000	850	920000	1430	1550000
	1-6x12	1070	1160000	1250	1360000	1050	1080000
	3-3x12	750	810000	880	945000	1050	1140000
	1-8x12	790	850000	920	780000	830	895000
	1-10x12	620	670000	720	710000	750	815000
	4-3x12	560	610000	660	880000	1090	1010000
	2-3x14	810	755000	950			
21′	3-2x12	1490	1640000	1600	1700000	1480	1570000
	2-3x12	1380	1470000	1300	1370000	1330	1410000
	4-2x12	1110	1180000	1160	1240000	1190	1260000
	2-4x12	1000	1060000	1040	1100000	1220	1290000
	5-2x12	890	945000	1530	1620000	990	1360000
	3-3x12	1310	1400000	1070	1130000	1010	1450000
	1-8x12	920	975000	1020	1190000	920	970000
	1-10x12	970	1030000	880	940000	1330	1200000
	4-3x12	760	805000	800	850000	1270	1150000
	2-3x14	1000	730000	1160	1050000		
	1-6x14	950	905000	1110	1010000		
22′	4-2x12	1220	1310000	1420	1530000	1630	1740000
	2-4x12	1090	1180000	1280	1370000	1460	1570000
	5-2x12	980	1050000	1140	1225000	1300	1400000
	1-6x12	1430	1550000	1680	1800000	1340	1440000
	3-3x12	1010	1080000	1180	1260000	1410	1510000
	1-8x12	1050	1040000	1230	1330000	1110	1190000
	1-10x12	830	890000	970	1040000	1010	1080000
	4-3x12	750	810000	880	945000	1460	1340000
	2-3x14	1090	1000000	1280	1170000	1390	1280000
	1-6x14	1040	960000	1220	1120000	970	890000
	3-3x14	730	670000	850	780000	1060	965000
	2-4x14	790	725000	920	845000		

Table 17-20. Here are fiber stress and elasticity values for shown beam sizes to support a live load of 30 pounds per square foot within a deflection limitation of l/360 (courtesy National Forest Products Associaton). (Continued on page 345).

SPAN OF BEAM	NOMINAL SIZE OF BEAM	MINIMUM "f" & "E" IN psi FOR BEAMS SPACED: 6'-0" f	6'-0" E	7'-0" f	7'-0" E	8'-0" f	8'-0" E
10'	2-3x6	1360	1670000	1700	1540000	1950	1740000
	1-3x8	1460	1320000	1220	1120000	1400	1275000
	1-4x8	1050	955000	920	830000	1050	950000
	3-2x8	790	710000	850	770000	970	880000
	2-3x8	730	655000	610	560000	700	635000
	2-4x8	530	475000	860	615000	980	705000
	2-2x10	740	525000				
11'	1-3x8	1770	1750000	1490	1480000	1700	1690000
	1-4x8	1270	1270000	1110	1100000	1270	1260000
	3-2x8	950	950000	1030	1020000	1180	1170000
	2-3x8	880	875000	750	740000	850	845000
	2-4x8	640	635000	1040	815000	1180	930000
	2-2x10	890	700000	1290	1010000	1480	1150000
	1-3x10	1100	865000				
12'	1-4x8	1510	1650000	1320	1430000	1510	1640000
	3-2x8	1130	1230000	1230	1320000	1400	1510000
	2-3x8	1050	1040000	880	865000	1010	1100000
	2-4x8	760	825000	1170	1270000	1340	1450000
	1-6x8	1000	1090000	1230	1060000	1410	1210000
	2-2x10	1060	910000	820	705000	940	805000
	3-2x10	750	605000	760	655000	880	750000
	2-3x10	660	560000	1110	945000	1270	1080000
	1-4x10	950	810000				
13'	3-2x8	1330	1560000	1440	1690000	1190	1390000
	2-3x8	1230	1440000	1040	1220000	1650	1540000
	2-4x8	890	1050000	1370	1610000	1100	1030000
	1-6x8	1180	1380000	1450	1350000	1030	950000
	2-2x10	1240	1150000	970	900000	1480	1370000
	3-2x10	830	835000	900	830000	980	905000
	2-3x10	770	710000	1300	1080000		
	1-4x10	1110	1030000	860	795000		
	1-6x10	730					
17'	2-3x10	1320	1590000	1470	1770000	1270	1540000
	1-6x10	1260	1520000	1110	1340000	1420	1720000
	2-4x10	950	1150000	1240	1500000	1230	1490000
	1-8x10	1060	1290000	1080	1300000		
	2-2x12	920	1110000	1700	1690000	1750	1730000
	1-4x12	1460	1450000	1520	1520000	1300	1290000
	3-2x12	1310	1300000	1140	1130000	1210	1200000
	2-3x12	970	965000	1060	1050000	970	1080000
	4-2x12	900	900000	850	845000	870	870000
	5-2x12	730	725000	760	760000	780	775000
		650	650000	680	675000		
		580	580000				
18'	2-4x10	1070	1360000	1250	1590000	1380	1760000
	4-2x10	1190	1530000	1390	1780000		
	1-8x10	1040	1320000	1210	1540000		
	1-4x12	1470	1760000				
	3-2x12	1090	1540000	1270	1340000	1460	1530000
	2-3x12	1010	1140000	1180	1240000	1350	1420000
	4-2x12	820	1070000	960	1000000	1090	1150000
	2-4x12	730	860000	860	900000	980	1030000
	5-2x12	660	770000	770	800000	870	920000
	1-6x12	960	690000	1120	1180000	1280	1350000
	3-3x12	680	1010000	790	825000	900	945000
			710000				
19'	2-4x10	1190	1610000	1420	1580000	1500	1670000
	1-8x10	1150	1560000	1320	1460000	1210	1350000
	3-2x12	1220	1350000	1060	1180000	1090	1210000
	2-3x12	1140	1260000	950	1060000	970	1080000
	4-2x12	910	1010000	850	950000	1430	1600000
	2-4x12	820	910000	1250	1400000	1000	1110000
	5-2x12	730	810000	880	975000	1050	1170000
	1-6x12	1070	1200000	920	1030000	830	920000
	3-3x12	750	835000	720	810000		
	1-8x12	790	880000				
	1-10x12	620	690000				

Table header (both tables): **MINIMUM "f" & "E" IN psi FOR BEAMS SPACED:**

Spans 14', 15', 16'

SPAN OF BEAM	NOMINAL SIZE OF BEAM	6'-0" f	6'-0" E	7'-0" f	7'-0" E	8'-0" f	8'-0" E
14'	2-4x8	1030	1310000	1210	1520000	1380	1740000
	1-6x8	1370	1720000	1680	1680000	1280	1280000
	2-2x10	1490	1440000	1120	1120000	1200	1190000
	3-2x10	960	960000	1050	1040000	1720	1720000
	2-3x10	890	890000	1510	1500000	1140	1130000
	1-4x10	1290	1280000	1000	990000	860	860000
	1-6x10	850	850000	750	750000	960	960000
	2-4x10	650	645000	840	840000	840	830000
	4-2x10	720	720000	730	725000		
	1-8x10	630	620000				
15'	2-2x10	1650	1770000	1280	1380000	1470	1570000
	3-2x10	1100	1180000	1200	1280000	1370	1460000
	2-3x10	1030	1090000	1140	1220000	1300	1390000
	1-4x10	1480	1580000	865	925000	990	1060000
	1-6x10	980	1040000	960	1030000	1100	1180000
	2-4x10	740	790000	840	890000	960	1020000
	4-2x10	830	885000	1330	1160000	1510	1330000
	1-8x10	720	765000	1190	1040000	1350	1190000
	2-2x12	1040	995000	880	775000	1000	1020000
	1-4x12	1020	890000	820	720000	940	820000
	3-2x12	760	665000				
	2-3x12	700	615000				
16'	3-2x10	1250	1430000	1460	1670000	1550	1770000
	2-3x10	1170	1330000	1360	1550000	1480	1680000
	1-6x10	1110	1270000	1300	1450000	1120	1280000
	2-4x10	840	960000	980	1120000	1250	1430000
	4-2x10	940	1070000	1100	1250000	1090	1240000
	1-8x10	830	930000	950	1080000	1720	1610000
	2-2x12	1290	1210000	1510	1410000	1540	1450000
	1-4x12	1160	1080000	1350	1260000	1150	1070000
	3-2x12	860	805000	1000	940000	1070	1000000
	2-3x12	800	750000	930	875000	860	795000
	4-2x12	640	605000	750	700000	770	725000
	2-4x12	580	545000	670	635000		

Spans 20', 21', 22'

SPAN OF BEAM	NOMINAL SIZE OF BEAM	6'-0" f	6'-0" E	7'-0" f	7'-0" E	8'-0" f	8'-0" E
20'	3-2x12	1210	1570000	1310	1713000	1210	1570000
	2-3x12	1120	1460000	1060	1380000	1090	1410000
	4-2x12	910	1180000	950	1240000	970	1260000
	2-4x12	810	1060000	850	1100000	1430	1190000
	5-2x12	730	945000	1250	1620000	1000	1300000
	1-6x12	1070	1390000	880	1130000	1050	1370000
	3-3x12	750	970000	920	1190000	830	1070000
	1-8x12	790	1020000	720	940000	750	975000
	1-10x12	620	805000	660	850000	1090	1210000
	4-3x12	560	730000	950	1050000	1040	1150000
	2-3x14	810	905000	910	1010000		
	1-6x14	780	865000				
21'	2-3x12	1380	1760000	1300	1660000	1330	1700000
	4-2x12	1110	1420000	1160	1490000	1190	1520000
	2-4x12	1000	1280000	1040	1330000	1220	1560000
	5-2x12	890	1140000	1070	1370000	990	1640000
	1-6x12	1310	1680000	1020	1440000	1010	1290000
	3-3x12	920	1170000	880	1130000	920	1170000
	1-8x12	970	1230000	800	1030000	1330	1450000
	1-10x12	760	970000	1160	1270000	1270	1380000
	4-3x12	690	880000	1110	1210000	880	970000
	2-3x14	1000	1090000	850	850000		
	1-6x14	950	1040000				
	3-3x14	670	730000				
22'	4-2x12	1220	1570000	1280	1650000	1300	1680000
	2-4x12	1090	1410000	1140	1470000	1340	1720000
	5-2x12	980	1260000	1180	1510000	1110	1430000
	3-3x12	1010	1290000	1230	1590000	1010	1300000
	1-8x12	1050	1360000	970	1250000	1460	1610000
	1-10x12	830	1070000	880	1130000	1390	1540000
	4-3x12	750	970000	1280	1400000	970	1070000
	2-3x14	1080	1200000	1220	1340000	1060	1160000
	1-6x14	1040	1150000	850	935000	730	800000
	3-3x14	730	800000	920	1010000		
	2-4x14	790	870000	640	700000		
	4-3x14	550	600000				

Table 17-21. These stress and elasticity values for beam sizes shown will support a live load of 40 pounds per square foot within a deflection limitation of I/240 (courtesy National Forest Products Association). (Continued on page 347).

Left portion (spans 10'–13')

SPAN OF BEAM	NOMINAL SIZE OF BEAM	6'-0" f	6'-0" E	7'-0" f	7'-0" E	8'-0" f	8'-0" E
10'	2-3x6	1700	1480000	1980	1730000	2440	1560000
	1-3x8	1820	1160000	2130	1360000	1970	1270000
	2-2x8	1480	950000	1720	1110000	1750	1130000
	1-4x8	1320	850000	1540	990000		
	1-6x8	870	560000	1020	650000	1160	745000
	2-2x10	920	470000	1070	545000	1220	625000
	1-3x10	1140	580000	1330	675000	1520	770000
11'	2-2x8	1780	1260000	1860	1320000	1410	990000
	1-4x8	1600	1130000	1230	870000	1490	830000
	1-6x8	1060	745000	1300	725000	1840	1020000
	2-2x10	1110	620000	1610	900000	1330	740000
	1-3x10	1380	770000	1160	650000	990	550000
	3-2x10	740	415000	860	485000		
12'	1-4x8	1890	1490000	1460	1150000	1670	1310000
	1-6x8	1250	980000	1650	1290000	1890	1480000
	3-2x8	1410	1110000	1560	955000	1760	1090000
	2-2x10	1630	820000	1910	1180000	2190	1350000
	1-3x10	1180	1010000	1380	855000	1580	980000
	1-4x10	880	730000	1030	640000	1170	730000
	3-2x10	810	545000	950	590000	1090	675000
	2-3x10		505000				
13'	1-6x8	1470	1220000	1720	1430000	1960	1640000
	2-3x8	1540	1290000	1800	1590000	2050	1710000
	2-4x8	1110	930000	1300	1090000	1490	1240000
	2-2x10	1550	1020000	1810	1200000	2070	1370000
	3-2x10	1010	685000	1180	795000	1380	915000
	1-3x10	1920	1270000	1120	740000	1280	845000
	1-4x10	1390	915000	1620	1070000	1850	1220000
	2-4x10	690	455000	810	535000	920	610000

Right portion (spans 17'–19')

SPAN OF BEAM	NOMINAL SIZE OF BEAM	6'-0" f	6'-0" E	7'-0" f	7'-0" E	8'-0" f	8'-0" E
17'	2-3x10	1640	1420000	1920	1650000	1580	1370000
	2-4x10	1190	1200000	1390	1200000	1460	1260000
	3-3x10	1100	945000	1280	1200000	1530	1320000
	1-8x10	1150	990000	1340	1160000	1620	1150000
	3-2x12	1220	860000	1420	1000000	1210	860000
	4-2x12	910	720000	1060	755000	970	690000
	5-2x12	730	515000	850	605000		
	2-3x12	1130	800000	1310	930000	1500	1070000
	3-3x12	750	530000	880	620000	1000	710000
	2-4x12	820	580000	950	680000	1090	775000
	1-6x12	1070	760000	1250	890000	1430	1020000
	1-8x12	790	560000	920	655000	1050	750000
18'	2-3x10	1850	1680000	1550	1420000	1780	1620000
	2-4x10	1330	1210000	1430	1310000	1640	1500000
	3-3x10	1230	1120000	1510	1370000	1720	1570000
	1-8x10	1290	1170000	1590	1190000	1810	1360000
	3-2x12	1360	1120000	1190	890000	1360	1020000
	4-2x12	1020	765000	950	715000	1090	815000
	5-2x12	820	610000				
	2-3x12	1270	945000	1480	1100000	1680	1260000
	3-3x12	840	630000	980	735000	1120	840000
	2-4x12	920	685000	1070	800000	1220	920000
	1-6x12	1200	900000	1400	1050000	1600	1210000
	1-8x12	880	660000	1030	775000	1180	885000
19'	1-8x10	1440	1380000	1680	1610000	2020	1600000
	3-2x12	1520	1200000	1770	1460000	1520	1200000
	4-2x12	1140	900000	1330	1050000	1210	960000
	5-2x12	910	720000	1060	840000	1880	1480000
	2-3x12	1410	1110000	1650	1300000	1250	985000
	3-3x12	940	740000	1100	860000	1360	1080000
	1-6x12	1340	1060000	1560	1240000	1790	1410000
	1-8x12	990	780000	1150	910000	1310	1040000
	3-4x12	680	540000	790	630000	910	720000
	4-3x12	700	555000	820	650000	940	740000
	2-6x12	670	530000	780	620000	890	710000

MINIMUM "f" & "E" IN psi FOR BEAMS SPACED:

SPAN OF BEAM	NOMINAL SIZE OF BEAM	6'-0" f	6'-0" E	7'-0" f	7'-0" E	8'-0" f	8'-0" E
14'	2-4x8	1290	1160000	1510	1360000	1720	1550000
	3-2x10	1200	855000	1400	995000	1600	1140000
	2-3x10	1110	790000	1300	920000	1490	1050000
	1-4x10	1610	1140000	1890	1330000	2150	1530000
	2-4x10	800	570000	940	665000	1070	760000
	3-3x10	740	530000	870	615000	990	700000
	1-6x10	1060	755000	1240	880000	1420	1000000
	1-8x10	780	555000	910	645000	1040	735000
	4-2x12	900	640000	1050	745000	1200	850000
	2-2x12	1230	720000	1440	840000	1650	960000
15'	3-2x10	1380	1050000	1610	1220000	1840	1400000
	2-3x10	1290	970000	1500	1130000	1710	1300000
	2-4x10	930	700000	1080	820000	1240	940000
	3-3x10	860	650000	1000	755000	1140	865000
	1-6x10	1220	925000	1430	1080000	1630	1230000
	1-8x10	900	680000	1050	795000	1200	910000
	4-2x10	1030	785000	1210	920000	1380	1050000
	2-2x12	1420	885000	1660	1030000	1900	1180000
	3-2x12	950	590000	1110	690000	1260	785000
	1-3x12	1760	1100000	2050	1280000	2350	1460000
	4-2x12	710	440000	830	515000	950	590000
	2-3x12	880	550000	1030	640000	1170	730000
16'	3-2x10	1570	1270000	1830	1490000	2090	1700000
	2-3x10	1460	1180000	1700	1380000	1950	1570000
	2-4x10	1050	855000	1230	1000000	1410	1140000
	3-3x10	970	785000	1130	920000	1290	1050000
	1-6x10	1390	1130000	1630	1310000	1850	1500000
	1-8x10	1020	825000	1190	965000	1360	1100000
	4-2x12	1170	955000	1370	1110000	1570	1270000
	2-2x12	1610	1080000	1880	1260000		
	3-2x12	1080	715000	1260	845000	1440	955000
	4-2x12	810	540000	940	630000	1080	715000
	5-2x12	640	430000	750	500000	860	575000
	2-3x12	1000	665000	1170	775000	1330	885000

SPAN OF BEAM	NOMINAL SIZE OF BEAM	6'-0" f	6'-0" E	7'-0" f	7'-0" E	8'-0" f	8'-0" E
20'	3-2x12	1680	1400000	1960	1630000	1680	1400000
	4-2x12	1260	1050000	1470	1220000	1350	1120000
	5-2x12	1010	840000	1180	980000	1390	1150000
	3-3x12	1040	865000	1210	1010000	1510	1260000
	2-4x12	1130	945000	1320	1090000	1980	1650000
	1-6x12	1460	1240000	1730	1440000	1450	1210000
	1-8x12	1090	910000	1270	1160000	1000	835000
	3-4x12	780	630000	880	730000	1040	865010
	4-3x12	740	650000	910	760000	990	825000
	2-6x12	850	620000	870	725000	1140	950000
	1-10x12	850	715000	1000	835000	1510	1070000
	2-3x14	1130	805000	1320	940000		
21'	3-2x12	1850	1610000	1620	1420000	1850	1620000
	4-2x12	1390	1210000	1300	1130000	1490	1300000
	5-2x12	1110	970000	1340	1170000	1530	1330000
	3-3x12	1150	1000000	1450	1270000	1660	1450000
	2-4x12	1240	1090000	1400	1230000	1600	1400000
	1-8x12	1200	1050000	970	850000	1110	970000
	3-4x12	830	730000	1000	880000	1150	1000000
	4-3x12	860	750000	960	840000	1090	960000
	2-6x12	820	720000	1100	970000	1260	1100000
	1-10x12	940	930000	1450	1090000	1660	1240000
	2-3x14	1240	890000	1390	1040000	1590	1180000
	1-6x14	1190					
22'	4-2x12	1530	1400000	1780	1630000	1630	1490000
	5-2x12	1220	1120000	1430	1300000	1680	1530000
	3-3x12	1260	1150000	1470	1340000	1210	1110000
	3-4x12	910	840000	1060	975000	1260	1150000
	4-3x12	940	870000	1100	1010000	1200	1100000
	2-6x12	900	830000	1050	960000	1380	1270000
	1-10x12	1040	950000	1210	1110000	1820	1430000
	2-3x14	1360	1070000	1590	1250000	1740	1360000
	1-6x14	1310	1020000	1530	1190000	1320	1030000
	2-4x14	990	775000	1160	900000	1210	950000
	3-3x14	910	715000	1060	830000	880	690000
	3-4x14	660	515000	770	600000		

Table 17-22. Stress and elasticity values for beam sizes shown in this table will support a live load of 40 pounds per square foot within a deflection limitation of I/300 (courtesy National Forest Products Association). (Continued on page 349).

SPAN OF BEAM	NOMINAL SIZE OF BEAM	MINIMUM "f" & "E" IN psi FOR BEAMS SPACED:					
		6'-0" f	6'-0" E	7'-0" f	7'-0" E	8'-0" f	8'-0" E
10'	1-3x8	1820	1460000	2130	1690000		
	2-2x8	1480	1180000	1720	1380000	1970	1580000
	1-4x8	1320	1060000	1540	1230000	1750	1410000
	1-6x8	870	700000	1020	815000	1160	930000
	2-2x10	920	585000	1070	680000	1220	775000
	1-3x10	1140	885000	1330	840000	1520	960000
	1-4x10	820	520000	960	610000	1090	695000
11'	2-2x8	1780	1570000	1860	1650000		
	1-4x8	1600	1410000				
	1-6x8	1060	930000	1230	1090000	1410	1240000
	2-2x10	1110	775000	1300	905000	1490	1035000
	1-3x10	1380	960000	1610	1120000	1840	1280000
	1-4x10	1000	695000	1160	810000	1330	925000
	3-2x10	740	515000	860	605000	990	690000
12'	1-6x8	1250	1210000	1460	1410000	1670	1610000
	3-2x8	1410	1360000	1650	1590000	1890	1820000
	2-2x10	1360	1010000	1560	1180000	1760	1340000
	1-3x10	1630	1250000	1910	1450000	2190	1660000
	1-4x10	1180	900000	1380	1050000	1580	1200000
	3-2x10	880	670000	1030	785000	1170	895000
	2-3x10	810	620000	950	730000	1090	830000
	1-6x10	780	595000	910	695000	1040	790000
	2-4x10	590	450000	690	535000	790	600000
13'	1-6x8	1470	1530000				
	2-3x8	1540	1600000				
	2-4x8	1110	1170000	1300	1360000	1490	1550000
	3-2x10	1010	855000	1180	1000000	1380	1140000
	2-2x10	1550	1280000	1810	1500000	2070	1710000
	1-3x10	1920	1580000				
	2-3x10	960	790000	1120	925000	1280	1150000
	1-__x10 (bottom cut off)			1620	1340000	1850	1530000

SPAN OF BEAM	NOMINAL SIZE OF BEAM	MINIMUM "f" & "E" IN psi FOR BEAMS SPACED:					
		6'-0" f	6'-0" E	7'-0" f	7'-0" E	8'-0" f	8'-0" E
17'	2-3x10	1640	1760000				
	2-4x10	1190	1280000	1390	1490000	1580	1700000
	3-3x10	1100	1180000	1280	1370000	1460	1570000
	1-8x10	1150	1240000	1340	1440000	1530	1650000
	3-2x12	1220	1070000	1420	1250000	1620	1430000
	4-2x12	910	805000	1060	940000	1210	1070000
	5-2x10	730	645000	850	750000	970	860000
	2-3x12	1130	995000	1310	1160000	1500	1330000
	3-3x12	750	665000	880	770000	1000	885000
	2-4x12	820	725000	950	840000	1090	965000
	1-6x12	1070	950000	1250	1110000	1430	1270000
	1-8x12	790	700000	920	810000	1050	930000
18'	2-4x10	1330	1510000	1550	1770000		
	3-3x10	1230	1390000	1430	1630000		
	1-8x10	1290	1460000	1510	1720000		
	3-2x12	1360	1270000	1590	1490000	1810	1700000
	4-2x12	1020	950000	1190	1120000	1360	1270000
	5-2x12	820	760000	950	890000	1090	1020000
	2-3x12	1270	1180000	1480	1380000	1680	1580000
	3-3x12	840	785000	980	920000	1120	1050000
	2-4x12	920	855000	1070	1000000	1220	1145000
	1-6x12	1200	1120000	1400	1320000	1600	1520000
	1-8x12	880	825000	1030	970000	1180	1100000
	3-4x12	610	570000	710	665000	810	760000
19'	3-3x10	1370	1640000				
	3-2x12	1520	1500000	1770	1750000		
	4-2x12	1140	1130000	1330	1310000	1520	1500000
	5-2x12	910	900000	1060	1050000	1210	1200000
	2-3x12	1410	1390000	1650	1620000		
	3-3x12	940	925000	1100	1080000	1250	1230000
	2-4x12	1020	1010000	1190	1180000	1360	1350000
	1-6x12	1340	1330000	1560	1550000	1790	885000
	1-8x12	990	975000	1150	1140000	1310	1300000
	3-4x12	680	675000	790	785000	910	895000

Minimum "f" & "E" in psi for beams spaced — span tables.

Left section (spans 14', 15', 16')

SPAN OF BEAM	NOMINAL SIZE OF BEAM	6'-0" f	6'-0" E	7'-0" f	7'-0" E	8'-0" f	8'-0" E
14'	2-4x8	1290	1450000	1510	1690000	1600	1420000
	3-2x10	1200	1070000	1400	1240000	1490	1320000
	2-3x10	1110	990000	1300	1150000		
	1-4x10	1610	1430000	1890	1660000		
	2-4x10	890	715000	940	830000	1070	950000
	3-3x10	740	660000	870	765000	990	880000
	1-6x10	1060	940000	1240	1100000	1420	1260000
	1-8x10	780	690000	910	805000	1040	920000
	4-2x10	900	800000	1050	930000	1200	1060000
	2-2x12	1250	900000	1440	1050000	1650	1200000
15'	3-2x10	1380	1310000	1610	1530000	1840	1750000
	2-3x10	1290	1220000	1500	1420000	1710	1620000
	2-4x10	930	880000	1080	1020000	1240	1170000
	3-3x10	860	810000	1000	945000	1140	1080000
	1-6x10	1220	1160000	1430	1350000	1630	1540000
	1-8x10	900	850000	1050	990000	1200	1130000
	4-2x10	1030	985000	1210	1150000	1380	1310000
	2-2x12	1420	1110000	1660	1290000	1900	1480000
	3-2x12	950	735000	1110	860000	1260	985000
	1-3x12	1760	1370000	2050	1600000		
	4-2x12	710	555000	830	645000	950	740000
	2-3x12	880	685000	1030	800000	1170	915000
16'	3-2x10	1570	1590000	1700	1720000	1410	1430000
	2-3x10	1460	1480000	1230	1250000	1290	1310000
	2-4x10	1050	1070000	1130	1150000	1360	1380000
	3-3x10	970	985000	1630	1640000	1570	1590000
	1-6x10	1390	1410000	1190	1200000	1440	1200000
	1-8x10	1020	1030000	1370	1390000	1080	895000
	4-2x10	1170	1190000	1880	1570000	860	720000
	2-2x12	1610	1340000	1260	1050000	1330	1110000
	3-2x12	1080	895000	940	785000		
	4-2x12	810	670000	750	630000		
	5-2x12	640	550000	1170	970000		
	2-3x12	1000	830000				

Right section (spans 20', 21', 22')

SPAN OF BEAM	NOMINAL SIZE OF BEAM	6'-0" f	6'-0" E	7'-0" f	7'-0" E	8'-0" f	8'-0" E
20'	3-2x12	1680	1750000	1470	1530000	1680	1750000
	4-2x12	1260	1310000	1180	1230000	1350	1400000
	5-2x12	1010	1050000	1210	1260000	1390	1440000
	3-3x12	1040	1080000	1320	1370000	1510	1570000
	2-4x12	1130	1180000	1270	1330000	1450	1520000
	1-6x12	1090	1140000	880	920000	1000	1050000
	1-8x12	750	785000	910	950000	1040	950000
	3-4x12	740	810000	870	905000	990	1030000
	4-3x12	850	890000	1000	1040000	1140	1190000
	2-6x12	1130	1000000	1320	1170000	1510	1340000
	1-10x12						
	2-3x14						
21'	4-2x12	1390	1520000	1620	1770000	1490	1620000
	5-2x12	1110	1210000	1300	1420000	1530	1670000
	3-3x12	1150	1250000	1340	1460000	1600	1750000
	2-4x12	1240	1360000	1450	1590000	1110	3210000
	1-8x12	1200	1320000	1400	1540000	1150	1210000
	3-4x12	830	910000	970	1060000	1090	1260000
	4-3x12	860	940000	1000	1100000	1260	1190000
	2-6x12	820	895000	960	1040000	1660	1380000
	1-10x12	940	1030000	1100	1210000	1590	1550000
	2-3x14	1240	1160000	1450	1360000	1200	1480000
	1-6x14	1190	1110000	1390	1300000		1120000
	2-4x14	900	840000	1050	980000		
22'	4-2x12	1530	1750000	1430	1620000	1210	1390000
	5-2x12	1220	1400000	1470	1680000	1260	1440000
	3-3x12	1260	1440000	1060	1220000	1200	1370000
	3-4x12	910	1050000	1100	1260000	1380	1590000
	2-6x12	940	1080000	1050	1190000	1820	1780000
	1-10x12	900	1030000	1210	1390000	1740	1700000
	2-3x14	1040	1190000	1590	1560000	1320	1280000
	1-6x14	1360	1280000	1530	1490000	1210	1190000
	2-4x14	1310	970000	1160	1130000	880	865000
	3-3x14	990	895000	1060	1040000		
	3-4x14	660	645000	770	750000		

Table 17-23. This beam design table applies for straight, simply supported, laminated timber beams. Other beam support systems may be used to meet changing design conditions (courtesy American Institute of Timber Construction). (Continued on page 351).

SPAN FT.	SPACING FT.	ROOF BEAMS—TOTAL LOAD CARRYING CAPACITY								FLOOR BEAMS TOTAL LOAD
		20 PSF	25 PSF	30 PSF	35 PSF	40 PSF	45 PSF	50 PSF	55 PSF	50 PSF
8	4			3⅛x4½	3⅛x4½	3⅛x6	3⅛x6	3⅛x6	3⅛x6	3⅛x6
	6			3⅛x4½	3⅛x4½	3⅛x6	3⅛x6	3⅛x6	3⅛x6	3⅛x6
	8			3⅛x4½	3⅛x4½	3⅛x6	3⅛x6	3⅛x6	3⅛x6	3⅛x7½
10	4			3⅛x4½	3⅛x4½	3⅛x6	3⅛x6	3⅛x6	3⅛x6	3⅛x7½
	6			3⅛x4½	3⅛x6	3⅛x6	3⅛x6	3⅛x6	3⅛x7½	3⅛x7½
	8			3⅛x6	3⅛x6	3⅛x7½	3⅛x7½	3⅛x7½	3⅛x7½	3⅛x9
	10			3⅛x6	3⅛x7½	3⅛x7½	3⅛x7½	3⅛x7½	3⅛x9	3⅛x9
12	6			3⅛x6	3⅛x6	3⅛x7½	3⅛x7½	3⅛x7½	3⅛x7½	3⅛x9
	8			3⅛x6	3⅛x7½	3⅛x9	3⅛x9	3⅛x9	3⅛x9	3⅛x10½
	10			3⅛x7½	3⅛x7½	3⅛x9	3⅛x9	3⅛x9	3⅛x10½	3⅛x10½
	12			3⅛x7½	3⅛x9	3⅛x9	3⅛x9	3⅛x10½	3⅛x10½	3⅛x12
14	S			3⅛x7½	3⅛x9	3⅛x9	3⅛x9	3⅛x10½	3⅛x10½	3⅛x12
	10			3⅛x9	3⅛x9	3⅛x10½	3⅛x10½	3⅛x10½	3⅛x12	3⅛x12
	12			3⅛x9	3⅛x10½	3⅛x10½	3⅛x10½	3⅛x12	3⅛x12	3⅛x13½
	14			3⅛x10½	3⅛x10½	3⅛x12	3⅛x12	3⅛x12	3⅛x13½	3⅛x13½
16	8			3⅛x9	3⅛x9	3⅛x10½	3⅛x10½	3⅛x12	3⅛x12	3⅛x13½
	12			3⅛x10½	3⅛x12	3⅛x12	3⅛x12	3⅛3x1½	3⅛x13½	3⅛x15
	14		3⅛x10½	3⅛x12	3⅛x12	3⅛x13½	3⅛x13½	3⅛x15	3⅛x15	3⅛x15
	16		3⅛x10½	3⅛x12	3⅛x13½	3⅛x13½	3⅛x15	3⅛x15	3⅛x16½	3⅛x15
18	8			3⅛x9	3⅛x10½	3⅛x12	3⅛x12	3⅛x12	3⅛x13½	3⅛x15
	12		3⅛x10½	3⅛x12	3⅛x12	3⅛x13½	3⅛x13½	3⅛x15	3⅛x16½	3⅛x16½
	16		3⅛x12	3⅛x13½	3⅛x15	3⅛x15	3⅛x16½	5⅛x13½	5⅛x13½	5⅛x15
	20		3⅛x13½	3⅛x15	3⅛x16½	3⅛x18	3⅛x18	5⅛x15	5⅛x16½	5⅛x16½
20	8			3⅛x12	3⅛x12	3⅛x13½	3⅛x13½	3⅛x13½	3⅛x15	3⅛x16½
	12		3⅛x12	3⅛x13½	3⅛x13½	3⅛x15	3⅛x16½	3⅛x16½	5⅛x13½	5⅛x15
	16		3⅛x13½	3⅛x15	3⅛x16½	3⅛x18	3⅛x18	5⅛x15	5⅛x16½	5⅛x18
	20		3⅛x15	3⅛x16½	3⅛x18	5⅛x15	5⅛x16½	5⅛x16½	5⅛x18	5⅛x18

SPAN FT.	SPACING FT.	ROOF BEAMS—TOTAL LOAD CARRYING CAPACITY								FLOOR BEAMS TOTAL LOAD
		20 PSF	25 PSF	30 PSF	35 PSF	40 PSF	45 PSF	50 PSF	55 PSF	50 PSF
24	8	—	—	3⅛x13½	3⅛x15	3⅛x15	3⅛x16½	3⅛x16½	3⅛x18	5⅛x16½
	12	—	3⅛x15	3⅛x16½	3⅛x16½	3⅛x18	5⅛x15	5⅛x16½	5⅛x16½	5⅛x18
	16	—	3⅛x16½	3⅛x18	5⅛x16½	5⅛x16½	5⅛x18	5⅛x18	5⅛x19½	5⅛x21
	20	—	3⅛x18	5⅛x16½	5⅛x16½	5⅛x18	5⅛x19½	5⅛x19½	5⅛x21	5⅛x22½
28	8	—	3⅛x13½	3⅛x16½	3⅛x16½	3⅛x18	3⅛x18	5⅛x16½	5⅛x16½	5⅛x19½
	12	—	3⅛x18	3⅛x18	5⅛x16½	5⅛x18	5⅛x18	5⅛x18	5⅛x19½	5⅛x21
	16	—	5⅛x16½	5⅛x18	5⅛x18	5⅛x19½	5⅛x19½	5⅛x21	5⅛x22½	5⅛x24
	20	—	5⅛x18	5⅛x18	5⅛x19½	5⅛x21	5⅛x22½	5⅛x24	5⅛x25½	5⅛x25½
32	8	—	3⅛x18	3⅛x18	5⅛x16½	5⅛x18	5⅛x18	5⅛x18	5⅛x19½	5⅛x21
	12	—	5⅛x16½	5⅛x18	5⅛x19½	5⅛x19½	5⅛x21	5⅛x21	5⅛x22½	5⅛x24
	16	—	5⅛x18	5⅛x19½	5⅛x21	5⅛x22½	5⅛x22½	5⅛x24	5⅛x25½	5⅛x27
	20	5⅛x18	5⅛x19½	5⅛x21	5⅛x22½	5⅛x24	5⅛x25½	5⅛x27	5⅛x28½	6¾x27
36	12	—	5⅛x19½	5⅛x19½	5⅛x21	5⅛x22½	5⅛x22½	5⅛x24	5⅛x25½	6¾x25½
	16	—	5⅛x21	5⅛x22½	5⅛x24	5⅛x24	5⅛x25½	5⅛x27	5⅛x28½	6¾x27
	20	5⅛x21	5⅛x22½	5⅛x24	5⅛x25½	5⅛x27	5⅛x30	6¾x27	6¾x28½	6¾x30
	24	5⅛x22½	5⅛x24	5⅛x25½	5⅛x28½	5⅛x30	6¾x27	6¾x28½	6¾x30	6¾x31½
40	12	5⅛x19½	5⅛x21	5⅛x22½	5⅛x24	5⅛x24	5⅛x25½	5⅛x27	6¾x25½	6¾x28½
	16	5⅛x21	5⅛x22½	5⅛x24	5⅛x25½	5⅛x27	5⅛x28½	6¾x27	6¾x28½	6¾x31½
	20	5⅛x22½	5⅛x25½	5⅛x27	5⅛x28½	6¾x27	6¾x28½	6¾x30	6¾x31½	6¾x33
	24	5⅛x24	5⅛x27	5⅛x28½	6¾x27	6¾x28½	6¾x31½	6¾x33	6¾x34½	6¾x36
44	12	5⅛x21	5⅛x22½	5⅛x24	5⅛x25½	5⅛x27	5⅛x27	6¾x25½	6¾x27	6¾x31½
	16	5⅛x24	5⅛x25½	5⅛x27	5⅛x28½	5⅛x30	6¾x28½	6¾x30	6¾x31½	6¾x33
	20	5⅛x25½	5⅛x27	5⅛x30	6¾x27	6¾x30	6¾x30	6¾x33	6¾x34½	6¾x36
	24	5⅛x27	5⅛x28½	6¾x28½	6¾x30	6¾x31½	6¾x34½	6¾x36	6¾x37½	6¾x39
48	12	5⅛x24	5⅛x25½	5⅛x27	5⅛x28½	5⅛x30	5⅛x30	6¾x28½	6¾x30	6¾x33
	16	5⅛x25½	5⅛x27	5⅛x30	6¾x28½	6¾x30	6¾x30	6¾x31½	6¾x34½	6¾x37½
	20	5⅛x27	5⅛x30	6¾x28½	6¾x30	6¾x31½	6¾x34½	6¾x36	6¾x37½	8¾x36
	24	5⅛x30	6¾x28½	6¾x30	6¾x33	6¾x34½	6¾x37½	6¾x39	8¾x36	8¾x39

Roofs should have a minimum slope of ¼ inch per foot to eliminate water ponding.

Total load carrying capacity includes beam weight. Floor beams are designed for uniform loads of 40 psf live load and 10 psf dead load.

Allowable stresses:
Bending stress, Fb = 2400 psi (reduced by size factor). C_F

Shear stress, Fv = 165 psi.
Modulus of elasticity, E = 1,800,000 psi.
For roof beams, Fb and Fv were increased 15% for short duration of loading.

Deflection limits:
Roof beams — 1/180 span for total load.
Floor beams — 1/360 span for 40 psf live load only.

Values for preliminary design purposes only. For more complete design information, see the AITC "Timber Construction Manual."

Table 17-24. Use this chart in determining total load carrying capacities for roof beams (courtesy American Institute of Timber Construction). (Continued on page 353).

SPAN FT.	SPACING FT.	ROOF BEAMS—TOTAL LOAD CARRYING CAPACITY								FLOOR BEAMS TOTAL LOAD
		20 PSF	25 PSF	30 PSF	35 PSF	40 PSF	45 PSF	50 PSF	55 PSF	[illegible] PSF
52	12	5⅛x25½	5⅛x27	5⅛x28½	5⅛x30	6¾x28½	6¾x30	6¾x31½	6¾x31½	6¾x36
	16	5⅛x28½	5⅛x30	6¾x28½	6¾x30	6¾x31½	6¾x33	6¾x34½	6¾x37½	8¾x36
	20	5⅛x30	6¾x30	6¾x31½	6¾x33	6¾x34½	6¾x37½	6¾x39	8¾x36	8¾x39
	24	6¾x28½	6¾x31½	6¾x33	6¾x36	6¾x37½	6¾x40½	8¾x37½	8¾x39	8¾x42
56	12	5⅛x27	5⅛x28½	6¾x28½	6¾x30	6¾x31½	6¾x33	6¾x33	6¾x34½	8¾x36
	16	5⅛x30	6¾x30	6¾x31½	6¾x33	6¾x34½	6¾x36	6¾x37½	8¾x34½	8¾x39
	20	6¾x28½	6¾x31½	6¾x33	6¾x36	6¾x37½	8¾x34½	8¾x37½	8¾x39	8¾x42
	24	6¾x31½	6¾x33	6¾x36	6¾x39	8¾x36	8¾x39	8¾x40½	8¾x42	8¾x45
60	12	5⅛x28½	6¾x28½	6¾x30	6¾x31½	6¾x33	6¾x34½	6¾x36	6¾x37½	8¾x39
	16	6¾x28½	6¾x31½	6¾x33	6¾x34½	6¾x36	6¾x39	8¾x36	8¾x37½	8¾x42
	20	6¾x31½	6¾x34½	6¾x36	6¾x37½	8¾x36	8¾x37½	8¾x40½	8¾x42	8¾x45
	24	6¾x33	6¾x36	6¾x39	8¾x36	8¾x39	8¾x42	8¾x43½	8¾x45	8¾x48
64	12	6¾x28½	6¾x30	6¾x33	6¾x34½	6¾x36	6¾x37½	6¾x39	6¾x40½	8¾x40½
	16	6¾x31½	6¾x33	6¾x36	6¾x37½	6¾x39	6¾x40½	8¾x39	8¾x40½	8¾x45
	20	6¾x33	6¾x36	6¾x37½	6¾x40½	8¾x39	8¾x40½	8¾x42	8¾x45	8¾x48
	24	6¾x36	6¾x37½	6¾x40½	8¾x39	8¾x42	8¾x43½	8¾x46½	8¾x49½	8¾x51
68	12	6¾x30	6¾x33	6¾x34½	6¾x36	6¾x37½	6¾x39	6¾x40½	8¾x39	8¾x43½
	16	6¾x33	6¾x36	6¾x37½	6¾x39	8¾x37½	8¾x39	8¾x40½	8¾x43½	8¾x48
	20	6¾x36	6¾x37½	6¾x40½	8¾x39	8¾x40½	8¾x43½	8¾x45	8¾x48	8¾x51
	24	6¾x37½	6¾x40½	8¾x39	8¾x42	8¾x45	8¾x46½	8¾x49½	8¾x52½	10¾x51
72	12	6¾x31½	6¾x34½	6¾x36	6¾x37½	6¾x40½	8¾x37½	8¾x39	8¾x40½	8¾x46½
	16	6¾x34½	6¾x37½	6¾x40½	8¾x39	8¾x40½	8¾x42	8¾x43½	8¾x45	8¾x51
	20	6¾x37½	6¾x40½	8¾x39	8¾x42	8¾x43½	8¾x45	8¾x48	8¾x51	10¾x51
	24	6¾x40½	8¾x39	8¾x42	8¾x43½	8¾x46½	8¾x49½	8¾x52½	10¾x49½	10¾x54
76	12	6¾x33	6¾x36	6¾x37½	6¾x40½	8¾x39	8¾x40½	8¾x42	8¾x43½	8¾x48
	16	6¾x37½	6¾x39	8¾x39	8¾x40½	8¾x42	8¾x43½	8¾x45	8¾x48	8¾x52½
	20	6¾x39	8¾x39	8¾x42	8¾x43½	8¾x45	8¾x48	8¾x51	10¾x48	10¾x54
	24	8¾x39	8¾x42	8¾x43½	8¾x46½	8¾x49½	8¾x52½	10¾x49½	10¾x52½	10¾x57
80	12	6¾x34½	6¾x37½	6¾x40½	8¾x39	8¼x40½	8¾x42	8¾x43½	8¾x45	8¾x51
	16	6¾x39	8¾x37½	8¾x40½	8¾x42	8¾x45	8¾x45	8¾x48	8¾x51	10¾x52½
	20	8¾x37½	8¾x40½	8¾x43½	8¾x46½	8¾x48	8¾x51	10¾x48	10¾x51	10¾x57
	24	8¾x40½	8¾x43½	8¾x46½	8¾x49½	8¾x52½	10¾x49½	10¾x52½	10¾x55½	10¾x60

SPAN FT.	SPACING FT.	ROOF BEAMS—TOTAL LOAD CARRYING CAPACITY								FLOOR BEAMS TOTAL LOAD
		20 PSF	25 PSF	30 PSF	35 PSF	40 PSF	45 PSF	50 PSF	55 PSF	50 PSF
84	12	6¾x37½	6¾x39	8¾x39	8¾x40½	8¾x42	8¾x43½	8¾x46½	8¾x48	10¾x49½
	16	6¾x40½	8¾x40½	8¾x42	8¾x45	8¾x46½	8¾x48	8¾x51	8¾x52½	10¾x55½
	20	8¾x40½	8¾x43½	8¾x46½	8¾x48	8¾x51	10¾x49½	10¾x51	10¼x54	10¾x58½
	24	8¾x42	8¾x46½	8¾x48	8¾x51	10¾x49½	10¾x52½	10¾x55½	10¾x58½	10¾x63
88	12	6¾x39	8¾x37½	8¾x40½	8¾x42	8¾x45	8¾x46½	8¾x48	8¾x49½	10¾x52½
	16	8¾x39	8¾x42	8¾x45	8¾x46½	8¾x49½	8¾x51	8¾x52½	10¾x51	10¾x57
	20	8¾x42	8¾x45	8¾x48	8¾x51	8¾x52½	10¾x51	10¾x54	10¾x55½	10¾x61½
	24	8¾x45	8¾x48	8¾x51	10¾x49½	10¾x52½	10¾x55½	10¾x58½	10¾x61½	—
92	12	6¾x40½	8¾x40½	8¾x42	8¾x45	8¾x46½	8¾x48	8¾x51	8¾x52½	10¾x54
	16	8¾x40½	8¾x43½	8¾x46½	8¾x49½	8¾x51	8¾x52½	10¾x51	10¾x54	10¾x60
	20	8¾x43½	8¾x46½	8¾x49½	8¾x52½	10¾x51	10¾x54	10¾x55½	10¾x58½	10¾x64½
	24	8¾x46½	8¾x49½	8¾x52½	10¾x52½	10¾x54	10¾x58½	10¾x61½	10¾x64½	—
96	12	8¾x39	8¾x42	8¾x43½	8¾x46½	8¾x48	8¾x51	8¾x52½	10¾x51	10¾x57
	16	8¾x42	8¾x45	8¾x48	8¾x51	10¾x49½	10¾x52½	10¾x54	10¾x55½	10¾x63
	20	8¾x45	8¾x49½	8¾x52½	10¾x51	10¾x54	10¾x55½	10¾x58½	10¾x61½	
	24	8¾x48	8¾x52½	10¾x52½	10¾x54	10¾x57	10¾x60	10¾x64½	—	—
100	12	8¾x40½	8¾x43½	8¾x46½	8¾x48	8¾x51	8¾x52½	10¾x51	10¾x52½	10¾x60
	16	8¾x43½	8¾x48	8¾x51	8¾x52½	10¾x52½	10¾x54	10¾x55½	10¾x58½	10¾x64½
	20	8¾x48	8¾x51	10¾x51	10¾x54	10¾x55½	10¾x58½	10¾x61½	10¾x64½	—
	24	8¾x51	10¾x51	10¾x54	10¾x57	10¾x60	10¾x63	—	—	—

CANTILEVERED AND CONTINUOUS SPAN SYSTEMS

Cantilever beam systems may be comprised of any of the various types and combinations of beam illustrated below. Cantilever systems permit longer spans or larger loads for a given size member than do simple span systems, provided member size is not controlled by compression perpendicular to grain at the supports or by horizontal shear. Substantial design economies can be effected by decreasing the depths of the members in the suspended portions of a cantilever system.

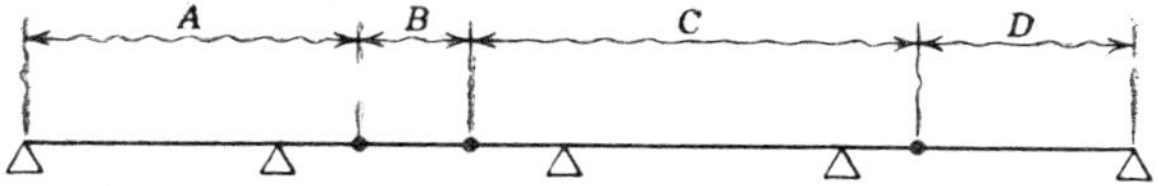

CANTILEVERED BEAM SYSTEMS. A is single cantilever, B is a suspended beam, C has a double cantilever, and D is a beam with one end suspended.

For economy, the negative bending moment at the supports of a cantilevered beam should be equal in magnitude to the positive moment.

Consideration must be given to deflection and camber in cantilevered multiple spans. When possible, roofs should be sloped the equivalent of ¼ inch per foot of horizontal distance between the level of the drain and the high point of the roof to eliminate water pockets, or provisions should be made to ensure that accumulation of water does not produce greater deflection and live loads than anticipated. Unbalanced loading conditions should be investigated for maximum bending moment, deflection, and stability.

Continuous span beams are commonly used in both building and bridge construction to reduce maximum moments, thus reducing the section size required.

Design aids for cantilever and continuous span beam systems may be found in the AITC "Timber Construction Manual."

Glued laminated timber beams are often tapered or curved to meet architectural requirements, to provide pitched roofs, or to provide a minimum depth of beam at the point of bearing.

Table 17-25. This chart can be used to calculate the needed size of plates, purlins and load-bearing girts. If there is a floor section 18 feet by 8 feet wide, this floor section is 144 square feet. If it is designed with a 50 psf (pounds per square foot) load, the floor section's total weight is 7,200 pounds. If the floor is supported by a line of central posts or a girder, ½ of this total load will be exerted on the header joist which spans between the posts to support the joists. The load will be 3,600 pounds. To carry this load, (2) 2x10s or a 4x10 will be needed. Two 2x10s with a piece of ½-inch plywood laminated between them will surpass the strength of a 4x10.

LUMBER SIZE	TOTAL WEIGHT	POUNDS PER LINEAL FOOT
2×4	306	38
4×4	714	89
2×6	756	94
4×6	1764	220
2×8	1314	164
4×8	2810	351
2×10	1960	245
4×10	4991	623
2×12	3164	395
4×12	7382	922

Table 17-26. This table gives load carrying capacities of circular concrete footing pads in different soils. (Courtesy Northeast Regional Agricultural Engineering Service).

Soil Description	Bearing Capacity ksf[a]	Pad Diameter, inches								
		8	10	12	14	16	18	20	22	24
		Minimum Pad Thickness, inches								
		4	4	5	5	6	6	7	8	8
		Load Carrying Capacity, 1000 pounds								
Soft limestone, partially cemented gravels and hardpan	16	5.6	8.7	12.6	17.1	22.3	28.3	34.9	42.2	50.3
Well drained gravel or gravel sand mixtures in natural thick beds with little clay or silt (GW, GP)*	12	4.2	6.5	9.4	12.8	16.8	21.2	26.2	31.7	37.7
Well drained sand with little or no clay or silt (SW, SP)*	8	2.8	4.4	6.3	8.6	11.2	14.1	17.4	21.1	25.1
Well drained gravel with silt or clay (GM, GC)*	6	2.1	3.3	4.7	6.4	8.4	10.6	13.1	15.8	18.8
Well drained sand with silt or clay (SM, SC)*	4	1.4	2.2	3.1	4.3	5.6	7.1	8.7	10.6	12.6
Well drained soft clay, silts or fine sand (CL, MH, ML)*	3	1.0	1.6	2.4	3.2	4.2	5.3	6.5	7.9	9.4
Poorly drained soft clay (CH)*	2	0.7	1.1	1.6	2.1	2.8	3.5	4.4	5.3	6.3
Organic soils, fills	By test only	-	-	-	-	-	-	-	-	-

*Unified Soil Classification System

[a] ksf equals 1000 pounds per square foot

Table 17-27. The chart lists frequently used circle diameters and the corresponding number of square feet needed for footings.

CIRCLE DIAMETER	NUMBER OF SQUARE FEET
13	.9
14	1.0
15	1.2
16	1.4
17	1.5
18	1.7
19	1.9
20	2.2
21	2.4
22	2.6
23	2.9
24	3.1
25	3.4
26	3.7
27	3.9
28	4.2
29	4.6
30	4.9

Table 17-28. Use this chart for determining needed thicknesses of concrete footings.

WEIGHT EXERTED UPON FOOTING	THICKNESS NEEDED
2,500 pounds	6″
3,500 pounds	7″
4,500 pounds	8″
5,500 pounds	9″
6,500 pounds (or more)	10″

Table 17-29. The diagram gives types of soils and their design properties (courtesy National Forest Products Association).

Soil group	Unified soil classification system symbol	Soil description	Allowable bearing in pounds per square foot with medium compaction or stiffness[1]	Drainage Characteristics[2]	Frost heave potential	Volume change potential expansion
Group 1 Excellent	GW	Well-graded gravels, gravel sand mixtures, little or no fines.	8000	Good	Low	Low
	GP	Poorly graded gravels or gravel sand mixtures little or no fines.	8000	Good	Low	Low
	SW	Well-graded sands, gravelly sands, little or no fines	6000	Good	Low	Low
	SP	Poorly graded sands or gravelly sands, little or no fines	5000	Good	Low	Low
	GM	Silty gravels, gravel-sand-silt mixtures.	4000	Good	Medium	Low
	SM	Silty sand, sand-silt mixtures.	4000	Good	Medium	Low
Group II Fair to Good	GC	Clayey gravels, gravel-sand-clay mixtures.	4000	Medium	Medium	Low
	SC	Clayey sands, sand-clay mixture.	4000	Medium	Medium	Low
	ML	Inorganic silts and very fine sands, rock flour, silty or clayey fine sands or clayey silts with slight plasticity.	2000	Medium	High	Low
	CL	Inorganic clays of low to medium plasticity, gravelly clays, sands clays, silty clays, lean clays.	2000	Medium	Medium	Medium[3]
Group III Poor	CH	Inorganic clays of high plasticity, fat clays	2000	Poor	Medium	High[3]
	MH	Inorganic silts, micaceous or diatomaceous fine sandy or silty soils, elastic silts	2000	Poor	High	High
Group IV Unsatisfactory	OL	Organic silts and organic silty clays of low plasticity.	400	Poor	Medium	Medium
	OH	Organic clays of medium to high plasticity, organic silts.	-0-	Unsatisfactory	Medium	High
	Pt	Peat and other highly organic soils.	-0-	Unsatisfactory	Medium	High

[1] Allowable bearing value may be increased 25 percent for very compact, coarse grained gravelly or sandy soils or very stiff fine-grained clayey or silty soils. Allowable bearing value shall be decreased 25 percent for loose, coarse-grained gravelly or sandy soils, or soft, fine-grained clayey or silty soils. See Table A-1, Appendix A.

[2] The percolation rate for good drainage is over 4 inches per hour, medium drainage is 2 to 4 inches per hour, and poor is less than 2 inches per hour.

[3] Dangerous expansion might occur if these soil types are dry but subject to future wetting.

Table 17-30. This chart lists minimum plywood grades and thicknesses for foundation construction and corresponding heights of fill and stud spacings (courtesy National Forest Products Association).

Height of fill (inches)	Stud spacing (inches)	Face grain across studs[2]			Face grain parallel to studs		
		Grade[3]	Minimum thickness[1]	Identification index	Grade[3]	Minimum thickness[1,5]	Identification index
24	12	B	½	32/16	B	½	32/16
	16	B	½	32/16	B	½ (4,5 ply)	32/16
48	12	B	½	32/16	B / A	½[6] (5 ply) / ½	32/16 / 32/16
	16	B	½	32/16	A / B	⅝ / ¾	42/20 / 48/24
72	12	B	½	32/16	A	⅝[6] (5 ply)	42/20
	16	A[4]	½[6]	32/16	B	¾[6]	48/24
86	12	B	½[6]	32/16	A / B	⅝[6] / ¾[6]	42/20 / 48/24
	16	A / B	⅝ / ¾	48/24 / 42/20	A	⅝[7]	42/20

[1] Minimum thickness ½ inch except crawl space sheathing may be ⅜ inch for face grain across studs and maximum 3 foot depth of unequal fill.
[2] Minimum 2 inch blocking between studs required at all horizontal panel joints more than 4 feet below adjacent ground level.
[3] Plywood shall be not less than the following minimum grades conforming to U.S. Product Standard PS 1, Construction and Industrial Plywood:
   A. Structural I C-D
   B. C-D (Exterior glue)
If a major portion of the wall is exposed above ground, a better appearance may be desired. The following Exterior grades would be suitable;
   A. Structural I A-C, Structural I B-C or Structural I C-C (Plugged)
   B. A-C Exterior Group 1, B-C Exterior Group 1, C-C (Plugged) Exterior Group 1 or MDO Exterior Group 1.
[4] For this combination of fill height and panel grade, only Structural I A-C or Structural I C-C may be substituted for improved appearance.
[5] When face grain is parallel to studs, plywood panels of the required thickness, grade and identification index may be any construction permitted under Article 2.2 except as noted in the table for minimum number of plys required.
[6] For this fill height, thickness and grade combination, panels which are continuous over less than three spans (across less than three stud spacings) require blocking 2 feet above bottom plate. Offset adjacent blocks and fasten through studs with two 16d corrosion resistant nails at each end.
[7] For this fill height, thickness and grade combination, panels require blocking 16 inches above bottom plate. Offset adjacent blocks and fasten through studs with two 16d corrosion resistant nails at each end.

**Table 17-31. The chart shows total allowable weight
in pounds to be supported by yellow pine or Douglas fir posts.**

POST SIZE

	4×4	4×6	6×6	6×8	8×8
6'	14,528	21,792	35,352	47,136	64,000
7'	13,264	19,896	34,776	46,368	
8'	11,328	16,992	33,912	45,216	62,848
9'	9,021	13,531	32,688	43,584	
10'	7,307	10,960	30,924	41,232	61,120
11'	6,039	9,058	28,584	38,112	
12'	5,074	7,611	25,488	33,984	58,112
13'	4,323	5,592	21,888	29,183	
14'	3,728	4,871	18,872	25,163	53,056
15'	3,247	4,281	16,440	21,920	
16'	2,854		14,449	16,857	45,312
17'					
18'			11,417	15,272	36,082
20'			9,247	12,330	29,227
22'					24,154
24'					20,296

Table 17-32. Most post sizes that you will need are covered in this table.

POST SPACING

		4'	8'	12'	16'	20'
E A V E H E I G H T	8'	4×4	4×4	4×6	6×6	6×6
	10'	4×4	4×6	6×6	6×6	6×8
	12'	4×6	6×6	6×6	6×8	8×8
	14'	6×6	6×6	6×8	8×8	8×8
	16'	6×6	6×8	8×8	8×8	
	18'	6×6	8×8	8×8		
	20'	6×6	8×8			

MINIMUM POST SIZES

Table 17-33. Use this chart to determine how deep to insert posts.

Depth of Embedment

Post Size	10,000 PSF Soil	6,000 PSF Soil	2,000 PSF Soil
4×4	3′	4′	5′
4×6 6×6	4′	5′	6′
6×8 8×8	5′	6′	7′

REFER TO TABLE 5-4
ON SOIL CLASSIFICATIONS

Fig. 17-34. The table shows the number of
square feet covered per cubic yard for concrete.

THICKNESS	Square feet covered
3″	108
4″	81
5″	67
6″	54

Table 17-35. Use this table for minimum plate footing
sizes (courtesy National Forest Products Association).

House width (feet)	Roof-40 psf live; 10 psf dead Ceiling-10 psf 1st floor-50 psf live & dead 2nd floor-50 psf live & dead		Roof-30 psf live; 10 psf dead Ceiling-10 psf 1st floor-50 psf live & dead 2nd floor-50 psf live & dead	
	2 stories	1 story	2 stories	1 story
32	2×10	2×8	2×10[2]	2×8
28	2×10	2×8	2×8	2×6
24	2×8	2×6	2×8	2×6

[1] Where width of footing plate is 4 inches or more wider than that of stud and bottom plate, use ¾ inch thick continuous treated plywood strips with face grain perpendicular to footing; minimum grade C-D (Exterior glue). Use plywood of same width as footing and fasten to footing with two 6d nails spaced 16 inches.

[2] This combination of house width and height may have 2×8 footing plate when second floor design load is 40 psf live and dead total load.

Table 17-36. The chart gives insulating values of rigid materials.

MATERIAL	"R"/INCH	¢/S.F/INCH	¢/"R"/S.F.	PROVIDES STRUCTURAL PURPOSE	PROVIDES NAILBASE
plywood	1.26	54	43	X	X
fiberboard	2.38	16	7	X	
softwood	3.23	56	17	X	X
styrofoam	5.40	25	5	X	
uretane panels	6.67	45	7	X	X

Fig. 17-37. Use this table to find insulating values of fill materials.

MATERIAL	"R"/INCH	¢/S.F./INCH	¢/"R"/S.F.	CAN BE USED IN WALLS	CAN BE USED IN CEILINGS
cellulose	3.7	4	1	X	X
fiberglass batts	3.17	4	1	X	X
fiberglass fill	2.2	5	2	X	X
Urea-formaldehyde (foam)	4.8	14*	3*·	X	

*INSTALLED PRICE

Table 17-38. Here are installed prices of fill insulation materials.

MATERIAL	¢/S.F./INCH	¢/"R"/S.F.
cellulose	14	4
fiberglass batts	7	2
fiberglass fill	14	6
urea-formaldehyde (foam)	14	3

Table 17-39. Refer to this chart to learn good and bad points concerning structural and insulating materials.

PROPERTIES OF STRUCTURAL AND INSULATING MATERIALS

PLYWOOD	+ good nailing surface, good durability, great strength − would not be used for insulation because of its expense
FIBERBOARD	+ inexpensive sheathing material, decent insulating value − not a good nailing surface, not waterproof
SOFTWOOD T&G DECKING	+ provides roof structure over beams 8′ on center, attractive ceiling material, nominal insulating value, great nailing surface − would not be used solely for insulation because of its expense
STYROFOAM	+ provides walls with flat surface, easily installed directly over studs, lightweight, good insulator, can be used below-grade − expensive, not a good nailing surface
URETHANE	+ superb insulator, provides adequate nailing surface, can be used on roofs − expensive, extremely flammable, when it burns it emits toxic fumes
CELLULOSE	+ inexpensive, needs less cavity for same insulating value as fiberglass, fireproof − may settle in walls, may collect moisture
FIBERGLASS	+ inexpensive, easily installed, can be bought with vapor barrier, foil-faced stops reflective heat loss, may be used in walls and ceilings, batts won't settle in walls − needs more space to match other insulations' "R" value
UREA-FORMAL-DEHYDE FOAM	+ can be installed in uninsulated homes, highest "R" value per inch of all the fill insulations − must be properly formulated by the installer, cannot be used in ceilings, inferior products may deteriorate

Table 17-40. Use this list when acquiring materials for building a survival cabin.

3,872 Board feet treated yellow pine 2×6 t&g @ $307/m (This equals 242 16' planks)	1,188
14 12 foot 4×4 treated posts @ 354/m	80
1 50# carton 16d coated nails	18
6 cases (60 tubes total) ½ barrel tubes Rely-on caulk @ .50/tube	30
13 yards fill sand delivered @ $4.00/yard	52
1 roll 10×100 foot 4 mil plastic	14
8 yards concrete delivered @ $33/yard	264
6 24 foot 2×10 fir @ 354/m	101
6 12 foot 2×10 yellow pine / $6.08/piece	37
2 12 foot 2×10 treated yellow pine @ $354/m	14
3 gusset plates	2
4 8 foot × 15¼ inch plate glass @ $3.00/square foot	120
1 ½ barrel tube silicone: clear	5
5 ½ barrel tubes construction adhesive	8
3 432 square foot rolls 15# felt	30
10 rolls 108 square feet roll roofing (65#)	100
1 5-gallon bucket plastic roof cement	10
1 50# carton 1 inch galvanized roofing nails	27
4 ⅜-inch diameter × 3 inch lag bolts	1
12 ¾ inch diameter × 8 inch hex-head bolts	12
1 power post-hole digger, rental	15
2 pounds 10d nails	1
6 pounds 50d spikes	4
	$2,133

Art credits:

Terry Alexander: Figures 1-2 thru 1-7, 6-1 thru 6-3, and 11-1 thru 11-10.

Ron and Judy Botan: Figures 3-2 thru 3-6, 15-9 thru 15-29, 15-31, and 15-32.

Shirley Roebuck: Figures 12-7 and 15-30, 15-31, and 15-32.

Billy Welker: Figures 1-1, 2-1, 5-1 thru 5-8, 7-1, 8-1 thru 8-16, 9-1 thru 9-19, 10-1, 10-2, 10-9, 13-1, and 16-1 thru 16-7.

Roger Zeman: Figures 12-1 thru 12-7, and 15-2 thru 15-8.

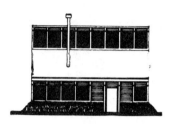

Glossary

ballast: any substance used to weight down roofing material.

berm: a mound of dirt sometimes placed against a building for insulation and frost protection.

bottom plate: the lowest part of a stud wall to which the studs are attached.

drywell: any area, usually underground, that has been furnished with stone or gravel for drainage. Storm drain pipes are sometimes run into a drywell.

end joist: the joist that runs perpendicular to the other joists at a building's perimeter; it is also called a header.

footing: the part of a building that is between the earth and the foundation.

girt: a horizontal wall member usually nailed onto the face of the posts.

glulam: a laminated wood system with the pieces glued together; it is short for glue-laminated.

interceptor trench: a trench filled with stone or gravel which intercepts excess water runoff before it reaches a building.

joist: the supporting members of a roof or floor which are 2 inches wide.

plate: loadbearing members spanning between posts which hold either the roof or floor joists.

psf: pounds per square foot.

purlin: a secondary roof or floor member spanning between beams, running perpendicular to them.

sheathing: solid wall covering which is covered with siding.

siding: the finish wall covering.

splashboard: a horizontal wall member which serves as form around the perimeter of the building for the slab.

stud: a vertical wall member separate from the posts.

tee: in plumbing, a component which is shaped like the letter "T".

toenail: to nail on an angle through the side of a joist or stud.

tongue-and-groove: abbreviated "t&g;" a design where the tongue of one member fits into the groove of another member.

top plate: the highest part of a stud wall to which the studs are nailed to.

wye: a component of plumbing shaped like the letter "Y".

Index

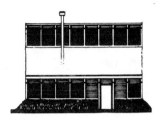

Index

A

American Wood Preservers
    Institute 57
Angles 46
Angles, right 44
Animal forms 52
Assessments 27
Auger 75

B

Backhoes 264
Batt insulation 112
.Beams 11
Beam and purlin 139
Beamed floor 166
Below-grade structure 92
Below-slab work 122
Box beam 287
Building perimeter 48
Building with an attic 141
Built-up roofing 128
By plank and beam 137

C

Cabinets 295
Cantilever 174
Carpeting 297, 310
Cedar 60
Ceiling height 189
Cellulose 220
Chalk 42
Char 60
Concrete 77, 284
Concrete floor 101, 151
Concrete patios 86
Construction adhesive 292
Continuous beam 124
Continuous footing 264

Continuous vent 148
Corners 42
Corner posts 267, 304
Countertops 295
Creosote 59

D

Decay fungi 51
Deed restrictions 32
Determining the building's
    location 244
Determining the exact perimeter
    of the building 258
Digging the hokles 75
Digging the perimeter trench 263
Bitch bitchd264
Door height 190
Drains 95
Drywall 113, 292
Drywall tape 294
Dual treatment 54
Duo-plane roof 136

E

Elevated floor 87
Elevated wood floor 101, 180

F

Fabricated beams 124
Face-to-face contact 164
Factory treatments 62
Felt paper 90
Fiberglass 213
Fiberglass batts 215
Field treatment 58
Fill insulations 213
Finish electrical 295
Finish grade 297

Finish heating	295
Finish plumbing	295
Floor plans	196, 198, 200
Flat roof	128
Floor trusses	161
Foam, Urea-formaldehyde	217
Foam, urethane	219
Foil facing	214
Foundation	263
Frost barrier	263
Frost heave	86
Frost line	105

G

Gable roof	132
Girts	94
Glass, single pane	227
Glue	159
Glulam beam	124
Grass whip	42
Gravel	91, 153
Gusset plates	281

H

Hammer	42
Hanging the beams	280

I

I-beam	156
Identification	57
Interior doors	295
Interior doors, hallow-core	295
Interior doors, pre-hung	295
Interior holes	261
Interior trim and molding	296
Interior walls	290
Installing the foam	270
Insulation	291
Insulation concerns	225

J

Joints	146
Joint compound	294

K

Kitchen	192

L

Land contract	33
Laying the slab floor	282
Level design number	171

Leveling the site	256
Limnoria tripunctata	54
Living area	192

M

Making the beams	276
Marine borers	54
Mason's line	42
Moisture	86
Moisture barriers	210
Monoplane roof	130
Mortgage	14
Multi-lists	21

N

Nails	42
Neighborhood	30
Normal earth pressure	87
Number 30 felt	288

O

Open ceiling	196
Overhangs	145

P

Painting	294
Pen	42
Penta	55
Perforated aluminum	145
Perk test	23
Pigeon-hole vent	147
Planks	11
Plank-and-beam roof	11
Plant forms	51
Plastic	90
Plastic membrane, CPE	130
Plastic membrane, EDPM	130
Plastic membrane, PVC	130
Plywood strips	276
Pointed stakes	42
Post-frame home	11
Post-hole diggers	76
Professionals	234
Property line	41
Purchase agreement	31
Pythagorean Therorem	42

R

"R" Value	212
Raftered ceiling	138
Realtors	21
Redwood	60

Reinforcing rod	78
Retainer wall	179
Rigid foam	115
Rigid insulation, molded polystyrene	223
Rigid insulations, styrofoam	222
Rigid insulation, urethane	224
Roof coating	310
Roof planking	281, 309
Rough electrical third	291
Rough heating	281
Rough heating first	291
Rough plumbing	266
Rough plumbing second	291
Round vent	148

S

Sand	153
Sales agreement	34
Sanitary hook-ups	258
Setting up the posts	266
Schools	31
Shipworms	54
Side entrance	198
Siding	288
Siding, channel	288
Siding, plywood	289
Silicone	60
Single story house	182
Skylights, double pane	228
Skylights, single pane	228
Slab floor	11, 90
Slab on grade	90
Sledgehammer	42
Sliding doors	194
Slope of the site	105
Soil	105
Spacing	104
Splashboard	109
Splashboard, 1 × 8	274
Split rings	164
Spreading the sand	256
Square vent	148
Steel	62
Stressed-skin beam	158
Subdivision map	41
Support wall	190

T

Tape measures	42
Tar	59
Tax base	26

Tear molding	296
Termites, subterranean	52
The backfill	275
The drains	274
The plastic	272
The size	71
Thermopane windows	228
Tongue-and-groove plywood	158
Topping compound	294
Trench footing	82
Triangle, right	44
Trimming the posts	277
Trussed roof	142
Trusses	11
Two step roof	229
Two story house	172
Types of footings	77

W

Wall designs	109, 110, 113, 116, 119, 121, 123, 124
Wall structure	285
Water-borne salt preservatives	56
Windows	287
casement	288
fixed	288
thermopane	288
unframed fixed	288
Wood	62
Wood deck	200
Wood floors	11, 155
Wood floors vs. concrete flooors	167

U

Unfaced batts	214
Utilities	28
Utility area	192

V

Vapor barriers	211
Ventilation	190
Vents	141
Visqueen	90

Y

Yard	152
Yellow pine	62

Z

Zoning	26

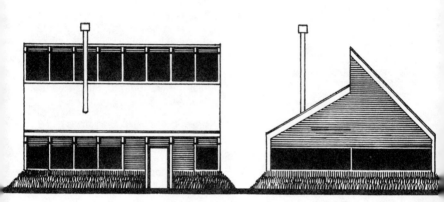

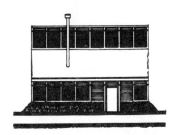

About the Artists

Billy H. Welker lives in the heart of Michigan's cherry and apple country on the Old Mission Penninsula above Traverse City. Billy attended Wayne State University's school of art in Detroit after graduating from a Detroit high school. He has lived in northern Michigan for the last five years where he now works as a licensed custom builder constructing architect-designed homes. With hired helpers, he completes all carpentry tasks of these homes. These tasks include the rough framing and finish carpentry as well as ceramic tile work, fabricating custom laminated counter-tops, and detail molding work.

Billy provided the basis of the artwork for this book.

Terry Lee Alexander is a registered architect living and working in Ann Arbor, Michigan. His speciality is single family dwellings. Terry worked for the city of Ann Arbor as their building code administrator, and gained the reputation as being fair and open-minded in a job where there is much potential for difficult times. He left this job to return to the design aspects of architecture. Currently he is working on several home projects and is incorporating with an Ann Arbor design firm.

Ron and Judy Botan both graduated from Eastern Michigan University in April 1979 with Bachelors of Fine Arts degrees. Ron is involved with sculpture, oil painting, and watercolor. Judy deals with photography, focusing on diverse, and sometimes experimental forms. Judy and Ron both do pen and ink sketches. They now live by Judy's native area on the coast of Ontario by the northern part of the Georgean Bay where they successfully freelance their artwork. Current plans include documenting the Canadian north coast through drawings and photography.

Rodger Zeman graduated from the University of Detroit's School of Architecture in 1969. He now works in an architecture firm in Ann Arbor functioning as a visual communications specialist. Although he has worked in firms throughout the United States, his concentration has always been on the visual aspects of architecture and design. His specialty is completing sketch studies and renderings for preliminary designs. He has also done extensive work in photography and is an excellent graphic and sketch artist.

Shirley Roebuck recently graduated with a Bachelors of Landscape Architecture degree from Michigan State University. She has worked on many different projects, including residential and commercial designs. She has also been involved with the Detroit Waterfront Project, rejuvenating and connecting downtown Detroit's park, riverside, and conference center areas. Shirley, like her brother Al Roebuck, has lived in several of Michigan's southeastern cities where she has been constantly involved in the field of landscape design.